AFRICA AND THE WEST

• • •

VOLUME 2

AFRICA AND THE WEST

A Documentary History

SECOND EDITION

◆ ◆ ◆

VOLUME 2

From Colonialism to Independence, 1875 to the Present

79

EDWARD A. ALPERS

OXFORD
UNIVERSITY PRESS

2010

OXFORD

UNIVERSITY PRESS

Oxford University Press, Inc., publishes works that further
Oxford University's objective of excellence
in research, scholarship, and education.

Oxford   New York
Auckland   Cape Town   Dar es Salaam   Hong Kong   Karachi
Kuala Lumpur   Madrid   Melbourne   Mexico City   Nairobi
New Delhi   Shanghai   Taipei   Toronto

With offices in
Argentina   Austria   Brazil   Chile   Czech Republic   France   Greece
Guatemala   Hungary   Italy   Japan   Poland   Portugal   Singapore
South Korea   Switzerland   Thailand   Turkey   Ukraine   Vietnam

Library of Congress Cataloging-in-Publication Data
Africa and the West : a documentary history / [edited by] William H. Worger, Nancy L. Clark, Edward A. Alpers.—2nd ed.
v.   cm.
Includes bibliographical references and index.
Contents: v. 1. From the slave trade to conquest, 1441–1905 — v. 2. From colonialism to independence, 1875 to the present.
ISBN 978-0-19-537313-4
1. Africa, Sub-Saharan—Relations—Europe—History—Sources. 2. Europe—Relations—Africa, Sub-Saharan—History—
Sources. 3. Africa, Sub-Saharan—Relations—America—History—Sources. 4. America—Relations—Africa, Sub-Saharan—
History—Sources. 5. Slave-trade—History—Sources. I. Worger, William H. II. Clark, Nancy L. III. Alpers, Edward A.
DT353.5.E9A34 2010
303.48'26701821—dc22   2009034387

Printed in the United States of America
on acid-free paper

PREFACE

This two-volume work presents the story of Africa's relationship with the West through the perspective of those who lived its history. The words of African kings, slaves, and politicians, as well as European officials, missionaries, and slave traders, reproduced here in 133 select primary documents, tell the story of the colonial encounter between Africa and the West from the beginning of the fifteenth century to the beginning of the twenty-first. Although direct contact between Europe and North Africa has existed since ancient times, a fundamentally new relationship developed between Africa and Europe with the advent of the Atlantic slave trade. We have chosen to follow the developing contours of this relationship, particularly the ways in which Africans were incorporated into an Atlantic world that used their labor and their agricultural produce to build wealth in the West but caused poverty in Africa.

The story begins with Portuguese explorers who came looking for the source of West Africa's gold in reputed rivers of the precious metal and with the establishment of the first Portuguese settlements along the northwest coast of Africa (especially on the Atlantic islands of the Azores, Madeira, Cape Verde, and the Canaries). It continues, from the latter part of the fifteenth century well into the nineteenth, with the consequent forcible removal of Africans, who were taken across the Atlantic not as free settlers but as servile laborers to colonize the Americas. With the gradual ending of the slave trade, the story continues as European nations that had prospered from the slave trade identified new products for export and worked for nearly a century to gain control over those resources and African land and to maintain their control over African labor. The period of colonialism—the apex of European intervention and the means for the reshaping of the continent—was the culmination of the drive from the West to control Africa's resources. It also sowed the seeds for the emergence of new African leaders and a quest for independence that finally succeeded at the end of the twentieth century. The book ends at the beginning of a new millennium, with international energy companies drawn to the continent by reports of veritable lakes of oil beneath areas such as Darfur and with African nations facing a host of challenges—poverty and hunger among the most important, and most of them the legacy of the six-hundred-year relationship with the West.

The two volumes of this book are organized both chronologically and thematically. Attempting comprehensiveness across a continent with an area so large and with populations as diverse as those of Africa would be impossible (though we have focused on two countries in particular—Ghana and South Africa—because of the importance of each in the history of the encounter between Africa and the West and because of the richness of the sources that allow us to document that encounter). Volume 1 focuses on the initiation of contact with Africa through the slave trade, the so-called legitimate trade of the nineteenth century, and the eventual military conquest of most parts of Africa. Despite the eloquent pleas of Africans that they could initiate whatever changes they wanted free of outside intervention, this volume ends

with the deaths of tens of thousands of Africans defending their autonomy against the inevitable military intervention of European powers. Volume 2 starts with discussions of the
aims of colonialism, as expressed by some of its architects, and the concurrent criticisms made
by colonial subjects (or victims, as increasingly they saw themselves). It examines the linkages between nineteenth- and twentieth-century political and economic practices, especially
in the development of authoritarian forms of colonial rule, and the transformation of slavery
into new forms of forced labor. Volume 2 ends with the struggle (ultimately successful) of
people in the Portuguese and white-settler-ruled areas of Africa (Angola, Guinea-Bissau,
Mozambique, Namibia, South Africa, and Zimbabwe) to achieve independence and the difficulties and contradictions of life after colonialism for people in the rest of Africa. While "freedom," in Nkrumah's stirring words, came to Africa with the end of formal colonialism, political independence has not translated into the types of freedom that most people expected.

In revising this work, originally published in one volume in 2001, we find continuing
signs of hope and concern in Africa's most recent history. When we completed the first edition of this book, we ended the volume with a stirring speech given by Nelson Mandela at his
inauguration as president of South Africa in May 1994, an oration that he concluded with the
words "Let freedom reign!" But we also noted the continuing evidence of what we termed
"reminders of the harsh legacy of colonialism," including genocide in Rwanda with a million
dead in a hundred days; civil war in Sierra Leone, where all of the vying parties, "government"
and "rebel" alike, used child soldiers and committed atrocities shockingly similar—dismemberment especially—to those carried out by Belgian colonialists in the Congo a century earlier; and riots in northern Nigeria, with Muslims being blamed for the killing of several hundred
Nigerian Christians. As we complete the second edition of this book in 2009, the perpetrators
of the Rwandan genocide have been sentenced to life in prison. Charles Taylor, considered
responsible for the deaths of thousands in the wars that raged in Sierra Leone and Liberia
throughout the 1990s, remains on trial. Riots have again taken place in Nigeria with evident
tensions between Muslims and Christians.

At the same time, we find new challenges and reminders of the troubled past. Africans
have the lowest life expectancy in the world, sometimes half that of people living in the West.
They have the highest under-five child mortality rates in the world. There are more poor
people (three hundred million) living in Africa than in any other part of the world, and they
account for 76 percent of the world's "ultrapoor," as those living on less than fifty cents a day
have been defined. They are hungry. In 2007 a survey of food intake in seven African countries (Burundi, Ethiopia, Kenya, Malawi, Rwanda, Senegal, and Zambia) found that the percentage of the population defined as the "ultrahungry" (consuming fewer than sixteen hundred calories a day) ranged from 27 percent of the people living in Kenya to 60 percent of
Burundi's population.[1] In Africa, more people are dying of AIDS than in the rest of the world
combined, with twelve million children orphaned by the disease by 2008. In the past five
years, five million people have died in the Congo as a result of violence, and few people elsewhere seem to have noticed. Darfur captures the world's attention with concerns about geno-

1. Akhter U. Ahmed, Ruth Vargas Hill, Lisa C. Smith, Doris M. Wiesmann, and Tim Frankenberger, *The
World's Most Deprived: Characteristics and Causes of Extreme Poverty and Hunger* (Washington, D.C.: International Food Policy Research Institute, 2007), xii; http://www.ifpri.org/sites/default/files/publications/
vp43.pdf.

cide, but few perceive the growing importance of oil in the Sudan and Chad as world powers embark on a new quest for dominance, one based on the control of strategic minerals rather than the land mass so common during colonialism and still evident during the Cold War. Our hope is that the injustices and brutality that so characterized interactions between Africa and the West, as recounted in these two volumes, will not be repeated in the future.

We have endeavored in this collection to compile a text that will be of interest to a wide range of audiences from middle school, high school, and college students and beyond to anyone interested in the history of the African continent. For some of us—and we are of a generation that came of age in the 1960s and the 1970s—the decolonizing of Africa was a time of hope, and the names of people like Frantz Fanon, Kwame Nkrumah, and Julius Nyerere are very familiar. Later generations are likely to be more familiar with those who fought against continuing oppression in Africa, whether it be Nelson Mandela and his struggles to end apartheid in South Africa or Jack Mapanje, who denounced the shortcomings of Malawi's president for life, Hastings Banda, or perhaps they will be aware of Africa mainly as a place of poverty and political unrest. Believing as historians that the present cannot be explained without a grasp of the past, we hope that readers of every generation will find these documents of value in understanding the history of Africa and gaining some insight into the problems and the potential with which the continent is currently contending.

The documents collected here were written by people who participated in the events described. They capture, in first-person narratives, poetry, letters, formal political speeches, and many other forms of writing, the hopes, aspirations, doubts, and sometimes hypocrisy that mark all human endeavors. Editorially, we have aimed to present selections lengthy enough to enable the reader to capture a sense of what each author intended. We have avoided cutting texts to reflect certain lines of interpretation, and we have kept the explanatory text to a minimum (though clearly the selection of the documents itself reflects our collective and individual points of view). With the exception of minor changes in punctuation, the replacement of the letter ƒ by s in some of the older English documents, and the reduction of some excessive capitalization (by today's standards), we have maintained the spelling, grammatical forms, and some capitalization from the original documents. In addition, we have dated the documents to reflect the period of time in which the events described took place, sometimes different from the actual publication date. Most important, we have retained without exception the documents' original language—always powerful, moving, and sometimes rough. The people whose words you read here were and still are exceptionally eloquent.

ACKNOWLEDGMENTS

In preparing the first edition of this work, we benefited at Cal Poly and UCLA from the research skills of Henry Trotter (who did much of the groundwork), Gibril Cole, Karen Flint, and Kristin Haynes and at Oryx Press from the editorial expertise of Jake Goldberg, Sean Tape, and Ann Thompson.

This second, revised, two-volume edition would not have happened without the energy and determination of the indefatigable Nancy Toff of Oxford University Press. Claire Cox of Greenwood Press went the extra step in sorting out the complex copyright issues. The three anonymous readers selected by Oxford provided numerous helpful suggestions for additions to and revisions of the first edition. We have benefited from answers to questions and a generous willingness to share material offered by Nwando Achebe, Gibril Cole, Jeremy Ball, Richard L. Betz, Elri Liebenberg, Bill Minter, Honoré Vinck, and David Rumsey. Ruby Bell-Gam of the Young Research Library (YRL) at UCLA answered every difficult bibliographic question with immense skill and alacrity. The YRL staff in circulation and interlibrary loan efficiently and graciously fielded an inordinate number of requests. Members of Special Collections at YRL provided high-quality reproductions of some of the illustrations. The Dean of Libraries at LSU, Jennifer Cargill, and the staffs of the Hill and Middleton libraries were always ready to help. The Dean of Social Sciences at UCLA provided a subvention for the costs of obtaining reprint permission for the copyrighted material included in this work. At OUP, we have also benefited from the sterling work of Jane Slusser, Leora Bersohn, Liz Smith, and Carol Hoke.

CONTENTS

PART II
The Emergence of Independent Africa (1961–2008)   145

◆ ◆ ◆

CHAPTER FIVE
African Ideologies of Independence (1961–71)   149

CHAPTER SIX
Colonial Legacies of Authoritarianism (1960–79)   184

ILLUSTRATIONS

PART I

Reshaping Africa (1875–1961)

INTRODUCTION

The entrance of European powers into the African continent during the colonial period changed Africa fundamentally. They established new borders based solely on commercial resources; shifted production away from internal sustenance to exports for external profits; interjected new values and standards through missionary education; and replaced African rule with governance by foreign dictate. This was a massive—and marginally successful—enterprise for the Europeans. Profits did not always outweigh the costs of imposing such thoroughgoing change on an entire continent. Force was always there to be used, but the high cost of maintaining standing armies and employing large numbers of European bureaucrats was more than most proponents of empire were prepared to support. Under colonialism, most Europeans sought to use their own settlers or, if none were available, the Africans who were products of expanding Western education. What they experienced was ongoing resistance to change, sometimes organized and sometimes spontaneous, but increasingly costly throughout the colonial period. In the end and after massive brutality and violence, the European powers left the societies they had so devastated, content to resume the trade patterns that began with the slave trade, exporting goods without incurring the costs of colonialism.

To institute effective methods of rule in the colonies, Europeans used different strategies, but they always relied on white authority. At the very beginning of the "scramble," the British fashioned a model of rule in southern Africa (Natal) in the 1870s—autocratic, hierarchical, completely undemocratic—that they claimed mirrored "traditional" indigenous practice and placed at its head as the all-powerful, unquestionable "supreme chief"—none other than the governor of the colony. More attuned to effective control over Africans than to "traditional" rule, this model was imposed over every ethnic group in the vicinity, now grouped as one, regardless of their identity. Elsewhere in Africa systems of indirect and direct rule differed somewhat in form, but the substance experienced by Africans was usually much the same. Colonialism was expressed by its masters in the language of command, and the only role allocated to and expected of Africans was obedience. Colonial rule rested also on a new class of Africans, very different from the "traditional" chiefs so favored in Natal. These were the people who had been attracted to Christianity. In mission schools they learned the vernacular of their new masters, and they found employment as agents of the colonial state as translators, clerks, and tax collectors.

Colonial officials adopted this combination of force and African intermediaries because they wanted colonialism to pay—to pay enough to return a profit to the colonizing country, to pay enough to support imperial administration (especially white civil servants) in the colonies and in the twentieth century, and to pay enough to subsidize the war-torn economies of Europe. To ensure profitability, the colonial authorities, in various ways in different countries, required Africans to grow cash crops for the export market rather than items for trade within Africa or food for their own sustenance; to work on the new plantations established and the new industries developed, many of them highly labor intensive, such as tobacco in Tanganyika or gold mining in South Africa. To force people to engage in these economic activities on terms set by the employers and not open to negotiation (black workers in South Africa, for example, were not recognized in the law as workers and therefore did not have the right to engage in collective bargaining), Europeans confiscated the land of Africans (especially in South Africa, southern Rhodesia, and Kenya), forced people to work on European and state-owned farms and roads (in French and Belgian territories, as well as those of the British), and imposed taxes at every possible opportunity (one of the favorites was a tax on African dogs). The worst extreme was probably that of the Congo, King Leopold's private domain, where Africans who failed to collect enough rubber had their hands chopped off as a warning to others to work faster.

Such atrocities and oppression did not go unopposed. Paradoxically, it was often missionaries who unwittingly fostered the leadership responsible for African opposition. Africans at mission stations not only learned to read and write but also became increasingly aware of the overarching nature of colonial rule and began to self-identify as Africans, not exclusively as Zulu, Kikuyu, or Shona. From the late nineteenth century onward, these mission-educated Africans established a vibrant indigenous press. Often they traveled overseas, usually under missionary sponsorship, to obtain the higher education that they could not obtain on a continent where the colonial authorities established no universities open to blacks until the middle decades of the twentieth century. Many of these travelers in search of higher education went to the United States, where, frequently attending universities for African Americans, they gained a sense of brotherhood with the descendants of former slaves and an appreciation that white rule did not necessarily lead to the improvements in society that missionaries had promised. People like John Chilembwe and John Dube returned to Africa determined to improve the lot of their fellow Africans: Chilembwe took the path of armed revolt and, like so many of his peers, was killed; Dube chose the politics of protest and petition and lived, though not without constant police harassment. Aware of their shared oppression, blacks on both sides of the Atlantic demanded an end to racism and white oppression and called for all peoples of African descent to join together in a movement for pan-African unity.

Growing opposition to the repressive nature of colonialism spurred the growth of new political movements, no longer based exclusively on ethnic identification and led primarily by members of the new educated "elite." Although the new leaders, Western educated and re-moved from traditional power bases, did not repudiate the West, they denounced the practices of colonialism. They aimed to bring together people across ethnic and regional boundaries and combine them in movements that would gain strength from their mass membership and hope-fully win democratic rights for Africans. Perhaps the most successful and distinctive of these movements in the early twentieth century was the Industrial and Commercial Workers Union in South Africa, where under the leadership of Clements Kadalie a combination of labor or-ganization and messianic appeal produced a strong enough threat that colonial authorities did everything that they could to bring about (successfully) its demise.

Despite the successful repression of their indigenous opponents during the 1920s and the 1930s, in the 1940s colonial rulers found their ability to rule profoundly challenged. Africans, many of whom had battled Axis imperialism during World War II, returned home after the war, dismayed that the prodemocracy rhetoric of the West did not apply to their own commu-nities, where they found the levels of exploitation to which they were subjected even greater than before as European colonizers tried to rebuild their war-torn economies on profits from their overseas possessions. People like the returned soldier Waruhui Itote and his near contempo-raries Anton Lembede and Mugo Gatheru wanted freedom "now," not later, and they turned from the politics of petition to those of labor struggle and mass protest to achieve their goals.

Though white settlers living in South Africa, Southern Rhodesia, and Kenya, as well as the Belgians and the Portuguese, determined to strengthen white supremacy as a means of main-taining their economic privilege, metropolitan officials in Britain and France realized, some-times hesitantly, that the price of repression was beginning to exceed the profits of colonialism. In the 1950s the British and the French began searching for ways to grant political autonomy to their colonial territories while at the same time securing the economic linkages that had made conquest so attractive in the first place and ensured the continued presence of Europe in Africa. They wanted to keep their profits and cut their losses.

Formal colonialism ended for most Africans in the late 1950s and the early 1960s, but its conclusion was a costly business. The British hanged a thousand Kenyans accused of insurrec-tion as part of the Mau Mau rebellion before they let go. At much the same time that Kwame Nkrumah celebrated Ghana's independence—the first of any African country—with ringing cries of "Freedom! Freedom! Freedom!" Hendrik Verwoerd committed South Africa to an-other forty years of race hatred. Nelson Mandela would spend twenty-seven years in prison while the rest of Africa slowly escaped colonialism. And Patrice Lumumba, the first president of the newly independent Congo, caught up in an international cold war not of Africa's making, lost his life in a secessionist war encouraged by European and South African investors who feared losing the country's mineral riches to a populist government. Colonialism ended as it had begun, in false promises, boundless expectations, and blood.

CHAPTER ONE

Methods of Rule (1875–1919)

1 ◆ Making colonialism appear "traditional" (1875)

The cost of rule was always of paramount concern to colonial officials. Having acquired empire in most instances for economic reasons, the colonial powers were not prepared to bear the heavy cost involved in employing large numbers of European administrators or maintaining expensive armies of occupation. Better to get Africans to rule themselves for less money. However, that meant identifying or, as was often the case, inventing "traditional" indigenous institutions through which Europeans could exercise their control.

For the British, the most pressing case in the latter half of the nineteenth century was that of the Zulu in southeastern Africa. Militarily powerful under the early kings, Shaka and Dingane, and capable of inflicting on the British their greatest defeat in a nineteenth-century colonial war (Isandlwana in 1879), the Zulu state remained potentially the most formidable challenge to British might, even after the defeat of King Cetshwayo's forces in the aftermath of Isandlwana. Natal officials, primarily Theophilus Shepstone, who was in charge of "native affairs" in the colony from 1845 until 1876, fashioned in the mid-1870s an administrative structure that they claimed reflected traditional African practices—a strictly hierarchical system headed by an all-powerful "supreme chief" supposedly modeled on Shaka (in colonial practice the lieutenant governor would act as Shaka)—but improved upon because of the introduction of formal trials (though with no jury). The system would be regulated by European administrators of native law since foreigners were deemed more knowledgeable about African practices than were Africans themselves. The 1877 Natal Native Administration Law, modeled on systems of indirect rule developed in India and itself a model for later systems of indirect rule elsewhere in Africa, was enacted into law by none other than Sir Garnet Wolseley, recently arrived in South Africa as lieutenant governor of Natal after his triumphal campaign against the Asante.[1]

Native Administration Law no. 26, December 17, 1875

Law: To make better provision for the Administration of justice among the Native Population of Natal, and for the gradual assimilation of Native Law to the Laws of the Colony . . .

2. It shall be lawful for the Lieutenant-Governor for the time being to appoint persons of European descent, who shall be called Administrators of Native Law, as also [Africans as] Native Chiefs or other Native Officers, to preside and exercise authority over and to administer

---

1. G. W. Eybers, ed., *Select Constitutional Documents Illustrating South African History, 1795–1910* (New York: Routledge and Sons, 1918), 247–51.

FIGURE 1 This drawing of a colonial chain gang was made by Salim Matola, a seventeen- or eighteen-year-old youth who accompanied German ethnographer Karl Weule on a six-month expedition in German East Africa in 1906. Wherever they traveled, the Maji Maji rebellion still formed the chief topic of conversation among the local people. Karl Weule, *Native Life in East Africa: The Results of an Ethnological Research Expedition*, 1909.

justice among Natives living under Native Law, within such districts as may be hereafter determined, and the Lieutenant-Governor shall have power summarily to remove such Native Chiefs or other Native Officers, so appointed, and to appoint others in their stead.

3. Every Administrator of Native Law, or Native Chief, or other Native Officer so appointed, shall have power to try and decide all civil disputes between native and native in the tribe or community placed under his charge, and within such limits as may from time to time be prescribed by the Lieutenant-Governor, except upon such cases as are hereinafter excepted, or may from time to time be excepted in manner hereinafter provided: Provided, however, that in all cases decided by any Native Chief or other Native Officer, a new trial may be had in conformity with such rules, of procedure as may be framed under the provisions of the 10th Section of this Law, before the Administrator of Native Law appointed over the district in which such Native Chief or other Native Officer resides, and that every such Native Chief or other Native Officer shall within ten days after the decision of any such civil case, communicate to the Administrator of Native Law having jurisdiction, the names of the plaintiff and defendant, the cause of the action, the decision arrived at, and the grounds of such decision; and each such officer is hereby required to record the same.

4. In all such civil cases there shall be an appeal to the Native High Court in this Law specified.

5. All matters and disputes in the nature of civil cases between Natives living under Native Law shall be tried under the provisions of this Law and not otherwise, and according to Native Laws, customs, and usages for the time being prevailing, so far as the same shall not be of a nature to work some manifest injustice, or be repugnant to the settled principles and policy of natural equity; except that all civil cases arising out of transactions in trade, or out of the ownership of or succession to land, shall be adjudicated upon according to the principles laid down by the ordinary Colonial Law in such cases; Provided always, that in the district or districts referred to in the proviso to Section —, of this Law, all matters and things required

to be done and observed by an Administrator of Native Law appointed under this Law, may, and shall be done and observed by an Administrator of Native Law appointed under Ordinance 3, 1849, until appointments under this Law shall have been made therein.

6. Subject to the exceptions in this Law specified, all crimes and offences committed by Natives shall be tried before the ordinary Courts of Law in this Colony in the same manner as if they had been committed by persons of European descent: Provided, however, that the following classes of crime shall be excepted:

(a) All crimes and offences of a political character, which shall be tried at the discretion of the Attorney-General, either before the Supreme Court of the Colony or the Native High Court: Provided that the Native High Court shall not have the power of passing sentence of capital punishment.

(b) All homicides, assaults, or other injury to the person or property of any Native caused by or arising out of riots by Natives or faction fights between Natives, or in which any tribe or section of a tribe or community of Natives may have taken part, and which in the judgment of the Attorney-General may be more conveniently tried according to the provisions of Native Law.

(c) All crimes or offences with respect to which it has been or may hereafter be enacted by any Law that they shall be tried by Native Law or before any special Court. And all crimes and offences so excepted, except those for the trial of which special provision has been made, shall be tried by the Native High Court in this Law specified: Provided, always, that it shall be lawful for the Native High Court to remit the trial of any such assault or injury aforesaid to one or more Administrators of Native Law, and such Administrators of Native Law may thereupon try the case subject to an appeal to the Native High Court, whose decision shall in such case be final.

7. There shall be constituted a Court, to be termed the Native High Court, and such High Court shall be presided over by a judge specially appointed by the Lieutenant-Governor, and such judge shall sit as sole judge, or may be assisted, as occasion may require, by Administrators of Native Law, or Native Chiefs, or other Native Officers, as assessors, in manner hereafter to be provided; and such Court shall hear and try all appeal cases from the Courts of the Administrators of Native Law, all civil cases that may be brought before it under the provisions of this Law, and all criminal cases, the trial of which is in this Law specially reserved to such High Court.

8. [Judge to hold office during good behaviour.]

9. All appeals from the Native High Court shall be to a Court of Appeal, which shall be held to be, and shall be a branch of the Supreme Court of the Colony, and shall consist of the Chief justice or one of the Puisne judges of the said Supreme Court, the Secretary for Native Affairs for the time being, and the judge of the Native High Court established under this Law; and the Court so constituted shall hear and determine all appeals that shall be brought before it under provisions of this Law . . .

THE SUPREME CHIEF

32. The Supreme Chief for the time being exercises in and over all Natives in the Colony of Natal all political power and authority, subject to the provisions of Section 7 of Law 44 of 1887.

33. The Supreme Chief appoints all Chiefs to preside over tribes, or sections of tribes; and also divides existing tribes into two or more parts, or amalgamates tribes or parts of tribes into one tribe, as necessity or the good government of the Natives may, in his opinion, require.

34. The Supreme Chief in Council may remove any Chief found guilty of any political offence, or for incompetency or other just cause, from his position as such Chief, and may also order his removal with his family and property, to another part of the Colony.

35. The Supreme Chief has absolute power to call upon Chiefs, District Headmen, and all other Natives, to supply armed men or levies for the defence of the Colony, and for the suppression of disorder and rebellion within its borders, and may call upon such chiefs, District Headmen, and all other Natives to personally render such military and other service.

36. The Supreme Chief has power to call upon all Natives to supply labour for public works, or for the general needs of the colony. This call or command may be transmitted by any person authorised so to do, and each native so called upon is bound to obey such call, and render such service in person, unless lawfully released from such duty.

37. The Supreme Chief, acting in conjunction with the Natal Native Trust, may, when deemed expedient in the general public good, remove any tribe or tribes, or portion thereof, or any native, from any part of the Colony or Location, to any other part of the Colony or Location, upon such terms and conditions and arrangements as he may determine.

38. The orders and directions of the Supreme Chief, or of the Supreme Chief in Council, may be carried into execution by the Secretary for Native Affairs, or by the Administrators of Native Law, or by other officers authorised for the purpose, and in respect of all such acts the various officers so employed shall be regarded as the deputies or representatives of the Supreme Chief, or of the Supreme Chief in Council, as the case may be.

39. The Supreme Chief, in the exercise of the political powers which attach to his office, has authority to punish by fine or imprisonment, or by both, for disobedience of his orders or for disregard of his authority.

40. The Supreme Chief is not subject to the Supreme Court, or to any other court of Law in the Colony of Natal, for, or by reason of, any order or proclamation, or of any other act or matter whatsoever, committed, ordered, permitted, or done either personally or in council.

41. The Supreme Chief is, by virtue of his office, Upper Guardian of all orphans and minors in law.

42. The Supreme Chief has power to regulate and fix from time to time the least number of houses which shall compose a kraal. He may, in his discretion, permit of exceptions to any such general rule in special cases.

2 • Africa for the African (1897)

Christianity appealed to many Africans, but often in ways the European missionaries did not intend. It offered a body of thought and attendant language to criticize the ways in which colonialism was imposed and practiced. There was no basis in the Bible for the exclusion of Africans from the higher reaches of church and state as was practiced without exception throughout colonial Africa. There was no basis in the Christian message for the harsh treatment of African workers in the Bel-

gian Congo rubber industry, the South African gold mines, or the tea and coffee plantations of East Africa. Indeed, African converts to Christianity became some of the most powerful critics of colonial hypocrisy.

One of the most notable of these critics was John Chilembwe, born around 1871 in present-day Malawi, the son of a Yao slave trader and a woman initially captured for trade. Chilembwe grew up to become the first convert of Joseph Booth, an Englishman who had become a born-again Christian while living in New Zealand and who then traveled as a missionary to central Africa, following consciously in the footsteps of David Livingstone. Under Booth's sponsorship, Chilembwe traveled to the United States in 1898 and studied at the Virginia Theological Seminary and College in Lynchburg, an institution established in 1890 "to prepare Christian preachers, teachers and workers for work among Negroes." After two years of study, Chilembwe returned to Nyasaland (as Malawi was then called) as a Baptist missionary and worked together with African American missionaries to establish an industrial school at which Africans could learn practical skills. Over time he became a strong critic of the ways in which Europeans treated Africans, particularly of the ways in which African land was forcibly taken and African workers were cruelly treated. Chilembwe aimed his criticism especially at the Bruce Estates, a large cotton and coffee plantation owned by a family that had, with George Mackinnon, founded the British East Africa Company and that was managed by a distant relative of David Livingstone.

In 1915 John Chilembwe, using biblical texts (Acts 20:29–32) to justify forceful action, led an armed uprising against British colonial rule, ordering the beheading of Livingstone's relative and torching European-run mission stations. British retribution was harsh. Chilembwe was hunted down and killed; his body was buried in secret so that a grave would not provide a symbol for further resistance. While overall casualties were small compared with those of the Maji Maji uprising, Chilembwe, too, despite British attempts at cover-up, served as a powerful symbol to later proponents of African independence.

The African Christian Union, first established in 1896 in Natal by Booth, was extended to Nyasaland by Chilembwe, working with his mentor, in 1897. The aim of the mission was to raise funds from local people in order to establish an industrial mission for Africans independent of the organizations run by European mission societies. The chief tenets of the organization were laid out in a broadsheet issued January 14, 1897.[2]

Objects of the Society:

1. To unite together in the name of Jesus Christ such persons as desire to see full justice done to the African race and are resolved to work towards and pray for the day when the African people shall become an African Christian Nation.

2. To provide capital to equip and develop Industrial Mission Stations worked by competent Native Christians or others of the African race; such stations to be placed on a self-supporting and self-propagating basis.

3. To steadfastly demand by Christian and lawful methods the equal recognition of the African and those having blood relationship, to the rights and privileges accorded to Europeans.

2. George Shepperson and Thomas Price, *Independent African: John Chilembwe and the Origins, Setting, and Significance of the Nyasaland Native Rising of 1915* (Edinburgh: Edinburgh University Press, 1958; paperback ed. 1987), 541–43.

4. To call upon every man, woman and child of the African race, as far as may be practicable, to take part in the redemption of Africa during this generation, by gift, loan, or personal service.

5. To specially call upon the Afro-American Christians, and those of the West Indies to join hearts and hands in the work either by coming in person to take an active part or by generous, systematic contributions.

6. To solicit funds in Great Britain, America and Australia for the purpose of restoring at their own wish carefully selected Christian Negro families, or adults of either sex, back to their fatherland in pursuance of the objects of the Union; and to organize an adequate propaganda to compass the work.

7. To apply such funds in equal parts to the founding of Industrial Mission centres and to the establishing of Christian Negro settlements.

8. To firmly, judiciously and repeatedly place on record by voice and pen for the information of the uninformed, the great wrongs inflicted upon the African race in the past and in the present, and to urge upon those who wish to be clear of African blood in the day of God's judgments, to make restitution for the wrongs of the past and to withstand the appropriation of the African's land in the present.

9. To initiate or develop the culture of Tea, Coffee, Cocoa, Sugar, etc. etc., and to establish profitable mining or other industries or manufactures.

10. To establish such transport agencies by land, river, lakes or ocean as shall give the African free access to the different parts of his great country and people, and to the general commerce of the world.

11. To engage qualified persons to train and teach African learners any department of Commercial, Engineering, nautical, professional or other necessary knowledge.

12. To mould and guide the labor of Africa's millions into channels that shall develop the vast God-given wealth of Africa for the uplifting and commonwealth of the people, rather than for the aggrandisement of a few already rich persons.

13. To promote the formation of Companies on a Christian basis devoted to special aspects of the work; whose liability shall be limited, whose shares shall not be transferable without the society's consent; whose shareholders shall receive a moderate rate of interest only; whose profits shall permanently become the property of the Trustees of the African Christian Union, for the prosecution of the defined objects of the Union.

14. To petition the government of the United States of America to make a substantial monetary grant to each adult Afro-American desiring to be restored to African soil, as some recognition of the 250 years of unpaid slave labor and the violent abduction of millions of Africans from their native land.

15. To petition the British and other European governments holding or claiming African territory to generously restore the same to the African people or at least to make adequate inalienable native reserve lands, such reserves to be convenient to the locality of the different tribes.

16. To petition the British and other European governments occupying portions of Africa to make substantial and free grants of land to expatriated Africans or their descendents desiring restoration to their fatherland, such grants to be made inalienable from the African race.

17. To provide for all representatives, officials or agents of the Union and its auxiliaries, inclusive of the Companies it may promote modest, economical yet efficient and as far as may be, equable, maintenance, together with due provision for periods of sickness, incapacity, widowhood or orphanage.

18. To print and publish literature in the interests of the African race and to furnish periodical accounts of the transactions of the Society and its auxiliary agencies, the same to be certified by recognized auditors and to be open to the fullest scrutiny of the Union's supporters.

19. To vest all funds, properties, products or other sources of income in the hands of Trustees, not less than seven in number, to be held in perpetuity in the distinct interest of the African race and for the accomplishment of the objects herein set forth in 21 clauses.

20. Finally, to pursue steadily and unswervingly the policy:

"AFRICA FOR THE AFRICAN"

and look for and hasten by prayer and united effort the forming of a united

AFRICAN CHRISTIAN NATION

By God's power and blessing and in His own time and way.

[Signed]

JOSEPH BOOTH, English missionary.

JOHN CHILEMBWE, Ajawa Christian Native.

ALEXANDER DICKIE, English missionary.

MORRISON MALINKA, Native Christian Chipeta Tribe.

Dated January 14th, 1897 at Blantyre, Nyassaland, East Central Africa.

3 • West African warfare (1905)

Though quinine and other drugs, as well as better medical treatment in general, reduced the death rate of European troops in Africa, they still got sick and died at a higher rate than did African troops. Local people, moreover, were much cheaper soldiers than were Europeans, and as a result every colonial power depended on African troops for the bulk of their armed forces.

More remarkable, however, in light of the deprecating comments so often made by Europeans about the people they ruled, they made a real exception for those men who served in their armies and police forces and whose endeavors made colonialism possible and profitable for their rulers and employers. The importance of African troops and the admiration with which they could be viewed are captured in a military manual written by C. Braithwaite Wallis, a London lawyer who had formerly served in the Frontier Force and been district commissioner for the Sierra Leone Protectorate.[3]

It is a fact incontrovertible, that our expansion of Empire has been very largely brought about by the subjugation of the savage and lawless races who were the original inhabitants of the soil. Looked at from this point of view—the point of view of empire building that is to say—the significance and importance of many of our "little wars" can scarcely be over-estimated. And, that being the case, it obviously behooves every officer who is serving or about to serve

---

3. C. Braithwaite Wallis, *West African Warfare* (London: Harrison and Sons, 1905), 1, 4–6, 13–16.

in any of the far-away corners of the earth, to make himself thoroughly master of the local conditions and of the hundred and one other points of a military nature, a complete knowledge of which is absolutely indispensable for the successful prosecution of a campaign in those lands . . .

In recent times most of the fighting in West Africa has been done by native troops and locally raised levies, commanded by that indispensable factor in the machine of West African warfare—the British officer. With the exception of the Ashanti Expedition of 1896, no large force of white troops has, at least to my knowledge, been employed in West Africa since Lord Wolseley's Expedition to Ashanti in 1874. These native troops, for the most part recruited and trained locally, have, so far, amply justified the confidence that has been placed in them. Their discipline has generally been excellent, and when under fire their bravery, endurance, and dash have been altogether beyond reproach. The employment of white soldiers in a climate so enervating and unhealthy as that of West Africa is certainly a mistake, and entails on those connected with the transport an enormous amount of unnecessary trouble and work, as well as costing the nation a great deal more in money. It must be admitted, however, that the moral effect of using white troops against a savage foe, and in conjunction with native troops, is great, and sometimes even a necessity. At the same time, with the splendid material we have at our disposal in West Africa, and the fine troops we have manufactured therefrom, we ought to be able to overcome any resistance that is likely to be offered against British arms in that part of the world . . .

One of the great advantages of being able to employ native soldiers—men born and bred in the country—is that we are then enabled to a great extent, to play the enemy's own game, to follow him into his fastnesses and favourite haunts, and generally to adopt his own strategy and tactics. We have, moreover, the great advantage of superior discipline and arms; and when a savage foe finds that we are able to strike him in the same way, strategically and tactically, that he is endeavouring to strike us, he at once becomes demoralized and uncertain how to act. It is then that an attack should, whenever possible, be followed up and pressed home. When once a savage foe begins to run, he will, as a rule, continue to do so, and a panic amongst these people is even more contagious than among civilised troops . . .

Native troops when going into action should, so far as it is possible, be led by their own officers, who know and are known by their men. The West African soldier is an excellent fellow when properly handled and understood. He is extraordinarily quick in finding out the stuff his officers are made of, and he has, like every one else, his likes and dislikes, and these in marked degrees. *He has a wonderful sense of justice;* and the officer who treats his men firmly and kindly, looks after their interests, proves himself capable of sustaining privations and undergoing hardships, and of sharing unselfishly the vicissitudes of a campaign with his men, will be beloved, respected, and followed to the death. In a tight corner this makes all the difference in the world.

If the position is serious, and an attack is being made by overwhelming odds against you, never let the men perceive that anything is wrong. These native soldiers watch every action and almost every look of the "Captain"—the white man—and would immediately notice the slightest timidity or hesitation, which might have a grave effect on their *morale*. A confident front, a few words of encouragement, a smile, a quick and determined order, will act like a spark and will carry them anywhere, even to certain death. During the relief of Kumasi, after several hours' severe fighting, when nearly every officer was hit, and every man tired and hungry, an order was given to a detachment of Hausa troops to charge and take a stockade with the bayonet in the face of heavy fire. It was one of those crises, lasting for only the fraction of a second, when the best troops in the world are liable to waiver. In this case, seeing the hesitation of the men, a native officer rushed to the front, and waving his sword above his head, and calling in his native language to the men to follow him in the name of Allah, rushed at the stockade. This conduct acted like an electric spark; and enthusiastically shouting their war cry, the men dashed headlong at the stockade, and drove the enemy out of it. And this is only a single example of the moral effect produced, and sometimes by very slight and unexpected causes, upon the minds of soldiers of all races and conditions. It helps to demonstrate the fact that, after all, there is much the same sentiment, more or less deeply rooted, underlying all human nature, whatever the nationality, creed, or colour. But it requires the ascendancy of a superior or enthusiastic mind, or determined will, to awaken this dormant flame, and fan it into noble and heroic action.

4 • Evidence of colonial atrocities in the Belgian Congo (1903–5)

While conditions for African workers in South Africa and elsewhere in Africa were always harsh, seldom did they reach the horrendous conditions found in King Leopold's Congo. Indeed, the Belgian king's private preserve served as something of a welcome change of focus for other European colonizers, who could condemn Leopold's practices while deflecting attention from, for example, the appalling death rates in South African mines or the brutal treatment meted out to plantation workers in German East Africa. In 1903 Roger Casement, working on behalf of the British government, wrote a powerful exposé of the conditions that African rubber collectors had to endure. His descriptions of the mutilations inflicted by Leopold's employees on Africans to make them produce more rubber shocked the world and forced the king to hand control of his colony over to the Belgian government (which, however, continued to use forced labor). In an ironic postscript to the affair, Casement himself became a victim of imperialism. A fervent supporter of Irish nationalism, he was hanged by the British on August 3, 1916, for having negotiated with Germany for support for an armed uprising in Ireland.

The publication of Casement's report set off a public firestorm, fueled especially by testimony provided and photographs taken by Leopold's critics, particularly missionaries such as Emily Banks, of the hideous effects of the punishments inflicted by the king's troops on the Congolese. These atrocity photographs often circulated without the victims being individually identified (see, for example, Mark Twain's biting satire, King Leopold's Soliloquy: A Defense of His Congo Rule, *1905). However, E. D. Morel, one of Leopold's most trenchant critics, provided for his readers detailed information on the victims, such as the young boy, Lokota, and the circumstances of their ill treatment. Despite such evidence, the Belgians at the time argued that the atrocities were exceptional cases and likely the result of supposed indigenous practices of maiming, unsupervised African soldiers, or perhaps wild animals.*

The debate continues to the present day, with Belgian denials of responsibility throughout the past century, that is, whenever they have admitted to the existence of such events. More common than denial has been avoidance, as is evidenced in a brief history of the Belgian Congo as taught to African students in missionary-run schools in the 1940s.[4]

A. Casement's report on the Congo submitted to the Marquess of Lansdowne, December 11, 1903

The town of N * consists approximately of seventy-one K * houses and seventy-three occupied by L *. These latter seemed industrious, simple folk, many weaving palm fibre into mats or native cloth; others had smithies, working brass wire into bracelets, chains and anklets; some iron workers making knives. Sitting down in one of these blacksmith's sheds, the five men at work ceased and came over to talk to us. I counted ten women, six grown-up men and eight lads and women in this shed of L *. I then asked them to tell me why they had left their homes. Three of the men sat down in front of me, and told a tale which I cannot think can be true, but it seemed to come straight from their hearts. I repeatedly asked certain parts to be gone over again while I wrote in my note-book. The fact of my writing down and asking for names, etc., seemed to impress them, and they spoke with what certainly impressed me as being great sincerity.

I asked, first, why they had left their homes, and had come to live in a strange, far-off country among the K * where they owned nothing, and were little better than servitors. All, when this question was put, women as well, shouted out: "On account of the rubber tax levied by the Government posts" . . .

I asked, then, how this tax was imposed. One of them, who had been hammering out an iron collar on my arrival, spoke first. He said:—

"I am N.N. These two beside me are O.O. and P.P. all of us Y **. From our country each village had to take twenty loads of rubber. These loads were big; they were as big as this . . ." (Producing an empty basket which came nearly up to the handle of my walking stick). "That was the first size. We had to fill that up, but as rubber got scarcer the white man reduced the amount. We had to take these loads in four times a month."

Q.: "How much pay do you get for this?"

A. (entire audience): "We got no pay. We got nothing."

And then N.N., whom I asked again, said:—

"Our village got cloth and a little salt but not the people who did the work. Our Chiefs ate up the cloth; the workers got nothing. The pay was a fathom of cloth and a little salt for every basket full, but it was given to the Chief, never to the men. It used to take ten days to get the twenty baskets of rubber—we were always in the forest and then when we were late

---

4. A, *Correspondence and Report from His Majesty's Counsel at Boma Respecting the Administration of the Independent State of the Congo*, Cd 1933 [Command Paper no. 1933] (London: Harrison and Sons, 1904), 60–61; B, declaration of Emily Banks in H. Grattan Guinness, *Congo Slavery: A Brief Survey of the Congo Question from the Humanitarian Point of View* (London: R. B. M. U. Publication Department, [1905]), 22; C, photograph of Lokota by Rev. W. D. Armstrong, published in E. D. Morel, *King Leopold's Rule in Africa* (London: Heinemann, 1904), photo facing p. 113; explanation, 377; D, Van Hullebusch, *Some Facts That Took Place in the Congo*, V, lesson 31 (trans. from Lingala, *Botondoli mambi ma nse, Mobu bwa mitano*, Lisala, 1944), 27–29.

FIGURE 2 Roger Casement, an Irish diplomat and poet, gained world renown for his work to expose the labor abuses in the Congo Free State and Peru. He was hanged by the British during World War I for high treason following his involvement with the importation of German arms to support the Irish struggle for freedom from colonial rule; here, he is escorted to the gallows at London's Pentonville Prison. Library of Congress.

FIGURE 3 Congolese forced rubber laborers display the severed hands of two fellow workers, murdered by sentries of the Anglo-Belgian India Rubber Company (ABIR) in 1904. They are flanked by two pith-helmeted American Presbyterian missionaries. Anti-Slavery International.

FIGURE 4 For this formal portrait taken about 1904, the men, who were forced to collect rubber in King Leopold's Congo, were tied together with ropes around their necks. The image, like that drawn by Salim Matola of a chain gang in German East Africa in 1906, harkens back to David Livingstone's drawing of Arab slavers in 1861. Anti-Slavery International.

we were killed. We had to go further and further into the forest to find the rubber vines, to go without food, and our women had to give up cultivating the fields and gardens. Then we starved. Wild beasts—the leopards—killed some of us when we were working away in the forest, and others got lost or died from exposure and starvation and we begged the white men to leave us alone, saying we could get no more rubber, but the white men and their soldiers said: 'Go! You are only beasts yourselves, you are only nyama (meat).' We tried, always going further into the forest, and when we failed and our rubber was short, the soldiers came to our towns and killed us. Many were shot, some had their ears cut off; others were tied up with ropes round their necks and bodies and taken away. The white men sometimes at the posts did not know of the bad things the soldiers did to us, but it was the white men who sent the soldiers to punish us for not bringing in enough rubber."

Here P.P. took up the story from N.N:—

"We said to the white man: 'We are not enough people now to do what you want of us. Our country has not many people in it and we are dying fast. We are killed by the work you make us do, by the stoppage of our plantations, and the breaking up of our homes.' The white man looked at us and said: 'There are lots of people in Mputu' (Europe, the white man's country). 'If there are lots of people in the white man's country there must be many people in the black man's country.' The white man who said this was the chief white man at F.F *, his name was A.B., he was a very bad man. Other white men of Bula Matadi who had been bad and wicked were B.C., C.D., and D.E. These had killed us often, and killed us by their own hands as well as by their soldiers. Some men were good" . . .

FIGURE 5 A line of female slaves in King Leopold's Congo (1908) dig a trench by hand, while others behind them work in a field overseen by a European supervisor. Anti-Slavery International.

"These ones told them to stay in their homes, and did not hunt and chase them as the others had done, but after what they had suffered they did not trust more any one's word and they had fled from their country and were now going to stay here, far from their homes, in this country where there was no rubber."

Q.: "How long is it since you left your homes, since the big trouble you speak of?"

A.: "It lasted three full seasons, and it is now four seasons since we fled and came into the K * country."

Q.: "How many days is it from N * to your own country?"

A.: "Six days of quick marching. We fled because we could not endure the things done to us. Our Chiefs were hanged and we were killed and starved and worked beyond endurance to get rubber."

Q.: "How do you know it was the white men themselves who ordered these cruel things to be done to you? These things must have been done without the white men's knowledge by the black soldiers."

A. (P.P.): "The white men told their soldiers: 'You kill only women; you cannot kill men. You must prove that you kill men.' So then the soldiers when they killed us" (here he stopped and hesitated, and then pointing to the private parts of my bulldog—it was lying asleep at my feet) he said: "then they cut off those things and took them to the white men, who said: 'It is true, you have killed men.'"

Q.: "You mean to tell me that any white man ordered your bodies to be mutilated like that and those parts of you carried to him?"

P.P., O.O., and all (shouting): "Yes! many white man. D.E. did it."

Q. "You say this is true? Were many of you so treated after being shot?"

All (shouting out): "Nkoto! Nkoto!" (Very many! Very many!)

There was no doubt. Their vehemence, their flashing eyes, their excitement was not simulated. Doubtless they exaggerated the numbers, but they were clearly telling me what they knew and loathed.

B. The affidavit of the American missionary, Emily Banks, relating to events in 1895

I, EMILY BANKS, now residing at Congo Villa, Uppleby Road, Upper Parkstone, in the county of Dorset, Widow, do hereby solemnly and sincerely declare as follows:—

1. I resided in the Congo Free State with my late husband, Rev. Charles Blair Banks, as Missionaries under the American Baptist Missionary Union from the year 1887 to the year 1899 save and except two furloughs of eighteen months each. During the first two years we were stationed at Wangata and during the rest of the time at Bolengi both places being in the Equator District.

2. On December 14th, 1895, a sentinel passed our station at Bolengi driving before him a poor woman who was carrying a basket of human hands. My husband, now dead, Mr. Sjoblom now dead, and myself went down the road and ordered the sentinel to put the hands on the road that we might see how many there were. We counted eighteen right hands, all of them smoked, and from their size we could judge that they had belonged to men, women and children. The sentinel was very angry with the woman because she had dropped one hand on the way, and there should have been nineteen. Doubtless some of the victims were relations of the poor creature who was forced to carry the basket of hands from her village to the State Commissaire.

The following is a verbatim entry of the event taken from my diary, which entry was made therein on the very day of the recurrence.

December 14th, 1895. The poor people amongst whom we live are sadly treated by the State. Only just now I saw with my husband and his colleague Mr. Sjoblom, 18 hands dried and which had been cut off their victims four days ago by the servants of the State.

A slave caught alive from the same town was made to carry the basket containing the right hands of the people.

This has been the practice of the Commissaire of our district for a long time, but this is the first time I have seen the dried right hands we have heard so much about, and which are carried to the Commissaire so that he may know without doubt how many have been killed, and thus giving his soldiers no chance of letting their fellow country-men off.

If food is wanted and the natives say they have none, they are shot down, their huts burnt, and all their stuff stolen. This is called war, and the stolen goods spoils of war.

O how cruel is man when placed over the weak and ignorant. They call this "Congo Free State!" Alas, never was such bondage known till the "Free State" came turning out the natives of the soil, slaying, burning and capturing them every month of the year.

The Commissaire told Charlie (my husband) he would burn out "Bolengi if we were not here!"

And I make this solemn Declaration conscientiously believing the same to be true, and by virtue of the provisions of the Statutory Declarations Act, 1835.

C. The experiences of the boy Lokota, based on his testimony given in 1903

This child—a boy—was brought to the Mission at Bonginda, on September 7, 1903, during the visit of His Majesty's Consul [Casement].

This photograph of the mutilated child was taken by the Rev. W. D. Armstrong, on the occasion of the visit to the Mission.

The village of Mpelengi lies only some three miles away from the Mission of Bonginda. This child was only able to run at the date of his mutilation, which is stated to have occurred under the following circumstances about four and a half or five years ago, at a period when the *régime* of the rubber blessing was being worked to the utmost in the lower Lulonga:—

Mpelengi was "attacked" for its failure to bring in enough rubber . . . Sentries of the trading organization appointed to the moral and material regeneration of Mpelengi were sent against it, with the usual supply of Government-distributed guns and ammunition.

The sentries, under a leader named Mokwolo, were named Ebomi, Mokuba, and Bomolo. These four well-armed men set out from a neighbouring town named Bolondo, and attacked Mpelengi at dawn. One of the first to fall was a principal chief of the town, a man named Eliba. The people fled to the forest, and the child Lokota toddled after. Mokwolo pursued and knocked the baby down with the butt of his rifle, and cut off its hand.

The hand of Eliba was also cut off and taken away in triumph, to attest that the sentries had done their duty and had punished the "rebel" town, which dared to fail in supplying the fixed quantity of India rubber. These methods of tax-collecting are simplicity itself, and involve no formalities, such as receipt-signing.

They are now so popular that the Congo State is believed to meditate a new Coat of Arms—or Hands.

The design will closely follow that in the Shield of Ulster—where the Red-Hand shines conspicuous; but in the Congo shield, I understand, the hands will be numerous and all black—while the motto to be substituted for the existing "Travail et progress," is, I am informed, to be "HANDS OFF!" Truly an appropriate motto for this poor little State, menaced by the intrigues of perfidious Albion!

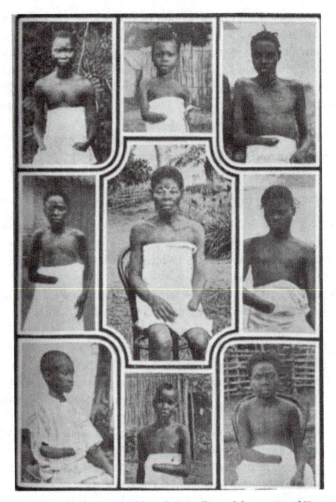

FIGURE 6 Mark Twain published this collage of the victims of King
Leopold's atrocities in a biting satire that he wrote on the monarch's
misrule, *King Leopold's Soliloquy: A Defense of His Congo Rule,* published
in 1905. "The pictures," Twain wrote, "get sneaked around everywhere."
The boy in the top center is Lokota, who was maimed by employees of
King Leopold. Mark Twain, *King Leopold's Soliloquy: A Defense of His
Congo Rule,* 1905.

D. A school lesson on the history of the Congo taught originally in Lingala to children in a mission school in 1944

Children, listen to the facts that took place in the Belgian Congo until today
   1. In 1489, the Portuguese reached the mouth of the Congo River. They called it Zaire.
Since about 415 years, the tradesmen and the priests came close to the mouth. They didn't go
up from there. They were afraid of the rapids, the stones, and the mountains.

2. Nearly 100 years later, other Portuguese explored the Congo, to the South and to the East.

3. Those that arrived the first to the Congo, in the heart of Africa, are the next three persons: Livingstone, an Englishman, from 1866 to 1868; he discovered the big lakes Tanganyika, and the other. In 1871, he discovered our river at Nyangwe. He died in Tabora in 1873. At the death of Livingstone, Cameron took the relief. He discovered Tanganyika, Nyangwe and the Indian ocean from 1873 to 1875. Stanley descended the River in 1877 from Nyangwe to Boma during 82 days. There were with him 4 Whites and 356 Blacks. In Boma there were Stanley and 115 Blacks only, the others died on the way because of wars and illnesses.

4. From there Stanley returned to Europe. He remained there during two years. He came back here, accompanied of other Whites. They went back up the river. They concluded some pacts with the chiefs and created stations of the State. In August 1879, Stanley arrived to the port of the river, close to Matadi. There, they looked for people. They had brought sufficient metal sheets to assemble three small crafts. They transported them until Kitambo (Leopoldville). There, they were assembled. Stanley and 4 Whites explored several regions and concluded some alliances with 500 customary chiefs, creating 40 stations of the State. They had spent five years on this work.

5. They had discovered a new country just to make it better. Some sovereigns of Europe chose Leopold II, king of the Belgians, to become also the king of the Congo. Leopold II, is a big civiliser, an intelligent man.

6. In 1885, Leopold II gave to the Congo its first Governor. He was placed in Boma. He also assigned some Whites everywhere. The Katanga submitted to the authority of the State in 1890. To this time the Blacks of the East and the Budja were suffering the cruelties of the Arabs (the Slave trade). The commanders who fought the Arabs are the following: Dhanis, Lippens, Debruyne, Ponthier, Jacques. The Whites could not expulse the Arabs before 1894. Afterwards, they put an end to their depredations.

7. After these wars many priests arrived to civilize the Blacks of the Congo. In the beginning, they travelled on foot from Matadi to Leopoldville. What sufferings! Then a railroad was built. Since 1898, the priests came by train. The train transported men and luggage.

8. Leopold II reigned on the Congo from Europe with great wisdom during 24 years. The whole world congratulated him about it. In 1908, Leopold II offered to its Belgian compatriots the country of the Congo. From then on one calls it the Belgian Congo. That is why all Belgians put their mind on civilizing the Blacks: the body, the intelligence, and the heart.

9. In 1909, Albert, the son of Leopold II, came to visit the Congo. At the end of that year Leopold II died. All wept. Albert was invested as King of the Belgians and of the Congo. Albert also governed us with wisdom during 25 years. He died in 1934. Albert's son went up to the throne: he is Leopold III, our beloved King.

10. Children, if there were no Whites, one would not know of a more prosperous Congo than previously. People do not wage big battles anymore between villages. They don't kill themselves anymore. They put on some clothes. The Whites have constructed beautiful houses. The State created some roads, big paths everywhere for vehicles and bicycles. One doesn't carry any heavy burden anymore. The Whites provide work, and the Blacks help them. To day, many Blacks do the works of the Whites. The priests take care of the soul and of the body. They build hospitals and schools. They also constructed numerous Missions to

teach the people God's true religion. They taught the children all kinds of professions: carpenters, masons, teachers, clerks, etc. The business became profitable. The doctors heal the patients. The judges settle the palavers.

The State governs and orders the country. Now we notice that the country is prosperous! The Church calls people to the prayer. All is in order. Let's return graces to God for these big and numerous kindnesses.

5 • Frederick Lugard instructs his officials on how to implement indirect rule (1913–18)

The most acclaimed theoretician of British colonial rule was Frederick Lugard, the same man who had waxed enthusiastic about the prospects of commercial empire in East Africa and who went on to govern Britain's largest possession by far in West Africa, Nigeria, for most of the first three decades of the twentieth century. Lugard's name has become synonymous with the theory of indirect rule, the process by which a very few Europeans would supposedly use indigenous institutions and practices to rule vast numbers of Africans. Over time, the memoranda that Lugard wrote to his officers regarding their duties became a sort of "bible" of colonial practice. As the following instructions demonstrate, there are clear links to the ideas developed by Shepstone and implemented by Wolseley decades earlier in Natal. As with their system, also, though rule is meant to be indirect, the governor is always given the powers of an autocrat, and, in the final analysis, colonial control rests on a readiness to use armed force to crush all opposition.[5]

Memo. 1. Duties of Political Officers

3. The British rôle here [Nigeria] is to bring to the country all the gains of civilisation by applied science (whether in the development of material resources, or the eradication of disease, &c.), with as little interference as possible with Native customs and modes of thought. Where new ideas are to be presented to the native mind, patient explanation of the objects in view will be well rewarded, and new methods may often be clothed in a familiar garb. Thus the object of Vaccination and its practical results may be sufficiently obvious, while the prejudice which exists among some Moslems may perhaps be removed by pointing out that it is a preventive of disease by contagion, no less than the circumcision enforced by their own law.

4. The term "Resident" implies duties rather of a Political or advisory nature, while the term "Commissioner" connotes names of ranks, functions of a more directly Administrative character. The former is therefore applicable to the Chief Government Officer in a Province of which large areas are under the immediate rule of a Paramount Chief, who, with Native Officials, himself administers a form of Government. The latter is more adapted to Provinces,

5. Frederick Lugard, *Political Memoranda: Revision of Instructions to Political Officers on Subjects Chiefly Political and Administrative, 1913–1918* (London: Waterlow and Sons, 1919, 2d ed.), 9–11, 166–67, 223–26, 254–56.

or parts of Provinces, less advanced in civilisation, where the authority of the Native Chiefs is small, and a large measure of direct Administration must devolve upon the Protectorate Government . . .

5. It is the duty of Residents to carry out loyally the policy of the Governor, and not to inaugurate policies of their own. The Governor, through the Lieutenant-Governor: is at all times ready and anxious to hear, and to give full and careful consideration to the views of Residents, but, when once a decision has been arrived at, he expects Residents to give effect to it in a thorough and loyal spirit, and to inculcate the same spirit in their juniors. This does not mean a rigid adherence to the letter of a ruling. Among such diverse races in widely varying degrees of advancement, it is inevitable and desirable that there should be diversity in the application of a general policy by the Resident, who knows the local conditions and feelings of his people. It does mean, however, that the principles underlying the policy are to be observed and the Resident in modifying their application will fully inform and obtain the approval of the Governor.

As I have said . . . we are all working not only with a common object but as parts of one organisation. The Government relies on its Administrative Officers to keep in close touch with Native opinion and feeling and to report for the information of the Governor. It is thus only that we can produce the best results, that the Governor and Lieutenant-Governors can keep in touch and gain information, and the Political Officer can count on support and on recognition of his work.

6. The degree to which a Political Officer may be called upon to act in an administrative capacity, will thus depend upon the influence and ability of the Native Chiefs in each part of the Province, though in every case he will endeavour to rule through the Native Chiefs.

In those parts of Provinces which are under the immediate authority of a Chief of the first or of the second grade, the primary duty and object of a Political Officer will be to educate them in the duties of Rulers according to a civilised standard; to convince them that oppression of the people is not sound policy, or to the eventual benefit of the rulers; to bring home to their intelligence, as far as may be, the evils attendant on a system which holds the lower classes in a state of slavery or serfdom, and so destroys individual responsibility, ambition, and development amongst them; to impress upon them the advantage of delegating the control of districts to subordinate Chiefs, and of trusting and encouraging these subordinates, while keeping a strict supervision over them; to see that there is no favouritism in such appointments; and to inculcate the unspeakable benefit of justice, free from bribery and open to all . . .

In districts where there is no Chief of the first or second grade, a Political Officer's functions become more largely Administrative, and among uncivilised Pagan tribes he must assume the full onus of Administration, to the extent to which time and opportunity permit. In such communities he will constantly endeavour to support the authority of the Chief, and encourage him to show initiative. If there is no Chief who exercises authority beyond his own village, he will encourage any village Chief of influence and character to control a group of villages, with a view to making him Chief of a district later if he shows ability for the charge. Native Court clerks or scribes, constables or couriers will never be allowed to usurp the authority of the Native Chief or Village Head . . .

Memo. No. 5. Taxation

4. "Experience (I wrote) seems to point, to the conclusion that in a country so fertile as this, direct taxation is a moral benefit to the people by stimulating industry and production. Hitherto the male population has been largely engaged in tribal war, and the men have depended on the labour of their women and the great fertility of the soil to supply their needs in food. Where taxes were formerly paid and have lapsed, it is stated that large areas have gone out of cultivation and the male population, deprived of the necessity for producing a surplus to pay their taxes, and of the pastime of war, have become indolent and addicted to drinking and quarrelling" . . .

5. [Direct taxation] . . . imposes on the freed slave, on the one hand, the obligation to render to the State, to which he owes his liberty, some portion, however small, of the labour or its equivalent which was formerly the sole property of his master, while the latter, deprived of the forced labour of his slaves, is compelled to lead a more useful life, either by personal effort, or by taking an active part in the labours of administration in return for a salary provided by means of taxation . . .

6. There is no civilised State in the world where direct taxation has not been found to be a necessity, and African communities which aspire to be regarded as civilised must share the common burden of civilisation . . .

7. Apart from the beneficial results of taxation described in the foregoing paragraphs . . . the immediate object of direct taxation is to provide a revenue . . .

Memo. No. 6. Slavery (Forced Labour, etc.)

11. Since slavery . . . stands condemned, why, it may be asked, was it not at once summarily abolished? If, however, slaves had been encouraged to assert their freedom unnecessarily in large numbers, or if those so asserting it, by leaving their masters without some good cause, had been indiscriminately upheld in their action by Political Officers, a state of anarchy and chaos would have resulted, and the whole social system of the Mohammedan States would, as I have said, have been dislocated. It might even have become necessary to legalise the institution under some other name, as was in effect done by the House Rule Proclamation in Southern Nigeria . . .

Such a sudden repudiation of their obligations to their employers by the mass of the slave population would, moreover, have involved equal misery to the slaves and to their masters. The former would have had no immediate means of livelihood, while the latter would have been reduced to beggary, and to detestation of British rule which had brought this result about. The great cities would have been filled with vagrants, criminals, and prostitutes; indeed in the early days of British Administration the large majority of the criminal class consisted of runaway slaves.

Moreover, to abolish prematurely the almost universal form of labour contract, before a better system had been developed to take its place, would not only have been an act of administrative folly, but would have been an injustice to the masters, since domestic slavery is an institution sanctioned by the law of Islam, and property in slaves was as real as any other form of property among the Mohammedan population at the time that the British assumed the Government, a nullification of which would have amounted to nothing less than whole-sale confiscation. This is equally true of either household or farm slaves, and it was very important that the latter should not leave their accustomed employment as agriculturists, and flock into the cities as "free" vagrants without means of subsistence. Residents were therefore instructed to discourage wholesale assertion of freedom, and where, similar circumstances still exist the same course will be pursued . . .

13. The introduction of a coin currency, and the enormous quantity put into circulation by the development of mining and trade, has greatly facilitated the employment of paid labour. Even the Native employer can now pay for his labour in cash. Payment in kind is always to be deprecated and discouraged for the employee so paid is unable to save his wages to purchase when and what he likes, and is dependent on instalments as they become available at arbitrary rates. The conditions in fact approximate to the slavery system, and free labour will not readily engage except for a money wage.

But above all the Government rule that each labourer must be paid up fully in cash, at short intervals, and without the intermediary of any middleman or Chief, has done more than anything else to popularise the system of paid labour, and to create a free labour market . . .

15. These results, so far as they have been achieved, have only been won at the cost of un-wearied patience and sympathetic counsel on the part of the Political Staff—and the task is by no means ended. It is still as necessary as ever, not merely to warn the ruling classes that slavery must eventually cease under British rule, but to explain to them the *practical* advantages of free labour.

One advantage to the master is that he is no longer responsible for the faults committed by his slave, or for his maintenance and that of his family in case of sickness. The labourer can no longer claim a share of the produce of the land, and is entitled to his day's wage and no more. Even the right of the freeman to terminate his contract when he pleases, on giving the agreed notice, produces no more inconvenience than the claim of the slave to run away, now that the master is unable to force him to return.

Another practical advantage of free labour to the master lies in the fact that, whereas the British Courts lend him no assistance in compelling his slave to do his proper day's work, or in punishing him if he runs away—while the legitimate assistance of the Native Courts is also strictly limited—he can, if he employs free labour, obtain the full assistance of the Administration in enforcing the contract, and punishing its breach, and it should be explained to him how he should enter into a contract enforceable at law. That slave owners were quick to recognise the advantage of free labour was shown by the voluntary emancipation of a large number of his slaves by the Sarkin Kwotto . . .

Memo. No. 7. *The Use of Armed Force*

12. When nearing the village where opposition is expected, the Political Officer will (if he can do so without too great risk to the envoy) send a message ahead, informing the people in unmistakable terms of the object of his visit, and what it is that they are, required to do or to refrain from doing, and which has given rise to the advent of all armed force . . .

If the terms are accepted, he will proceed with the troops to the village and meet the Chiefs there, subsequently withdrawing and awaiting the fulfillment of the pledges to the limit of the time allowed. He, will, meantime use every effort to get in touch with the Chiefs and people, and reassure them that no hostilities, will take place if the demands are met.

13. If, however, the message is ignored, or the attempt to get into communication has failed, and it is obvious that preparations are being made for resistance, the Civil Officer, after allowing time for the non-combatants to escape, will request the Officer Commanding the Patrol to advance and occupy the village.

Fire will not be opened until the party has been actually fired upon, or is beyond all possibility of doubt about to be attacked in force. Even then, the object will be to occupy the village—which will usually be found to have been deserted with the infliction only of such loss on the opponents as is necessary for the purpose, and firm discipline will be strictly maintained.

14. If the advance has been resisted, sufficient livestock and food will, if possible, be collected in and around the village to pay the fine demanded, and the Political Officer will again endeavour to get into communication with the Chiefs by means of any prisoner captured. He will repeat his ultimatum, and summon the Chiefs and Elders under a promise that their lives will be safe, and that they will not be carried off as prisoners, but will inform them that failure to obey the summons will result in the burning of the principal huts and of the seizure, of food supplies for the troops. The Patrol will pay for its supplies unless it has been wantonly attacked, but will *insist* on having them, and take them by force if necessary.

15. If this second summons is ineffectual, he will proceed to destroy the houses of the Chiefs and those of the persons or faction known to be implicated in the original outrages (if any) and of the ringleaders in the disturbance. If in spite of this resistance is maintained, he will request the Officer Commanding the Patrol to proceed to break down the opposition, and if this is of a determined character it will be necessary to inflict a severe blow, and thoroughly disperse the opponents. The party will remain in possession of the village, the Patrol being fed from local supplies, but no looting will ever be allowed.

This, in most cases, will have the desired effect, and the Chiefs will come in and comply with the demands. If, however, the people prefer to carry on active hostilities, the Officer Commanding the Patrol will search the surrounding bush and attack and destroy the "war-camps." Before leaving the place, sufficient livestock and food will, if possible, be collected to liquidate an increased fine. This, however, is rarely feasible, for such determined resistance will only be offered by a tribe which has been guilty of repeated crimes, and which has made every preparation for a fight by removing their belongings. In such a case it may be necessary before leaving to burn the entire village and destroy the crops . . .

17. Experience has shown that where resistance is obstinate the only way to avoid the perpetration of crimes and recurrent expeditions, is to inflict sufficiently deterrent punishment. Uncivilised man regrettably only recognises force, and measures its potency by his own losses.

6 • The French practice direct rule
to enforce submission (1908)

In apparent contrast to the British, the French believed in the direct administration of their colonial possessions, that is, ruling without the use of indigenous intermediaries other than the Africans who composed the bulk of their armies. This policy was clearly expressed by G. L. Angoulvant, governor of French West Africa, in a set of instructions that he wrote for civilian administrators in November 1908. Despite the stress on direct as distinct from indirect management, many of Angoulvant's ideas about colonial rule would have found considerable support among his British contemporaries. Angoulvant argued that before the advent of European rule most Africans had lived in a perpetual state of subjugation and were largely incapable of expressing their political views. For him, a necessary goal of colonial rule was to change completely the "Negro mentality." Furthermore, a necessary start to such a revolutionary process would be the "suppression of all resistance," physical and mental, by Africans to their rulers.[6]

General instructions to civilian administrators, November 26, 1908

One of the greatest difficulties we have encountered in establishing our influence lies in the natives' attitude of mind, or in short in the moral condition of the country. I do not refer to the northern regions, whose inhabitants have too many links with the Sudan not to share, from the mental and even intellectual point of view, in the relative but undeniable degree of civilisation of the sudanic peoples. The peoples of these regions have been softened up by forced subjection to the yoke of black conquerors. They do not dispute our supremacy, which for them means an incomparable improvement in their moral and material condition.

Among the natives of the centre of the Colony and the lower Ivory Coast the previous state of anarchy, with the solid advantages it brought to savage peoples, is still all too persistent, and where it has ceased it has left deep traces; its gradual disappearance is causing too many regrets for there to be no after-effects. These are manifested by the survival of internal disputes, feuds and rivalries, which are too often translated into sudden attacks, fights between villages, or individual crimes. Order, which in this country should ideally develop through the sacrifices of particular liberties for the sake of the liberty of all, seems to the masses to mean painful, almost intolerable, interference with all their conscious aspirations ... The native is so incapable of reflection that he does not spontaneously compare the present with the past, does not consider that we have brought him peace, the right to circulate freely, to enrich himself by his labour and to enjoy its fruits. We are the masters, and so people whose power must be respected but whose actions, however full of justice and goodwill, arouse no affection.

To make ourselves understood we must totally change the Negro mentality. It is not those who lived through the periods of anarchy who will follow us, welcome us, and love us. If we had any illusions about this they would be destroyed by the way our favourites—those who have been able to serve us and earn our special interests—often hasten to profit from their position at the public expense. Let's face it; at present the native is still hostile to our institutions and indifferent to the efforts we are making to improve his miserable lot.

This is a sad conclusion but we must recognise it; even if it does not modify our aims it should dictate our actions. For a long time yet our subjects must be led to progress despite themselves, as some children are educated despite their reluctance to work. We must play the

6. John D. Hargreaves, ed., *France and West Africa: An Anthology of Historical Documents* (London: Macmillan, 1969), 200–206.

role of strong, strict, parents towards the natives, obtaining through authority what persuasion would not gain.

The most urgent task is to check every sign of insubordination or ill-will . . .

I was quickly struck, when talking with administrators or reading their reports, by the false ideas which natives have about our occupation. In many parts of the Colony they regard it as temporary, and do not hesitate to say so. Again, when making contact with certain tribes I was greatly astonished by the lack of deference in their chief's attitude towards us, and by the independence of character which even led them to try to discuss with us the advisability of our best-justified measures.

Henceforth I wish there to be no hesitation about the political attitude to be adopted. Our line of conduct must be uniform throughout the Colony, even though, in its present immaturity, the Colony is in a state of continuous evolution and may present, within a single region, radically different situations requiring different forms of action in matters of detail. Even if the exact methods of action cannot be defined, since they must follow the development of the country and adapt themselves to circumstances, they must nevertheless share one invariable inspiration, one fixed principle, namely the principle of authority.

This principle is derived from the purposes we pursue, purposes—which I have already clearly stated in special instructions addressed to certain administrators, and which may be defined as follows. To subdue all hostile elements; to win over the waverers; to encourage the masses, who can always be drawn to our side by self-interest until one day they are drawn there by sympathy; in short, to establish our authority beyond dispute; and finally to express these results in such tangible ways as the full collection of taxes, the rendering of assistance by the natives in the creation of public fixed capital, and economic and social progress . . .

What I want us to avoid, in this country where minds have still to be conquered, is making a display of fruitless sentimentalism. We ought not to start off by seeming to set great value on the natives' wishes; the essential thing is to follow, without weakening, the only road capable of leading us to our goal. Make no mistake, these wishes of the natives are essentially unproductive, and hindrances to progress. To respect them would mean deferring indefinitely the establishment of order.

In a new country where the natives have hitherto been guided almost exclusively by instinct, order cannot be secured without provoking misunderstandings and clashes. These originate with the bad elements, that is to say with the tiny minority which unfortunately commonly has the gift of leading the masses astray. The masses are then the first to deplore the consequences of these errors, and to repudiate the real authors.

The native policy to be followed in this country must therefore be, literally, benevolent but firm; its firmness will be shown by the suppression of all resistance (which does not mean that we may depart for a moment from the humane principles by which our colonial policy is inspired). If it is important to avoid abuses and excesses by individuals, to aim always to appeal to the native's reason and to win his goodwill, to use patience, diplomacy and forbearance, it is as dangerous to show weakness as it is unwise. It is desirable to avoid the use of force, but if it is used against us we must not be afraid to use it in our turn; I am determined to teach the natives a very sharp lesson whenever, wearying of our gentleness, they think they can flout our authority.

Although our policy is a benevolent one, it does not follow that this should mean exaggerated condescension towards the native or excessive respect for the interests of a few privileged ones, mostly chiefs. These are usually unworthy of respect since they owe their prestige to excesses at the expense of the masses, of whom they all too often lead us to lose sight.

It is futile to suppose that at the present time native policy can be based solely upon reciprocal sympathies. To believe this is to risk placing blind trust in people who will abuse it. The administrator must never drop his vigilance; in fact he will do well to be mistrustful for the most trifling symptoms may conceal broad and deep movements.

In short, I cannot repeat too often that the first condition for achieving anything practical and useful in our Colony is to establish our authority on unshakeable foundations. If there is the slightest crack, all our work will be at risk; hence we must not tolerate even the slightest breach in security. In native countries events may have extraordinary reverberations and the slightest incident, especially if troublesome for us, is at once blown up and misrepresented. Administrators must thus keep an attentive watch, and even eavesdrop. Demonstrations of impatience or disrespect for our authority, or any deliberate lack of goodwill must be suppressed without delay. Populations must be kept in suspense, held on the right lines by repeated visits from those whose mission it is to command them. It is essential that bad characters, who are generally the only instigators of disorders, should be isolated and eliminated.

Now I have indicated the attitude to be adopted towards the populations [at large] I can raise the question of native administration . . . We may consider our purpose as almost fulfilled when we can administer with the help of native elements, instead of finding them in our way. This result has been achieved in the Northern districts. We must now bring it about in the forest zone and in Baoulé . . .

Not that I have the slightest notion of attempting here any experiment in indirect administration. Except in a few northern districts the Ivory Coast does not have, among its own natives, any subjects capable of even roughly discharging the role of native official, of holding even the slightest fragment of public authority. Long years will be needed before we can find individuals who are at once relatively well educated, energetic, active, honest, loyal, ready to face the dangers involved for a native in exercising of power in his own country, and sufficiently disinterested to serve us as administrative auxiliaries, even at the price of close and continuing control.

We must thus confine ourselves to practising direct administration, which is in any case the most moral system in Negro countries, for it involves far fewer of those excesses which are the undeniable consequence of any participation by natives in public affairs . . .

Some will doubtless think that innovations of the sort which I have outlined and will enlarge on later would gravely jeopardise an existing social order for which they do not believe we can safely substitute an organisation made out of nothing.

On the contrary, I believe that we are in this country precisely in order to change the social order of the people now submitted to our laws. What this social order amounts to, among the forest-dwellers and the Baoulé, is permanent and general anarchy, resulting from the absence of any authority and obstructing the realisation of any useful reform . . . It is our mission to bring civilisation, moral and social progress, economic prosperity. We shall never succeed in this if we think ourselves obliged to preserve a deplorable situation where the weight of the past prevents any reform; or if we do succeed it will be at a speed out of keeping with the importance of the sacrifices we have made and the interests which are involved.

In colonial politics nothing is more dangerous than a conservative policy. Why make firm resolutions if they are to weaken in the face of a situation which it was their very purpose to bring to an end? Why make such efforts if we doom them to failure in advance, condemning them to remain platonic on the pretext of respecting the customs and instincts of the natives?

7 • A German school examination for African children (1909)

In the 1860s Edward Blyden proposed a new university for Africa based on the teaching of classical languages, literature, and history (he was referring to Greece and Rome), combined with study of the Arab world, as well as the history and culture of African societies. Although the imperialists of the late nineteenth century argued that one of their chief goals in extending direct rule over Africans peoples was to "civilize" them, the following school examination, administered to fifty-five pupils at Catholic and Protestant mission stations in German Togo in November 1909, illustrates the limits of colonial education in practice.[7]

Saturday, November 20, 1909

10–10.30 A.M. *Calligraphy.* A passage was written on the blackboard and the pupils had to copy it.

10.30–11 A.M. *Spelling.* The chairman of the commission dictated a simple passage from a short story, with which none of them were acquainted.

11–12 A.M. *Geography.* The following questions had been set as a task:

(a) The large states of Europe and their capitals.
(b) What are the names of Germany's most important mountains?
(c) What are the names of the most important rivers in Germany and in what direction do they run?

The last question was intended to show whether the pupils could not only reproduce the names mechanically, but could also visualize a map.

3–4.30 P.M. *An Essay.* The subject set was: "What good things have the Europeans brought us?"

5.30–6 P.M. *Reading.* In addition to passages known to the pupils, they had to read aloud an unfamiliar article from a little book, called "Drei Kaiserbüchlein," out of the bookshop of the North German Mission.

•

Monday, November 22, 1909

7.30–9 A.M. *Oral Arithmetic.* The questions were asked by the teachers themselves.

10–11 A.M. *Written Arithmetic.* One question each was chosen from amongst those proposed by the school associations:

7. Bruce Fetter, ed., *Colonial Rule in Africa: Readings from Primary Sources* (Madison: University of Wisconsin Press, 1979), 128–29.

(1) Multiply 118.92 by 67¼ and then divide the number obtained by 3,964.

(2) In 1906 Togo exported copra worth 8,000 marks. In 1907 11,000 marks' worth. What was the increase per cent on the export of 1907?

(3) A labourer drinks brandy worth 0.25 marks a day. (a) How much does he pay for the brandy in a year? (b) How many days must he work for the brandy, if he earns 2 marks a day? (c) How many kgs of pork could he have bought with this sum, if pork costs 65 pfennige a kg?

From 11–12 and from 3–6 in the afternoon, *useful knowledge, grammar* and *translation* were examined.

•

Tuesday, November 23, 1909

7–8 A.M. *History*. The task set was: The reign of emperor William I and the wars he had waged. Name those men who had specially supported his government.

From 8–11.30 A.M. the examinations in translation were completed.

8 • The Natives Land Act, South Africa (1913)

After the formal establishment of the Union of South Africa in 1910, under a constitution that in practice guaranteed that whites would remain in control of the state, the new government led by Boers but working in league with the English-speaking owners of the gold-mining industry, implemented legislation to protect their respective economic interests. The Mines and Works Act of 1911 formally introduced a legal color bar into the mining industry by preventing Africans from having jobs beyond the level of manual laborer and thereby helping ensure that labor costs would remain low. The Natives Land Act of 1913, discussed in draft form for several years before its passage, was much more far reaching. It would set up the mechanism to allocate land in South Africa on the basis of race. An official government body, known popularly as the Beaumont Commission, determined the exact proportions of this allocation. Ninety-three percent of the land in South Africa—the best land, as well the most—went to 20 percent of the population (the whites); the balance went to the Africans, who comprised 80 percent of the country's population. Africans were prohibited from owning or acquiring land in areas designated for whites. Nor could they legally lease or farm on shares on white land. Their only occupation, at least as recognized by law, would be as laborers. The introduction of the legislation spurred the formation of the South African Native National Congress (SANNC), a body that aimed to represent the concerns of all Africans in South Africa. In this resolution, dated October 2, 1916, the leaders of the SANNC express their objections to the new legislation.[8]

Having heard the main features of the Report of the Natives Land Commission on the Natives Land Act of 1913, and having learnt its principal recommendations, this meeting of the

---

8. Thomas Karis and Gwendolen M. Carter, *From Protest to Challenge: A Documentary History of African Politics in South Africa, 1882–1964* (Stanford: Hoover Institution Press, 1972), vol. 1, *Protest and Hope, 1882–1934,* ed. Sheridan Johns, 86–88.

South African Native National Congress held at Pietermaritzburg, Natal, this 2nd day of October 1916, resolves:

THAT looking to the interests and welfare of the Bantu people within the Union, the Report of the Natives Land Commission presented to Parliament is disappointing and unsatisfactory, and fails to carry out the alleged principal of territorial separation of the races on an equitable basis for the following reasons:

THAT it confirms all our previous apprehensions prior to the passing of the Act: That it offers no alternative for the restriction of the free right to acquire land or interest in land: It recommends no practical or equitable remedy for the removal of the manifold objectionable disabilities imposed on the Natives by the Natives Land Act.

THAT it has failed to fulfill the official promises made to the Natives and also to satisfy their anticipations that the Report of the Commission would provide more land sufficient for occupation for themselves and their stock.

WHEREAS the land now demarcated or recommended by the Commission is inadequate for permanent settlement or occupation in proportion to the needs of the present and future Native population: And Whereas the said land is, in most parts, unsuitable for human habitation as also for agricultural or pastoral requirements, seeing that it has been studiously selected on the barren, marshy and malarial districts more especially in the Provinces of the Transvaal and the Orange Free State:

AND WHEREAS according to the evidence given before the Commission there is conflict of opinion amongst the whites as to the approval or disapproval of the principle of the Natives Land Act—the majority of the whites in the Northern Provinces are opposed to the Natives having the right to purchase land or acquire any interest in land in their own names: Nor are they in favour of any large tracts of land being granted to Natives for occupation or settlement except in the unsuitable districts as aforesaid.

BY REASON of these facts the Report of the Commission as presented for consideration by Parliament cannot be acceptable as a basis for the alleged intended territorial separation of the races or as a fair application of the alleged principles of the Act, on just and equitable lines.

ON THE OTHER HAND, while the ostensible aim of the Natives Land Act is that of territorial separation of the races, the evidence in the Report of the Commission shows that the ulterior object of the Government as well as the real desire of the white population of the country is:

To deprive the Natives as a people of their freedom to acquire more land in their own right: To restrict or limit their right to bargain mutually on even terms for the occupation of or settlement on land: To reduce by gradual process and by artificial means the Bantu people as a race to a status of permanent labourers or subordinates for all purposes and for all times with little or no freedom to sell their labour by bargaining on even terms with employers in the open markets of labour either in the agricultural or industrial centres: To limit all opportunities for their economic improvement and independence: To lessen their chances as a people of competing freely and fairly in all commercial enterprises.

THEREFORE this Congress, representing all the tribes of the Bantu Races within the Union, earnestly prays that Parliament unhesitantly reject the Report of the Natives Land Commission and instantly withdraw the Natives Land Act 1913 from operation as a statute.

II

With regard to ZULULAND it can only be pointed out as an acknowledged historical fact that the parcelling out of this territory into private farms for whites by the successive Colonial Governments was a breach of the Royal proclamation especially making this territory of Zululand a permanent reserve for the original owners. Having regard to the breaches of the aforesaid Royal proclamations and apart from the Natives Land Act 1913, this Congress urges Parliament to take the bold step of restoring the status quo in Zululand by proclaiming it a territory and a permanent place for the original owners thus securing an act of justice where it is due.

III

FINALLY, this Congress begs to point out that the great bulk of the Native population in South Africa has no protection or any privilege under the Constitution of the Union, no legal safeguard of their interest and vested rights as subjects of the British Empire, no channel for any other intervention on their behalf in the redress of their just grievances, no recognised means whereby they can effectively make their legitimate objections felt on any proposed legislation in the Union Parliament; and that as things stand the Executive for the time being in its own initiative and their interest and that of their supporters may (without any previous consultation with the Natives and their Chiefs) impose any law on the Native people without let or hindrance and regardless of the principles of that law and its effects on the people concerned. Guided by these facts and by the light of political experiences in the past we cannot accept the projected solution of the land question. We regard the Natives Land Act as one-sided and as inconsistent with the ideals of fair Government by reason of the disabilities it imposes on the Native people of the Union, while the Report of the Lands Commission is based on the objections of the European people only. Consequently, instead of establishing good relationship it is creating friction and racial antipathies between the blacks and the whites.

That the welfare of this country depends upon its economic development while this Act is calculated to retard the law of supply and demand. The Act as designed is wrong in principle as violating the laws of nature that every man is a free agent and has a right to live where he chooses according to his circumstances and his inclinations. Any system therefore of settlement on land to be lasting and beneficial without the least injury to any section of the community can only be on natural lines, and not by means of artificial legislation. Further that partial territorial separation of the races already obtains in every sphere of life in the urban and rural places: and therefore this cannot effectively be met by retaining the Natives Land Act on the statute Book. We submit there should be no interference with the existing conditions and vested rights of the Natives, and there should be no removal or ejectment of *them* from their ancestral lands or from lands they have occupied for generations past: but they should have unrestricted liberty in every Province to acquire land wherever and whenever opportunity permits.

For these and diverse reasons this Congress consisting of delegates representing the various Native tribes of South Africa in declaring its unshakable opposition to the Natives Land Act 1913 reiterated all its former resolutions with respect thereto and hereby further resolves to employ all means within its power to secure the repeal of this mischievous Act and the nonenforcement of the Commission's Report.

In spite of our previous promises to desist from agitation in connection with the Natives Land Act 1913, and recognising the Act is still in operation with detrimental effects to our people, the Executive Committee is instructed to immediately inaugurate a campaign for the collection of funds for the purposes of this resolution and to educate the Bantu people by directing their attention towards this iniquitous law.

That this resolution be sent to the Governor-General, the Missionary Societies and other interested bodies, and to the Anti-Slavery and Aborigines Protection Society. That the Chief Executive appoint a deputation of three to place this resolution before the Union Government at the earliest opportunity and also to lay same before the Union Parliament next session.

9 • The African National Congress in South Africa (1919)

While colonial administrators such as Lugard and Angoulvant argued for continuing European guardianship until such time—usually viewed as being several centuries in the future—as Africans would be capable of ruling themselves, many Africans pushed for a much more accelerated process of change. In South Africa, people distressed by the post–South African war failure of the British to oppose the racially discriminatory policies of local officials and settlers established a number of political organizations, the most significant of which was the South African Native National Congress (SANNC), formed in 1912 and renamed the African National Congress (ANC) in 1923. The principal founder of this organization was Pixley Seme, who grew up at an American mission station in Natal and, through the assistance of a Congregationalist missionary, traveled to the United States to attend high school in Massachusetts. Seme went on to obtain a BA from Columbia University in 1906 and then, after moving to Britain, studied law at Oxford University and was admitted to the London bar in 1910. He then returned to South Africa to practice as an attorney.

The first president of the organization was John L. Dube, a Zulu educated by American missionaries in the 1870s and 1880s, who in 1887 traveled to the United States to enroll at Oberlin College. In the late 1890s Dube spent another three years in America, studying theology at a seminary in Brooklyn, New York. On his return to South Africa he established a vocational school based on the model of Booker T. Washington's Tuskegee Institute and later helped launch Natal's first African newspaper.

Under the influence of Seme and Dube, the SANNC aimed to represent the concerns of all Africans in South Africa but did not call for an immediate end to British colonial rule. Its leaders praised the benefits of British civilization, while arguing that Africans should not be deprived of all of the rights and privileges of citizenship simply because of their color. The organization's constitution, drawn up in 1919, stressed the importance of mutual understanding among civilized peoples.[9]

1. To form a National Vigilant Association and a deliberative Assembly or Council, without legislative pretentions.

2. To unite, absorb, consolidate and preserve under its aegis existing political and educational Associations, Vigilance Committees and other public and private bodies whose aims are the promotion and safeguarding of the interests of the aboriginal races.

9. Http://www.anc.org.za/ancdocs/history/const/constitution_sannc.html.

3. To be the medium of expression of representative opinion and to formulate a standard policy on Native Affairs for the benefit and guidance of the Union Government and Parliament.

4. To educate Parliament and Provincial Councils, Municipalities, other bodies and the public generally regarding the requirements and aspirations of the native people; and to enlist the sympathy and support of such European Societies, Leagues or Unions as might be willing to espouse the cause of right and fair treatment of coloured races.

5. To educate Bantu people on their rights, duties and obligations to the state and to themselves individually and collectively; and to promote mutual help, feeling of fellowship and a spirit of brotherhood among them.

6. To encourage mutual understanding and to bring together into common action as one political people all tribes and clans of various tribes or races and by means of combined effort and united political organisation to defend their freedom, rights and privileges.

7. To discourage and contend against racialism and tribal feuds or to secure the elimination of racialism and tribal feuds; jealousy and petty quarrels by economic combination, education, goodwill and by other means.

8. To recommend, propose and lay before the Government for consideration and adoption laws for the benefit and protection of the Native races. And also to watch Bills introduced in Parliament for proposed legislation as well as in other bodies for legislation affecting Natives and to draft and present amendments thereto.

9. To agitate and advocate by just means for the removal of the "Colour Bar" in political education and industrial fields and for equitable representation of Natives in Parliament or in those public bodies that are vested with legislative powers or in those charged with the duty of administering matters affecting the Coloured races.

10. To promote and advocate the establishment in Parliament and other public bodies of representatives to be under the control of and for the purpose of the Association.

11. To record all grievances and wants of native peoples and to seek by constitutional means the redress thereof, and to obtain legal advice and assistance for members of the Association and its branches and to render financial [aid] where necessary with the objects hereof.

12. To encourage and promote union of Churches free from all sectarian and denominational anomalies.

13. To establish or assist the establishment of national Colleges or Public Institutions free from denominationalism or State control.

14. To originate and expound the right system of education in all schools and colleges and to advocate for its adoption by State and Churches and by all other independent bodies in respect thereto.

15. To encourage inculcation and practice of habits of industry, thrift and cleanliness among the people and propagate the gospel of the dignity of labour.

16. To acquire land by purchase, lease, exchange, gift or otherwise for erection of halls and other public buildings for the use and purposes of the Association.

17. To sell, dispose, manage, develop, let and deal in any way with all or any part of the property of the Association.

18. To borrow or raise money by mortgage or charge of all or any part of the property of the Association; and also to grant loans on security of mortgages in the manner hereinafter provided.

19. To establish a National Fund for the purposes of the Association either by means of voluntary contributions, periodical subscriptions, levies, contributions, charges or other payments; and to hold and manage all funds raised for the objects of the Association.

20. To [do] all and everything directly or indirectly to maintain and uplift the standard of the race morally and spiritually, mentally and materially, socially and politically.

21. AND GENERALLY, to do all such things as are incidental or conducive to the attainment of the above objects or any of them.

10 • W. E. B. Du Bois describes an Atlantic world bounded by racial exploitation (1915)

As with the African American missionaries who joined people like John Chilembwe in working to ameliorate the worst excesses of European rule in Africa, other African American critics of colonialism called attention to the economic exploitation of black people on both sides of the Atlantic. Perhaps the most prominent of these individuals was W. E. B. Du Bois, the first African American to earn a PhD in the United States (from Harvard University). His book The Souls of Black Folk, a powerful indictment of the discrimination that African Americans faced in the South, had found sympathetic readers throughout the world. In The Negro, published during the First World War, Du Bois tackled the history of Africans in Africa, using the same written sources as European historians of the continent did but focusing critically on the economic exploitation and political repression that he considered integral features of colonialism. Du Bois argued that black people everywhere should join together to resist the oppression to which they were subjected solely on the basis of their race.[10]

It is impossible to separate the population of the world accurately by race, since that is no scientific criterion by which to divide races. If we divide the world, however, roughly into African Negroes and Negroids, European whites, and Asiatic and American brown and yellow peoples, we have approximately 150,000,000 Negroes, 500,000,000 whites, and 900,000,000 yellow and brown peoples. Of the 150,000,000 Negroes, 121,000,000 live in Africa, 27,000,000 in the new world, and 9,000,000 in Asia.

What is to be the future relation of the Negro race to the rest of the world? The visitor from Altruria might see here no peculiar problem. He would expect the Negro race to develop along the lines of other human races. In Africa his economic and political development would restore and eventually outrun the ancient glories of Egypt, Ethiopia, and Yoruba; overseas the West Indies would become a new and nobler Africa, built in the very pathway of the new highway of commerce between East and West—the real sea route to India; while in the United States a large part of its citizenship (showing for perhaps centuries their dark descent, but nevertheless equal sharers of and contributors to the civilization of the West) would be the descendants of the wretched victims of the seventeenth, eighteenth, and nineteenth century slave trade.

10. W. E. B. Du Bois, *The Negro* (New York: Henry Holt, 1915), 232–42.

This natural assumption of a stranger finds, however, lodging in the minds of few present-day thinkers. On the contrary, such an outcome is usually dismissed summarily. Most persons have accepted that tacit but clear modern philosophy which assigns to the white race alone the hegemony of the world and assumes that other races, and particularly the Negro race, will either be content to serve the interests of the whites or die out before their all-conquering march. This philosophy is the child of the African slave trade and of the expansion of Europe during the nineteenth century.

The Negro slave trade was the first step in modern world commerce, followed by the modern theory of colonial expansion. Slaves as an article of commerce were shipped as long as the traffic paid. When the Americas had enough black laborers for their immediate demand, the moral action of the eighteenth century had a chance to make its faint voice heard.

The moral repugnance was powerfully reinforced by the revolt of the slaves in the West Indies and South America, and by the fact that North America early began to regard itself as the seat of advanced ideas in politics, religion, and humanity.

Finally European capital began to find better investments than slave shipping and flew to them. These better investments were the fruit of the new industrial revolution of the nineteenth century, with its factory system; they were also in part the result of the cheapened price of gold and silver, brought about by slavery and the slave trade to the new world. Commodities other than gold, and commodities capable of manufacture and exploitation in Europe out of materials furnishable by America, became enhanced in value; the bottom fell out of the commercial slave trade and its suppression became possible.

The middle of the nineteenth century saw the beginning of the rise of the modern working class. By means of political power the laborers slowly but surely began to demand a larger share in the profiting industry. In the United States their demand bade fair to be halted by the competition of slave labor. The labor vote, therefore, first confined slavery to limits in which it could not live, and when the slave power sought to exceed these territorial limits, it was suddenly and unintentionally abolished.

As the emancipation of millions of dark workers took place in the West Indies, North and South America, and parts of Africa at this time, it was natural to assume that the uplift of this working class lay along the same paths with that of European and American whites. This was the *first* suggested solution of the Negro problem. Consequently these Negroes received partial enfranchisement, the beginnings of education, and some of the elementary rights of wage earners and property holders, while the independence of Liberia and Hayti was recognized. However, long before they were strong enough to assert the rights thus granted or to gather intelligence enough for proper group leadership, the new colonialism of the later nineteenth and twentieth centuries began to dawn. The new colonial theory transferred the reign of commercial privilege and extraordinary profit from the exploitation of the European working class to the exploitation of backward races under the political domination of Europe. For the purpose of carrying out this idea the European and white American working class was practically invited to share in this new exploitation, and particularly were flattered by popular appeals to their inherent superiority to "Dagoes," "Chinks," "Japs," and "Niggers."

This tendency was strengthened by the fact that the new colonial expansion centered in Africa. Thus in 1875 something less than one-tenth of Africa was under nominal European control, but the Franco-Prussian War and the exploration of the Congo led to new and fateful things. Germany desired economic expansion and, being shut out from America by the Monroe Doctrine, turned to Africa. France, humiliated in war, dreamed of an African empire from the Atlantic to the Red Sea. Italy became ambitious for Tripoli and Abyssinia. Great Britain began to take new interest in her African realm, but found herself largely checkmated by the jealousy of all Europe. Portugal sought to make good her ancient claim to the larger part of the whole southern peninsula. It was Leopold of Belgium who started to make the exploration and civilization of Africa an international movement. This project failed, and the Congo Free State became in time simply a Belgian colony. While the project was under discussion, the international scramble for Africa began. As a result the Berlin Conference and subsequent wars and treaties gave Great Britain control of 2,101,411 square miles of African territory, in addition to Egypt and the Egyptian Sudan with 1,600,000 square miles. This includes South Africa, Bechuanaland and Rhodesia, East Africa, Uganda and Zanzibar, Nigeria, and British West Africa. The French hold 4,106,950 square miles, including nearly all North Africa (except Tripoli) west of the Niger valley and Libyan Desert, and touching the Atlantic at four points. To this is added the Island of Madagascar. The Germans have 910,150 square miles, principally in Southeast and Southwest Africa and the Kamerun. The Portuguese retain 787,500 square miles in Southeast and Southwest Africa. The Belgians have 900,000 square miles, while Liberia (43,000 square miles) and Abyssinia (350,000 square miles) are independent. The Italians have about 600,000 square miles and the Spanish less than 100,000 square miles.

This partition of Africa brought revision of the ideas of Negro uplift. Why was it necessary, the European investors argued, to push a continent of black workers along the paths of social uplift by education, trades-unionism, property holding, and the electoral franchise when the workers desired no change, and the rate of European profit would suffer?

There quickly arose then the *second* suggestion for settling the Negro problem. It called for the virtual enslavement of natives in certain industries, as rubber and ivory collecting in the Belgian Congo, cocoa raising in Portuguese Angola, and diamond mining in South Africa. This new slavery or "forced" labor was stoutly defended as a necessary foundation for implanting modern industry in a barbarous land; but its likeness to slavery was too clear and it has been modified, but not wholly abolished.

The *third* attempted solution of the Negro sought the result of the *second* by less direct methods. Negroes in Africa, the West Indies, and America were to be forced to work by land monopoly, taxation, and little or no education. In this way a docile industrial class working for low wages, and not intelligent enough to unite in labor unions, was to be developed. The peonage systems in parts of the United States and the labor systems of many of the African colonies of Great Britain and Germany illustrate this phase of solution. (footnote text: The South African natives, in an appeal to the English Parliament, show in an astonishing way the confiscation of their land by the English. They say that in the Union of South Africa 1,250,000 whites own 264,000,000 acres of land, while the 4,500,000 natives have only 21,000,000 acres. On top of this the Union Parliament has passed a law making even the future purchase of land by Negroes illegal save in restricted areas!) It is also illustrated in many of the West Indian islands where we have a predominant Negro population, and this population freed from slavery and partially enfranchised. Land and capital, however, have for the most part been so managed and monopolized that the black peasantry have been reduced to straits to earn a living in one of the richest parts of the world. The problem is now going to be intensified when the world's commerce begins to sweep through the Panama Canal.

All these solutions and methods, however, run directly counter to modern philanthropy, and have to be carried on with a certain concealment and half-hypocrisy which is not only distasteful in itself, but always liable to be discovered and exposed by some liberal or religious movement of the masses of men and suddenly overthrown. These solutions are, therefore, gradually merging into a *fourth* solution, which is to-day very popular. This solution says: Negroes differ from whites in their inherent genius and stage of development. Their development must not, therefore, be sought along European lines, but along their own native lines. Consequently the effort is made to-day in British Nigeria, in the French Congo and Sudan, in Uganda and Rhodesia to leave so far as possible the outward structure of native life intact; the king or chief reigns, the popular assemblies meet and act, the native courts adjudicate, and native social and family life and religion prevail. All this, however, is subject to the veto and command of a European magistracy supported by a native army with European officers. The advantage of this method is that on its face it carries no clue to its real working. Indeed it can always point to certain undoubted advantages: the abolition of the slave trade, the suppression of war and feud, the encouragement of peaceful industry. On the other hand, back of practically all these experiments stands the economic motive—the determination to use the organization, the land, and the people, not for their own benefit, but for the benefit of white Europe. For this reason education is seldom encouraged, modern religious ideas are carefully limited, sound political development is sternly frowned upon, and industry is degraded and changed to the demands of European markets. The most ruthless class of white mercantile exploiters is allowed large liberty, if not a free hand, and protected by a concerted attempt to deify white men as such in the eyes of the native and in their own imagination. (footnote text: The traveler Glave writes . . . "Formerly [in the Congo Free State] an ordinary white man was merely called 'bwana' or 'Mzunga'; now the merest insect of a pale face earns the title of 'bwana Mkubwa' [big master].")

White missionary societies are spending perhaps as much as five million dollars a year in Africa and accomplishing much good, but at the same time white merchants are sending at least twenty million dollars' worth of European liquor into Africa each year, and the debauchery of the almost unrestricted rum traffic goes far to neutralize missionary effort.

Under this last mentioned solution of the Negro problems we may put the attempts at the segregation of Negroes and mulattoes in the United States and to some extent in the West Indies. Ostensibly this is "separation" of the races in society, civil rights, etc. In practice it is the subordination of colored people of all grades under white tutelage, and their separation as far as possible from contact with civilization in dwelling place, in education, and in public life.

On the other hand the economic significance of the Negro to-day is tremendous. Black Africa to-day exports annually nearly two hundred million dollars' worth of goods, and its economic development has scarcely begun. The black West Indies export nearly one hundred million dollars' worth of goods; to this must be added the labor value of Negroes in South Africa, Egypt, the West Indies, North, Central, and South America, where the result is blended in the common output of many races. The economic foundation of the Negro problem can easily be seen to be a matter of many hundreds of millions to-day, and ready to rise to the billions tomorrow.

Such figures and facts give some slight idea of the economic meaning of the Negro to-day as a worker and industrial factor . . .

What do Negroes themselves think of these their problems and the attitude of the world toward them? First and most significant, they are thinking. There is as yet no great single centralizing of thought or unification of opinion, but there are centers which are growing larger and larger and touching edges. The most significant centers of this new thinking are, perhaps naturally, outside Africa and in America: in the United States and in the West Indies; this is followed by South Africa and West Africa and then, more vaguely, by South America, with faint beginnings in East Central Africa, Nigeria, and the Sudan.

The Pan-African movement when it comes will not, however, be merely a narrow racial propaganda. Already the more far-seeing Negroes sense the coming unities: a unity of the working classes everywhere, a unity of the colored races, a new unity of men. The proposed economic solution of the Negro problem in Africa and America has turned the thoughts of Negroes toward a realization of the fact that the modern white laborer of Europe and America has the key to the serfdom of black folk, in his support of militarism and colonial expansion. He is beginning to say to these workingmen that, so long as black laborers are slaves, white laborers cannot be free. Already there are signs in South Africa and the United States of the beginning of understanding between the two classes.

In a conscious sense of unity among colored races there is to-day only a growing interest. There is slowly arising not only a curiously strong brotherhood of Negro blood throughout the world, but the common cause of the darker races against the intolerable assumptions and insults of Europeans has already found expression. Most men in this world are colored. A belief in humanity means a belief in colored men. The future world will, in all reasonable probability, be what colored men make it. In order for this colored world to come into its heritage, must the earth again be drenched in the blood of fighting, snarling human beasts, or will Reason and Good Will prevail? That such may be true, the character of the Negro race is the best and greatest hope; for in its normal condition it is at once the strongest and gentlest of the races of men: "Semper novi quid ex Africa!"

CHAPTER TWO

The Interwar Years

Supporting the Metropoles (1919–36)

11 ♦ An appeal for the equal treatment of Africans and people of African descent (1919)

Joined by other black leaders from the United States, the Caribbean, and Africa, W. E. B. Du Bois attended the peace treaty negotiations held in Versailles in 1919 at the conclusion of World War I. None of the European powers present (including the United States) accepted the arguments of Du Bois and his colleagues that representatives of colonized people should officially participate in the negotiations, nor did they agree to the request that the former colonies of Germany be turned over to an international organization rather than divided up among the other colonial powers. Germany's colonial possessions were apportioned between Britain and France. Du Bois and his colleagues, however, passed a series of resolutions that likely influenced the establishment by the newly formed League of Nations of the Mandate Commission, an international body responsible for overseeing the treatment of the former colonial subjects of Germany. Their presence at the negotiations and their unity in speaking on behalf of oppressed people of color on both sides of the Atlantic demonstrated the potential for the development of a pan-African movement, evident especially in the resolutions that their Pan-African Congress passed in Paris in February 1919.[1]

The resolutions of the Congress asked in part:

    A. That the Allied and Associated Powers establish a code of law for the international protection of the natives of Africa, similar to the proposed international code for labor.

    B. That the League of Nations establish a permanent Bureau charged with the special duty of overseeing the application of these laws to the political, social, and economic welfare of the natives.

    C. The Negroes of the world demand that hereafter the natives of Africa and the peoples of African descent be governed according to the following principles:

1.   *The land:* the land and its natural resources shall be held in trust for the natives and at all times they shall have effective ownership of as much land as they can profitably develop.

2.   *Capital:* the investment of capital and granting of concessions shall be so regulated as to prevent the exploitation of the natives and the exhaustion of the natural wealth of

---

1. W. E. B. Du Bois, *The World and Africa: An Inquiry into the Part Which Africa Has Played in World History* (New York: International Publishers, 1965), 11–12.

the country. Concessions shall always be limited in time and subject to State control. The growing social needs of the natives must be regarded and the profits taxed for social and material benefit of the natives.

3. *Labor:* slavery and corporal punishment shall be abolished and forced labor except in punishment for crime, and the general conditions of labor shall be prescribed and regulated by the State.

4. *Education:* it shall be the right of every native child to learn to read and write his own language, and the language of the trustee nation, at public expense, and to be given technical instruction in some branch of industry. The State shall also educate as large a number of natives as possible in higher technical and cultural training and maintain a corps of native teachers.

5. *The State:* the natives of Africa must have the right to participate in the government as fast as their development permits, in conformity with the principle that the government exists for the natives, and not the natives for the government. They shall at once be allowed to participate in local and tribal government, according to ancient usage, and this participation shall gradually extend, as education and experience proceed, to the higher offices of State; to that end, in time, Africa be ruled by consent of the Africans . . . Whenever it is proven that African natives are not receiving just treatment at the hands of any State or that any State deliberately excludes its civilized citizens or subjects of Negro descent from its body politic and cultural, it shall be the duty of the League of Nations to bring the matter to the notice of the civilized World.

12 • Harry Thuku explains why he formed a political movement for all East Africans (1921)

Harry Thuku was born in what is now Kenya in 1895 and educated at a school run by American missionaries. As a teenager, he moved to Nairobi and worked as a clerk. His employment there made him aware for the first time that he was part of a larger community than his own Gikuyu people and that it was a multiethnic community as well. ("Gikuyu" is the indigenous spelling of the more common term "kikuyu.") In many ways, this transformation was a typical experience for the newly emerging elite class of missionary-educated Africans. Thuku was also representative of this first generation coming of age under colonialism in his perception and condemnation of the daily practices of white settler rule, practices that seemed contrary to the claims of upliftment, civilization, and development emanating from the distant imperial capital of London. In 1921 Thuku established the East Africa Association, a political organization to represent Africans throughout British East Africa. He was motivated in particular by legislation, passed between 1915 and 1920, that dispossessed Africans of most of their land, restricted lease holding to Europeans, and began the process of placing Africans in rural reserves (usually on the poorest land), a policy already implemented in South Africa. For his attempts to develop a political movement, Thuku was arrested by the British in 1922 and kept in prison until 1930, again an experience that was common for those Africans who attempted to resist colonialism through peaceful means during the first half of the twentieth century.[2]

2. Harry Thuku, *Harry Thuku: An Autobiography* (Nairobi: Oxford University Press, 1970), 1–3, 5–6, 8–9, 11, 14–15, 16, 18–20, 22–23, 29–30, 32, 33–34.

I can tell you how I know I was born in 1895; my elder brother, who died recently, was circumcised in that year. My father's village was here on the site of my house, and this brother, Kigume, was circumcised just a few yards away beyond my present hedge; in fact it was on the land of one of my father's tenants. But the reason I know my year of birth was that later on my mother told me that she could not attend the ceremony, even though it was close by, because she had just delivered me and had no strength to go. And I have since then found out from the books of government officers that my brother's age-set, Mutung'u, was circumcised in 1895.

My father's village was about two miles from Kambui Hill, on one of the ridges between the Chomba River and the Mukuyu. In his compound there were the huts of his four wives, the eldest wife being nearest his hut, and my mother, Wanjiku, furthest from the centre. According to the custom of my clan, Anjiru, the village entrance faced south, just like my present house; I am not sure why this is, for other Kikuyu clans, such as Achera, and my wife's clan, Agachiku, actually face north. My father's cattle stayed some distance from his village in a *manyatta* (kraal), but each night the sheep and the goats returned; they all knew their way to the huts of the various wives.

My mother was also a cultivator, and grew her maize, beans, and sweet potatoes along with delicious arrowroot, on a small patch behind my house. As soon as I was able to walk a little I would accompany my elder brothers—it would not be very far, but we loved to go, just as my children now cry to go and herd, when I want them to go to school. I used also to accompany my mother to her little patch where my coffee now grows. Indeed I buried her when she died in 1934 right in her old garden. She was very old. But with us children she was very kind, showing it in many ways; she never punished or beat any of the children including myself. Also she had a lot of food for us, since she was a good cultivator. In this work she was much helped by these unpaid female labourers we call *ndungata*. They would work on the land of a rich man, getting their food supplied, and gradually acquire goats and sheep of their own. You know, I remember a woman who died just a few years ago who had been one of my mother's *ndungata*.

Kairianja, my father, died in 1899, when I was only four years old; so Kigume became the *muramati* of all our land and property. At this time Kigume used to do a little work for a European who had quietly, slipped on to our land. We did not know he was coming to stay, since he had just built a little mud and grass house where the present manager of Mchana Estate lives. The Kikuyu gave him the nickname Kibara for he was always beating people, but he did not seem to do much actual planting; he did not plant any crops or coffee, and did not come into any Kikuyu village—I think because he was afraid probably, But anyway I did go sometimes to take food to my brother who was working with him. No one thought that Kibara had come permanently. In fact it was only in 1915 that some of us finally heard that this part of our land had been sold to a Mr. Noon, one of the government transport officers, who I happened to know quite well. Then our people, including Waweru, the chief, were asked to move a little further west. Of course it was government policy to sell land without telling the occupiers. Then later the new "owner" would come along and say, "This land is mine; I bought it from government." Naturally the people were afraid of government. And if you asked these early white settlers and government people how they had sold off our land they would reply, "You have no land. The land belongs to God. God has given it to the white man, and they have it now." Indeed I remember one man told me he had gone to see Mr.

Ainsworth, the Commissioner in Nairobi, and after protesting about land sales, Ainsworth had told him that amongst the Kikuyu, land belonged to the *hiti* (hyena)!

When I was about five, the government had made a large encampment with Nubian soldiers near Ruiru, which was about seven miles from my home. And there they had brought some Amerikani (cotton cloth) for people to buy. One day I had been given one rupee by my brother and I went along with some other boys to buy my first cloth. I bought it and wore it like a Maasai, over my shoulder. But the first European I saw with my eyes was in 1902. It was Mr. Knapp of the Gospel Missionary Society (GMS) who had come to the village of my cousin, Mburu, just beneath our village. I and some other small boys heard there was to be a white man speaking, so we went along. His Kikuyu was very poor, but we were so interested in him that when he asked us to pray, we looked through our fingers just to see him.

Eventually, he had discussions with the elders of our clan about land for a mission station, and it was agreed to give the mission one hundred acres. Included in that was Kambui Hill which had also belonged to our family. It was there that my oldest brother, Njongoro, had had his village, but he had died earlier at the turn of the century...

I got my name Thuku from my grandfather on my mother's side. Originally he had been called Karanja, but then the Arabs came into the country selling that brass wire in exchange for elephant tusks. They called it *ruthuku*. So my grandfather took that name and forgot his first one, and I in turn was given it later.

I have nothing belonging to my mother or my father except my mother's photograph. Some people when they became Christians, including myself, were no longer interested in Kikuyu things. The man, however, who kept some things of Kikuyu tradition was Kenyatta. But I was not interested. I did not have to destroy anything when I became a Christian because I did not own anything—not even a snuff box! And these were the commonest things that I saw being thrown on the fire at the mission when I was a boy. The Gospel Mission did not order people to destroy such things; it simply preached that witchcraft, greasing the body, and wearing ornaments were not God's way. But people did not throw their necklaces and bracelets on the mission fires, only snuff boxes and the things the witchdoctor used for doctoring people...

In 1908, when I had been at the mission one year, two important things happened. First, I was baptized—they gave me the name Harry—and I had to go completely under water in a deep pool in the Mukuyu River. With baptism, my mother and brother did not seem to mind at all; they did not object certainly...

I did not get any political education from the missionaries, for they did not discuss political matters with us. But I found out later that they fought for us out of our presence amongst other Europeans. I have said that Dr. Henderson fought for African rights, and he was certainly a very fearless man. I know this because of evidence that he gave to a Commission; the settlers wanted to take all Kikuyu lands, and some suggested, with Lord Delamere's encouragement, that the Kikuyu should be moved three hundred miles to the north. Now, Dr. Henderson was on this commission at the time, and when he gave his evidence, I remember he said: "If you interfere or try to move the Kikuyu people from their land completely, all Europeans in Kikuyu country will be killed in one night"...

My time in the mission came to an end in 1911, and I set off for employment in Nairobi...

You know, there were only two churches in Nairobi for Africans at that time, the CMS and the Roman Catholics (RC). At that time the Catholics were all Italian and French fathers (the Italians north of the Chania River, and the others nearer Nairobi). Funnily enough the Catholics were always trying to sow hatred between the RC and the CMS mission boys, and one father I remember even refused to come into Mr. Knapp's house. The Catholic policy was only to teach Africans religion, but no fuller education. So there were no Catholics working in those days in government offices in Nairobi; instead almost everybody was CMS. Indeed I only remember that I knew one Catholic friend, a man Matthew who worked with me in my second job. But later on when I founded the East African Association, there were no Catholic members—although there were many Muslims. I think this was because the Italian and French fathers did not give Africans good English, and also because they taught their students that it was a sin to take part in politics. When there were political troubles in Nairobi after my arrest in 1922, they thought this showed their policy had been right. For they wrote in their mission newspaper published in Nyeri, "You British people, you have made a mistake. You sharpened a knife which is now cutting you." They meant the knife of education . . .

Several of my friends, including Josiah Njonjo, were at that time working on the newspaper, the *Leader* of British East Africa; so in 1914 I joined these boys and was given the job of composing type. Later I was taught to print, and I spent my time between those two jobs of compositor and machine man. Of course some people did not think it a very honourable position, but looking back I can see I was rather lucky to be there. All my further education, or self-education, I gained from there. Whenever there were words or phrases I did not understand, I consulted Goan or Indian friends working there.

And beyond this, when the war came to East Africa, I was also taught by a military sergeant how to print maps and sketches of war positions. This was a special skill, and as only the sergeant and I knew how to do it, the *Leader* did not allow me to go and fight in the East Africa Campaign. Also I read many of the articles that the settlers wrote to the *Leader* (the paper was strongly in favour of the white settlers), and when I saw something there about the treatment of Africans, it entered into my head and lay quiet until later on.

While I was at the *Leader,* I used to get a monthly wage of 46 rupees, and usually 12 rupees out of this I spent on my lodgings. At the time, I lived in River Road, in one room in various Asians' houses. I did not have any transport, so it was easier to live in River Road than over at Pangani village. River Road was also the place where many of the first government African clerks lived, and these came from Freretown and Rabai at the Coast, or from Buganda. This was why most of my friends at this time were Coast men, all good Swahili speakers, and it was how I got a grasp of good pronunciation . . .

It was at the *Leader,* from about 1915, that I first began to think seriously about some of our troubles as Africans—especially this question of forced labour. Before then only men had been made to work, but at about that time women and girls too were compelled to go out to work. This was what happened: a settler who wanted labour for his farm would write to the D.C. [District Commissioner] saying he required thirty young men, women or girls for work on his farm. The D.C. sent a letter to a chief or headman to supply such and such a number, and the chief in turn had his tribal retainers to carry out this business. They would simply go to people's houses—very often where there were beautiful women and daughters—and point out which were to come to work. Sometimes they had to work a distance from home, and the number of girls who got pregnant in this way was very great . . .

1916 was the year I first began meeting Koinange—old, Chief Koinange—and later on when I was living in Pangani itself, he once came to my single room and spent the night there.

We discussed many matters, and I saw he was quite fearless. He was very opposed to what had happened with Kikuyu land, and the government had done a very stupid thing over his own land. A road divided it in two, and the government had declared that on one side of the road was European, and on the other African land. Yet it was across the road from Koinange's house that both his father's and grandfather's graves were. And every morning when Koinange got up he would look across the road at the European coffee which he was not allowed to grow . . .

The War ended, and after it, things began to warm up in the British East Africa Protectorate (that was Kenya's old name). First there were many thousands of porters who came back from very very difficult conditions in the East Africa Campaign, and found that they would not get any gratuity. Instead the government under General Northey decided that the white soldiers, and especially the officers, should be rewarded. So they alienated many thousands of acres in the area round Kericho for a Soldier Settlement Scheme. Also in my own Kiambu area, more land was taken at this time and given to white settlers. However, I want to make one thing clear about this land business; back at that time we Africans who were a little educated were not saying that all Europeans should leave the country, or that we should get self-government. There was no idea of that. What we objected to was that the Europeans did not treat us as we had treated the Dorobos. I mean, we bought our land from the Dorobo according to agreed prices, and as I said earlier, we planted *itoka* lilies to confirm these sales. We did not simply claim land without the Dorobo knowing anything about it. And I am not saying that one or two Europeans did not do things in a proper manner. Take the way Mr. Krieger bought his farm from a Kikuyu, Gichinga, just nearby here at Thembigwa. He paid him 70 female goats in the presence of Mr. Knapp, and I always told my people that they should not fight to get that piece back, for it was not taken secretly or by force . . .

The second thing that was making Africans angrier after the War was this thing called *kipande*. This was Swahili for a container in which a registration paper was carried. Now General Northey, Kenya's Governor after the War, decided in 1919 to implement the recommendations of an earlier committee which had suggested that Africans be registered. The ordinary people did not understand what this registration was, but even more educated ones like me did not oppose it to begin with, for we knew that many countries asked their citizens to register. So we did not object until we found out that it was a very different business in Kenya. First of all you had to wear this quite heavy metal box round your neck on a string all the time; then in the columns on the paper inside there were many things that were against Africans. There was one space where the employer had to sign when he engaged you and also when you left. You could not leave employment without permission, and if you did, you could be taken to the D.C.'s court. Also, no other employer would take you if the space for discharge was not filled up. Another thing in the early kind of *kipande* was a space for remarks; and here, if an employer did not like you, he could spoil your name completely by putting "lazy," "disobedient," or "cheeky." That column made me very angry. *Kipande* was only for Africans; and in 1919, at that old building still standing opposite Nairobi General Post Office, I collected my one.

There was also the question of rising tax for Africans. It kept on going up even though we did not see anything like schools or clinics which we get nowadays for our high taxes. The reason for it was to pull African workers out of their houses to work for the European settlers;

you see, they could not get the money to pay their tax unless they left their homes and worked for some months . . .

The final thing was when we heard that the settlers were going to reduce African wages by one third. Many of us got very angry, and we called a meeting in Pangani on 7 June 1921 to see if we could form a Young Kikuyu Association. The reason we called it "Young" was this. For a long time in Nairobi I had known Baganda people. There was one Muganda called Ssentongo who had his own newspaper, *Sekanyolya,* and there were clerical workers. Then there was a Buganda football team which used to come through and play us in Nairobi. Indeed a little later on it was through football that I met Prince Suna of Buganda—he was the uncle of Kabaka Daudi Chwa. He had come to Nairobi accompanying his team; his secretary came and found me, and Suna and I had our photograph taken together. From some of these people I learnt that they had a body called the Young Baganda Association in their country. "Does that mean," I asked them, "that only young people can join it?" "No!" they told me, "even men of seventy years old, for it is the Association which is young and not the members!" So we thought of doing the same . . .

Once I got back to Nairobi, I began to have discussions with my friends. We saw clearly that if we sent anything coming from the Kikuyu tribe alone, we would carry no weight. But if we could show that it came from all tribes—the Maasai, the Kamba etc., then we should have a great voice. At the same time, over the next few days, we continued our discussions for the proper name for our Association, and finally decided that we should change it from the Young Kikuyu to the East African Association (EAA), so that anyone in the whole area could join. This we agreed in committee on 1 July.

To acquaint the people of Nairobi with our plans, I called a meeting on Sunday, 10 July, 1921, for all Africans. The site was where the present Arya Samaj Girls' School is, near Ngara Road, and we had an attendance of about 2,000. I was voted into the Chair, and we had a long discussion on our grievances. I do not remember all the speakers, but I do remember two men in particular—how powerfully James Mwanthi from Kamba country spoke; and also how a Luo, Abednego, jumped up on the table and gave a fiery speech. By the end we had passed a number of resolutions on the Indians, forced labour, taxation and education, and the mass meeting agreed that we should send the substance of our resolutions direct to the Colonial Office in London . . .

Within Kenya itself, the EAA had by now many members from different tribes. The Maasai had been in it from the beginnings with people like Haikoko, the chauffeur of Mr. Jeevanjee. Then there were my very close Kamba friends, Ali Kironjo [Kilonzo], James Mwanthi, and Mohamed Sheikh, who helped us to spread out into Kamba country. We had a few Luo (we called them Kavirondo then), and even some Nandi. What all of us wanted was to show people that we were all one family and that there was no difference between all the tribes of Kenya.

Once, for instance, I went to hold a meeting at Waiganjo's place, Ng'enda; it was deep in Kikuyu country. But in order to show that there were many other people in Kenya, I deliberately took along Juma Mnandi (a Nandi who was a gardener in Government House), Samuel Okoth the Kavirondo pastor, and Ali Kironjo, the Kamba Muslim . . .

I was very delighted to be travelling to the meeting at Ng'enda, because I was accompanied by the school teacher, Samuel Okoth, a Christian from Maseno, and two Moslems, their names were Abdulla Tairara and Ali Kironjo. We were very pleased at our trip for we travelled as brothers. And I saw no difference between the Kavirondo and the man from Kikuyu, or even between the Christian believer and the believer in Islam. I was pleased too in that we fulfilled the command of our Lord God—that you should love your neighbour as yourself . . .

The chiefs, as I said, had been continuing to preach against us. So this time we decided to follow them up by car. None of us drove, so we hired an Indian taxi (the driver was in Nairobi until quite recently) and set off. All the main members went along, including Waiganjo, Muchuchu and Tairara. And we toured a number of places like Wangindu and Kiguoya's. Everywhere I gave advice to carry on underground if the Association was stopped and I was arrested . . .

We returned to Nairobi and paid about 1,300 rupees for the hire of the car. But I knew that chiefs and missionaries had been collecting affidavits against me, and I suppose I was not really surprised when at 6 o'clock on 14 March I was arrested . . .

Soon fifty members of the Association had been arrested, and the government decided to deport three of us—Waiganjo, Mugekenyi and me. I think they felt that if they left either of those free, the movement would continue. As it was, Waiganjo heard that they were looking for him, and as he was a fearless man, he rode his mule right into the D.C.'s compound at Kiambu, and said, "I understand you are looking for me." He was arrested.

13 • Creating a national movement for all West Africans (1920)

In 1919, the same year that W. E. B. Du Bois was presenting the grievances of colonial people at Versailles, the South African Native National Congress (SANNC) was agreeing upon a constitution for a body to represent all "native peoples" in southern Africa, and Harry Thuku was becoming increasingly appalled by the racist treatment meted out to Africans in British East Africa, representatives from all of the British colonial possessions in West Africa met to form a political organization of their own, the National Congress for British West Africa. The members of this new organization, most of them merchants and missionary-educated professionals (doctors and lawyers) petitioned the British government on October 19, 1920, to allow Africans to elect their own political representatives, especially to the administrative bodies that determined the type and amount of taxes levied in colonial territories. They also objected to the repartitioning of Africa that they saw taking place at Versailles. The British government ignored their representatives.[3]

To his most Gracious Majesty George the Fifth, King of Great Britain and Ireland, and the Dominions beyond the Seas in Council. The Humble Petition of the National Congress of British West Africa by Its Delegates Now in London,
Sheweth:

That your Petitioners are the accredited representatives of the National Congress of British West Africa, which was brought into being after the first Conference of Africans of British West Africa [held in Accra, March 1919, with delegates from Ghana, Nigeria, Sierra

3. George Metcalfe, ed., *Great Britain and Ghana: Documents of Ghana History, 1807–1957* (Legon: University of Ghana, 1964), 583–85.

Leone, and Gambia], for the purpose of continuing and perpetuating the work of the Conference.

That your Petitioners would respectfully seize the opportunity of expressing their loyalty, devotion, and attachment to Your Majesty's person and throne and would further beg to refer to the sentiment of the Conference in one of its Resolutions, to the effect "That this Conference desires to place on record the attachment of the peoples of British West Africa to the British Empire, and their unfeigned loyalty and devotion to the throne and person of His Majesty the King-Emperor, and direct that copies of these Resolutions be forwarded in due course to His Majesty's Principal Secretary of State for the Colonies and to each of the Governors of the several Dependencies." Further it may be noted that the policy of the Congress is "to preserve strictly and inviolate the connection of the British West African Dependencies with the British Empire and to maintain unreservedly all and every right of free citizenship of the Empire and the fundamental principle that taxation goes with effective representation" ...

That your Petitioners desire to bring to the notice of Your Majesty, that the administrations of the several British West African Dependencies are composed of Executive and Legislative Councils. The Members of the Executive Councils are all Government officials who also, together with Members nominated by the Governors, compose the Legislative Councils. As such the nominated members do not really represent the people, and they are not directly in touch with them ...

That apart from the fact that the National Congress of British West Africa represents substantially the intelligentsia and the advanced thought of British West Africa, and that the principles it stands for are some of those fundamental ones that have always actuated communities that have arrived at the stage of national consciousness, it also represents the bulk of the inhabitants of the various indigenous communities and with them claims, as sons of the soil, the inherent right to make representations [as] to existing disabilities, and to submit recommendations for the necessary reforms.

That your Petitioners would respectfully beg leave to point out that in asking for the franchise, the people of British West Africa are not seeking to copy a foreign institution. On the contrary, it is important to notice that the principle of electing representatives to local councils and bodies is inherent in all the [political] systems of British West Africa, which are essentially democratic in nature, as may be gathered from standard works on the subject.

That, further, according to the African system, no Headman, Chief, or Paramount Ruler has an inherent right to exercise Jurisdiction unless he is duly elected by the people to represent them, and that the appointment to political offices also entirely depends upon the election and the will of the people.

That such being the British West African system of representation the arrangement by which the Governor of a Crown Colony nominates whom he thinks proper to represent the people, cannot but strike them as a great anomaly and does constitute a grievance and a disability which they now respectfully pray may be remedied ...

That in order that Your Majesty may appreciate how detrimentally the present system of appointment to the Legislative Councils by Government nomination works, attention is respectfully drawn to the passage of the Palm Kernels Ordinance against the will of the people ...

That your Petitioners, therefore, humbly pray your Majesty to grant an amendment of the existing letters patent for the several British West African Dependencies whereby the present system of Government may be altered so as to provide for the reconstruction of the several Legislative Councils by giving the people the right of electing one-half of the Members thereof, and by the constitution of Houses of Assembly which shall be composed of the Members of the Legislative Council besides six other financial representatives elected by the people, who shall have the power of imposing all taxes and of discussing freely and without reserve the items on the annual estimates of revenue and expenditure prepared by the Governors in the Executive Council and approving of them . . .

That your Petitioners would respectfully submit that the time has come for the establishment of Municipal Corporations in all the principal towns of British West Africa with full power of local self-government, and that the people may have the power of electing four-fifths of the Members thereof and the remaining one-fifth nominated by the Government, such elected and nominated members having the power of electing the Mayor of the Corporation, who, however, must be an elected member.

That your Petitioners desire the establishment of a British West African University, and are prepared to promote the necessary funds for its establishment, supported by Government subsidies.

That in the opinion of your Petitioners the time has arrived for the introduction of Emigration Laws so as to keep out "undesirables," and the opinion of Your Majesty's Government is invited as to whether Syrians are not "undesirables" . . .

That your Petitioners view with marked disfavour the scheme of the Empire Resources Development Committee, and regret that British publicists should be found capable of advocating a policy which, if adopted, would bring Imperial Britain on a par with pre-war German attitude with regard to African Proprietary rights. In this connection, it is submitted that the principle of Trusteeship may easily be made to operate detrimentally to African proprietary rights, and that the people are well able to control their own lands and to watch and protect their proprietary interests . . .

That Your Majesty's Petitioners view with grave alarm the right assumed by the European Powers of exchanging or partitioning African countries between them without regard to the wishes of the people, and beg leave respectfully to request that the partitioning of Togoland between the English and the French be reconsidered . . .

Signed for and on behalf of the National Congress of British West Africa.

T. Hutton-Mills, Barrister-at-Law, President

Casely Hayford, M.B.E., M.L.C., Barrister-at-Law, Vice President and Gold Coast Delegate

Edward Francis Small, Gambia Delegate

Henry Maurice Jones, Merchant, Gambia Delegate

Fred. W. Dove, Merchant, Sierra Leone Delegate

H. C. Bankole-Bright, Physician and Surgeon, Editor "Aurora," Secretary London Committee, Delegate Sierra Leone

H. Van Hien, Merchant, Treasurer, Gold Coast Delegate

J. Egerton-Shyngle, Barrister-at-Law, Nigeria Delegate

Chief Oluwa, of Lagos, Nigeria Delegate

14 • Forced labor in Portuguese Africa (1924)

Labor conditions in colonial Africa were uniformly appalling irrespective of the particular European country in control. Nonetheless, conditions in the Portuguese territories were considered exceptional even by this low standard. In 1924 American critics of the labor situation in Africa persuaded a professor of sociology at the University of Wisconsin, Madison, Edward Ross, to combine an investigative tour of the Portuguese colonies in Africa with an already planned research trip that Ross was making to India later that year. Ross avoided working with the local Portuguese officials, who, he believed, would simply claim that everything was being done in accordance with the law.

Between July 19 and September 3, 1924, Ross and a colleague traveled throughout the countryside of Angola and Mozambique, where, they reported, they "visited the native villages in the bush, gathered the people together and, through an interpreter known to them and in whom they had confidence, questioned them as to their compulsory labor. In Angola nineteen villages were visited from three centres not less than two hundred miles apart. The facts as to many other villages were elicited from conversation with the chief, the native pastor or the native teacher. The statements were taken down just as they fell from the lips of the interpreter, and such notes form the basis of this report. Data were secured also from labor groups encountered on the highway and from individuals. Altogether for Angola we have the experiences of from six thousand to seven thousand of the native population in three different provinces" (Ross 1925, 91).

Partly as a result of Ross's investigations, the International Labour Organisation (ILO), founded in 1919 on the premise that "universal and lasting peace" could be established "only if it is based upon social justice" (ILO Constitution), in 1930 adopted the "Forced Labour Convention." This convention, which aimed "to suppress the use of forced or compulsory labour in all its forms within the shortest possible period," was ratified by Great Britain in 1931, Italy in 1934, and France in 1937, but not by Belgium until 1944 or by Portugal until 1956. The following reports on the situation in individual villages were written by Ross based on the personal observations that he and his colleague made in Angola and Mozambique in July, August, and September 1924.[4]

VILLAGE No. 2

In the late afternoon we sat in the shade of big trees and interrogated about seventy Ambaquistas. They are of a superior type, and I saw many faces of worthy, mild and excellent men.

Case 1.—Had to labor two weeks at a stint on the Government plantation, supplying his own food. This is in addition to paying taxes. Since December 1st this village has been furnishing workers on this plantation. Generally the recruits worked two weeks out of six, i.e. in the six months this lasted the average villager worked two months on the plantation. They were under the hippo-hide whip and came back thin. No pay.

Case 2.—Some have been taken from here to work on routes leading out of Malange. They are worked two weeks at a time and get nothing. This has lasted eight months and the family still have to furnish members for this work. The soldiers come, catch the people, children included, and tie them up. They take about half of the family, leaving the other half to change off with it.

4. Edward Alsworth Ross, *Report on Employment of Native Labor in Portuguese Africa* (New York: Abbott, 1925), 8–9, 11–12, 18–19, 23–24.

Case 3.—Was working as a mason for a building contractor in town, left him because he was allowed but six cents a day for food—which was insufficient—and he got no pay on the ground that he was a learner. The contractor retaliated by giving his name to the Government, so he was recruited. After two months as a carrier on Government jobs in Malange, he was sent to Benguela where he worked six months on street work for which he received rations but no pay. He had already paid his head tax. On both jobs he was maltreated. They would flog a man until he could hardly stand up and then send him to work just the same. Some died, but none from this village.

Spokesmen of the village say that from fear of rebellion the Government keeps ammunition from the people, so that they hunt only with bows and spears. They cannot get ammunition for their old muzzle-loaders. In recent years, much greater care has been exercised in keeping powder and cartridges from the natives.

In practice, forced labor works out as follows. A laborer works for the coffee planter and at the close of his term of service the planter says, "I can't pay you anything for I have deposited the stipulated wage for you with the Government; go to such and such an office and you will get your pay." The worker applies there and is told to come around in a couple of months. If he has the temerity to do so, he is threatened with the calaboose and that ends it. It is all a system of bare-faced labor stealing. They think that the planter has really paid for their labor, but that the official does them out of it. It is frequently observed that the official comes suddenly into prosperity and this is suspected to be the source of it.

If a private employer wants to retain a worker, he advances the man's tax and the man is unmolested. If, on the other hand, one has worked for a private employer for months but for any reason leaves that employment, he is liable to be recruited by the Government. Past employment affords him no protection. The villagers insist that times are worse for them than they used to be under the king. More unrequited toil is exacted now than a few years ago . . .

•

VILLAGE No. 4

Fifty villagers are gathered—Ambaquistas. They say that in the time of the monarchy (before 1910), although they were slaves, they were better off and got more for their work. Their lot is getting harder. Things got abruptly worse for them 1917–1918. The Government makes them work but gives them nothing. They return to find their fields neglected, no crops growing. They would rather be slaves than what they are now. As slaves they would have value and are not underfed, but now nobody cares whether they live or die. This Government serfdom is more heartless than the old domestic slavery, which was cruel only when the master was of cruel character. Now they are in the iron grasp of a system which makes no allowance for the circumstances of the individual and ignores the fate of the families of the labor recruits.

There are 140 huts in this area, which extends five miles by two. For fifteen months no less than 50 have been required to work on the roads, and some months more than one hundred. The quota is maintained by shifts.

When a white man applies to the *administrador* for workers a soldier is sent with him to the village who calls out the chief and notifies him that so many men must be forthcoming from that village. When men are taken for distant plantations, they are provided with a thin jersey, a *pano,* and in the cool season a blanket. Two months ago thirty from this area were taken to an unknown destination.

In 1922 twenty from this area were requisitioned to work as carriers between L—and P—. Their taxes had already been paid. For six months service they got the equivalent of $1.80. They think that the Government gets twelve dollars for every man who works for the planter six months. Somebody keeps most of it so that the laborer gets no pay.

The law contemplates that the laborer shall enter into labor contracts with a free will. These *Ambaquistas* say that they put their thumb prints on some papers but do not know what these papers contain and would be flogged should they dare refuse to sign them. The Government keeps all these contracts. They are *para Ingleza ver,* i.e., *"for the English to see"* ...

◆

VILLAGE No. 10

This village which has sixty-three payers of head tax, must keep three men regularly on road work, five men are now working for the Benguela Government and five are on Government work at G—. Those at Benguela may be there six months or a year and will get nothing but a tax receipt. Those at G— have been called for a month, but when they come back others must take their places. They supply their own food and will not get even their tax receipt. The men at Benguela work from dark to dark and are given wormy meal which often brings on dysentery. Labor extractions are on the increase and it is now six years that the pressure has been getting worse. This district once produced tons and tons of rice, but this branch of cultivation has all but died out because the labor requisitions made it impossible to care for it. Villages deep in the bush suffer as much from labor exactions as those near. More is required from villages with skilled workers than from those without trades. Hence parents hesitate to let their boys learn a trade.

During our palaver we ask eleven men sitting in a row "How much forced labor have you performed in the last twelve months?" The replies are: two months, seven weeks, nine weeks, three months, two months, twenty weeks, nine weeks, four months, eight weeks, seven weeks, six months—in all thirty-three months or an average of three months. In no case were there rations, pay or tax receipt. Their wives not only did road work but had to carry on their heads to the Post, forty miles away, the boards and planks their husbands had sawed in the woods ...

◆

VILLAGE No. 16

A policeman will come to the village with an order for so many men to work at Silva Porto, the Post. There they are assigned to various people who wish servants—hotel keepers, traders, residents. They serve six months, get their food but no clothes and are paid enough to equal their head tax. Generally the work is hard, the hours are long, and the whip is used. At the end of six months the village sends a replacing gang. The year around ten [gangs] must be maintained in this service. Then six, chiefly boys and girls, work from dark to dark on the highway under a policeman with a whip ...

I asked, "Why don't you protest against such treatment?" The school teacher stated that he had complained to the secretary of the administration of the blackmailing of the villagers by the policeman. That official promptly flared up and said, "Get out of here! It's none of your business what the authorities do." Although these policemen are under no supervision in their dealings with the villagers, the authorities will harken to no complaints against them. Thanks to this the *cipaio* sometimes makes money faster than a successful trader. He is given an order to comb out so many men from the district, but it is within his discretion how many shall be required of a particular village. So under threat of being tied up the villagers compete in bribing him not to hit them too hard. He demands men even of villages all of whose able-bodied men are away on duty. In order to avoid being beaten they will have to pay him. Thus a *cipaio* rakes in money, corn, sheep, goats and chickens until sometimes not a domestic animal is left in the village. The *cipaio* is often a criminal or a bad character and his field of operation is always a strange tribe, preferably one with which his tribe is at enmity. The Portuguese have been very skillful in playing off one tribe against another so as to use the black man in carrying out the white man's evil purpose. We were told that in the eastern part of Angola the unexpected appearance of a strange white man in the village is a signal for the precipitate abandonment of huts and firesides. Across the border in the Belgian-Congo such panic is unknown.

15 • Organizing African workers (1928)

While the African National Congress (ANC) focused primarily on representing the concerns of the urban, newly educated professional classes, Clements Kadalie aimed at developing a trade union movement for the people he regarded as the most oppressed by colonialism: "workers." Kadalie was born in Nyasaland around 1896 and schooled by his uncle (a brother of the first prime minister of independent Malawi, Hastings Banda) and later at a mission station.

Kadalie worked as a clerk in Portuguese East Africa and in Rhodesia before coming to South Africa, where in 1919 he established the Industrial and Commercial Workers Union (ICU) to represent African dock workers. All African workers in South Africa were excluded from the legal definition of "worker" under South African law and therefore were not entitled to be formally represented in contract or wage negotiations. Despite this obstacle, the ICU grew enormously in the early to mid-1920s and benefited from Kadalie's charisma as a public speaker and his readiness to develop the organization into a movement that aimed to bring together all Africans opposed to racial segregation and to challenge the ruling order by threatening strikes rather than using the petitions the ANC relied upon. Although the ICU claimed a membership of 100,000 by 1928 (when the ANC had only a few thousand dues-paying members), it collapsed because of a combination of internal conflicts and police action. The fundamental problem for people who adopted the same approach as Kadalie was that, while direct challenges to the ruling system engendered a great deal of popular support, the readiness of the South African state (like that of every other colonial ruler in Africa) to use force, and its monopoly of arms, to repress opposition meant that the challenge could not succeed without unacceptable levels (to the protestors) of bloodshed. Kadalie was charged with "promoting racial hostility" under legislation introduced in 1927 and thereafter became an increasingly marginal figure in South African politics. For a time, though, his was the most eloquent voice opposing racial discrimination in South Africa. The document that follows is the ICU's program for 1928.[5]

5. Thomas Karis and Gwendolen M. Carter, eds., *From Protest to Challenge: A Documentary History of African Politics in South Africa, 1882–1962* (Stanford: Hoover Institution Press, 1972), vol. 1, *Protest and Hope, 1882–1934,* ed. Sheridan Johns, 331–33.

Opponents of the I.C.U. have frequently asserted that the Organisation is not a trade union in the sense that the term is generally understood in South Africa, but that it is a kind of pseudo-political body. The ground on which this assertion has been based is the fact that I.C.U. has concentrated its attention on matters in which the issues involved have not been "purely economic" whilst these "purely economic" issues have been very largely neglected.

The new constitution, which was adopted at the Special Congress at Kimberley in December last, definitely establishes the I.C.U. as a trade union, albeit one of the native workers whose rights of organisation are only now earning recognition. In these circumstances it has become necessary for the organisation to have a clearly defined economic programme, corresponding to the interests of the membership at large. At the same time it must be clearly understood that we have no intention of copying the stupid and futile "Non-political" attitude of our White contemporaries. As Karl Marx said, every economic question is, in the last analysis, a political question also, and we must recognise that in neglecting to concern ourselves with current politics, in leaving the political machines to the unchallenged control of our class enemies, we are rendering a disservice to those tens of thousands of our members who are groaning under oppressive laws and who are looking to the I.C.U. for a lead.

In the past, the officers of the I.C.U. in the field have had no definite programme to follow, and this has resulted not merely in confusion of ideas, but it has led to the dissemination of conflicting politics. This being so, I make no apology for introducing the subject of an Economic and Political Programme for the Organisation at this stage. The I.C.U. is a homogeneous national organisation. As such it must have a national policy, consonant with the terms of its constitution, which will serve as a programme of action by which its officials will be guided in their work. The framing of such a policy or programme is essentially the work of Congress, and I propose to give here the broad outlines for a programme, which I trust will serve as a basis of discussion. In view of what I said above it will be realised that it is not necessary to divide the programme into political and economic sections, the two being closely bound up with each other.

I will further preface the proposals I have to make by remarking that our programme must be largely of an agrarian character, for the reason that the greater proportion of our membership comprises rural workers, landless peasants, whose dissatisfaction with conditions is with good reason greater than that of the workers in urban areas. These conditions are only too well known to you to require any restatement from me. The town workers must not, however, be neglected. More attention must in the future be given to their grievances, desires and aspirations if their loyalty to the I.C.U. is to be secured. At the present stage of our development it is inevitable that our activities should be almost entirely of an agitational character for we are not recognised as citizens in our own country, being almost entirely disfranchised and debarred from exercising a say in state affairs closely affecting our lives and welfare. Our programme will therefore be almost entirely agitational in character.

I now detail my proposals, as follows:

(1) WAGES: A consistent and persistent agitation for improved wages for native workers must be conducted by all branches of the Union. The agitation must be Union-wide, and regard must always be had to local conditions and circumstances. Improvements, however small in themselves, must be welcomed and made the basis on which to agitate for further advances. Every endeavour should be made to enter into friendly negotiations with farmers'

associations, employers' organisations and individual employers in the towns, with a view to securing improvements. If no results are obtained branch secretaries should, wherever practicable, invoke the aid of the Wage Board. In this connection a study of the Wage Act, 1925, is urged.

As an immediate objective, a minimum wage of £5 per month (plus food and housing in country districts) should be striven for. The reasonableness of this claim cannot be disputed by anyone. The attainment of this admittedly low rate, which it must be said few native workers are receiving, is not to be regarded as an end in itself, but as a stepping stone to the ultimate achievement of the full economic rights of the native workers.

(2) HOURS: Insistence should be made on a maximum working day of eight hours and a working week of 5 ½ days for town and country workers alike. This demand will have the support of all right-thinking and justice-loving people, and members who refuse to exceed this working-time should be given every possible support and encouragement.

(3) ILLEGAL PRACTICES: Illegal practices by employers, such as withholding wages, seizing stock, etc. should be reported to the local Magistrate and Native Affairs Department, with fullest particulars. Any refusal by these officials to deal with complaints, or failure to secure satisfaction for the members concerned should be reported to the Head Office of the Organisation for submission to the higher authorities.

(4) THE FRANCHISE: The proposal of the present government to withdraw the very limited franchise granted to Natives in the Cape Province should be unequivocally condemned at every public gathering of the I.C.U. Further, on the principle: "No taxation without representation" an extension of the franchise to Natives should be demanded. We would suggest that a monster petition be organised by the I.C.U. against the present reactionary proposal and presented to Parliament during the present session.

In the event of the Bill being passed and the franchise being withdrawn a protest should be made by means of a mammoth petition calling into question the necessity and legality of taxing and legislating for a section of the population and citizens without granting them the same representation as provided for the Europeans, at the same time asking for tangible and unbiased reasons why the Natives should not refuse to pay taxes without representation.

(5) PASS LAWS: The Pass Laws are a legal expression of Native enslavement, corresponding with the dark days of Tzarist Russia. They manufacture criminals and possess no moral or ethical justification. It is therefore the duty of the I.C.U. to oppose them by every possible means at its disposal. I would propose that the government be petitioned to suspend the Pass Laws for, say, a period of six months. If, during that period it is found that there has been no increase of lawlessness among the Natives, but that they are just as law-abiding without passes as with them, then the Government should be asked to repeal the Pass Laws in their entirety as there will no longer be any reason or justification, either real or imaginary, for their continuance.

In the event of the government refusing to comply with such a petition, Congress should fix a day of national protest against the Pass Laws, to be marked by mass demonstrations at which all natives should be asked to hand in their passports, the same to be burned in public, by the demonstrations. In addition, those assembled should be pledged by solemn resolution to refuse to carry any further passports or to give any further recognition to the Pass Laws.

(6) LAND: The total area of land set aside for exclusive native occupation in the Union is notoriously inadequate. Parliament should be petitioned through one or more of its members to increase the Native reserves so as to make provision for the landless native farmers. The assistance of labour organisation overseas should be invoked in this matter. In addition, an agitation should be started against the laws prohibiting native squatting.

(7) FREE SPEECH: Vigorous propaganda must be carried on against those provisions in the Native Administration Act which place restrictions on the right of free speech. Ostensibly these provisions are designed to prevent the stirring-up of hostility between the white and black races. Actually they are intended to limit the opportunities for trade union propaganda and organisation among the native workers. These provisions must therefore be strenuously fought against and their legality challenged where wrongful arrests are carried out. In this connection, no opportunity must be lost of stressing the fact that the I.C.U. is not an anti-European organisation, and that where it has occasion to criticise Europeans it is on the grounds of their actions (usually as employers of labour) towards the natives and not on account of the colour of their skins.

(8) PROPAGANDA: Members must be kept fully informed of the activities of the organisation and of all happenings affecting their interests. For this purpose regular members' meetings must be called by Branch Secretaries and the speeches made thereat must not, as heretofore, be of a vague or general agitational character but must deal with concrete and immediate problems. Every endeavour must be made to stimulate a direct personal interest in the affairs of the organisation and to this end questions and discussions by the audience must be encouraged.

The "Workers Herald," our official organ, must be further popularised among the members. If every member bought the paper its circulation could be easily quadrupled and more. The paper could be made to possess an interest for each district if Branch Secretaries would take the trouble to contribute notes concerning local happenings with their comments thereon.

(9) NEW RECRUITS: There are large numbers of native workers to whom the I.C.U. is scarcely known. I refer to the workers on the Witwatersrand gold mines, the Natal Coal Mines and the Railways. Branch Secretaries in these areas should make every endeavour to rope these men in as members of the I.C.U. as they would be an undoubted source of strength. The good work commenced some years ago among Dock Workers has unfortunately been discontinued very largely. Renewed efforts must be made during the ensuing year to bring the strayed ones back to the fold.

(10) REPRESENTATION ON PUBLIC BODIES: It was decided at a previous Congress that advantage be taken of the laws governing Provincial Council elections in the Cape to run official I.C.U. candidates. Native Parliamentary voters are qualified to enter the Cape Provincial Council, and definite steps should be taken to select candidates to stand on behalf of the I.C.U. in Cape constituencies where there is a possibility of securing a fair vote at least. An instruction should be issued to the National Council accordingly, and full preparations should be made by the branch or branches concerned for a thorough election campaign in the next Cape Provincial Council elections. Propaganda must be the main consideration, although every effort must be made to secure the return of any candidates put up. The question of candidates in the Parliamentary General Elections forms a separate item on the agenda. In submitting the

above outline, I trust that delegates will see with me the urgent necessity for a national policy for the organisation. Once a policy is adopted, and a programme arranged, it must not be allowed to remain on paper, and every official will be expected to do his utmost to translate the same into practice. Only in this way can the organisation grow and become an effective agency for liberating the African workers from the thraldom of slavery.

16 • Charlotte Maxeke describes the impact of colonialism on women and the family (1930)

While Clements Kadalie focused primarily on the concerns of male African workers, other critics of European rule drew attention to the way in which colonialism had a particularly harsh impact on women. Charlotte Maxeke, born in South Africa in 1874 and educated by missionaries, had traveled overseas with a choral group in the 1890s and visited Great Britain, Canada, and the United States. When she graduated from Wilberforce University in 1905, she became the first African woman to earn a bachelor's degree. Upon her return to South Africa, she founded the Women's League of the African National Congress. In a speech titled "Social Conditions among Bantu Women and Girls," given in 1930 at Fort Hare, a university college established by the South African government for blacks only, Maxeke describes the ways in which the loss of land and the development of migrant labor had a profound impact on African family life, especially on the lives of women and girls.[6]

In speaking of Bantu women in urban areas, the first thing to be considered is the Home, around which and in which the whole activity of family life circulates. First of all, the Home is the residence of the family, and home and family life are successful only where husband and wife live happily together, bringing up their family in a sensible way, sharing the responsibilities naturally involved in a fair and wholehearted spirit. The woman, the wife, is the keystone of the household: she holds a position of supreme importance, for is she not directly and intimately concerned with the nurturing and upbringing of the *children* of the family, the future generation? She is their first counsellor, and teacher; on her rests the responsibility of implanting in the flexible minds of her young, the right principles and teachings of modern civilisation. Indeed, on her rests the failure or success of her children when they go out into life. It is therefore essential that the home atmosphere be right, that the mother be the real "queen" of the home, the inspiration of her family, if her children are to go out into the world equipped for the battles of life.

There are many problems pressing in upon us Bantu, to disturb the peaceful working of our homes. One of the chief is perhaps the stream of Native life into the towns. Men leave their homes, and go into big towns like Johannesburg, where they get a glimpse of a life such as they had never dreamed existed. At the end of their term of employment they receive the wages for which they have worked hard, and which should be used for the sustenance of their families, but the attractive luxuries of civilisation are in many instances too much for them,

6. Karis and Carter, *From Protest to Challenge,* vol. 1, *Protest and Hope,* ed. Johns, 344–46.

they waste their hard earned wages, and seem to forget completely the crying need of their family out in the veld.

The wife finds that her husband has apparently forgotten her existence, and she therefore makes her hard and weary way to the town in search of him. When she gets there, and starts looking round for a house of some sort in which to accommodate herself and her children, she meets with the first rebuff. The Location Superintendent informs her that she cannot rent accommodation unless she has a husband. Thus she is driven to the first step on the downward path, for if she would have a roof to cover her children's heads a husband must be found, and so we get these Poor women forced by circumstances to consort with men in order to provide shelter for their families. Thus we see that the authorities in enforcing the restrictions in regard to accommodation are often doing Bantu society a grievous harm, for they are forcing its womanhood, its wedded womanhood, to the first step on the downward path of sin and crime.

Many Bantu women live in the cities at a great price, the price of their children; for these women, even when they live with their husbands, are forced in most cases to go out and work, to bring sufficient into the homes to keep their children alive. The children of these unfortunate people therefore run wild, and as there are not sufficient schools to house them, it is easy for them to live an aimless existence, learning crime of all sorts in their infancy almost.

If these circumstances obtain when husband and wife live together in the towns, imagine the case of the woman, whose husband has gone to town and left her, forgetting apparently all his responsibilities. Here we get young women, the flower of the youth of the Bantu, going up to towns in search of their husbands, and as I have already stated, living as the reputed wives of other men, because of the location requirements, or becoming housekeepers to men in the locations and towns, and eventually their nominal wives.

In Johannesburg, and other large towns, the male Natives are employed to do domestic work, in the majority of instances, and a female domestic servant is a rarity. We thus have a very dangerous environment existing for any woman who goes into any kind of domestic service in these towns, and naturally immorality of various kinds ensues, as the inevitable outcome of this situation. Thus we see that the European is by his treatment of the Native in these ways which I have mentioned, only pushing him further and further down in the social scale, forgetting that it was he and his kind who brought these conditions about in South Africa, forgetting his responsibilities to those who labour for him and to whom he introduced the benefits, and evils, of civilisation. These facts do not sound very pleasant I know, but this Conference is, according to my belief, intended to give us all the opportunity of expressing our views, our problems, and of discussing them in an attitude of friendliness and fairmindedness, so that we may perhaps be enabled to see some way out of them.

Then we come to the *Land Question.* This is very acute in South Africa, especially from the Bantu point of view. South Africa in terms of available land is shrinking daily owing to increased population, and to many other economic and climatic causes. Cattle diseases have crept into the country, ruining many a stock farmer, and thus Bantu wealth is gradually decaying. As a result there are more and more workers making their way to the towns and cities such as Johannesburg to earn a living. And what a living! The majority earn about £3 10s. per month, out of which they must pay 25s. for rent, and 10s. for tram fares, so I leave you to imagine what sort of existence they lead on the remainder.

Here again we come back to the same old problem that I outlined before, that of the woman of the home being obliged to find work in order to supplement her husband's wages, with the children growing up undisciplined and uncared for, and the natural following rapid decay of morality among the people. We find that in this state of affairs, the woman in despair very often decides that she cannot leave her children thus uncared for, and she therefore throws up her employment in order to care for them, but is naturally forced into some form of home industry, which, as there is very little choice for her in this direction, more often than not takes the form of the brewing and selling of Skokiaan [beer]. Thus the woman starts on a career of crime for herself and her children, a career which often takes her and her children right down the depths of immorality and misery.

The woman, poor unfortunate victim of circumstances, goes to prison, and the children are left even more desolate than when their mother left them to earn her living. Again they are uncared for, undisciplined, no-one's responsibility, the prey of the undesirables with whom their mother has come into contact in her frantic endeavour to provide for them by selling skokiaan. The children thus become decadent, never having had a chance in life. About ten years ago, there was talk of Industrial schools being started for such unfortunate children, but it was only talk, and we are to-day in the same position, aggravated by the increased numbers steadily streaming in from the rural areas, all undergoing very similar experiences to those I have just outlined.

I would suggest that there might be a conference of Native and European women, where we could get to understand each others point of view, each others difficulties and problems, and where, actuated by the real spirit of love, we might find some basis on which we could work for the common good of European and Bantu womanhood.

Many of the Bantu feel and rightly too that the laws of the land are not made for Black and White alike. Take the question of permits for the right to look for work. To look for work, mark you! The poor unfortunate Native, fresh from the country does not know of these rules and regulations, naturally breaks them and is thrown into prison; or if he does happen to know the regulations and obtains a pass for six days, and is obliged to renew it several times, as is of course very often the case, he will find that when he turns up for the third or fourth time for the renewal of his permit, he is put into prison, because he has been unsuccessful in obtaining work. And not only do the Bantu feel that the law for the White and the Black is not similar, but we even find some of them convinced that there are two Gods, one for the White and one for the Black. I had an instance of this in an old Native woman who had suffered much and could not be convinced that the same God watched over and cared for us all, but felt that the God who gave the Europeans their life of comparative comfort and ease, could not possibly be the same God who allowed his poor Bantu to suffer so. As another instance of the inequalities existing in our social scheme, we have the fact of Natives not being allowed to travel on buses and trams in many towns, except those specially designed for them.

In connection with the difficulty experienced through men being employed almost exclusively in domestic work in the cities, I would mention that this is of course one of the chief reasons for young women, who should rightly be doing that work, going rapidly down in the social life of the community; and it is here that joint service councils of Bantu and White women would be able to do so much for the good of the community. The solution to the problem seems to me to be to get women into service, and to give them proper accommodation, where they know they are safe. Provide hostels, and club-rooms, and rest rooms for these

social justice

domestic servants, where they may spend their leisure hours, and I think you will find the
problem of the employment of female domestic servants will solve itself, and that a better and
happier condition of life will come into being for the Bantu.

If you definitely and earnestly set out to lift women and children up in the social life of
the Bantu, you will find the men will benefit, and thus the whole community, both White and
Black. Johannesburg is, to my knowledge, a great example of endeavour for the uplift of the
Bantu woman, but we must put all our energies into this task if we would succeed. What we
want is more co-operation and friendship between the two races, and more definite display of
real Christianity to help us in the solving of these riddles. Let us try to make our Christianity
practical.

17 • Education in the United States of America (1925–33)

*Colonial officials preferred that Africans not go overseas for higher education because they would
likely be influenced by people that the officials considered radical, such as W. E. B. Du Bois. Cases
like that of John Chilembwe, for example, convinced colonial officials of the potentially subversive
nature of American education. Yet the limited development of local universities—only a few in
British territories and none in Portuguese- or French-ruled areas—and the long-term linkages that
existed between Africa and African American communities in the United States meant that large
numbers of Africans continued to go overseas for their higher education. Nnamdi Azikiwe was one
such individual. He studied at Lincoln University, Pennsylvania, where one of his classmates was
Thurgood Marshall, and continued his education at Howard University and later, at the graduate
level, at the University of Pennsylvania. He became the leader of the independence movement in
Nigeria during the 1940s and 1950s, the first African governor general of that country in 1960, and
its first president when Nigeria became a republic in 1963. In his autobiography, he reflects on the
decade that he spent living in the United States, a country that both shocked and impressed him.*[7]

On the eve of my sixtieth birthday in 1964, "Peter Pan," the satirical columnist of the *Daily
Times,* asked me whether there were any events that haunted me and which had registered unfavourable impressions on my memory during my nine years' sojourn in the United States . . .

As far as the unfavourable impressions were concerned, I replied that four lynchings had
shocked me. With the aid of the magazine *Fact,* I was able to recollect the details of these
macabre holocausts. In December 1925, two months after my arrival in the United States,
Lindsay Coleman, a Negro, was tried by a Circuit Court for alleged murder of a plantation
manager. He was found not guilty by a jury in Clarksdale, Mississippi; nevertheless he was
lynched.

In June 1926, Albert Blades, a twenty-two-year-old Negro, was lynched, by hanging and
burning, because he was suspected of having criminally assaulted a small white girl. The official physicians who examined the girl exonerated the Negro and declared that the girl was
never attacked but was merely startled by the presence of a black man. This happened in
Osceola, Arkansas.

7. Nnamdi Azikiwe, *My Odyssey: An Autobiography* (London: Hurst, 1970), 193–97.

In November 1927, at Columbia, Tennessee, a Negro named Henry Choate was accused of attacking a white girl. It was Armistice Day and the court-house where he was to be
tried was festooned with flags and bunting. A mob of white men transformed the balcony of
the court into a gallows, wrested him from the police and lynched him without a fair trial.

In October 1933 a crowd of 3,000 white men, women and children in Princess Anne,
Maryland, overpowered fifty policemen, smashed the doors of a prison cell, dragged out and
lynched George Armwood, aged twenty-four, in one of the wildest lynching orgies ever
staged in America. He was accused of attacking an aged white woman; and without giving
him a fair chance to defend himself or to be tried by a lawfully constituted court, the mob took
the law into their hands. The lynching was especially ghastly because one white boy, aged
eighteen years, was reported by the *New York Times* of October 19, 1933, to have slashed off
Armwood's ear with a knife.

On the favourable impressions, the victory of Franklin Delano Roosevelt in the presidential elections of 1932, and the introduction of the "New Deal" reinforced my faith in the
ultimate emergence of the United States as a moral force in the twentieth-century world.
Roosevelt's policy was radical, because with imagination and confidence he courageously
departed from the beaten path of the traditional capitalist practice of leaving private entrepreneurs to determine the factors for employing labour on an inequitable basis of the "law" of
supply and demand. The "New Deal" was designed to deploy public funds to create employment opportunities in public works and other units of the public sector, so that the unemployed would be kept employed. This philosophy laid a solid foundation for the elaborate
machinery of social security introduced later to guarantee the welfare of what Roosevelt and
his "brains trust" characterised as "the Forgotten Man."

These unfavourable and favourable impressions combined to mould my ideas and construct in my mind the image of America which has lingered. On the one side of the balance
sheet, we have an America saturated with racial intolerance, bigotry and lawlessness. This was
a passing phase in the saga of American history, in spite of the colourful roles of certain American politicians. The fact that successive administrations tightened the screw on the law enforcement agencies, compelling them to perform their sworn duties and protect the lives and
properties of American citizens, was a clear indication that the era of unbridled fanaticism
and anarchy was in process of becoming an unlamented closed chapter in American history.

On the other side of the balance sheet, we have a great and sprawling country, peopled
by self-reliant, hard-working, and philanthropic go-getters, descendants of hardy pioneers
who defied the elements in order to crystallise democracy as a way of life. If we examine more
closely the adjectives I have employed to describe this species of humanity, we should be able
to appreciate the soul of the real American.

Self-reliance has enabled Americans to build the mightiest nation on the face of the
earth. Hard work has enabled them to establish the highest standard of living and remuneration for work in the whole world. Philanthropy demonstrates the humanistic philosophy
of these pioneers and the spiritual nature of their make-up as fellow human beings, thus jus-
tifying the exodus of the "Pilgrim Fathers" in the seventeenth century, who defied the dangers
of the Atlantic, fervently believing that, although their ancestors were "chained in prisons
dark," yet they did not mortgage their conscience to the forces of oppression, intolerance and
inhumanity.

Go-getting is an American trait. It implies the exercise of initiative and enterprising ability. Hardy pioneering means an adventurous spirit that ignores all hazards. It is an exempli-
fication of willpower that is resolute, undaunted and irresistible. Democracy is the legacy
bequeathed to those who are now privileged to live as full-fledged citizens of the fifty states
comprising the United States of America. It means living in an atmosphere in which the state
concedes to the citizen certain fundamental freedoms and basic rights: the freedom to life,
the freedom of speech, the freedom of the press, the freedom to acquire and possess property,
the freedom of movement, the freedom of peaceful assembly and the freedom of association.
Protection of these basic freedoms is guaranteed under the provisions of a written constitution, which can not be abridged, denied or violated excepting under due process of law.

If such a country is described as "God's country," the exaggeration can be excused. But
deep in my heart I can honestly confess that the United States of America impressed me as a
haven of refuge for the oppressed sections of humanity in Europe, Africa, Asia and the rest of
the world. It is only in the United States that any human being can live in a free environment
which will give that individual full scope to develop his personality to the full, in spite of the
vagaries of human life, some of which I have spotlighted above.

Therefore, if one should ask me why tears trickled down my cheek as the *Aquitania* sailed
away [in 1933] from the shores of the United States of America, my simple reply would be
that, despite the fact that some people who looked like me were fed "with bread of bitterness"
by a microscopic section of the backward elements of this progressive and philanthropically-
minded segment of human society, this great country is still the bulwark of liberty and the
haven of the children of God. Don't blame me for calling it "God's country." In the words of
Louis F. Benson:

> "Who shares his life's pure pleasures
> And walks the honest road,
> Who trades with heaping measures
> And lifts his brother's load,
> Who turns the wrong down bluntly
> And lends the right a hand,
> He dwells in God's own country,
> And tills the holy land."

I lived in the United States for close on nine years. My life is a testimonial that Americans
shared life's pleasures and walked the honest road with me. They traded with heaping measures and lifted the heavy load off my shoulders. They turned the wrong of inhumanity down
bluntly and lent a helping hand to the forces of righteousness. Surely, people of this nature
dwell in God's country and till the holy land. I am a living witness.

18 • Colonial rule equals taxes and forced labor (1934)

*Despite imperial rhetoric about the civilizing mission to uplift African peoples, the main aspects of
colonialism experienced by all Africans on a daily basis were the Europeans' constant demands for
taxes and labor. Geoffrey Gorer here describes the practices of colonialism, which he witnessed while*

making an extended tour through French West Africa in 1934. Gorer, a young man at the time and not yet embarked on a career, was led in his travels by Féral Benga, an African dancer with the Folies Bergère, who invited the author to accompany him on a trip to study dance in West Africa. Gorer later moved to the United States, where he studied anthropology briefly with Ruth Benedict and Margaret Mead. Benga returned to France, where, after a period underground during the Nazi occupation, he eventually owned a café that catered to Africans resident in Paris.[8]

"The idea of colonization becomes increasingly more repugnant to me. To collect taxes, that is the chief preoccupation. Pacification, medical aid, have only one aim: to tame the people so that they will be docile and pay their taxes. What is the object of tours, sometimes accompanied by bloodshed? To bring in the taxes. What is the object of studies? To learn how to govern more subtly so that the taxes shall come in better. I think of the Negroes of the A.O.F. who paid with their lungs and their blood in the 1914–1918 war to give to the least 'nigger' among them the right to vote for M. [Blaise] Diagne; of the Negroes of the A.E.F. who are the prey of the big concessionary companies and the railway builders . . ." So writes Michel Leiris in the diary which he kept while working for the Griaule ethnographical expedition. It is, at least as far as concerns French West Africa, a judgment which it is difficult to quarrel with. (Except that the Negroes did not even get the right to vote for M. Diagne by the sacrifice of their lungs and blood; they had had that for several years before. The victims of the 1914–1918 war were simply blood sacrifices on the altars of the white fetishes Gloire and Patrie; they didn't get any more out of the transaction than sacrificial animals usually do.)

All Negroes, with the exception of a few town dwellers, are subject to taxation in two forms—"capitation" or head-tax, and "prestation," which is defined by Larousse as "a local tax used for the upkeep of roads in the neighborhood, payable either in money or work." As far as I know this latter is assessed everywhere except in the towns at twenty francs a head; but except as a favor Negroes are not allowed to pay in money; they have to work off the tax under conditions which I shall describe in the next section.

The amount and incidence of the head-tax varies with each district. In the most favored it is only levied on all males over the age of fifteen; in the majority on all people over that age; in the most unfortunate on all people. The amount varies between six and fifty francs a year. It is usually the smallest sums which are the hardest to pay, for the taxes are assessed more or less according to the richness of the country; if they are under fifteen francs a head it is a pretty safe bet that there is no work to be found in the district and no produce which can be sold.

The district administrator is instructed from Dakar of the amount of taxes he has to collect—a sum usually calculated on the last census figures; the administrator is made responsible for seeing that the stipulated amount is brought in. He in turn assigns to the *chefs de canton* the sum for which each is responsible in his district, and they in their turn tell each village chief how much his village must contribute. The village chief is personally responsible for the taxes of the entire village; if he is unable to get enough out of the villagers he has to make up the sum himself; if the village does not pay to the full the administration takes a hand,

---

8. Geoffrey Gorer, *Africa Dances: A Book about West African Negroes* (New York: Norton, 1962; first published in 1935), 92–97.

Revenue

	Estimates Francs	Receipts Francs
I. Ordinary Revenue		
Direct taxes	7,844,000	7,933,000
Customs and excise	21,002,000	22,870,000
Posts, telegraphs, &c.	781,000	1,130,000
Grants and subsidies	1,669,700	1,750,000
Receipts from previous financial year	200,000	630,000
II. Extraordinary Revenue		
Sundry receipts	3,500,000	1,000,000
Exceptional withdrawals from the Reserve Bank	2,000,000	3,300,000
General funds	4,000,000	5,444,000
TOTALS	40,996,700	44,057,000

Expenditure

	Estimates Francs	Payments Francs
I. Ordinary Expenditure		
Debt charges	5,845,500	5,845,000
Salaries of administrative staffs	7,750,000	7,720,000
Other administrative expenses	1,463,000	1,450,000
Posts, telegraphs, &c. (salaries and wages)	2,632,500	2,630,000
Posts, telegraphs, &c. (plant and materials)	962,500	955,000
Public works	2,910,000	2,830,000
Social and economic departments (salaries)	3,866,000	3,850,000
Social and economic departments (other expenditure)	1,965,000	1,950,000
Sundry disbursements	4,099,200	3,967,000
Secret funds	3,000	3,000
II. Extraordinary Expenditure		
Sleeping-sickness units (salaries)	1,145,000	700,000
Sleeping-sickness units (other expenditure)	2,355,000	2,000,000
Public works	2,000,000	1,100,000
General funds	4,000,000	5,444,000
TOTALS	40,996,700	40,444,000

FIGURE 7 The tally of revenue and expenditures for the French colony of Togo in 1938 indicates that the great bulk of expenditures was for the salaries of Europeans employed in the colonial service. This fact is usually absent from most attempts at a balance sheet of empire, which generally assume that any spending was for the benefit of Africans. Great Britain, Naval Intelligence Division, *French West Africa*, 1943–44.

and the village chief is the first to suffer. The village chiefs will consequently go to almost any lengths to collect the required sum, and it is on them that the chief onus is thrown.

If the money can be earned, either by selling produce or labor, the tax is not unduly hard. Moreover the census figures—which were, I think, last taken in 1931—then probably bear a reasonable relation to the population. But the districts which fulfil these conditions are almost exclusively situated within a hundred miles or so of the coast—that is to say the forest region of the Ivory Coast, with its numerous and flourishing coffee plantations, the banana area of New Guinea, and at any rate until the slump in Senegal and lower Dahomey, with groundnuts and palms respectively. But between this prolific band and the Sahara to the north there is a large area of savannah, save on the banks of the Niger indifferently watered, which can produce little beyond the food needed to support a scanty population. It is this very extensive region on which the taxation falls hardest. There is no money to be earned locally; except for rice or cotton in a few small areas there is no exportable product; however moderate the tax, it is almost impossible for the natives to acquire any money unless they go south to seek work. A considerable number do this, and all do not return, which is one of the numerous reasons why the census figure is in most districts far higher than the present population—in Bodi in North Dahomey, for instance, the 1926 census figures on which the tax is collected give the population as three thousand: according to a native estimate it is now six hundred, a statement which the number of abandoned huts confirmed—and consequently the tax which is demanded of the village works out at far more per head than the official figure. To pay the sum required is almost an impossibility; and there are numerous cases of unscrupulous administrators and/or *chefs de canton* demanding the tax two or three times in the year. There is no redress against this, except a personal appeal to the governor; and that is made very difficult.

When a village fails to pay its taxes the administration steps in brutally and ruthlessly. When punitive measures are taken, as they frequently are, the administrator himself is never present, and therefore has a complete alibi; he sends his Negro soldiers—naturally always of a different race to the people they are sent out against, most usually Bambara—with instructions to collect the money. It is axiomatic that no one treats servants so badly as a servant set in authority; no one could be more heartlessly brutal to the Negroes than the uniformed Negroes who act for the administrators. This employment of Negroes for the dirty work serves a double aim; it keeps lively the interracial hatred which is so essential for colonies where the subject races are more numerous than the colonizers, and it enables the administration to deny forthright the more inhuman practices in which they tacitly acquiesce, or should the facts be irrefutable, to lay the blame on the excessive zeal of their subordinates.

I heard on my journey a very great number of stories nauseatingly horrible, but obviously unproved. I shall only tell of those incidents which I know to be true, either from personal experience or from abundant evidence. I am not indicating the district exactly for fear of getting my informants into trouble. None of the cases are exceptional.

A village in the southern Sudan was unable to pay the taxes; the native guards were sent, took all the women and children of the village, put them into a compound in the center, burned the huts, and told the men they could have their families back when the taxes were paid.

In North Dahomey two men who had not paid their taxes fully (they were twenty-five francs short of the hundred at the proper date) were flogged with the *chacoute* (a heavy leather whip) in front of the assembled village until they fainted, were taken to prison without medical attention where they had to work for fifty days, and were then sent back with the remainder of the tax still owing. I spoke to one of the men in question and saw his back covered with suppurating sores.

In a village in the northern Ivory Coast, the chief's son had been taken as hostage until the tax was paid. The chief had not seen his son for nearly two years. Incidentally this practice of hostage-taking is very common; and I cannot remember how many times I have been offered young girls and boys to enjoy or keep as servants for the price of the head-tax.

The following letter was received by the servant of a doctor from his father: "Envoie vite 30 francs pour impôt. Ils nous avons pris tout le bétail et tout le mil et nous crevons de faim." (Send thirty francs for taxes at once. They have taken all our animals and millet and we are starving.) In a village in the Upper Volta, people were collecting winged ants; they explained that they had nothing to eat, for the whole of their livestock and grain had been taken for taxes.

In the whole of the western Ivory Coast flogging with the *chacoute*—legally nonexistent—and imprisonment follow unpunctuality in taxpaying.

On the way to Abengourou in the Ivory Coast, though not in that *cercle,* I was stopped by a native guard who mistook my car for the administrator's. The guard was slightly wounded in the head and had with him the most miserable man I have ever seen. He was naked with his genitals much swollen, his belly puffed and bruised, his eyes closed and bloody, and blood pouring from his nearly toothless mouth. His hands were tied, but he could barely stand, much less run away. The guard explained that the man was behindhand with his taxes; he had therefore gone to fetch him to work on the road, and the man had refused on the ground that if he left his plantation at such a critical moment he would never be able to pay taxes. He had tried to resist, slightly wounding the guard, who thereupon "lui avait foutu dans la gueule." He was obviously very pleased with himself and waited anxiously for my commendation. I told him that he deserved the legion of honor.

"Forced labor" and "prison labor" were a few years ago the two most popular anti-Bolshevik war cries; with Russia's increasing respectability they have now become rather old-fashioned; but they are very adequate descriptions of how nine-tenths of the public work in the French West African colonies are performed. Fifty centimes—one penny at the normal rate of exchange—is considered the proper rate of remuneration for a ten-hour working day; and the "prestation" or work tax, fines, and arrears of taxes are worked off at that rate. Consequently every adult male Negro—in some districts also women and children—does at least forty days' work for the state, chiefly road making, and if it happens that he has to make roads when he should be cultivating his fields, that is just too bad. The more conscientious administrators try to avoid this contingency, but the fields have to be worked during the rainy season, which is also the time when the roads need the most attention.

Except in the districts where there are railways, the roads in French West Africa are reasonably plentiful and good. They have been built and kept in repair by unpaid laborers working without any tools except the short-handled hatchet which is the Negro's sole agricultural instrument. The roads are made of earth and in the southern part of the colony the sod is laterite, which makes a particularly good and hard surface. The best roads are slightly raised above the surrounding country, on account of the rains; the earth to make them up is scooped out of the neighboring land with these hatchets into wicker baskets which are then carried on to the road and dumped. The surface is smoothed by having mud poured on to it which is beaten by women standing in serried lines holding pieces of wood and beating the earth to the time given out by the forewoman. They keep this up for ten hours, continually stooping, many of them pregnant or with babies strapped to their backs . . .

Except in the case of a couple of bridges being built by private contractors, I did not see any instruments of any sort being used in public works in French West Africa. Albert Londres has already described the building of the Congo-Océan railway, where each sleeper literally represents a Negro life, and where the only instruments he found were one hammer and one pickaxe for making tunnels, and I have no reason to believe that conditions are better in French West Africa. Negroes cost far less than shovels, not to mention cranes. I did not see any railway building, but the Thiess-Niger line is so bad that part of it will have to be relaid shortly; still, after the strike of 1925 the government may take a few more precautions.

In the forest regions of the Ivory Coast there is a great deal of work to be done with woodcutting and plantations and a very sparse population; consequently workers have to be recruited elsewhere, and particularly among the Mossi of the Upper Volta (now part of the Ivory Coast) who were by far the most populous tribe of the savannah; this is done both by public and private enterprise. On several occasions the administration have settled large groups of the Mossi in the Ivory Coast—sixty thousand have been moved to the neighborhood of Yammossoukro, in the middle of the forest, this year; but the Negroes support the changed climatic and dietary conditions so badly—not to mention hard work on inadequate pay—that something like half die in the first year. Private woodcutters and planters can also get permission to go and recruit the men they need; the local administrator merely tells the chiefs that so many men are required and are to be delivered at such a place and date. The men cannot refuse to go.

When men are working away from their village, they are meant to be fed and housed. What is more they sometimes are, though in more than one case that I have seen the Society for the Prevention of Cruelty to Animals would have prosecuted me if I had given a dog the same quantity and quality of food and shelter.

19 • Colonial rule equals police harassment (1920s–30s)

Control of labor was a keystone of colonial policy in Africa. In South Africa this took the form of the hated pass; in Kenya it was the "kipande." Rural peasants and urban workers were the principal victims of this system, but it also affected educated Africans like Mugo Gatheru. Gatheru, born in 1925, was the son of a squatter in the area of Kenya designated by colonial officials as the white highlands (where only Europeans could own the land). He learned to read and write at missionary schools and became the editor of a newspaper. For men of his emerging class, the affront of being stopped and having to produce evidence that he was not an "idler" and should not be sent to a rural "reserve" or forced to work for a European employer was especially grating. Gatheru became a thorn in the side of the British. In 1951 he traveled to the United States and enrolled as a student at Lincoln University. Despite being subjected to investigation by the FBI and the INS as a suspected Communist (the American authorities were following up on a request to investigate made by British colonial officials), Gatheru remained in the United States throughout the 1950s and earned a BA from Lincoln and an MA from New York University before returning to independent Kenya in the 1960s. The following excerpt is from Gatheru's autobiography.[9]

9. R. Mugo Gatheru, *Child of Two Worlds: A Kikuyu's Story* (New York: Praeger, 1964), pp. 88–95.

What was the Kipande System?

The Kipande system was officially introduced in Kenya in 1921. Every male African above sixteen years of age had to be registered, finger-printed, and issued with a registration certificate—Kipande. Kipande was different from the passport, the birth certificate, the identity cards in Britain, or social security numbers in the United States of America.

In Kenya a policeman could stop an African on the road or in the street and demand that he produce his Kipande—regardless of whether the African concerned was as wise as Socrates, as holy as St. Francis, or as piratical as Sir Francis Drake.

Kipande was also used to prevent the African labourer escaping distasteful employment or from unjust employers who had power to have him arrested and then fined, imprisoned, or both. When Kenyatta took over the leadership of the Kenya African Union from James Gichuru he announced publicly that the Africans had carried "Vipande" (plural for Kipande) long enough and that they should burn them if the Kenya Government refused to repeal the ordinance which had instituted the system. The alternative, Kenyatta explained, was for the Kenya Government to issue Vipande to all the races of Kenya—the Europeans, the Asians, and the Africans. The Africans, at that time, were seriously prepared to take action, illegal if necessary, to abolish Vipande whether the Government liked it or not. Mass meetings were held all over Kenya at which a lot of money was collected to buy wood for a big fire at the centre of Nairobi city on which all the Africans would burn their Vipande. This was to be an historic fire!

Quickly and wisely the Kenya Government promised the African leaders that the Kipande system would be repealed forthwith and that a system of identity cards for all the races in Kenya would replace it.

The Africans welcomed the government promise and in 1950 the Kipande system was abolished. But the scars of Kipande remained. In the thirty years of its existence Kipande caused great humiliation and hardship and was a constant grievance among my people. It cannot be said that the British Government knew nothing of this: when sending Kenyatta to England on various occasions from 1929 onwards the Africans instructed him to speak not only about the thorny problems of land but also to protest about Kipande.

A well-known missionary, and one of the few well-wishers of the Kenya Africans among the Europeans there, complained in a letter to the London *Times* of June 1938 that not less than 50,000 Africans in Kenya had been jailed since 1920 for failure to produce Vipande—an average of 5000 Africans per year!

When the Kenya Government announced officially in 1948 that the Kipande system would be abolished the Kenya settlers, as was expected, resisted strongly. The instrument which they had used so long in keeping the African labourers in a state of serfdom was now being lifted. They accused the Government of yielding to "African agitators" and "irresponsible demagogues"! The settlers did not stop to ask themselves what would be the effect of the frustrated anger of the Kenya Africans. They did not understand that no human being, of whatever nationality, can keep on indefinitely without breaking through such frustration. After all, the Kenya Africans had carried their Vipande on their persons from 1921 to 1950, and yet the Kipande was only one of innumerable grievances.

The Europeans and the Asians were free from having Vipande. The psychological effect of the Kipande system was equal to that of an African calling a European "Bwana" instead of "Mr.," or of a European calling a seventy-year-old African "boy," or referring to "natives" without a capital "N," or "native locations" in the city instead of "African sections."

The Africans were constantly worried by these passes. I remember full well that, whenever my father mislaid his Kipande he was as much worried and unhappy as if he had been an important government official accused of accepting a vicuna coat from a private citizen!

There were also numerous other passes which were equally insulting, and principally the so-called "The Red-Book" issued by the Labour Exchange and which every African domestic servant was required to carry. In the Red-Book the character of the African concerned, the amount of pay he was receiving, and the cause of dismissal were to be recorded.

I remember well one afternoon when I was walking with Muchaba who had been my chief aide during my *irua* or circumcision ceremony. We were in Pangani, one of the sections of Nairobi, when we heard a voice far away call "Simama" or "Halt!" We did not pay too much attention since we were discussing family matters. Suddenly, we heard another voice shouting loudly: "You! Stop there!" We looked back and saw two policemen hurrying towards us. We suddenly had butterflies in our stomachs. We stopped and waited for them and, as they were approaching us, I whispered to Muchaba:

"Do you have your Kipande with you?" "No, I don't have it," he replied. "I don't have mine either."

"We'll catch hell now," Muchaba said. The two policemen came up to us.

"Why didn't you stop at once when we called you?" the first one asked. And the second one, sarcastically:

"Who do you think you are?" even before we had a chance to reply.

"At first we didn't know you were calling to us, sirs," Muchaba said. "We are very sorry."

"No, you look like law breakers, like most of the Kikuyu," one policeman said.

"Show us your Kipande quickly!" the second one demanded. "I don't have mine. I have just forgotten it," Muchaba replied.

"Where?"

"Where I work," Muchaba said.

"Where and for whom do you work?" asked the policeman.

"I work for a European lady just near the Fair View Hotel."

"What do you do?"

"I am a cook," Muchaba replied.

"Do you have any other pass as an identification?" asked the policeman.

"No. But I can give you my employer's address and the telephone number if you like," Muchaba said.

"Idiot!" shouted the policeman. "How stupid can you get? Do you expect us to make telephone calls for all criminals we arrest without their Vipande? We are not your telephone operators."

"What can I do then?" asked Muchaba.

"Carry your Kipande with you,'" replied the policeman. "Incidentally, who is this fellow here with his arms folded like a great bwana. Do you have your Kipande?" They turned to me.

"No, I don't have it. I have never had a formal Kipande," I said.

"What!" they both exclaimed thunderously.

"When I joined the Medical Department in 1945 the Senior Medical Officer sent me to the Labour Exchange to obtain my Kipande but I found out that the copies of the formal Kipande were exhausted. I was given an emergency certificate and told to get a formal Kipande later on," I explained.

"Are you still in the Medical Department?" they asked.

"No, I am working for the Kenya African Union as an assistant editor," I said.

"Where do you live?" they asked.

"Kaloleni," I replied.

"Just because you are working for that trouble-making KAU you think you don't have to carry Kipande?"

"No, that is not the reason. I just forgot my emergency certificate. I don't think that KAU is trouble making. We fight for the rights of everyone in Kenya, including the police," I said.

They looked at each other, confused. "Do you have any other papers as identification?" they asked.

"I have some papers with the letter-heading of the Kenya African Union."

"We are not interested in letter-heads. We want official documents. Any fool can produce letter-heads."

This comedy finally ended and they decided to take us to the police station.

We walked in front of them and they followed us. As we were walking I tried to get a handkerchief from my pocket to blow my nose. One policeman thought that I was insulting him by putting my hands in my pocket like a big bwana and hit me on my shoulder with his truncheon. He hit me hard. I tried to explain to him that my nose was running but I saw he was ready to hit me again, and so I kept quiet. Muchaba said nothing.

As we approached the police station I heard somebody calling:

"Hey you, that's Mr. Mathu's man. What did he do?"

Muchaba and I were afraid to look back in case we should be hit again. The two policemen answered the call and then suddenly told us to stop. We turned round and saw two other policemen coming towards us. I recognized one of them. He was my classmate at Kambui Primary School and he knew both Muchaba and I full well. We were relieved and happy! The four policemen conferred together and the one who knew us explained to his colleagues that we must have been telling the truth, and that we should not be arrested. Two of them agreed but the third still wanted to go to the police station.

At last they let us go but by then Muchaba was very late in returning to his work. His employer was very, very angry, as her dinner was late. Muchaba had not telephoned and she had no idea where to find him.

I advised Muchaba to take a taxi but there was none in sight. It was getting too late. Finally he took a bus and, when he arrived at his employer's home, he found her waiting near the gate holding a pen.

"Bring your Red-Book right away. You have no job now. You are entirely unreliable, a lazy, untrustworthy African. I hate you bloody niggers," she said.

Muchaba had no chance to explain anything. He was told to pack up his belongings and leave at once. He had some heavy luggage and couldn't move it all at once and so he took it bit by bit to the nearest street. Finally he took a taxi and came to my place. I took a chance and let him stay with me for the night! If the police had knocked me up in the night and found him with me, both of us would have been in trouble.

That evening, as he had never learnt to read or write English, Muchaba asked me to tell him what had been written in his Red-Book. I knew Muchaba very well to be a sensitive and intelligent man and was sickened to read: "He is quick in his work; he likes sweet things and may steal sugar if he has a chance; sometimes his thinking is like that of an eleven-year-old child." When Muchaba heard this he was so angry that he burnt the book. I cannot blame him for this but it put him in serious difficulty as no one would give him another job unless he produced the book, even this one with its permanent defamatory record. It was more than a month before the Labour Exchange agreed to issue Muchaba with a new book (I can only liken the process to that when one loses a passport), and then he was able to get another job working as a cook for a wealthy Indian businessman.

Muchaba's story can also illustrate the considerable licence allowed by their superiors to the ordinary police force, at that time largely illiterate, which in itself contributed to the atmosphere of European superiority and power which sapped the resistance of the unorganized African population.

In the evenings the police could knock on the door of any African in the African locations and demand to know how many people were sleeping there, how many had Kipande, and proof of where they were working. This could have happened to any African rooming place, and almost always the police called about eleven o'clock or midnight.

In some cases, a man and his wife might be sleeping peacefully but they had to open the door quickly. Police would then ask the man to produce Kipande and to say where he was working. They would search everywhere with their flash-lights and, if they were satisfied, would leave the place without even saying sorry to the couple they had awakened.

I remember full well when the police knocked up one of my uncles at about 12.45 A.M. When three policemen entered the room my uncle and his wife were trying to fix their pyjamas. One of the policemen shouted:

"How many people do you have in this room, eh?"

"Only my wife and myself, sir."

"How many people do you usually accommodate?" the second policeman demanded.

"None at all except my wife."

"My wife, my wife," the third policeman shouted. "How do we know she isn't just a prostitute from Manjengo eh?"

"No! No! You have it all wrong. This is my own legal wife and if you insist on disagreeing with me please take me to the police station," Uncle protested vehemently. His pride and dignity were badly shaken. Utterly hurt.

The three policemen left. They had caused great upset and inconvenience to my uncle and his wife but he had no remedy. He could not sue the Police Department which could always say "They did this in the course of their duty to uproot undesirable natives": an excuse invariably accepted by their superiors.

I would illustrate the general attitude of their superiors to the police by quoting from *The Report on the Committee on Police Terms of Service*, 1942, which among other things says:

The evidence submitted to us indicates that, in general, the illiterate African makes a better policeman than a literate African. The latter is less amenable to discipline and is reluctant to undertake the menial tasks which sometimes fall to the lot of ordinary constables. That being so, it seems to us that the policy of recruiting literates should be pursued with great caution, and that no special inducements by way of salary are necessary. In fact, we venture to go so far as to recommend the abolition of literacy allowance for new entrants.

In the rural area it was difficult for me to realize that the Africans were always accorded the last treatment. The city life taught me this.

It could well be asked why the Africans submit to the unjust domination of the police and the system of Kipande. For once the answer is quite simple: lack of good organization, one virtue of their civilization which the Europeans were not eager to pass on, and the determination of the Europeans to preserve their privileged system at any price. Thus, in 1943, there was only one African representative in the Kenya Legislative Council, none in the Executive Council, and in 1946 two were nominated in the City Council with no real voice in civic affairs. There was no effective organization to correlate the grievances of the Africans and present them with any force. Certainly neither the European settlers nor the British Colonial Government felt any inclination to remedy the appalling and obvious defects in the system which they had created, for which they were responsible, and which only they were strong enough to change.

20 • Colonial rule equals censorship (1936)

All of the colonial regimes kept a strict control over African speech. In every colony, whether British or French or Portuguese, criticism of the colonial administration was never acceptable and was always subject to criminal penalty. Critical comments, whether spoken or written, were frequently deemed seditious on the grounds that they would promote hostility between the races, a legal labeling process that was never applied to settlers' comments on Africans. Censorship became a major source of conflict between African and European, especially because of the huge growth in the African press. While African-run newspapers had been in existence since the mid-nineteenth century, many of these had been published under the auspices of missionary societies. From the 1920s on, however, throughout Africa new publications addressed the suffering of Africans under colonialism and the need for a swift movement toward independence.

One of the leaders of this critical journalism was Nnamdi Azikiwe, who, after leaving the United States, went to Ghana, where he became editor of the African Morning Post. *On May 15, 1936, Azikiwe published a mocking article written by a prominent local opponent of British rule, Wallace Johnson. Azikiwe was arrested and charged with publishing a seditious document. Although found guilty at first, which judgment was upheld all the way up through the British judicial system to the Privy Council in London, Azikiwe was later found not guilty on a technicality—that the prosecution had not proved that he was the editor of the newspaper on the exact day that the article appeared. Azikiwe left Ghana in 1937 and returned to Nigeria, where he became a leader in the independence movement. The following extract from Azikiwe's autobiography reproduces the offending passage by Johnson and then lists the Privy Council's grounds for at first upholding Azikiwe's conviction.*[10]

"Personally, I [Wallace Johnson] believe the European has a God in whom he believes and whom he is representing in his churches all over Africa. He believes in the god whose name is spelt *deceit*. He believes in the god whose law is Ye strong, you must weaken the weak. Ye 'civilised' Europeans, you must 'civilise' the 'barbarous' Africans with machine guns. Ye 'Christian' Europeans, you must 'christianise' the 'pagan' Africans with bombs, poison gases, etc.

In the colonies the Europeans believe in the god that commands 'Ye administrators...' (meaning to include therein the Government of the Gold Coast) '... Sedition Bill...' (meaning to include therein the Criminal Code Amendment Ordinance No. 21 of 1934 of the Gold Coast) '... to keep the African gagged. Make Forced Labour Ordinance of the Gold Coast to work the Africans as slaves. Make Deportation Ordinance...' (meaning to include therein the Kofi Sechere Detention and Removal Ordinance No. 1 of 1936) '... to send the Africans to exile whenever they dare to question your authority.'

Make an ordinance to grab his money so that he cannot stand economically. Make Levy Bill (meaning to include therein the Native Administration Ordinance No. 25 of 1936 of the Gold Coast Colony) to force him to pay taxes for the importation of unemployed Europeans to serve as Stool Treasurers. Send detectives to stay around the house of any African who is nationally conscious and who is agitating for national independence and if possible to round him up in a 'criminal frame-up' (meaning thereby a criminal charge in which the evidence is fabricated) 'so that he could be kept behind the bars' (meaning thereby prison)."

Among the definitions of "A seditious intention" then operative in colonial law were the following:

1. To bring into hatred or contempt or to excite disaffection against the person of His Majesty, his heirs or successors of the Government of the Gold Coast as by law established; or
2. To bring about a change in the sovereignty of the Gold Coast; or
3. To excite His Majesty's subjects or inhabitants of the Gold Coast to attempt to procure the alteration, otherwise than by lawful means, of any matter in the Gold Coast as by law established; or
4. To bring into hatred or contempt or to excite disaffection against the administration of justice in the Gold Coast; or
5. To raise discontent or disaffection among His Majesty's subjects or inhabitants of the Gold Coast; or
6. To promote feelings of ill-will and hostility between different classes of the population of the Gold Coast.

10. Nnamdi Azikiwe, *My Odyssey: An Autobiography* (London: Hurst, 1970), 262–64.

CHAPTER THREE

World War II and Its
Immediate Aftermath (1941–50)

21 • The impact of World War II (1941–45)

World War II had a major impact on Africa in a variety of ways. On the continent it emphasized Great Britain's dependence on certain critical agricultural products, such as vegetable oils, to sustain its beleaguered economy. This dependence did not end with the war but was actually intensified in major agricultural campaigns like a disastrous groundnut plan in southern Tanganyika (mainland Tanzania) in 1947 that only aggravated colonial demands for taxes and labor. The other major impact was on the men who enlisted in the colonial armies of the French and the British and who fought against fascism in both the European and the Asian theaters of action. For soldiers of the King's African Rifles, composed of troops from Kenya, Uganda, Tanganyika, and Nyasaland, this meant that they were trained in Ceylon (Sri Lanka), fought against the Japanese in Burma (Myanmar), occupied Vichy French Madagascar, and, in some cases, were stationed in Mauritius after the war. Even before the war, some had fought in the 1930s against the Italians in Somalia.

Waruhui Itote was born in 1922. Schooled at a Church of Scotland mission, at the age of seventeen he went to Nairobi and worked at a grinding machine. In 1939 he started a vegetable business with some friends. Since the business was not going well and British officials told young African men that "unless we joined up and helped the Government, Kenya would be occupied by Germans and Italians," Itote enlisted in 1941. For African men such as him, their war experiences showed them how much Britain depended on the support and loyalty of African colonial troops to defend its empire and also that the supposedly invincible British could be defeated by people of "color" (the Japanese). The close connections between East Africa and India were a secondary influence with respect to the presence of Indian communities on the continent (so favored by Frederick Lugard), the role of India in fighting the Japanese in World War II, and the powerful symbol of the Indian campaign for self-rule that led to India's independence in 1947. In common with many of the African men who served overseas during the war, Waruhui Itote carried his experiences back home and eventually translated them into direct military action for the liberation of Kenya during the Mau Mau movement of the 1950s.[1]

The first time I ever thought of myself as a Kenyan was in 1943, in the Kalewa trenches on the Burma Front. I'd spent several evenings talking to a British soldier, and thought we had

---

1. Waruhiu Itote (General China), *"Mau Mau" General* (Nairobi: East African Institute Press, 1967), 9–12, 23–25.

FIGURE 8 An African recruit is sworn into Britain's Royal West African Frontier Force in 1942. All of the colonial powers relied on African recruits to help fight both World Wars I and II, and many served in combat roles in Europe. Despite this service, Africans returned to colonial subservience following both wars. AP Photo.

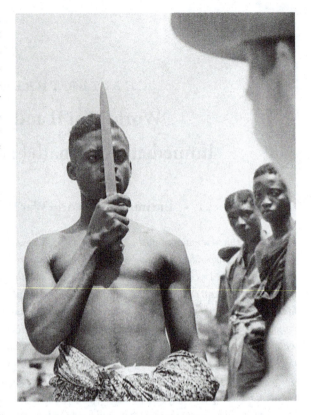

become friends. But I was rather surprised one evening when, after we had been talking for a while, he said, "You know, sometimes I don't understand you Africans who are out here fighting. What do you think you are fighting for?"

I didn't have to reflect much on that question—we had all had it drilled into our heads many times.

"I'm fighting for the same thing as you are, of course," I told him.

"In a funny way," he said, "I think you're right—and I'm not sure that's such a good idea."

I asked him to explain this.

"Look," he began, "I'm fighting for England, to preserve my country, my culture, all those things which we Englishmen have built up over the centuries of our history as a nation; it's really my 'national independence' that I'm fighting to preserve. And, I suppose, all that goes with it, including the British Empire. Does it seem right to you, that you should be fighting for the same things as I?"

I did not know how to answer this, so I said, "I doubt it, I don't think so."

"You'd better not think so," he replied. "Naturally, we're all fighting to protect not only our own countries but the whole world against Fascism and dictatorship; we know that. But I can't see why you Africans should fight to protect the Empire instead of fighting to free yourselves. Years from now, maybe, your children will fight a war to preserve the national independence of your country, but before that it's up to you to see that they get an independence in the first place, so they can preserve it later!"

He turned away for a moment, and then turned back for a last word before leaving me alone.

"At least if I die in this war," he said softly, "I know it will be for my country. But if you're killed here, what will your country have gained?"

A week later he was killed, in Burma and far from home, but still a link in the defence and preservation of his own Britain. What he'd told me never left my mind. At first I could only ease the conflicts in my head by thinking of myself simply and purely as a mercenary, fighting for a foreign power which just happened to be our colonial ruler. But being a mercenary seemed cheap and second-rate, especially when there were more worthy causes much nearer my own home.

The following year I was at the Calcutta Rest Camp, where I met a tall and powerful Negro from the American South. An English-speaking Tanganyikan, Ali, was with me and the three of us started chatting. "What's your real name?" I asked the Negro, when I read the name 'Stephenson' on his American Army bush jacket.

"What do you mean, 'real name'? That's my name right here, 'Stephenson,'" he replied.

I explained that I meant his African name. Since he was a black man like the rest of us, he must have an African name somewhere in his background.

"If I had an African name," he said, "it must have been lost a long time ago, probably on the slave ship that brought one of my grandfathers to America" . . .

"What about your tribe?" Ali asked him. "Can't you even remember that?"

Stephenson shook his head, looking round at the handful of other African soldiers who had gathered at the interesting sound of our conversation.

"You guys," he said very clearly, "are all looking at me as though I'm some freak, something strange, just because I don't have an African name. Well, I got this way because somewhere, a long time ago, some Arabs shipped my people to America, and after that we all grew up in a Christian country. But the same thing can happen to people when the Christians come to them—you don't have to be taken to England to lose not only your names but your whole way of life as well. You can lose it right out from under you in your own country! Right now you're being baptized as Christians generation after generation; one day you'll all wake up and think that you *are* Christians, Won't this make it easy for the white men to keep on ruling you? Some of you will believe it when you're told that the white way of life, the white religions, everything white is the best thing for Africans to believe in and follow. Then who will be willing to fight for your freedom?"

He must have seen that his conversation was turning into a speech, and I thought for a moment he was going to break off out of embarrassment. But we were all somehow held by his words, and fortunately, I think for all of us, he didn't stop. Instead he told us about the colour-bar in America, a fact, he said, which screamed at him in hotels, cinemas, buses and shops even though all Americans, from Roosevelt downwards, denied there was such a thing. America was a great nation, he said, but eaten away inside by racial discrimination; a nation of two standards and two faces, seemingly lacking the capacity to heal itself.

"We Negroes in America are always being told that it is the land of freedom," he continued, "that we have nothing to worry about as long as we work hard. So we go along, suffering for decades. And you'll be misled in the same way after this war, I'm sure. The British or whoever rules your countries will tell you that nothing is wrong, that you should leave everything to them and not worry. I don't know how much you've suffered in the past, but I know you'll suffer in the future if you don't have your own freedom."

I was listening very closely to all this, for it had called up in me memories of that other strange conversation I had had in Burma.

"All I can say," Stephenson went on, "is that you shouldn't be misled by white Christians who tell you they are superior with their holy names and their holy way of life. Jerusalem isn't in heaven, you know, it's just in Palestine and people are fighting there with bombs and shells, dying in the so-called Holy Places."

This rather shocked me, for I had always believed Jerusalem to be in Heaven. "White Christians are fighting each other right now, so don't you worry when they tell you not to fight for your own freedom," Stephenson told us, almost with a shout. "But the whites who are fighting now will be heroes in their own countries forever and amen, while you Africans will be heroes for a day and then you'll be forgotten. If you want to be heroes, why don't you fight for your own countries?"

Stephenson's speech and the long talks I had with him over the next few days were like being in school again. He was fond of talking about history, and especially about wars and revolutions—his favourite example was Haiti, where black men had fought and won their freedom from Napoleon, despite claims that they could never succeed. Before we parted, Stephenson told me he liked my 'guts' and that he would make arrangements for me to get to America, where I could find the education I would need to help my people. His promise was sincere, but the fortunes of war never brought us together again, and what was then a big part of my dreams never came true. Still, he had been a good teacher at an important moment in my life.

I was still in Calcutta when I lost my way in a subway and asked a passing Indian lady for directions. It turned out that her family had been in Tanganyika for many years and she herself spoke Swahili. She invited me to her home for a meal and I was only too glad to accept the chance of some conversation about Africa. Her husband was particularly interested in knowing what my fighting experiences had been, and what the war in Burma was like. We were taking tea when our conversation turned to political topics, in which, after my talks with Stephenson, I had begun to take a great interest. I was anxious to hear what somebody who knew Africa would have to say about our situation there.

"While you're here in India," the man was telling me, "you ought to pay attention to what we are doing, because you might learn something to help your own countries. We Indians are fighting for others in this war, but in return we've received a promise of Independence when it ends. I have seen many Africans fighting alongside our men, but I haven't heard what demands you've made for the end of the war?"

I certainly didn't know of any myself, and said so. "So you mean," he asked, "when the British in Kenya came and told you to fight, you just got up without a word and went?" I had to admit that was more or less the case, except of course that we had been told our country was threatened with invasion by the Germans and Italians, whom we could only imagine to be the worst monsters on earth.

"You should have demanded Independence as your minimum price for fighting," he said.

"But," I interrupted, "Europeans have all the land and schooling, and Africans have no factories or anything else to support themselves. How could we begin to run our own country right now?" My background on such topics was limited, and I could only feel a sense of wonder at the whole idea.

"If you must have them," the Indian replied, "you can keep all the Europeans you need after Independence—we will even be doing that for a while here in India. But at least you will have your say in what goes on, instead of being always at the mercy of foreigners. And it won't take long before you are running everything yourselves. If you remember, you were colonized in the first place because you had no education and no weapons to match the Europeans. Now some of you have got education, and some of you know how to use European weapons and can get them if necessary—is there anything else you have to wait for?"

Conversations like this continued throughout my stay in Calcutta. My new friends took a great interest in me, and often talked about the things we servicemen could do for ourselves once we were back in our home countries. Co-operatives were important, they told me, for a hundred ex-servicemen with gratuities could get rich much faster than one man alone, struggling against large organizations. Unity and trust seemed to my Indian friends to be the most important elements in any kind of social or political activity, and they transmitted to me a high regard for co-operation, as well, as a deepening awareness that I personally wanted to play an active part in bringing Independence to my people . . .

I join the KAR [Kenya African Rifles].

In 1941 Gachehe joined the army and Gakunga went to Kisumu. There was also some trouble with the money in our business and we agreed to close it down. Late in 1941 I decided to go into the army and on the second of January, 1942, I enlisted at Langata Camp, on the edge of the Nairobi Game Park. After three months Depot training at Ruiru, and a similar period at Nanyuki and Yatta, I was posted to 36 KAR at Moshi in Tanganyika. In the full battalion there were only nine Kikuyu and since we constituted one-fifth of Kenya's population this seemed curious. Although most Europeans condemned us as bad and disloyal people, it is more likely that they saw us as the greatest threat to their dominant position and to the strange feudal society they had created in Kenya.

Life in the Army training depot quickly revealed some of the humiliating absurdities of colour discrimination. There was a large difference between the pay packets of European and African corporals, although both of them had the same responsibilities. We shared the same chances of death and salvation, but used separate messes and separate lavatories.

From Moshi we were drafted to Ceylon, and travelled there in a troopship. It is probably difficult for others to understand how surprised we were to find ourselves doing P.T. in a house moving on water. New experiences were crowding in on me. When we were two days out from Ceylon the alarm was sounded as a practice, but one young Tanganyikan thought it was the real thing and jumped into the sea with his lifebelt on. We were astounded at the speed with which a destroyer rushed in like a hawk and plucked him out of the water. To us it was miraculous to watch.

After completing some rigorous training manoeuvres in Ceylon we left on 12 July, 1943 by ship, rail and road for the Burma Front. We were to relieve a section of the Indian Army that had been severely battered. Just before we reached the India/Burma border I was promoted to full corporal.

The Japanese knew how to fight, especially in the jungle. Their snipers always fired on our leaders, the officers, the sergeants and corporals, and so we removed all arm chevrons and wore wristbands of rank in their place. We developed extra instincts for danger. The Europeans covered their faces with black boot polish for no one wanted to stick out in any way. We all wanted to merge into one anonymous group.

I learnt many useful things about the spirit of men under the strain of fighting. In a crisis, the calibre and aspect of the leaders is all important. The Indians we replaced had poor officers and they were steadily defeated. Our colonel and his subordinates were excellent and we held our line, though at a heavy cost in men's lives and bodies. The Japanese split up into small groups and, as a result, greatly increased their effectiveness in this type of country. A group of three or four people can easily achieve the same results as a full company by rapid movement and careful shooting. The Japanese knew how to conceal themselves. They dug pits well behind our lines, camouflaged them with living grass, and used them as ammunition dumps and food stores and also as shelters. In order to survive anything at all a soldier must carry enough food and ammunition. Once he has lost either of these he becomes useless.

It was always raining in the Burma forests and we never changed our clothes. Leeches presented a problem that was never really solved. Food and other supplies were dropped by parachute, including the very welcome bottles of rum issued to warm us up spiritually as well as physically. I saw elephants being used to carry ammunition. The jungle trees were soft and not at all like those in our Kenya forests. They were easily chopped down with a panga [machete] and we used them to make a surface on the forest tracks for our transport. I was so busy merely surviving that I did not think much about Kenya and home at this time, although I used to send back the usual stereotyped letter-forms.

As the battle went on we suffered severe casualties and when we reached Kalewa we were relieved by another battalion. At one stage, morale dropped very low indeed and none of us could see any end to it at all but death. Many started malingering. Thomas, a Masai friend from Tanganyika, wanted to shoot himself through the middle of his hand so as to be returned home. I dissuaded him by pointing out that if he did this, even if he went back to Tanganyika, he would be crippled and poor, whereas by sticking it out he had at least an even chance of surviving intact.

During the see-saw Kalewa battle we were told to dig a slit-trench, but as soon as it was finished we were told to leave it and advance. After half a mile we stopped, buckled to and dug another slit-trench; as soon as we had made this one snug and comfortable we upped sticks again and advanced another half-mile, only to go through the whole rigmarole of digging and abandoning once more. By this time people were getting fed up and Private Massed showed his feelings by relieving himself in his trench and not even bothering to cover it up with earth. Many others followed his lead as we jerked our way forward. But then we had to retreat and when the Japanese airplanes strafed us we had to use our former trenches, muck and all! This taught me that if you have built something good, it is not right to destroy it, because you do not know when you will need it later.

After this no askari was ever angry again at being told to dig trenches. We all saw their importance in saving our lives. Even we corporals found it easier from then on. There was no more talk of "I've fifty rounds of ammunition and you've fifty rounds of ammunition, however many stripes you may have. Let's see who's who."

In Ceylon we were taught to swim and it seemed a complete waste of time. But when we crossed the Chindwin River, and saw boats capsize under bombing attacks and swimmers saving not only themselves but many others as well, we revised our opinions. We slowly realized that whenever anyone was instructing us we must listen carefully. We could never know when the lesson would come in useful.

In 1944 we returned to India from the Kalewa battlefront. I took back with me many lasting memories. Among the shells and bullets there had been no pride, no air of superiority from our European comrades-in-arms. We drank the same tea, used the same water and lavatories, and shared the same jokes. There were no racial insults, no references to "niggers," "baboons" and so on. The white heat of battle had blistered all that away and left only our common humanity and our common fate, either death or survival.

I had learnt much, too, about military organization. I was now familiar with the procedure and conduct of pre-battle meetings. I realized the importance of establishing a Headquarters in every camp as a centre for communications, reports, records, discipline and control. Information, not only about the enemy, but also about your own forces and their positions, is crucially important in war, especially in guerilla fighting.

Perhaps most important, I had become conscious of myself as a Kenya African, one among millions whose destinies were still in the hands of foreigners, yet also one who could see the need and the possibility of changing that situation.

Late in 1944 we returned to Nairobi and at the Railway Station our troop-train was met by Eliud Mathu, the first nominated African member of the Kenya Legislative Council. The military bands were playing and beautifully dressed European ladies chattered while they served us with tea and cakes on the platform. This was a very surprising thing, because we knew that, the next day, if we so much as looked at one of them in the Nairobi streets we would be arrested. But today we were heroes and they were grateful. Their tea and cakes nearly choked me.

When I went home on leave I found my darling Leah had been very worried and frightened, for people had said I was dead and many men had offered to marry her. However, she had remained faithful and our baby boy, Itote, had now grown very big. Leah was beside herself with joy at seeing me and we were very happy during our short time together.

On my return from leave in 1945 I was posted to the 3rd KAR Depot at Jinja, Uganda. I met and talked with many Baganda there. They told me that they had their own king, and I even osaw the police giving taxi money to the Kabaka, not to a European District Commissioner. We discussed these things with the other Kikuyu in the battalion and talked about the Kikuyu Central Association which had been proscribed in 1940 and about the iniquitous Carter Land Commission Report and of our leaders' attempts to get it revised. We talked about our great leader, Jomo Kenyatta, who had been fighting for us for so many years in England. It was time he came back to lead us, like Moses, into the Promised Land.

The KAR had been sent to Uganda because of some unrest there. I particularly remember one Muganda called Musa. We were drinking "Mwenge" at his house one day when he gave us a strong lecture.

"Why have you come here to plague us?" he asked, "and to punish us for trying to get our freedom? Why aren't you helping your own people to get theirs? The leaders of your Kikuyu Central Association were all deported and you do nothing. You have a duty to fight until you have made Kenyatta your Kabaka and until your taxes go to him, not to the English. You should be making your own armies and your own roads and building schools for your own kind of education. If you don't fight for Kenyatta to become your Kabaka you will be a useless lot of people. Are you Kikuyu just a collection of women?"

22 • The official mind of colonialism (1944)

Although World War II had a profound impact materially and intellectually on many Africans, it also provided an opportunity for the reinforcement of stereotypes in official thinking about colonies and colonized peoples. During the war, the British Division of Naval Intelligence solicited from "trained geographers drawn largely from the Universities, and working at sub-centres established at Oxford and Cambridge," a set of geographical handbooks to serve as reference texts on the areas of the world deemed most important to the imperial war effort. The only previous such set had been published just after World War I. The handbooks provided extensive information about resources, transportation networks, population concentrations, and other data. They also provided a brief introduction to the history of each country or area and some description of the local people. In the volume on French West Africa (1944), the authors, under the direction of Lieutenant Colonel K. Mason, professor of geography at Oxford University, and including Louis Leakey from Cambridge University and R. M. Cocks from Oxford, concluded their section on "The Negroes" with this sentence: "Indeed, in many ways he resembles a child, and in many cases should be treated as such" (235).

The authors of the volume on the Belgian Congo, all of them colonial officials rather than Oxbridge academics, avoided the "child" metaphor, but their description of the "character" of Africans still reeks of condescension and describes a person or a people unrecognizable in the writings of, for example, Azikiwe or Itote. In this description there is no comprehension of the changes wrought by several hundred years of contact between Africa and the West, of the trade in slaves, of the forced labor inflicted by the Belgians, or of the emergence of an articulate and literate group of indigenous leaders.[2]

CHARACTER

The native is good-tempered and not fanatical. His outlook is practical. He is clannish and therefore capable of loyalty. His intrepidity in hunting and river navigation is proof of his courage. In his private habits he is decent. He is accused, not without justification, of a lack of responsibility and of laziness. Living as he does in an easy-going generous community, there is no great incentive to work. If his crops fail someone will come to the rescue. He is not solely responsible, in fact, and he seldom looks ahead. Moreover, work for wages under a master is, to him, a new thought. The background of his life has been the looking after his family. His wants are few, and his concerns at home. In the interests of that home he can work. He carries heavy loads to market and paddles long distances, but nature is bountiful, to-morrow comes, and his activity is spasmodic. Within his own community, he is honest, and predial larceny is rare and considered detestable, but he thinks strangers fair game and his patriarchal upbringing induces him to consider his master's property as his own. Yet even here his lar-

---

2. H. S. L. Winterbotham, E. Gardiner Smith, and F. Longland, *The Belgian Congo* (Oxford: Naval Intelligence Division, 1944), 162–64.

FIGURE 9 Soldiers of the Ethiopian army kiss the ground in front of Emperor Haile Selassie (seated, on top step) in July 1941 following the defeat of Italian forces that had invaded Ethiopia in 1935. Selassie ruled Ethiopia from 1930 to 1974 and was a symbol of African independence until he was deposed and later assassinated in a military coup. His body was entombed below the office floor of the man who deposed him. AP Photo.

ceny is within reason. He will appropriate an Aertex vest, or a pair of shorts; he will take a nip from the whiskey-bottle, or a cigarette from the box, but he will, as a rule, be honest about money and will not do things which would seriously inconvenience "the Boss." The native is not particularly truthful, and when he is asked a leading question he usually gives the answer which he thinks is expected.

Misunderstandings are more likely to be on the European, than the native, side, for the African is very susceptible to atmosphere, understands more than one would think, and catches the drift of remarks even in languages with which he is little familiar.

Drunken bouts are common, and many villagers waken cross and with sore heads after a moonlight spree, but the native is not a toper. Those who have looked into an African cookhouse or slept in a native hut will not generally put cleanliness amongst the African virtues. Yet they are clean in person, and for ever washing themselves, their teeth, and their clothes. The lack of cleanliness in cookery and in their huts may be due to their habit of mind. Any illness is, to them, the result of the malignant action of some spirit and not a matter of infection.

It would be helpful to the European if he could see himself through native eyes. The African is a shrewd observer and often hits off the idiosyncrasies of a white man by a happy nickname. The explorer Stanley was known as Bula Matari (Breaker of Rocks) because of his road-making, and this has now become the native name for the Government. The native considers the European fussy and rigid. It is sometimes said that what the black man wants is justice without mercy, but this is misleading. The native point of view is rather that of the parable of the unmerciful servant (S. Matthew xviii. 23). He considers that there is a place for entreaty and pacification and the European seems to him very unbending. Humour of course varies with latitude and longitude. The native has a great sense of humour and enjoys a Rabelaisian joke, but words like "fool," said in fun, which to us seem harmless, may be taken as insulting. He resents injustice, favouritism, and sarcasm very keenly and can often find ways of getting his own back. In some spheres the European's failure to grasp the native point of view may cause a fiasco. This is especially true of witchcraft and "medicine" (spells), which to us seem absurd yet to the native are as real as they were to our ancestors. It need hardly be said that the native appreciates courtesy and resents brusqueness. Some of the chiefs have a great deal of dignity and self-control.

23 ◆ The dream of the warrior (1940s)

Mugo Gatheru's dream reveals the kind of class consciousness that developed among educated Africans (who were overwhelmingly male) after World War II. Full of contradictions, colonialism had enabled men like Gatheru to imagine a better life for themselves and their people while at the same time denying them the right to effect such change in practice. Frustration was a major force in post–World War II nationalism among these elites, and the possibility of bringing about rapid and forceful change was attractive. Yet the rhetoric of such dreams often reflected another contradiction: that between members of the elite's visions of a liberated nation and their hopes for their own class position within a free Africa.[3]

Day after day, as I lived and worked in Nairobi, my mind would drift into "The Dream of the Warrior," a fable I made up in which the main character was a Kikuyu boy named Gambuguatheru, a disguised form of my own name. My dream was, to me, also a kind of "revelation," in which it was "revealed" to me that it is wrong to think that heroism can be displayed in warfare only, though many people cling to that idea. A true hero may also display his mettle in fighting against the wrong deeds or ideas of those around him, just as much as in actual warfare. And so I kept on dreaming.

Gambuguatheru, of my dream, was a boy when the white men came. He became so curious to know who they were and what they wanted in his country that he was determined to go and question a European. One evening he told his father of his intent, and his father was so astonished at his son's daring that he would not allow him to sleep alone in his room for fear he might escape and go out to accomplish this dangerous mission. Next morning his father, still determined to dissuade Gambuguatheru, told him how the white men could shoot black men at a great distance and how they could make a box (gramophone) speak, but Gambuguatheru was still determined.

At noon he went to a certain missionary station and there he found an English missionary. He was told by the missionary that the sole aim of the white men was to preach the gospel.

3. R. Mugo Gatheru, *Child of Two Worlds: A Kikuyu's Story* (New York: Praeger, 1964), 101–4.

After receiving several presents he returned to his home. The whole family was amazed to hear of the boy's adventure since he was the first among them to talk to a white man. And he had returned unharmed.

In spite of his father's opposition to any more contact between his son and the missionary and the latter's plan to spread the new gospel, Gambuguatheru decided to take the leadership of his people so that their ignorance of the foreigners might not cause them loss in trade or menace their control of their country. How to do that was a serious problem. People began to fear him for his queer behaviour, but his personality was such that once he began talking people gathered round him to listen. In this way he was able to make most of the people trust him.

During this time there was a belief that if one wrote a letter trying to contact a European, or if one invented something like a machine, one's hands would be cut off by the white men. Gambuguatheru wanted to prove the truth or falsity of this belief so that he could rid his country of apprehension if it was false. "But what shall I write about?" he wondered. At last an idea struck him. He saw that the country was desperately in need of education and he wanted men and women to come who would concentrate only on educating his people. After much thinking and hesitation he wrote the letter and gave it to the missionary, who posted it for him to England. After a year he got a reply which promised him that he would get the men he wanted in a few months' time. And nothing was said about cutting off his hands for having written the letter.

Gambuguatheru then decided to turn to matters concerning the administration of his country. Already some administrative centres had been established in different parts of the country. He learned that the Europeans staying in these centres were called District Commissioners. They had already begun giving orders to the people around them. He very well knew that these District Commissioners would not agree to train him so that he could become a District Commissioner too since he would be trying to be their equal. So taking his spear and club he went out to go to the Governor to demand such training.

At the Governor's gate he was stopped from entering by gate-keepers. He was so dusty that they could not believe that such a man was entitled to talk to the Governor. Fortunately, the Governor happened to be walking round his garden and saw him. Gambuguatheru at once left the gate-keepers and ran to the nearest side of the garden. Then, speaking the bad English he had picked up from the missionaries, he shouted to the Governor. It was a wonder to hear an African talking to the Governor on such a subject in so loud and peremptory a manner!

Although he was the dirtiest man the Governor had ever seen, Gambuguatheru was admitted. It was arranged that he should be trained as a District Commissioner. The training took two years, after which he returned to his home and was made a D.C. He found that his people had abandoned all their old customs and copied the foreign ones. He was not impressed by all this. Within six months he had made his people see the mistake of giving up all their customs, so that it was easy for him to introduce subjects like African pottery, painting, the blacksmith's craft, and carving in the schools. Later, he established a school teaching only old things and trying to improve them by applying foreign methods where necessary.

The results of this school were so successful that years afterwards it was one of the biggest and most liked in Kikuyuland. After Gambuguatheru's death his statue was placed at the gate of the school, and the following words written on it:

A HERO HE WAS INDEED! IN BOTH THOUGHT
AND DEED. HE NEVER LEFT ANYTHING
UNDONE IF HE KNEW IT SHOULD BE DONE.

Now that I have had a college education I recognize that in this daydream, which I used to imagine at the age of twenty, my unconscious mind had condensed and disguised all sorts of ideas and images that I was getting from my reading and from the new experiences I was having in the big city of Nairobi. Now, for the first time in my life I was beginning to get interested in "politics"—those serious affairs that were affecting all Kenya Africans. My image of myself and of what the country needed was not yet clear. The vision of myself in the dream was a sort of combined image of "The Educated Ones"—that very small group of Kenya Africans who had been away to colleges and universities overseas and who were the acknowledged leaders among the Africans. Of these, three stood out above all the rest, Jomo Kenyatta, Mbiyu Koinange, and Eliud Wambu Mathu. To understand my dream, one needs to understand them.

24 • Freedom in our lifetime (1946)

World War II escalated economic and political tensions in South Africa. The demands of war production led to a huge expansion of African urbanization. Segregated areas such as Soweto (southwest townships) were built by the government to house the new immigrants, and the pass law was strictly enforced in order to maintain the supply and circulation of cheap black labor, on which the country's industries depended. In this context of urban expansion and impoverishment, the African National Congress (ANC) took the lead as the prime political representative of Africans' frustrations, especially in the person of younger people such as Anton Lembede and Nelson Mandela, who were more ready to demand immediate action than were their elders.

Lembede was born in 1914, the son of a farm laborer. Educated initially by his mother, he later won scholarships that enabled him to receive training as an elementary school teacher. Subsequently, while teaching full time, he earned a BA, a law degree, and an MA in philosophy. Along with Mandela he was a founder of the ANC's Youth League and became its first president in 1944. A fervent anti-Communist, Lembede believed that, contrary to its past policy of aiming to work with representatives of all groups opposed to racial discrimination in South Africa, the ANC should focus primarily on the concerns of Africans since they were the majority of the population and the segment most affected by colonialism. He also spoke against past policies of petitioning and sending letters of protest and argued that the ANC should take much more forceful steps to achieve its goals. He advocated strikes, boycotts, and stay-at-homes. Lembede died prematurely of natural causes in 1947 while working on a doctorate in law. His Africanist ideas lost favor in the ANC after his death but reappeared again in the Pan-Africanist Congress formed in 1958. Here he outlines the policy of the Youth League in May 1946.[4]

4. Thomas Karis and Gwendolen M. Carter, eds., *From Protest to Challenge: A Documentary History of African Politics in South Africa, 1882–1962* (Stanford: Hoover Institution Press, 1972), vol. 2, *Hope and Challenge, 1935–1952,* ed. Thomas Karis, 317–18.

The history of modern times is the history of nationalism. Nationalism has been tested in the people's struggles and the fires of battle and found to be the only effective weapon, the only antidote against foreign rule and modern imperialism. It is for that reason that the great imperialistic powers feverishly endeavour with all their might to discourage and eradicate all nationalistic tendencies among their alien subjects; for that purpose huge and enormous sums of money are lavishly expended on propaganda against nationalism which is dubbed, designated, or dismissed as "narrow," "barbarous," "uncultured," "devilish" etc. Some alien subjects become dupes of this sinister propaganda and consequently become tools or instruments of imperialism for which great service they are highly praised, extolled and eulogised by the imperialistic power and showered with such epithets as "cultured," "liberal," "progressive," "broadminded" etc.

All over the world nationalism is rising in revolt against foreign domination, conquest and oppression in India, in Indonesia, in Egypt, in Persia and several other countries. Among Africans also clear signs of national awakening, national renaissance, or rebirth are noticeable on the far-off horizon.

A new spirit of African nationalism, or Africanism, is pervading through and stirring the African society. A young virile nation is in the process of birth and emergence. The national movement imbued with and animated by the national spirit is gaining strength and momentum. The African National Congress Youth League is called upon to aid and participate in this historical process. African nationalism is based on the following cardinal principles:

1. *Africa is a blackman's country.* Africans are the natives of Africa and they have inhabited Africa, their Motherland, from times immemorial; Africa belongs to them.

2. *Africans are one.* Out of the heterogeneous tribes, there must emerge a homogeneous nation. The basis of national unity is the nationalistic feeling of the Africans, the feeling of being Africans irrespective of tribal connection, social status, educational attainment or economic class. This nationalistic feeling can only be realised in and interpreted by [a] national movement of which all Africans must be members.

3. *The Leader of the Africans will come out of their own loins.* No foreigner can ever be a true and genuine leader of the African people because no foreigner can ever truly and genuinely interpret the African spirit which is unique and peculiar to Africans only. Some foreigners Asiatic or European who pose as African leaders must be categorically denounced and rejected. An African must lead Africans. Africans must honour, venerate and find inspiration from African heroes of the past: Shaka, Moshoeshoe, Makana, Hintsa, Khama, Mzilikazi, Sekhukhuni, Sobhuza and many others.

4. *Cooperation between Africans and other Non-Europeans on common problems and issues may be highly desirable.* But this occasional cooperation can only take place between Africans as a single unit and other Non-European groups as separate units. Non-European unity is a fantastic dream which has no foundation in reality.

5. *The divine destiny of the African people is National Freedom.* Unless Africans achieve national freedom as early as possible they will be confronted with the impending doom and imminent catastrophe of extermination; they will not be able to survive the satanic forces, economic, social and political unleashed against them. Africans are being mowed down by such diseases as tuberculosis, typhus, venereal diseases etc. Infantile mortality is tremendously high. Moral and physical degeneration is assuming alarming dimensions. Moral and spiritual

degeneration manifests itself in such abnormal and pathological phenomena as loss of self confidence, inferiority complex, a feeling of frustration, the worship and idolisation of white men, foreign leaders and ideologies. All these are symptoms of a pathological state of mind.

As a result of educational and industrial colour bars, young African men and women are converted into juvenile delinquents.

Now the panacea of all these ills is National Freedom, in as much as when Africans are free, they will be in a position to pilot their own ship and, unhampered, work toward their own destiny and, without external hindrance or restriction devise ways and means of saving or rescuing their perishing race.

Freedom is an indispensable condition for all progress and development. It will only be when Africans are free that they will be able to exploit fully and bring to fruition their divine talent and contribute something new towards the general welfare and prosperity of Mankind; and it will only be then that Africans will enter on a footing of equality with other nations of the world into the commonwealth of nations; and only then will Africans occupy their rightful and honourable place among the nations of the world.

6. *Africans must aim at balanced progress or advancement.* We must guard against the temptation of lop-sided or one-sided progress. Our forces as it were, must march forward in a coordinated manner and in all theatres of the war, socially, educationally, culturally, morally, economically, and politically. Hence the Youth League must be all inclusive.

7. *After national freedom, then socialism.* Africans are naturally socialistic as illustrated in their social practices and customs. The achievement of national liberation will therefore, herald or usher in a new era, the era of African socialism. Our immediate task, however, is not socialism, but national liberation.

Our motto: *Freedom in Our Life Time.*

25 • Women and men on strike (1947–48)

In the immediate aftermath of World War II, colonial Africa was racked by labor conflict. Africans like Waruhui Itote had volunteered in large numbers to fight on the side of the allies and had listened to the anti-Axis rhetoric that the war was being fought to keep the world free of Nazi aggression and to liberate the peoples conquered by the Germans, the Italians, and the Japanese. Yet after the war, none of the European powers extended this essentially anticolonial rhetoric to their own empires. Instead they sought to rebuild their war-torn economies by imposing greater production targets and labor demands on their subject peoples. Africans responded with a series of massive strikes—in South Africa, Kenya, Senegal, Ghana, and elsewhere—that demonstrated that they would not passively accept these new demands. Perhaps the most famous of these strikes, both at the time that it took place and because of its celebration in a novel by the Senegalese author Sembene Ousmane, was that which took place in Senegal and lasted for six months. In this extract from Ousmane's novel God's Bits of Wood, *the strike, and particularly the role of women in its organization and success, serves as an opportunity to discuss issues of women and men, army camps, the early slave port of Gorée, demon possession, and illegitimate children.*[5]

5. Sembene Ousmane, *God's Bits of Wood* (London: Heinemann, 1985; first published in 1960 as *Les bouts de bois de dieu*), 184–202.

The crowd had preceded the delegates to the Place Aly N'Guer. Weary with the long hours of waiting, first at the union building and then before the offices of the company, most of them were sitting on the dusty ground, but others gathered in little animated groups, discussing the events of the day, while the sun blasted their sweaty shoulders and arms and skull with the last of that day's fires. Penda, Dieynaba, and Mariame Sonko tried as best they could to maintain some semblance of order among the excited women, but it was not until the delegation arrived and took up its position at the center of the square that the clamor finally subsided.

Lahbib spoke first. He gave them all of the details of the meeting with Dejean and his associates, but he was a bad speaker and he knew it, so he performed his duty as rapidly as possible and turned the platform over to Bakayoko. The trainman waited until the murmurs which had followed Lahbib's account died down. His voice was clear and distinct and could be heard at the farthest corners of the square. Since they already knew what had happened that afternoon, he spoke first of other things, beginning with a brief history of the events which had brought the [railway] line into being, and then speaking of the strike of September 1938 and of the men who had died in it. He knew that he would provoke the anger of the crowd when he concluded, "And now they refuse to give us what we are asking for, on the pretext that our wives and our mothers are concubines, and we and our sons are bastards!"

Again he had to wait for silence, and then he said, "Well, we are not going to give in to them and go back to work! And it is here that this strike must be won! In every town I have visited in these past months I have been told, 'If Thiès can hold out, we will hold out.' Workers of Thiès, it is here, in this city, that there is a Place du Premier Septembre, in honor of the men who died in 1938, and it is in their name that you must hold out now. You know that there is support for you everywhere—from Kaolack to Saint-Louis, from Guinea to Dahomey, and even in France itself. The time when we could be beaten by dividing us against ourselves is past. We will maintain the order for an unlimited strike, and we will continue to maintain it until we have won!"

Shouts and roars of approval came back to him from the crowd, where even the few who had remained seated were standing now and waving their fists with the others. But in the midst of this unleashed tumult, a little group of women managed to make its way through the crush and approach the delegates. Bakayoko saw them and raised his arms, calling for silence.

"Our gallant women have something to say to us," he cried. "They have the right to be heard!"

It was Penda who addressed them, hesitantly at first, but gathering assurance as she spoke.

"I speak in the name of all of the women, but I am just the voice they have chosen to tell you what they have decided to do. Yesterday we all laughed together, men and women, and today we weep together, but for us women this strike still means the possibility of a better life tomorrow. We owe it to ourselves to hold up our heads and not to give in now. So we have decided that tomorrow we will march together to Dakar."

For a moment Penda's voice was lost in a confused murmuring that linked astonishment and misgiving, and then she spoke again, more firmly.

"Yes—we will go together to Dakar to hear what these *toubabs* have to say and to let them see if we are concubines! Men, you must allow your wives to come with us! Every woman here who is capable of walking should be with us tomorrow!"

Again there was murmuring and shouting, and some applause, but there were also cries of remonstrance and protest. Bakayoko took Penda by the arm,

"Come to the union office with us," he said. "Your idea is good, but you can't start on something like this without thinking it over carefully."

As they crossed the square, through the gradually scattering crowd, they passed dozens of little groups discussing this new development. It was the first time in living memory that a woman had spoken in public in Thiès, and even the onslaught of night could not still the arguments.

The discussion at the union office was no less heated. Balla expressed the opinion of many when he said, "I'm against letting the women go. It's normal that they should support us; a wife should support her husband, but from that to a march on Dakar . . . No, I vote against it. The heat or their anger or something has gone to their heads! Lahbib, would you take the responsibility for letting the women go?"

"We can't possibly listen to everyone's ideas or opinions about it. If you wish, we can take a vote."

Bakayoko interrupted the argument that threatened to break out. "We have no right to discourage anyone who wants to strike a blow for us," he said brutally. "It may be just that blow that is needed. If the women have decided, all that is left for us to do is to help them. I move that the delegates from Dakar leave immediately to warn the local committee of their arrival. You're from Dakar, aren't you?" he asked, speaking to Beaugosse for the first time. "How long do you think it will take them to get there?"

"I've never gone to Dakar on foot," Beaugosse answered, "but I don't think it is anything for women to try. Besides, there is no water there; when I left, Alioune and all the other men were scouring the city for a cask or even a bottle of water—which is what the women should be doing. Instead of that, they have been battling troops in the streets and starting fires. Now the soldiers and the militia are patrolling everywhere. You would be sending those women straight into the jaws of a lion."

"You can keep your French for yourself," Bakayoko said. "The men will understand you better if you speak their language. As for the men in Dakar looking for water for their families, the time when our fathers would have considered that demeaning is past. If all the workers thought like you, we might as well say good-by to the strike and to all the months of sacrifice."

"All right, Bakayoko," Lahbib said. "Calm down, and let's get back to practical matters. If the women have decided to go, we must help them and prepare an escort for them. We'll have to do something about the children, too—at least about those whose mothers will be leaving. I suggest that we try to find some trucks and send them into the villages in the brush country. Everyone here has relatives in the villages. As for you, Penda, you will have to be sure that the men who come with you do not bother the women; and if you find that this march is too hard for the women, stop them and make them turn back. There will be no shame in that, and no one will hold it against you."

If the truth be told, although Bakayoko, with his manner of disregarding destiny or bending it to his will, was the soul of this strike, it was Lahbib, the serious, thoughtful, calm, and modest Lahbib, who was its brain. Lahbib counted each one of God's bits of wood, weighed them, and balanced them, but the strength that was in them came from Bakayoko.

While the men discussed the measures to be taken at the union office, the women prepared for their departure. An inky night flowed through the city, somber and viscid, as if the heavens had decanted a layer of crude oil across the earth. The cries and shouts that pierced the darkness were like fitful flashes of lightning, but the ceaseless sound of the tam-tams seemed to carry with it a promise that dawn would come.

The compound of Dieynaba, the market woman, had been turned into the major place of assembly, although she herself was not to leave because Gorgui was dying. Shadows came and went in the courtyard, challenging and calling to each other; the squalling of children and the excited chattering and laughter of the old women who were being left at home added to the hubbub and confusion, but at the same time there was a steady trampling of purposeful feet, like the sounds of a legion lifting camp.

Another group was making ready in the Place du Premier Septembre, just across from the militiamen who stood guard in front of the police station. Prevented by their orders from talking with the women, and uneasy in the flickering light of the lanterns they had brought from the guardhouse, they watched this gathering of shadows without knowing quite what to do, but there were some among them who listened to the drums and knew what was in the air.

At last, toward two o'clock in the morning, when a few venturesome stars had succeeded in stabbing through the obscurity, the two groups came together. A cloud of white dust, pushed up and out by a lazy wind, rose to the sky and a meeting with the darkness.

"Now we are leaving!" Penda cried. Like so many echoes, hundreds of voices answered her. "Now we are leaving . . . leaving . . . leaving . . ." Preceded, accompanied, and followed by the beating of the drums, the cortège moved out into the night.

At the first light of morning, some of the men who had gone out with the women to speed them on their way turned and went back to Thiès.

"Do you think they will get there safely?" Bakary asked. The bowl of Bakayoko's pipe glowed briefly in the gray dawn. "Yes, Uncle," he said, "We have faith in them."

To observe the ceremony of the women's departure properly, Bakary had girded his arms with amulets and fetishes. His upper arms were completely covered by circlets of red, black, and yellow leather, and his forearms with bracelets made of antelope horns edged with horsehair or covered with red cloth sewn with *cauris,* the little shells which once had been used as money. On the index finger of his right hand he wore an enormous ring of raw metal. He had sworn that none of these charms would leave his body until the women's journey had ended . . .

Ever since they left Thiès, the women had not stopped singing. As soon as one group allowed the refrain to die, another picked it up, and new verses were born at the hazard of chance or inspiration, one word leading to another and each finding, in its turn, its rhythm and its place. No one was very sure any longer where the song began, or if it had an ending. It rolled out over its own length, like the movement of a serpent. It was as long as a life . . .

The sun was behind them, beating ever harder on their backs, but they paid no attention to it; they knew it well. The sun was a native.

Penda, still wearing her soldier's cartridge belt, marched at the head of the procession with Mariame Sonko, the wife of Balla, and Maimouna, the blind woman, who had joined them in the darkness without being noticed by anyone. Her baby was strapped across her back with an old shawl.

The men of the little escort group followed at some distance behind the women, and several of them had brought bicycles in the event that they should be needed. Boubacar had strung a necklace of cans and gourds filled with water from the framework and handlebars on his. Samba N'Doulougou was perched like a scrawny bird on an elegant English machine. His rump beat irregularly against the saddle, and his feet parted company with the pedals at every turn.

They were traveling across a countryside laid waste by the dry season. The torrents of the sun had struck at the hearts of even the grasses and the wild plants and drained away their sap. The smallest leaves and stalks leaned toward the earth, preparing to fall and die. The only things that seemed alive were the thorny plants that thrived on drought and, far off toward the horizon, the lofty baobabs, to whom the comings and goings of seasons meant nothing. The soil was ridged and caked in an unwholesome crust, but it still bore traces of ancient cultivation; little squares of earth pierced by stumps of millet or corn, standing like the teeth of a broken comb. Once, a line of thatched roofs had been drawn here, against the bosom of a rich, brown earth; and countless little pathways—coming from no one knew where, going no one knew where—crossed this master road, and the hundreds of feet that trod them raised a cloud of reddish dust, for in those days there was no asphalt on the road from Dakar.

Quite early on the first night they came to a village. The inhabitants, bewildered at the sight of so many women, plied them with questions. But their hospitality was cordial, although a little ceremonious because of their surprise at such an event. At dawn, their thirst assuaged, their stomachs calmed, their feet still sore, they left again, to a concert of compliments and encouragement. Two hours later they passed the bus to Thiès, and some of the women performed a little dance in the road, to acknowledge the cheers and waving of the travelers. Then they took up their march again.

And the second day was very much like the first . . .

It was during the next stage of the march that the crisis occurred which seemed certain to bring about the failure of the whole enterprise.

It had not been easy to rouse the women, who groaned and complained bitterly, pressing their hands against their aching limbs and backs, trying to rid themselves of the stiffness brought on by an hour's rest. Penda tried to cheer them up by joking with the group of younger girls.

"Be sure you don't let the men get too close to you. I don't want to have to answer to your families when your bellies start to swell!"

"We haven't done anything," Aby said indignantly.

"And I suppose if you did you would come and tell me about it right away, hé?" But no one was in a mood to laugh. Water had become the only thing they thought about. The few cans Boubacar's men brought back had been enough to supply only a few drops to each person.

"I'm as filthy as a pig," one woman said, displaying the scales of dried sweat, raked with dust that had formed on her legs.

"I'd like to get in the water and stay in it, like a fish!" "When I get to Dakar, I'm going to do nothing but drink for the first hour!"

"Those beautiful, well-scrubbed boys in Dakar won't be interested in our dirty bodies!"

Little by little, however, the column reformed. There was no laughter or singing now, but a curious new thing seemed to have come to them: the sort of hope, or instinct, that will guide an animal searching for a new place to graze.

More and more often now, Penda left her own group and walked back along the length of the column, gathering in the stragglers, stopping to talk to the old and the more feeble, encouraging them to go on. On one such journey she heard Awa talking to a group of her friends, in a loud, frightened voice.

"I swear to you, there are evil spirits among us. My dream came back while we were resting—but I've taken precautions; they won't want me." Saying this, she untied a corner of her skirt, which she had made into a large knot. "Before we left, I covered myself with salt and every now and then I eat a little of it. That way, when the *deumes* come to devour me, they will find that they don't want me."

Several of the others held out their hands eagerly, and Awa gave them each a pinch of salt. In their fatigue and discouragement, the women were beset again by all the fears instilled in them by age-old legends. The sky itself seemed to threaten them; little clouds the color of Dahomey ivory, bordered in dark gray, raced across the horizon, throwing the bony fingers of the cade trees into stark relief.

"You are right, Awa." one of the women said. "We must be very careful. These offshoots of hell can change themselves into grains of dust, or into ants or thorns, or even into birds. I'm going to warn my sister."

"You're a bunch of fools," Penda said angrily, "and you ought to . . ."

But she was interrupted by a piercing, disjointed shriek, followed by the sound of hysterical screaming from the rear of the column. She began to run in that direction, and a few of the more curious among the other women followed her, but most of them remained frozen where they were, and some even fled in the opposite direction.

Séni was rolling in the dust in the middle of the road, her limbs writhing horribly, her back arched and twisted in convulsions. Her skirt had been torn off, a slimy foam dribbled from her mouth, and her eyes had rolled back into her head until only the whites stared out. "I told you!" Awa cried. "It's a *deume* who is devouring her! We've got to find it!"

The great orbs of her eyes, rolling in terror, suddenly came to rest on the tiny figure of Yaciné, seated by the side of the road a few feet away. The old woman had cut her big toe, and since it was bleeding profusely, she was trying to bring her foot up to her mouth to suck the blood away.

"There she is! There she is!" Awa screamed. "Look—she is sucking Séni's blood through her feet!"

Twenty mouths screamed with her now. "There she is! There is the *deume!* Catch her, catch her!"

Yaciné leaped to her feet, panic-stricken, and tried to run, but she was caught in an instant. A dozen hands seized her roughly, and others hurled branches and stones at her.

"You've all gone mad!" Penda shouted, trying to protect the old woman, whose face had been gashed by a stone and was beginning to bleed.

Awa was still screaming hysterically. "I told you so! I told you so! We have a *deume,* and Séni is going to die!"

"*Fermez vos gueules!*" Without realizing it, Penda had spoken in French. "You're the ones who are *deumes!* Let this woman go, or I'll eat you alive myself! Mariame! Go get Boubacar and the men and bring Maimouna, too!"

She succeeded at last in freeing Yaciné, half dead with fright, her clothing almost torn from her body. Séni was lying on her back in the road, surrounded by a circle of women. Her legs were straight and stiff, and her teeth were chattering violently.

Boubacar arrived, followed by five or six men on bicycles, one of them carrying Maimouna behind him. She leaned over the prostrate woman, her fingers moving swiftly over her face and feeling for her pulse.

"It isn't serious," she said. "It's just the heat. She'll have to inhale some urine."

"All right, some of you sluts go and piss!" Penda cried.

Some of the women climbed over to the other side of the embankment, and Maimouna followed them. She came back a few minutes later, carrying some clods of humid earth. Seating herself in the road, she kneaded them into little balls, which she passed back and forth under Séni's nostrils, while Penda held up the unconscious woman's head.

In all this time, Awa never once stopped shouting. "There are others! I tell you, there are others! Séni is going to die—I can smell the odor of death from her already. They brought us out here because it would be easier to devour us here—it's just like it was in my dream!"

Penda could no longer control herself. She rested Séni's head on the knees of the blind woman and hurled herself at Awa.

"Now, you are going to be quiet!" Her fists were as hard as a man's, and she hammered at the other woman's face and stomach until she stumbled and fell against the foot of a tree, screaming with pain and fear.

Then, her anger drained out of her by this explosion of physical energy, Penda walked over to the giant smith, who had been watching her in amazement.

"Boubacar, some of the men will have to carry the women who are sick," she said, pointing at Awa, the weeping Yaciné, and Séni, who was now sitting up, with her head resting calmly on Maimouna's shoulder, next to that of the baby sleeping on her mother's back.

The men lifted her from the ground and installed her on the seat of a bicycle, where they could support her as they pushed it along. Boubacar took Awa on his powerful back, and the column formed up once again . . .

The ranks of the original column from Thiès had been swollen by women from the villages, and by a delegation from Rufisque; and a large group of men had reinforced the escort. The women sang again and laughed and joked.

"We will surely see some beautiful houses at Dakar."

"But they are not for us; they are only for the *toubabs*."

"After the strike we will have them, too."

"After the strike I am going to do what the wives of the *toubabs* do, and take my husband's pay."

"And if there are two of you?"

"We'll each take half, and that way he won't have anything left to spend on other women. We will have won the strike, too!"

"The men have been good, though. Did you see how the smith was sweating while he was carrying Awa?"

"Bah! For once he had a woman on his back. They have us on our backs every night!"

In the last miles before they reached their goal they passed a point from which they could see the island of Gorée, a tiny black dot in the green expanse of the ocean; they saw the vast Lafarge cement factories and the remains of an American army camp. As they approached the first buildings of Dakar's suburbs, a breathless boy on a bicycle raced up to meet them, leaping off his machine in front of the little group at the head of the column.

"There are soldiers on the road at the entrance to the city," he gasped. "They say that the women from Thiès will not be allowed to pass."

The laughter and the singing stopped abruptly, and there was silence. A few of the women left the road and took shelter behind the walls, as if they expected the soldiers to appear at any minute; but the bulk of the column stood firm. Penda climbed up on a little slope.

"The soldiers can't eat us!" she cried. "They can't even kill us; there are too many of us! Don't be afraid—our friends are waiting for us in Dakar! We'll go on!"

The long, multi-colored mass began to move forward again. Maimouna, who was walking a little behind Penda, suddenly felt a hand on her arm.

"Who is it?"

"It's me."

"You, Samba? What's the matter?"

"There are soldiers . . ."

"Yes, I heard."

Samba N'Doulougou did not understand too clearly what force it was that had compelled him to come here now and seek out this woman whose body he had enjoyed one night. Was it pity for the weak and infirm, or was it for the mother and the child? He remembered the shame he had lived with for months as he watched her working in the sun while her belly grew large with the child, his child. And he remembered the way he had tried to alter his voice so she would not recognize him.

"Give me the child," he said. "It will be easier for me to avoid the soldiers."

"You want your child?" the blind woman said.

"The soldiers are going to be there . . ."

"And after that? . . . A father may die while a woman is big with child, but that does not prevent the child from living, because the mother is there. It is up to me to protect this child. Go away now. After I get to Dakar you will never see me again; and I have never seen you. No one knows who is the father of this child—you can sleep peacefully, and your honor will be safe. Now go back to the men."

Just outside the big racecourse of the city, the column confronted the red tarbooshes of the soldiers. A black non-commissioned officer who was standing with the captain commanding the little detachment called out to them.

"Go back to Thiès, women! We cannot let you pass!"

"We will pass if we have to walk on the body of your mother!" Penda cried.

And already the pressure of this human wall was forcing the soldiers to draw back. Reinforcements began to appear, from everywhere at once, but they were not for the men in uniform. A few rifle butts came up menacingly and were beaten down by clubs and stones. The unnerved soldiers hesitated, not knowing what to do, and then some shots rang out, and in the column two people fell—Penda and Samba N'Doulougou.

But how could a handful of men in red tarbooshes prevent this great river from rolling on to the sea?

26 • Only the dead are exempt from forced labor (1947)

Despite the report by Edward Ross on the appalling labor conditions he found in Portuguese Angola in 1924, conditions worsened over the succeeding decades. In 1947 Henrique Galvão, officially appointed as the Angolan deputy to the National Assembly of Portugal, presented to his colleagues a damning update on forced labor in the colony. As a result of his complaints, he was arrested in 1952 by the government of António de Oliveira Salazar (dictator of Portugal from 1932 until 1968) and imprisoned until his escape seven years later. In 1961 Galvão hijacked the Portuguese luxury cruise ship Santa Maria *in a successful effort to draw world attention to the conditions in Angola, an act that some scholars have suggested symbolized the beginning of the end of Portuguese rule in Africa.*[6]

1. THE DEMOGRAPHIC HEMORRHAGE OF THE PORTUGUESE COLONIES IN AFRICA. For many years there has been a stream of emigration from the Portuguese colonies on the continent of Africa (Guinea, Angola, and Mozambique) to neighboring colonies. The legally authorized emigration of 100,000 of the best of the natives to the Union of South Africa constitutes, of course, an important population loss. But it is the clandestine emigration that is depleting, in an even faster rhythm, the populations of these colonies . . . The elderly, the women, the children, the feeble, remain behind. The continual absence of the strongest individuals and the permanent settlement of an ever-increasing number of them in foreign colonies, as well as the remaining behind of the weakest, not only disorganizes and debilitates the native families but also creates very bad conditions affecting the birth rate . . .

Portugal, formerly a breeder of peoples, is now faced with a situation in which the populations of the colonies flee en masse, abandoning their homes, deserting their native lands. I figure the number of natives lost to Portugal in the last ten years through emigration to be one million, and the total number now absent from Angola and Mozambique to be about two million. The annual loss exceeds one hundred thousand and is tending to increase.

2. THE PHYSICAL DECADENCE OF THE PEOPLE. Population losses are caused by the physical incapacity and decadence of the people, lack of medical care, undernourishment, a declining birth rate, infant mortality, and disabilities and deaths resulting from work . . . The evils causing the decadence are consequences of the course of political and administrative action during the past years. In addition to these evils, the mass dislocation of the workers and the working conditions that have been established, not only in self-employment but also, and especially, in forced labor for others, have brought these colonies to a state of frightful demographic impoverishment. The clearest manifestation of this impoverishment is seen in the continually falling birth rate, in the horribly high infant mortality, in the ever-growing number of sick persons and invalids, and in the high death rate resulting from various causes, prominent among which are the working conditions and the labor recruitment methods . . .

3. LACK OF HEALTH SERVICES . . . There are far too few doctors and they continue to shun the interior and to concentrate in the cities and more important towns. The hospitals continue to lack the most elementary facilities, and many places that are strategic points for health services continue to have no hospitals . . . When important visitors are coming, a rush

6. Henrique Galvão, *My Crusade for Portugal* (Cleveland: World Publishing, 1961), 57–71.

job of cleaning is done, fresh linen is put on the beds, and everything is arranged to deceive them. I maintain that the health service to the natives in Angola, Mozambique, and Guinea (where, however, it is somewhat less bad)—both that for which the Government is directly responsible and that for which it relies on private enterprise—is virtually nonexistent . . .

4. ONLY THE DEAD ARE EXEMPT FROM FORCED LABOR . . . For the Government and for everyone else who exploits labor, the labor problem is, as one would expect in view of the population losses previously discussed, a problem of scarcity. This scarcity is not yet very appreciable in Guinea, but is felt with a certain acuteness in some parts of Mozambique and is reaching alarming proportions in all parts of Angola. This latter colony is rapidly approaching a demographic—and, therefore, an economic—catastrophe. Mozambique is on the same road. In Angola we lack the number of workers necessary to maintain the present level of production and development of the vast territory under humane conditions of labor utilization. In all the African colonies we lack the mass of workers that we need if we are even to consider the possibility of effecting great projects of social and economic progress . . . And if this situation is less perceptible than it should be, the reason is that to cover the deficit the most shameful outrages are committed, including forced labor of independent, self-employed workers, of women, of children, of the sick, of decrepit old men, etc. *Only the dead are really exempt from forced labor* . . .

5. HOW WORKERS ARE RECRUITED . . . [In Angola] the Government has so openly and deliberately made itself a recruiter and distributor of workers that individuals and enterprises come to the government offices and make written application for a supply of workers, just as brazenly as if they were asking for a supply of merchandise. In Mozambique pretty much the same practice is followed, but more surreptitiously. There the façade is preserved . . . The employer cares little whether the man lives or dies, provided he keeps on working while he can; for the employer can demand that another laborer be furnished if the first one becomes incapacitated or dies. There are employers who let as many as 35 per cent of the workers, received from the government agents, die during what is called the work-contract period. It is not recorded that any of them have been refused new workers to labor under the same conditions . . .

6. THE "CONTRACT" . . . In the African colonies, native labor is provided in the three following ways: *Voluntarily* . . . As a rule, the authorities prevent voluntary workers from choosing their employer or the kind of work they will do, and even from stipulating the wages for which they are willing to work. They are obliged to accept the minimum wage and the employer designated by the Government. Faced with this outrage, a large number of the voluntary workers go elsewhere—some to the big cities but most of them to other colonies . . . *Under Compulsion.* The natives call forced labor "contract." When they are moved to a place of forced labor, they say they are "going on contract"—for the Negroes thus herded to work are said by whites to be "contracted"—a euphemism apparently intended to dignify the outrage . . . It is a plain fact that this "contract," made possible only by the intervention of the Government, causes greater loss to the population, through death, sickness, and flight, than certain endemic diseases do. *To the Government.* The Government recruits workers for private enterprises but also for its own services. But, because there is a shortage of labor even for private enterprises, the Government frequently resorts to the conscription of women and of the infirm . . .

7. SLAVES OF THE SOIL. The self-employed workers comprise merchants, farmers, producers of raw materials, and, notably, herders of cattle. They create the wealth called native production, which is the most important element in the native economy. Organization of and aid to this mass of workers would automatically lead to an increase and improvement in native production. Temporarily, indeed, this production can be maintained and even increased without organization or aid, but only through extremely severe measures against the natives. This is the course that has been followed . . . The pressures exerted by the authorities on the native farmers, the herders of cattle, and the exploiters of raw materials such as wax and rubber, to force them to produce more, are indeed persistent and severe. But the authorities, usually beset by orders, circulars, and requirements of the central offices, soon force these men to abandon their farming or other independent work and send them to the "contract" . . . Under another pretext—this time to help the natives by promoting the production of certain products of great economic value (cotton, rice, castor beans)—there has been copied, almost without change, the system of exploitation adopted for the same purpose by the Belgian Congo and commonly known as the system of zones of influence . . . it may be appropriate for me to indicate some features of its real face, features that have caused our cotton to be classified, in certain well-informed circles, as "slave cotton" . . . The native is virtually reduced to a slave of the soil.

8. PHYSICAL ABUSES AND SPIRIT OF ANNIHILATION. The employers create obstacles to a humane solution of the labor problem. They do this against or under the protection of official regulations, sometimes deceiving the enforcement agencies and sometimes suborning them, exploiting to their own profit the lack of means of enforcement or the mildness of the authorities, and using whatever power and influence they can muster. These are the most salient facts about their conduct:

a. Resistance of every kind to a policy of wages that is economically and socially fair.

b. Bad treatment of the workers: corporal punishment is still practiced; the employers evade their obligations regarding food, clothing, and medical service; the idea that the Negro is just a beast of burden has been revived; there is manifest indifference to the physical and mental health of the workers; and a classification of the employers according to the way they treat their workers shows a fearful percentage of bad employers.

c. The waste of labor. Labor is used as if it were extremely abundant. Everything is done by Negro work hands, from the pulling of dump carts to the draining of swamps.

d. The inhuman quality of the labor recruiters.

e. The dislocation of workers to distant regions without consideration of the sudden change in climate. The hardships are especially severe when they are moved from the interior to the coastal strip and from healthful regions to regions infested by the tsetse fly.

f. The extortions, unrestrained by the authorities, practiced on the natives by merchants.

g. Disdainful unconcern about living conditions.

27 • Colonial officials take note of African discontent (1948)

Less celebrated than the strike in French West Africa but no less significant for the end of colonialism were the labor struggles (or "disturbances" in colonial parlance) that brought production to a halt in the Gold Coast for much of 1948. As the following excerpt from an official investigation into the causes of unrest indicates, British colonial officials concluded that political, economic, and social forces were all at play and that these different factors were closely interrelated. Indeed, so powerful was the challenge to colonialism, particularly its ability to produce cheap goods for a European market (the very rationale of empire), that from this time forward British officials in London (though not the local white settlers in Africa) began to consider policies that might enable them to disengage themselves politically from their possessions in West and East Africa while still maintaining a close economic relationship. To pursue that approach, the British realized that they would have to identify potential leaders in Africa with whom they felt that they could work and to whom could be given the responsibility for self-government. Unfortunately for the British, as for other colonial powers, their ideas of responsible leaders often were viewed as collaborators by Africans calling for immediate and unfettered independence.[7]

Report of the commission of enquiry into disturbances on the Gold Coast, 1948

... In the main, the underlying causes may be divided into three broad categories: political, economic and social. There is often no clear dividing line between them and they are frequently interrelated ... The remedy for the distrust and suspicion with which the African views the European, and which is to-day poisoning life in the Gold Coast, demands an attack on all three causes. None of them may be said to take precedence ...

These may be summarised as follows:

A. POLITICAL

(1) The large number of African soldiers returning from service with the Forces, where they had lived under different and better conditions, made for a general communicable state of unrest. Such Africans by reason of their contacts with other peoples, including Europeans, had developed a political and national consciousness. The fact that they were disappointed with conditions on their return, either from specious promises made before demobilisation or a general expectancy of a golden age for heroes, made them the natural focal point for any general movement against authority.

(2) A feeling of political frustration among the educated Africans who saw no prospect of ever experiencing political power under existing conditions and who regarded the 1946 Constitution as mere window-dressing designed to cover, but not to advance their natural aspirations.

(3) A failure of the Government to realise that, with the spread of liberal ideas, increasing literacy and a closer contact with political developments in other parts of the world, the star of rule through the Chiefs was on the wane. The achievement of self-government in India, Burma and Ceylon had not passed unnoticed on the Gold Coast.

7. G. E. Metcalfe, ed., *Great Britain and Ghana: Documents of Ghana History, 1807–1957* (Legon: University of Ghana, 1964), 682–83.

FIGURE 10 Nnamdi Azikiwe (wearing tie, center), led a delegation to meet the British colonial secretary in 1947 to ask for reforms in the Nigerian constitution. Azikiwe was educated in the United States and upon his return to West Africa became a well-known journalist arguing for African independence. He was elected the first president of an independent Nigeria in 1963. AP Photo.

(4) A universal feeling that Africanisation was merely a promise and not a driving force in Government policy, coupled with the suspicion that education had been slowed up, and directed in such a way as to impede Africanisation.

(5) A general suspicion of Government measures and intentions reinforced by a hostile press and heightened by the general failure of the Administration in the field of Public Relations.

(6) Increasing resentment at the growing concentration of certain trades in the hands of foreigners, particularly at the increase in the number of Syrian merchants.

B. ECONOMIC

(1) The announcement of the Government that it would remain neutral in the dispute which had arisen between the traders and the people of the Gold Coast over high prices of imported goods and which led to the organised boycott of January–February, 1948.

(2) The continuance of war-time control of imports, and the shortage and high prices of consumer goods which were widely attributed to the machinations of European importers.

(3) The alleged unfair allocation and distribution of goods in short supply, by the importing firms.

(4) The Government's acceptance of the scientists' finding that the only cure for Swollen Shoot disease of cocoa was to cut out diseased trees, and their adoption of that policy, combined with allegations of improper methods of carrying it out.

(5) The degree of control in the Cocoa Marketing Board, which limited the powers of the farmers' representatives to control the vast reserves which are accumulating under the Board's policy.

(6) The feeling that the Government had not formulated any plans for the future of industry and agriculture, and that, indeed, it was lukewarm about any development apart from production for export.

C. SOCIAL

(1) The alleged slow development of educational facilities in spite of a growing demand, and the almost complete failure to provide any technical or vocational training.

(2) The shortage of housing, particularly in the towns, and the low standards of houses for Africans as compared with those provided for Europeans.

(3) The fear of wholesale alienation of tribal lands leaving a landless peasantry.

(4) Inadequacy of the legal powers of Government necessary to deal with speeches designed to arouse disorder and violence . . .

28 • Hendrik Verwoerd explains apartheid (1950)

While British officials in Ghana, Kenya, and elsewhere in Africa considered how colonies might be moved toward political independence without breaking the economic ties that bound African producers to European markets, in South Africa a newly triumphant Afrikaner nationalist movement took power in the parliamentary election of 1948 (in which whites composed more than 90 percent of the electorate, and of those voters, Afrikaners about two-thirds) and took steps to ensure that racial discrimination was strengthened, not weakened. The policy associated with the Afrikaner nationalists and which they practiced for the next half century throughout South Africa was apartheid (apartness): the policy of favoring racial separation and, ultimately, the removal of all peoples of color from South Africa (Africans to other parts of Africa, Indians to India, Chinese to China) so that it could literally be a white man's country. For white South Africans the loss of political power and economic domination was not a scenario that they cared to face, even if it appeared to make little sense to call a country white in which more than 80 percent of the population was black and to plan for the removal of the very workforce that made possible the enormously high standard of living enjoyed by white settlers (English-speaking and Afrikaner alike).

* The most prominent spokesman for this extreme policy of racial separation was Hendrik Verwoerd, born in Amsterdam in 1901 but living in South Africa from 1903 on. Interested at first in following a career in theology, Verwoerd switched his university studies to psychology and philosophy and in the 1920s became a professor first of applied psychology and philosophy and later of sociology and social work. Attracted to Afrikaner nationalist politics, he became a newspaper editor in the 1930s and then entered parliament in 1948. He was minister of native affairs from 1950 to 1958 and then prime minister from 1958 until his assassination in 1966 (he was stabbed to death in the House of Assembly by a parliamentary messenger). On December 5, 1950, he gave the following address to the members of the Native Representative Council.[8]*

Next, I wish to accede to the wish which, I understand, has long been felt by members of this council, namely that a member of the Government should explain the main features of what is implied by the policy of Apartheid.

8. A. N. Pelzer, ed., *Verwoerd Speaks: Speeches 1948–1966* (Johannesburg: APB Publishers, 1966), 23–29.

FIGURE 11 A South African shows his passbook, which Africans were
required to carry for identification at all times under apartheid. During
the defiance campaign, launched in 1952 by the African National Congress Youth League, many Africans burned their passbooks in protest
against apartheid. AP Photo.

Within the compass of an address I have, naturally, to confine myself to the fundamen-
tals of the Apartheid policy and to the main steps following logically from the policy. Further
details and a fuller description of the reasons and value of what is being planned will have to
remain in abeyance today. Properly understood, however, these main features will elucidate
what will be done and how this will be as much in the interests of the Bantu as in those of the
European.

As a premise, the question may be put: Must Bantu and European in future develop as
intermixed communities, or as communities separated from one another in so far as this is
practically possible? If the reply is "intermingled communities," then the following must be
understood. There will be competition and conflict everywhere. So long as the points of contact are still comparatively few, as is the case now, friction and conflict will be few and less
evident. The more this intermixing develops, however, the stronger the conflict will become.
In such conflict, the Europeans will, at least for a long time, hold the stronger position, and
the Bantu be the defeated party in every phase of the struggle. This must cause to rise in him
an increasing sense of resentment and revenge. Neither for the European, nor for the Bantu,

can this, namely increasing tension and conflict, be an ideal future, because the intermixed development involves disadvantage to both.

Perhaps, in such an eventuality, it is best frankly to face the situation which must arise in the political sphere. In the event of an intermixed development, the Bantu will undoubtedly desire a share in the government of the intermixed country. He will, in due course, not be satisfied with a limited share in the form of communal representation, but will desire full participation in the country's government on the basis of an equal franchise. For the sake of simplicity, I shall not enlarge here on the fact that, simultaneously with the development of this demand, he will desire the same in the social, economic and other spheres of life, involving in due course, intermixed residence, intermixed labour, intermixed living, and, eventually, a miscegenated population—in spite of the well-known pride of both the Bantu and the European in their respective purity of descent. It follows logically, therefore, that, in an intermixed country, the Bantu must, in the political sphere, have as their object equal franchise with the European.

Now examine the same question from the European's point of view. A section of the Europeans, consisting of both Afrikaans- and English-speaking peoples, says equally clearly that, in regard to the above standpoint, the European must continue to dominate what will be the European part of South Africa. It should be noted that, notwithstanding false representations, these Europeans do not demand domination over the whole of South Africa, that is to say, over the Native territories according as the Bantu outgrow the need for their trusteeship. Because that section of the European population states its case very clearly, it must not be accepted, however, that the other section of the European population will support the above possible future demand of the Bantu. That section of the European population (English as well as Afrikaans) which is prepared to grant representation to the Bantu in the country's government does not wish to grant anything beyond communal representation, and that on a strictly limited basis. They do not yet realize that a balance of power may thereby be given to the non-European with which an attempt may later be made to secure full and equal franchise on the same voters' roll. The moment they realize that, or the moment when the attempt is made, this latter section of the European population will also throw in its weight with the first section in the interests of European supremacy in the European portion of the country. This appears clearly from its proposition that, in its belief on the basis of an inherent superiority, or greater knowledge, or whatever it may be, the European must remain master and leader. The section is, therefore, also a protagonist of separate residential areas, and of what it calls separation.

My point is this that, if mixed development is to be the policy of the future in South Africa, it will lead to the most terrific clash of interests imaginable. The endeavours and desires of the Bantu and the endeavours and objectives of all Europeans will be antagonistic. Such a clash can only bring unhappiness and misery to both. Both Bantu and European must, therefore, consider in good time how this misery can be averted from themselves and from their descendants. They must find a plan to provide the two population groups with opportunities for the full development of their respective powers and ambitions without coming into conflict.

The only possible way out is the second alternative, namely, that both adopt a development divorced from each other. That is all that the word apartheid means. Any word can be

equal false &
negative connotations of apartheid.

within theme

poisoned by attaching a false meaning to it. That has happened to this word. The Bantu have been made to believe that it means oppression, or even that the Native territories are to be taken away from them. In reality, however, exactly the opposite is intended with the policy of apartheid. To avoid the above-mentioned unpleasant and dangerous future for both sections of the population, the present Government adopts the attitude that it concedes and wishes to give to others precisely what it demands for itself. It believes in the supremacy (baasskap) of the European in his sphere but, then, it also believes equally in the supremacy (baasskap) of the Bantu in his own sphere. For the European child it wishes to create all the possible opportunities for its own development, prosperity and national service in its own sphere; but for the Bantu it also wishes to create all the opportunities for the realization of ambitions and the rendering of service to *their* own people. There is thus no policy of oppression here, but one of creating a situation which has never existed for the Bantu; namely, that, taking into consideration their languages, traditions, history and different national communities, they may pass through a development of their own. That opportunity arises for them as soon as such a division is brought into being between them and the Europeans that they need not be the imitators and henchmen of the latter.

The next question, then, is how the division is to be brought about so as to allow the European and the Bantu to pass through a development of their own, in accordance with their own traditions, under their own leaders in every sphere of life.

It is perfectly clear that it would have been the easiest—an ideal condition for each of the two groups—if the course of history had been different. Suppose there had arisen in Southern Africa a state in which only Bantu lived and worked, and another in which only Europeans lived and worked. Each could then have worked out its own destiny in its own way. This is not the situation today, however, and planning must in practice take present day actualities of life in the Union into account. We cannot escape from that which history has brought in its train. However, this easiest situation for peaceful association, self-government and development, each according to its own nature and completely apart from one another, may, in fact, be taken as a yardstick whereby to test plans for getting out of the present confusion and difficulties. One may, so far as is practicable, try to approach this objective in the future.

The realities of today are that a little over one-third of the Bantu resides, or still has its roots, in what are unambiguously termed Native territories. A little over a third lives in the countryside and on the farms of Europeans. A little less than a third lives and works in the cities, of whom a section have been detribalized and urbanized. The apartheid policy takes this reality into account.

Obviously, in order to grant equal opportunities to the Bantu, both in their interests as well as those of the Europeans, its starting-point is the Native territories. For the present, these territories cannot provide the desired opportunities for living and development to their inhabitants and their children, let alone to more people. Due to neglect of their soil and overpopulation by man and cattle, large numbers are even now being continuously forced to go and seek a living under the protection of the European and his industries. In these circumstances it cannot be expected that the Bantu community will so provide for itself and so progress as to allow ambitious and developed young people to be taken up by their own people in their own national service out of their own funds. According as a flourishing community arises in such territories, however, the need will develop for teachers, dealers, clerks, artisans, agricultural experts, leaders of local and general governing bodies of their own. In other words, the whole superstructure of administrative and professional people arising in every prosperous community will then become necessary. Our first aim as a Government is, therefore, to lay the foundation of a prosperous producing community through soil reclamation and conservation methods and through the systematic establishment in the Native territories of Bantu farming on an economic basis.

The limited territories are, however, as little able to carry the whole of the Bantu population of the reserves of the present and the future—if all were to be farmers—as the European area would be able to carry all the Europeans if they were all to be farmers, or as England would be able to carry its whole population if all of them had to be landowners, farmers and cattle breeders. Consequently, the systematic building up of the Native territories aims at a development precisely as in all prosperous countries. Side by side with agricultural development must also come an urban development founded on industrial growth. The future Bantu towns and cities in the reserves may arise partly in conjunction with Bantu industries of their own in those reserves. In their establishment Europeans must be prepared to help with money and knowledge, in the consciousness that such industries must, as soon as is possible, wholly pass over into the hands of the Bantu.

On account of the backlog, it is conceivable, however, that such industries may not develop sufficiently rapidly to meet adequately the needs of the Bantu requiring work. The European industrialist will, therefore, have to be encouraged to establish industries within the European areas near such towns and cities. Bantu working in those industries will then be able to live within their own territories, where they have their own schools, their own traders, and where they govern themselves. Indeed, the kernel of the apartheid policy is that, as the Bantu no longer need the European, the latter must wholly withdraw from the Native territories.

What length of time it will take the Bantu in the reserves to advance to that stage of self-sufficiency and self-government will depend on his own industry and preparedness to grasp this opportunity offered by the apartheid policy for self-development and service to his own nation. This development of the reserves will not, however, mean that all Natives from the cities or European countryside will be able, or wish, to trek to them. In the countryside there has, up to the present, not been a clash of social interests. The endeavour, at any rate for the time being, must be to grant the Bantu in town locations as much self-government as is practicable under the guardianship of the town councils, and to let tribal control of farm Natives function effectively. There the residential and working conditions will also have to enjoy special attention so that the Bantu community finding a livelihood as farm labourers may also be prosperous and happy. Here the problem is rather how to create better relationships, greater stability, correct training and good working conditions. Apart from the removal of black spots (like the removal of white spots in the Native areas), the policy of apartheid is for the time being, not so much an issue at this juncture, except if mechanization of farming should later cause a decrease in non-European labourers.

Finally, there are the implications of the apartheid policy in respect of European cities. The primary requirement of this policy is well known, namely, that not only must there be separation between European and non-European residential areas, but also that the different non-European groups, such as the Bantu, the Coloured, and the Indian, shall live in their own residential areas. Although considerable numbers of Bantu who are still rooted in the reserves may conceivably return thither, particularly according as urban and industrial development take place, or even many urbanized Bantu may proceed thence because of the opportunities to exercise their talents as artisans, traders, clerks or professionals, or to realize their political ambitions—large numbers will undoubtedly still remain behind in the big cities. For a long time to come, this will probably continue to be the case.

For these Bantu also the Apartheid policy and separate residential areas have great significance. The objective is, namely, to give them the greatest possible measure of self-government in such areas according to the degree in which local authorities, who construct these towns, can fall into line. In due course, too, depending on the ability of the Bantu community, all the work there will have to be done by their own people, as was described in connection with the reserves. Even within a European area, therefore, the Bantu communities would not be separated for the former to oppress them, but to form their own communities within which they may pursue a full life of work and service.

In view of all this, it will be appreciated why the Apartheid policy also takes an interest in suitable education for the Bantu. This, in fact, brings in its train the need for sufficiently competent Bantu in many spheres. The only and obvious reservation is that the Bantu will have to place his development and his knowledge exclusively at the service of his own people.

Co-operation in implementing the apartheid policy as described here is one of the greatest services the present leader of the Bantu population can render his people. Instead of striving after vague chimeras and trying to equal the European in an intermingled community with confused ideals and inevitable conflict, he can be a national figure helping to lead his own people along the road of peace and prosperity. He can help to give the children and educated men and women of his people an opportunity to find employment or fully to realize their ambitions within their own sphere or, where this is not possible, as within the Europeans' sphere, employment and service within segregated areas of their own.

I trust that every Bantu will forget the misunderstandings of the past and choose not the road leading to conflict, but that which leads to peace and happiness for both the separate communities. Are the present leaders of the Bantu, under the influence of Communist agitators, going to seek a form of equality which they will not get? For in the long run they will come up against the whole of the European community, as well as the large section of their own compatriots who prefer the many advantages of self-government within a community of their own. I cannot believe that they will. Nobody can reject a form of independence, obtainable with everybody's co-operation, in favour of a futile striving after that which promises to be not freedom but downfall.

CHAPTER FOUR

No Easy Road to Decolonization (1953–61)

29 • Nelson Mandela's "No Easy Walk to Freedom" (1953)

Nelson Mandela (born 1918) was one of the founding members of the ANC's Youth League and in 1950 became its president. A lawyer by training, he organized the ANC's "defiance campaign" in 1952 in collaboration with other antiapartheid organizations as an attempt to demonstrate the futility of apartheid by encouraging massive, popular noncompliance with the policy. Thousands of opponents of apartheid burned their passes, refused to travel on segregated forms of transportation, and ignored signs enforcing the color bar (such as those indicating separate entrances for each race into post offices and courts of law, as well as different parks, beaches, and other public facilities). The National Party government responded by arresting thousands of protestors, including Mandela and most of the leaders of the ANC. Mandela, along with several others, was charged under the terms of the Suppression of Communism Act (which made it legally possible to define as a Communist anyone who encouraged "feelings of hostility between the European and the non-European races of the Union" and who aimed at "bringing about any political, industrial, social, or economic change within the Union by the promotion of disturbance or disorder"). Mandela was convicted and initially given a suspended sentence, but then, under new legislation enacted to deal with the protest movement, he was banned from participating in any public activities in South Africa. The speech reproduced here, his presidential address to the Transvaal branch of the ANC, delivered on September 21, 1953, was the last public statement that he was able to make before his banning order went fully into effect.[1]

Since 1912 and year after year thereafter, in their homes and local areas, in provincial and national gatherings, on trains and buses, in the factories and on the farms, in cities, villages, shanty towns, schools and prisons, the African people have discussed the shameful misdeeds of those who rule the country. Year after year, they have raised their voices in condemnation of the grinding poverty of the people, the low wages, the acute shortage of land, the inhuman exploitation and the whole policy of white domination. But instead of more freedom repression began to grow in volume and intensity and it seemed that all their sacrifices would end up in smoke and dust. Today the entire country knows that their labours were not in vain for a new spirit and new ideas have gripped our people. Today the people speak the language of

---

1. Thomas Karis and Gwendolen M. Carter, eds., *From Protest to Challenge: A Documentary History of African Politics in South Africa, 1882–1962* (Stanford: Hoover Institution Press, 1972), vol. 3, *Challenge and Violence, 1953–1964*, ed. Thomas Karis and Gail M. Gerhart, 106–15.

action: there is a mighty awakening among the men and women of our country and the year 1952 stands out as the year of this upsurge of national consciousness.

In June, 1952, the AFRICAN NATIONAL CONGRESS and the SOUTH AFRICAN IN-DIAN CONGRESS [SAIC], bearing in mind their responsibility as the representatives of the downtrodden and oppressed people of South Africa, took the plunge and launched the Campaign for the Defiance of the Unjust Laws. Starting off in Port Elizabeth in the early hours of June 26 and with only thirty-three defiers in action and then in Johannesburg in the afternoon of the same day with one hundred and six defiers, it spread throughout the country like wild fire. Factory and office workers, doctors, lawyers, teachers, students and the clergy; Africans, Coloureds, Indians and Europeans, old and young, all rallied to the national call and defied the pass laws and the curfew and the railway apartheid regulations. At the end of the year, more than 8,000 people of all races had defied. The Campaign called for immediate and heavy sacrifices. Workers lost their jobs, chiefs and teachers were expelled from the service, doctors, lawyers and businessmen gave up their practices and businesses and elected to go to jail. Defiance was a step of great political significance. It released strong social forces which affected thousands of our countrymen. It was an effective way of getting the masses to function polit-ically; a powerful method of voicing our indignation against the reactionary policies of the Government. It was one of the best ways of exerting pressure on the Government and ex-tremely dangerous to the stability and security of the State. It inspired and aroused our people from a servile community of yesmen to a militant and uncompromising band of comrades-in-arms. The entire country was transformed into battle zones where the forces of liberation were locked up in immortal conflict against those of reaction and evil. Our flag flew in every battlefield and thousands of our countrymen rallied around it. We held the initiative and the forces of freedom were advancing on all fronts. It was against this background and at the height of this Campaign that we held our last annual provincial Conference in Pretoria from the 10th to the 12th of October last year. In a way, that Conference was a welcome reception for those who had returned from the battlefields and a farewell to those who were still going to action. The spirit of defiance and action dominated the entire conference.

Today we meet under totally different conditions. By the end of July last year, the Cam-paign had reached a stage where it had to be suppressed by the Government or it would im-pose its own policies on the country.

The government launched its reactionary offensive and struck at us. Between July last year and August this year forty-seven leading members from both Congresses in Johannes-burg, Port Elizabeth and Kimberley were arrested, tried and convicted for launching the De-fiance Campaign and given suspended sentences ranging from three months to two years on condition that they did not again participate in the defiance of the unjust laws. In November last year, a proclamation was passed which prohibited meetings of more than ten Africans and made it an offence for any person to call upon an African to defy. Contravention of this proclamation carried a penalty of three years or of a fine of three hundred pounds. In March this year the Government passed the so-called Public Safety Act which empowered it to de-clare a state of emergency and to create conditions which would permit of the most ruthless and pitiless methods of suppressing our movement. Almost simultaneously, the Criminal Laws Amendment Act was passed which provided heavy penalties for those convicted of Defiance offences. This Act also made provision for the whipping of defiers including women. It was under this Act that Mr. Arthur Matiala who was the local [leader] of the Central Branch during the Defiance Campaign, was convicted and sentenced to twelve months with hard labour plus eight strokes by the Magistrate of Villa Nora. The Government also made extensive use of the Suppression of Communism Act. You will remember that in May last year the Government ordered Moses Kotane, Yusuf Dadoo, J. B. Marks, David Bopape and Johnson Ngwevela to resign from the Congresses and many other organisations and were also prohibited from attending political gatherings. In consequence of these bans, Moses Kotane, J. B. Marks, and David Bopape did not attend our last provincial Conference. In December last year, the Secretary-General, Mr. W. M. Sisulu, and I were banned from attending gatherings and confined to Johannesburg for six months. Early this year, the President-General, Chief Luthuli, whilst in the midst of a national tour which he was prosecuting with remarkable energy and devotion, was prohibited for a period of twelve months from attending public gatherings and from visiting Durban, Johannesburg, Cape Town, Port Elizabeth and many other centres. A few days before the President-General was banned, the President of the S.A.I.C., Dr. G. M. Naicker, had been served with a similar notice. Many other active workers both from the African and Indian Congresses and from trade union organisations were also banned.

The Congresses realised that these measures created a new situation which did not prevail when the Campaign was launched in June 1952. The tide of defiance was bound to recede and we were forced to pause and to take stock of the new situation. We had to analyse the dangers that faced us, formulate plans to overcome them and evolve new plans of political struggle. A political movement must keep in touch with reality and the prevailing conditions. Long speeches, the shaking of fists, the banging of tables and strongly worded resolutions out of touch with the objective conditions do not bring about mass action and can do a great deal of harm to the organisation and the struggle we serve. The masses had to be prepared and made ready for new forms of political struggle. We had to recuperate our strength and muster our forces for another and more powerful offensive against the enemy. To have gone ahead blindly as if nothing had happened would have been suicidal and stupid. The conditions under which we meet today are, therefore, vastly different. The Defiance Campaign together with its thrills and adventures has receded. The old methods of bringing about mass action through public mass meetings, press statements and leaflets calling upon the people to go to action have become extremely dangerous and difficult to use effectively. The authorities will not easily permit a meeting called under the auspices of the A.N.C., few newspapers will publish statements openly criticising the policies of the Government and there is hardly a single printing press which will agree to print leaflets calling upon workers to embark on industrial action for fear of prosecution under the Suppression of Communism Act and similar measures. These developments require the evolution of new forms of political struggle which will make it reasonable for us to strive for action on a higher level than the Defiance Campaign. The Government, alarmed at the indomitable upsurge of national consciousness, is doing everything in its power to crush our movement by removing the genuine representatives of the people from the organisations. According to a statement made by [C. R.] Swart [minister of justice] in Parliament on the 18th September, 1953, there are thirty-three trade union officials and eighty-nine other people who have been served with notices in terms of the Suppression of

Communism Act. This does not include that formidable array of freedom fighters who have been named and blacklisted under the Suppression of Communism Act and those who have been banned under the Riotous Assemblies Act.

Meanwhile the living conditions of the people, already extremely difficult, are steadily worsening and becoming unbearable. The purchasing power of the masses is progressively declining and the cost of living is rocketing. Bread is now dearer than it was two months ago. The cost of milk, meat and vegetables is beyond the pockets of the average family and many of our people cannot afford them. The people are too poor to have enough food to feed their families and children. They cannot afford sufficient clothing, housing and medical care. They are denied the right to security in the event of unemployment, sickness, disability, old age and where these exist, they are of an extremely inferior and useless nature. Because of lack of proper medical amenities our people are ravaged by such dreaded diseases as tuberculosis, venereal disease, leprosy, pellagra, and infantile mortality is very high. The recent state budget made provision for the increase of the cost-of-living allowances for Europeans and not a word was said about the poorest and most hard-hit section of the population—the African people. The insane policies of the Government which have brought about an explosive situation in the country have definitely scared away foreign capital from South Africa and the financial crisis through which the country is now passing is forcing many industrial and business concerns to close down, to retrench their staffs and unemployment is growing every day. The farm labourers are in a particularly dire plight. You will perhaps recall the investigations and exposures of the semi-slave conditions on the Bethal farms made in 1948 by the Reverend Michael Scott and a *Guardian* Correspondent; by the *Drum* last year and the *Advance* in April this year. You will recall how human beings, wearing only sacks with holes for their heads and arms, never given enough food to eat, slept on cement floors on cold nights with only their sacks to cover their shivering bodies. You will remember how they are woken up as early as 4 A.M. and taken to work on the fields with the indunas sjamboking [whipping] those who tried to straighten their backs, who felt weak and dropped down because of hunger and sheer exhaustion. You will also recall the story of human beings toiling pathetically from the early hours of the morning till sunset, fed only on mealie [corn] meal served on filthy sacks spread on the ground and eating with their dirty hands. People falling ill and never once being given medical attention. You will also recall the revolting story of a farmer who was convicted for tying a labourer by his feet from a tree and had him flogged to death, pouring boiling water into his mouth whenever he cried for water. These things which have long vanished from many parts of the world still flourish in S. A. today. None will deny that they constitute a serious challenge to Congress and we are in duty bound to find an effective remedy for these obnoxious practices.

The Government has introduced in Parliament the Native Labour (Settlement of Disputes) Bill and the Bantu Education Bill. Speaking on the Labour Bill, the Minister of Labour, Ben Schoeman, openly stated that the aim of this wicked measure is to bleed African trade unions to death. By forbidding strikes and lockouts it deprives Africans of the one weapon the workers have to improve their position. The aim of the measure is to destroy the present African trade unions which are controlled by the workers themselves and which fight for the improvement of their working conditions in return for a Central Native Labour Board controlled by the Government and which will be used to frustrate the legitimate aspirations of the

African worker. The Minister of Native Affairs, Verwoerd, has also been brutally clear in explaining the objects of the Bantu Education Bill. According to him the aim of this law is to teach our children that Africans are inferior to Europeans. African education would be taken out of the hands of people who taught equality between black and white. When this Bill becomes law, it will not be the parents but the Department of Native Affairs which will decide whether an African child should receive higher or other education. It might well be that the children of those who criticise the Government and who fight its policies will almost certainly be taught how to drill rocks in the mines and how to plough potatoes on the farms of Bethal. High education might well be the privilege of those children whose families have a tradition of collaboration with the ruling circles.

The attitude of the Congress on these bills is very clear and unequivocal. Congress totally rejects both bills without reservation. The last provincial Conference strongly condemned the then proposed Labour Bill as a measure designed to rob the African workers of the universal right of free trade unionism and to undermine and destroy the existing African trade unions. Conference further called upon the African workers to boycott and defy the application of this sinister scheme which was calculated to further the exploitation of the African worker. To accept a measure of this nature even in a qualified manner would be a betrayal of the toiling masses. At a time when every genuine Congressite should fight unreservedly for the recognition of African trade unions and the realisation of the principle that everyone has the right to form and to join trade unions for the protection of his interests, we declare our firm belief in the principles enunciated in the Universal Declaration of Human Rights that everyone has the right to education; that education shall be directed to the full development of human personality and to the strengthening of respect for human rights and fundamental freedoms. It shall promote understanding, tolerance and friendship among the nations, racial or religious groups and shall further the activities of the United Nations for the maintenance of peace. That parents have the right to choose the kind of education that shall be given to their children.

The cumulative effect of all these measures is to prop up and perpetuate the artificial and decaying policy of the supremacy of the white men. The attitude of the government to us is that: "Let's beat them down with guns and batons and trample them under our feet. We must be ready to drown the whole country in blood if only there is the slightest chance of preserving white supremacy."

But there is nothing inherently superior about the herrenvolk idea of the supremacy of the whites. In China, India, Indonesia and Korea, American, British, Dutch and French Imperialism, based on the concept of the supremacy of Europeans over Asians, has been completely and perfectly exploded. In Malaya and Indo-China British and French imperialisms are being shaken to their foundations by powerful and revolutionary national liberation movements. In Africa, there are approximately 190,000,000 Africans as against 4,000,000 Europeans. The entire continent is seething with discontent and already there are powerful revolutionary eruptions in the Gold Coast, Nigeria, Tunisia, Kenya, the Rhodesias and South Africa. The oppressed people and the oppressors are at loggerheads. *The day of reckoning* between the forces of freedom and those of reaction is not very far off. I have not the slightest doubt that when that day comes truth and justice will prevail.

The intensification of repressions and the extensive use of the bans is designed to immobilise every active worker and to check the national liberation movement. But gone forever are the days when harsh and wicked laws provided the oppressors with years of peace and quiet. The racial policies of the Government have pricked the conscience of all men of good will and have aroused their deepest indignation. The feelings of the oppressed people have never been more bitter. If the ruling circles seek to maintain their position by such inhuman methods then a clash between the forces of freedom and those of reaction is certain. The grave plight of the people compels them to resist to the death the stinking policies of the gangsters that rule our country.

But in spite of all the difficulties outlined above, we have won important victories. The general political level of the people has been considerably raised and they are now more conscious of their strength. Action has become the language of the day. The ties between the working people and the Congress have been greatly strengthened. This is a development of the highest importance because in a country such as ours a political organisation that does not receive the support of the workers is in fact paralysed on the very ground on which it has chosen to wage battle. Leaders of trade union organisations are at the same time important officials of the provincial and local branches of the A.N.C. In the past we talked of the African, Indian and Coloured struggles. Though certain individuals raised the question of a united front of all the oppressed groups, the various non-European organisations stood miles apart from one another and the efforts of those for co-ordination and unity were like a voice crying in the wilderness and it seemed that the day would never dawn when the oppressed people would stand and fight together shoulder to shoulder against a common enemy. Today we talk of the struggle of the oppressed people which, though it is waged through their respective autonomous organisations, is gravitating towards one central command.

Our immediate task is to consolidate these victories, to preserve our organisations and to muster our forces for the resumption of the offensive. To achieve this important task the National Executive of the A.N.C. in consultation with the National Action Committee of the A.N.C. and the S.A.I.C. formulated a plan of action popularly known as the "M" Plan and the highest importance is [given] to it by the National Executives. Instructions were given to all provinces to implement the "M" Plan without delay.

The underlying principle of this plan is the understanding that it is no longer possible to wage our struggle mainly on the old methods of public meetings and printed circulars. The aim is:

(1) to consolidate the Congress machinery;

(2) to enable the transmission of important decisions taken on a national level to every member of the organisation without calling public meetings, issuing press statements and printing circulars;

(3) to build up in the local branches themselves local Congresses which will effectively represent the strength and will of the people;

(4) to extend and strengthen the ties between Congress and the people and to consolidate Congress leadership.

This plan is being implemented in many branches not only in the Transvaal but also in the other provinces and is producing excellent results. The Regional Conferences held in Sophiatown, Germiston, Kliptown and Benoni on the 28th June, 23rd and 30th August and on the 6th September, 1953, which were attended by large crowds, are a striking demonstration of the effectiveness of this plan, and the National Executives must be complimented for it. I appeal to all members of the Congress to redouble their efforts and play their part truly and well in its implementation. The hard, dirty and strenuous task of recruiting members and strengthening our organisation through a house to house campaign in every locality must be done by you all. From now on the activity of Congressites must not be confined to speeches and resolutions. Their activities must find expression in wide scale work among the masses, work which will enable them to make the greatest possible contact with the working people. You must protect and defend your trade unions. If you are not allowed to have your meetings publicly, then you must hold them over your machines in the factories, on the trains and buses as you travel home. You must have them in your villages and shantytowns. You must make every home, every shack and every mud structure where our people live, a branch of the trade union movement and *never surrender*.

You must defend the right of African parents to decide the kind of education that shall be given to their children. Teach the children that Africans are not one iota inferior to Europeans. Establish your own community schools where the right kind of education will be given to our children. If it becomes dangerous or impossible to have these alternative schools, then again you must make every home, every shack or rickety structure a centre of learning for our children. Never surrender to the inhuman and barbaric theories of Verwoerd.

The decision to defy the unjust laws enabled Congress to develop considerably wider contacts between itself and the masses and the urge to join Congress grew day by day. But due to the fact that the local branches did not exercise proper control and supervision, the admission of new members was not carried out satisfactorily. No careful examination was made of their past history and political characteristics. As a result of this, there were many shady characters ranging from political clowns, place-seekers, splitters, saboteurs, agents-provocateurs to informers and even policemen, who infiltrated into the ranks of Congress. One need only refer to the Johannesburg trial of Dr. Moroka and nineteen others, where a member of Congress who actually worked at the National Headquarters, turned out to be a detective-sergeant on special duty. Remember the case of Leballo of Brakpan who wormed himself into that Branch by producing faked naming letters from the Liquidator, De Villiers Louw, who had instructions to spy on us. There are many other similar instances that emerged during the Johannesburg, Port Elizabeth and Kimberley trials. Whilst some of these men were discovered there are many who have not been found out. In Congress there are still many shady characters, political clowns, place-seekers, saboteurs, provocateurs, informers and policemen who masquerade as Progressives but who are in fact the bitterest enemies of our organisation. Outside appearances are highly deceptive and we cannot classify these men by looking at their faces or by listening to their sweet tongues or their vehement speeches demanding immediate action. The friends of the people are distinguishable by the ready and disciplined manner in which they rally behind their organisation and their readiness to sacrifice when the preservation of the organisation has become a matter of life and death. Similarly, enemies and shady characters are detected by the extent to which they consistently attempt to wreck the organisation by creating fratricidal strife, disseminating confusion and undermining and even opposing important plans of action to vitalise the organisation. In this respect it is interesting to note that almost all the people who oppose the "M" Plan are people who have consistently refused to respond when sacrifices were called for, and whose political background leaves much to be desired. These shady characters by means of flattery, bribes and corruption, win the support of the weak-willed and politically backward individuals, detach them from Congress and use them in their own interests. The presence of such elements in Congress constitutes a serious threat to the struggle, for the capacity for political action of an organisation which is ravaged by such disruptive and splitting elements is considerably undermined. Here in South Africa, as in many parts of the world, a revolution is maturing: it is the profound desire, the determination and the urge of the overwhelming majority of the country to destroy for ever the shackles of oppression that condemn them to servitude and slavery. To overthrow oppression has been sanctioned by humanity and is the highest aspiration of every free man. If elements in our organisation seek to impede the realisation of this lofty purpose then these people have placed themselves outside the organisation and must be put out of action before they do more harm. To do otherwise would be a crime and a serious neglect of duty. We must rid ourselves of such elements and give our organisation the striking power of a real militant mass organisation.

Kotane, Marks, Bopape, Tloome and I have been banned from attending gatherings and we cannot join and counsel with you on the serious problems that are facing our country. We have been banned because we champion the freedom of the oppressed people of our country and because we have consistently fought against the policy of racial discrimination in favour of a policy which accords fundamental human rights to all, irrespective of race, colour, sex or language. We are exiled from our own people for we have uncompromisingly resisted the efforts of imperialist America and her satellites to drag the world into the rule of violence and brutal force, into the rule of the napalm, hydrogen and the cobalt bombs where millions of people will be wiped out to satisfy the criminal and greedy appetites of the imperial powers. We have been gagged because we have emphatically and openly condemned the criminal attacks by the imperialists against the people of Malaya, Vietnam, Indonesia, Tunisia and Tanganyika and called upon our people to identify themselves unreservedly with the cause of world peace and to fight against the war policies of America and her satellites. We are being shadowed, hounded and trailed because we fearlessly voiced our horror and indignation at the slaughter of the people of Korea and Kenya. The massacre of the Kenya people by Britain has aroused world-wide indignation and protest. Children are being burnt alive, women are raped, tortured, whipped and boiling water poured on their breasts to force confessions from them that Jomo Kenyatta had administered the Mau Mau oath to them. Men are being castrated and shot dead. In the Kikuyu country there are some villages in which the population has been completely wiped out. We are prisoners in our own country because we dared to raise our voices against these horrible atrocities and because we expressed our solidarity with the cause of the Kenya people.

You can see that "there is no easy walk to freedom anywhere, and many of us will have to pass through the valley of the shadow (of death) again and again before we reach the mountain tops of our desires.

Dangers and difficulties have not deterred us in the past, they will not frighten us now. But we must be prepared for them like men in business who do not waste energy in vain talk and idle action. The way of preparation (for action) lies in our rooting out all impurity and indiscipline from our organisation and making it the bright and shining instrument that will cleave its way to (Africa's) freedom." [The sentences Mandela quoted are from the speeches of Jawaharlal Nehru.]

30 • Jomo Kenyatta in court (1953)

The British sought to decolonize Africa on their own terms. They were not prepared to be forced out. The situation became even more complicated when there was a significant white settler population, as in South Africa, Southern Rhodesia, and Kenya, because those settlers saw themselves as the natural inheritors of imperial dominion, not the Africans who provided their labor force. In Kenya in the early 1950s some of the African opponents of the colonial regime, primarily people suffering from severe loss of land due to the encroachment of white settlers, went into the forest on the side of Mount Kenya and formed what became known among Europeans as the Mau Mau movement (and among Africans as the Land and Freedom Army). Mau Mau is arguably the most highly contended political movement in the history of modern Africa. So hotly disputed are its meaning and heritage among Kenyans and historians that there has never been a single monument erected in commemoration of the movement in Kenya. So although its intimate connection to the history of anticolonial liberation and, consequently, nationalism in Kenya is evident, just how that relationship should be interpreted remains unresolved, especially at the level of national politics.

Whatever else we do know about Mau Mau, it is certain that Jomo Kenyatta (c. 1894–1978), who, like Azikiwe and other African leaders of his generation, had spent an extended time overseas before returning to lead an independence movement in his country, was not its leader or even directly involved in the movement. However, as the leader of the Kenya African Union (KAU), deemed "radical" by the British, he represented all that was dangerous and feared in Africans by the closed community of white settlers in Kenya. Moreover, with Nkrumah he had participated in the organizing the Fifth Pan-African Congress held at Manchester, England, an occasion when Africans from throughout the continent joined together to denounce colonialism and call for immediate independence. In the early 1950s, when Nkrumah had just been released from an extended period of imprisonment for demanding self-rule for Ghana and Nelson Mandela and other leaders of the ANC were being criminally prosecuted for creating race hostility because they protested against apartheid, Kenyatta was brought to trial as the head of Mau Mau and charged with every heinous crime that the settlers' imagination and the colonial authorities could conjure up. Despite (or perhaps because of) the eloquent statement that he made at his trial, Kenyatta was convicted and sentenced to seven years of hard labor and exile in a remote part of the barren north of Kenya. At least Kenyatta's life was spared. British repression of Mau Mau was as severe as any taken by a colonizer on a colonized people, with tens of thousands of Africans forced off their land and into guarded encampments and more than a thousand hanged, the largest judicially organized process of mass execution in Africa's colonial history. Though the Land and Freedom Army was defeated militarily by the mid-1950s, Kenyan opposition to colonial rule could not be repressed. Faced by the mounting costs of staying in control, the British government decided that imperial interests would best be served by granting Kenya independence with the understanding that British economic interests would be protected. In one of the jolting compromises of the end of colonialism, British politicians had to accept their old nemesis, Kenyatta, as the first prime minister of independent Kenya in 1963. However, before these events unfolded, Kenyatta testified on January 26, 1953, at his trial on charges of organizing Mau Mau in the Kapenguria district.[2]

2. Jomo Kenyatta, *Suffering without Bitterness* (Nairobi: East African Publishing House, 1968), 24–28.

FIGURE 12 Jomo Kenyatta in 1953, the year he was imprisoned for alleged involvement in the Mau Mau movement against British colonialism. Kenyatta had earlier studied in England and upon his return to Kenya worked for the country's independence, helping to organize the Kenya Africa Union. He was held in prison from 1953 to 1959 and after his release continued to work for Kenya's independence, becoming its first president in 1964. AP Photo.

The East African Association in 1921, with which I sympathised, opposed such things as forced labour of both African men and women, and the Registration Certificate introduced soon after the war. It was also concerned about land, and that people should have better wages, education, hospitals and roads. The Association worked by constitutional means, making representations to the Government in the most peaceful way we possibly could.

The Kikuyu Central Association, from about 1925 onwards, pursued the same aims and objects, but by 1928 more grievances were added. Most of us had become aware of the Crown Lands Ordinance of 1915, which said something like: "all land previously occupied by native people becomes the property of the Crown, and the Africans or natives living thereon become tenants at the will of the Crown." When we realised this, we started a demand for its abolition, on the grounds that it was unfair for our people, because we were not informed of its enactment and had no say in its provisions.

We were also protesting against the country's status being changed to that of a Colony, instead of a Protectorate. We knew the Africans would have less legal claim to their territory in a Colony than in a Protectorate, since the latter would be guided by the British Government until we could be left to our own affairs. We were told that everybody would have rights in a Colony, but Africans would have the least rights.

If you woke up one morning and found that somebody had come to your house, and had declared that house belonged to him, you would naturally be surprised, and you would like to know by what arrangement. Many Africans at that time found that, on land which had been in the possession of their ancestors from time immemorial, they were now working as squatters or as labourers.

I became a member of the Kikuyu Central Association in 1928, after the visit of the Hilton Young Commission which came to investigate land problems in Kenya. My people approached me saying they would like me to represent them, so I left Government service and joined the KCA. I immediately started a paper—the first newspaper in this part of the world published by Africans—called "Muigwithania" [He who brings together].

The KCA sought the redress of grievances through constitutional means: by making representations to the Government of Kenya, to various Commissions, and to the home Government, in England.

In 1929, I was asked if I could go to England to represent my people. By then our demands had increased, to include direct representation of the African people in Legislative Council. We were told when we approached the Government: "Well, you know, we have no objection to you coming to Legislative Council or any other place of Government, providing you have education." We badly wanted to educate our children, so another reason why I went to Europe was to seek ways and means of establishing our schools.

When I arrived in London, I prepared my case, sent a memorandum to the Secretary of State—then Lord Passfield—and made contact with Members of Parliament. There were many negotiations. A White Paper was then published saying, in essence, that the Government has decided no more African land would be taken away from them, and what was left to them would remain their land for ever. I think this reaffirmed as well another declaration— by the Duke of Devonshire in 1923—to the effect that: "Kenya is an African territory and the African interest must be paramount, and whenever the interests of the African people and those of the immigrant races conflict, the African interests will always prevail."

I think this 1930 White Paper was known as: "Native Policy in East Africa." But I have been placed at a great disadvantage because I cannot get my papers to present my case, so I have to rely on what I can remember. All my documents and files were taken away . . . (*Note: Mzee Kenyatta's personal files and documents were never returned to him by the Administration or the Police. An exhaustive search since Independence has proved fruitless, and the assumption can only be that they were destroyed.*)

While in Europe, I had published the correspondence as between the KCA and the Secretary of State. I also had the opportunity of going to meet the Archbishop of Canterbury, and went to Edinburgh for an interview with the Moderator of the Church of Scotland.

Speaking to a Committee of the House of Commons, I said we could take some of the good European and Indian customs, and those of our customs which were good, and see how we could build a new kind of society in Kenya.

Whereas formerly it had been illegal for us to establish a school, we were now given permission by the Government to do so, if we could find land to build on, find the money to build, and find money to pay teachers. From about 1930, the Kikuyu Independent Schools Association and the Karinga ISA came into being. When I came back, I found they had over 300 schools educating more than 60,000 children, with no financial help at all from the Government.

I went to Europe again in 1931 and stayed till 1946, when I found the KCA had been proscribed. I saw the Governor . . . (Note: the late Sir Philip Mitchell) . . . twice on this question, and had interviews with the Chief Native Commissioner several times to investigate the position. The Governor told me the matter would be reconsidered. He said he himself could see no reason why the Association should not start functioning, but he left the matter to his officials and to the Member of Legislative Council representing African interests. The Chief Native Commissioner said some people had behaved rashly and got themselves into trouble, so the matter was dropped.

Our files show that the KCA was a constitutional organization, but the Police are keeping them.

Early in 1947, when I was very busy in the activities of schools, I came to know about and joined the Kenya African Union. At the annual meeting in June, I was elected as President. The aims of KAU were to unite the African people of Kenya; to prepare the way for introduction of democracy in Kenya; to defend and promote the interests of the African people by organizing and educating them in the struggle for better working and social conditions; to fight for equal rights for all Africans and break down racial barriers; to strive for extension to all African adults of the right to vote and to be elected to parliamentary and other representative bodies; to publish a political newspaper; to fight for freedom of assembly, press and movement.

To fight for equal rights does not mean fighting with fists or with a weapon, but to fight through negotiations and by constitutional means. We do not believe in violence at all, but in discussion and representation.

We feel that the racial barrier is one of the most diabolical things that we have in the Colony, and we see no reason at all why all races in this country cannot work harmoniously together without any discrimination. If people of goodwill can come together, they can eliminate this evil. God put everybody into this world to live happily, and to enjoy the gifts of Nature that God bestowed upon mankind. During my stay in Europe—and especially in England —I lived very happily, and made thousands of good friends. I do not see why people in this country cannot do the same thing. To my mind, colour is irrelevant.

Some time ago, I invited about 40 Europeans to meet me, and spent a whole day with them at our school at Githunguri. One of them said they expected to be chased away; then he apologised for the hatred that he had felt for us, and for believing that we hated the Europeans. That was a common attitude of many settlers who had never met me. I told him I was just an ordinary man, striving to fight for the rights of my people, and to better their conditions, without hating anybody.

31 • Mau Mau's daughter (1954)

Mau Mau involved virtually the entire Gikuyu people, whether as forest fighters, colonial soldiers, loyalist chiefs, urban dwellers who carried messages and materials from Nairobi into the reserves and forests, or rural villagers. Although men were at the center of the armed struggle, women and children played a critical role as messengers and carriers of provisions to the men hidden away in the forests. Some of these women and children, like Wambui Otieno (whose extract follows), were progressively drawn into the conflict through their experience of the abuse and exploitation to

which people were subjected in the reserves and participated in the oath taking that bound them
and their brothers together in the armed struggle.[3]

As a sixteen-year-old schoolgirl, I did not know much about being a freedom fighter, although
I read such newspapers as the *East African Standard* and *Daily Chronicle* and knew about
Jomo Kenyatta's pronouncements. I had read his book *Facing Mount Kenya* [published in
1938] and Kenyatta himself was a frequent visitor to our home. He and the late Mbiyu
Koinange would come and lie on the grass outside our house and have discussions with my
father for hours on end. But, as children, we did not know what they were discussing. By the
time the State of Emergency was declared, I had already taken my first Mau Mau oath, albeit
unknowingly. This happened during one of the school holidays in 1952. I had assumed the
oath to be associated with the Girl Guide movement, of which I was a member. A cousin
named Timothy Chege took me and another woman to a place called Gaitumbi. She worked
on our farm and was related to my mother. Both were aware of my intense resentment of the
brutal treatment my great-grandfather Waiyaki wa Hinga had suffered at the hands of the
colonialists [according to Gikuyu memories, Hinga was buried alive by the British in 1892;
the British claimed to the contrary that he had committed suicide], for I had openly said that
I was prepared to avenge him.

   I was told very little when we arrived at Gaitumbi. I was asked whether I was menstruating. (I later learned that a menstruating woman was disqualified from taking the oath at that
time, as menstruation was regarded as dirty and a cause of misfortune.) I answered "No," and
in turn received a hard slap, the purpose of which was not clear to me. I was then ordered to
shed all my clothes except my bra and knickers. I was led into a poorly lit room where a group
of people were casually sitting. On one side were two sugarcane poles standing erect with
their tips tied to form an arch. The poles were tall enough for a person to walk underneath.
Each initiate was told to walk through the arch seven times. Then I was tied to the other initi-
ates with a long goatskin, which I later learned was called "Rukwaro." In a single line, we again
walked through the two poles seven times. After that an old man brought a calabash and told
each of us to drink a mouthful of a concoction of blood and soil. I nearly threw up because it
smelled like goat's intestines. However, I remembered the words of my mother's relative—
freedom would not come easily. Kenyatta's similar sentiments had appeared in the newspapers on many occasions. I therefore forced myself to swallow everything. Then I took the
oath of allegiance. Repeating carefully after an instructor, I swore to:

1. Fight for the soil of Gikuyu and Mumbi's children, which had been stolen from them
   by the whites.
2. If possible, get a gun from a white or a black collaborator and any other valuables or
   money to help strengthen the movement.
3. Kill anyone who was against the movement, even if that person was my brother.

3. Wambui Otieno, *Mau Mau's Daughter: A Life History,* ed. and with an introduction by Cora Ann Presley
   (Boulder: Lynne Rienner, 1998), 32–37.

4. Never reveal what had just happened or any other information disclosed to me as a member of the movement, but always to do my utmost to strengthen the movement; and if I didn't keep my words, may the oath kill me.

This ceremony took place a few months before the Emergency was declared.

The State of Emergency kept me from studying abroad. I left school [in] 1953 and was supposed to join my elder sister and brothers who were studying in England, but because of the state of affairs in the country I couldn't leave. Finding myself with more time on my hands, I became even more eager to learn about freedom activities and followed the more closely. I continued helping with the farm and house chores and became friendly with a woman farm-worker to whom I often related matters concerning freedom-fighting activities. I told her of my indignation that Waiyaki had been brutally murdered by the whites and that Kinyanjui wa Gathirimu, the black collaborator, had been rewarded for his betrayal of our people with the office of paramount chief. She would talk to me about politics and I realized she knew more about Mau Mau than I did. Finally she trusted me enough to reveal her knowledge of the movement. She said that by joining it, I would assist in getting rid of colonialists and their black collaborators. I had not revealed to her that I had already taken the oath. I felt that I still did not really belong to the movement, despite having taken the oath. However, now that I was no longer in school, I wanted to participate more in its activities. So we made a plan. One night when everyone else was asleep, I sneaked out through the window. She and other members of Mau Mau were waiting for me. Together, we went again to Gaitumbi, to the home-stead of a man called Mumira, where I took my second oath, which was similar to the one I had taken two years earlier.

Shortly after this oath-taking, there occurred an incident that left me with a terrible feeling of guilt. One night at home we heard gunshots outside. My mother began to open a window to peep out. I already knew that an attack on the Kinoo Home Guard post was under way and had marked our gate with a special sign so the Mau Mau would know that our home helped the movement. Although I knew we would be left alone, I feared that a stray bullet might hit my mother, so I went after her, closing the windows. I was wrestling with her as she opened one window after another. She was puzzled by my strange behavior, but I did not explain because I was under oath. My real worry was that she might get hurt. Later I learned that was exactly what had happened to my uncle, Muchugia Wambaa, whose ear was injured. I protested to the Mau Mau War Council because, with the help of my cousin Chege, I had marked all my close relatives' homes as "safe." I could do this honestly because my relatives had not collaborated with the colonists.

After the attack on the Kinoo Home Guard post, I took my second oath at Kinoo in the bush near a river (I considered the first two oaths to be one oath). I took the third oath at Waithaka, at the home of Wairimu wa Wagaca, who was called "Nyina wa Andu" (mother of the people), a very determined freedom fighter. The other oaths I took varied according to reasons for taking them or actions one was supposed to complete after taking them. Some were meant to strengthen previous ones, while others like Kindu or Mbatuni (battalion or platoon) were very serious and were administered only to the real fighters and scouts. I took Mbatuni voluntarily and felt more commitment to Mau Mau thereafter, convinced it was the only way Kenya could be free. The oath made believers keep secrets. Above all, it brought unity to Mau Mau's members. Through certain signs and modes of greeting, we were able to identify one another. We also had a code of regulations that we adhered to. I took nine oaths altogether during my time as a Mau Mau.

From 1952 to 1954, the government was on the defensive against Mau Mau. On April 23, 1954, two years after the State of Emergency had been declared, government forces began Operation Anvil. The following day my father was arrested and detained at Langata Camp. He was later moved to the camp at Mackinnon Road and finally detained at Camp No. 6 in Manyani. From there he wrote us a letter that read; "I am in Manyani Camp. I am keeping well. I have sent this letter with an officer who will collect my clothes. Yours, T.W. Munyua."

Matters worsened as the State of Emergency continued. People were arrested arbitrarily by the panicked colonial administration. All it took was a little suspicion for one to be branded a Mau Mau. This also encouraged black collaborators to accuse people of being Mau Mau with little or no proof. I personally knew many people who got into trouble yet who had nothing whatsoever to do with our movement. It became increasingly difficult not to take sides. Despite all this, I felt as determined as ever. In my mind I had no doubt that I was fighting for a just cause, and I owe my gratitude to the late Muiruri Waiyaki, my cousin, who helped me survive those early trying days. He inspired me and boosted my morale during the lengthy hours I spent with him. I felt a great sense of loss when he was captured at Kahawa and hanged by court order. May God rest his soul in peace.

My fighting spirit was aroused to a frenzy one day when my mother was almost hit on the head by a European called Peter. The incident took place when I was in our homestead garden near Kiharu River. As I came up the path, I immediately sensed something had happened. My mother's unsteady gait and the way she carried herself brought tears to my eyes. I suggested that we lodge a complaint with the district officer at Kikuyu, but she was hesitant. She said we must exercise caution. "Times are bad," she said. However, I was not going to let the matter end there. If she was not prepared to do something about it, then I was. My mother suggested she go to Thogoto Mission to inform Reverend MacPherson. I had no time for that suggestion. To me, they were all colonialists, and indeed they were. Without informing her, I hurriedly dressed, took fifty cents for bus fare from her drawer, and left.

When I arrived at the district officer's office, I encountered a disgusting sight. The body of a Mukurinu preacher who had been killed near Muguga had been brought and put on public display. The Europeans had removed his turban to reveal his dreadlocks, and to the ignorant public was a convincing Mau Mau terrorist. There was a queue of people waiting for travel passes. I jumped to the head of the queue and stormed into the D.O.'s [district officer's] office. Mr. Martin, the assistant DO, was not amused by the intrusion.

But I was in no mood for compromise. He shouted at me and I shouted back. I intended to make as much of a scene as possible. My anger at my mother's treatment was so great that I did not care if they killed me for confronting them. The Home Guards cocked their rifles menacingly at me, and I dared them to shoot me. I was too angry to care. But their commander, Kiarie wa Wambari, did not give the order to fire. The senior DO, Mr. Kemble, ordered that I be taken to his office, and he asked me to compose myself so that we could discuss the matter rationally. I left his office only after he had agreed to have Peter removed from the Kinoo

Home Guard post. Luckily, as I walked out I met Senior Chief Josiah Njonjo Mugane and a police officer, Eli John, who assisted in seeing that Peter was removed from that area. Peter was a lunatic who, when he could not find an excuse to shoot at Africans, would ask for sheep or goats to be brought to him so he could mow them down with his gun, after which he would calm down.

Meanwhile, investigations were going on concerning my father, who was still in detention. Special policemen from the Criminal Investigation Division (CID) visited our home many times at night in a futile search for evidence to prove his role in Mau Mau. Finally they had to release him. I owe my gratitude to Peter Okola, who saved my life during those searches, as I could not resist battling with the colonial police. Okola, who had worked with my father on the police force, became the director of intelligence after independence. During my father's absence from home, our family suffered many hardships. For lack of money, my brothers in England had to discontinue their education. My mother took risky train trips to Nairobi to collect rent from our house, No. 490 in Pumwani. She traveled without a pass and would have gotten into much trouble had she been discovered. We also felled black wattle trees and sold the wood and bark to Muguga Ginnery to supplement our income. Through all these hardships, I was active in the movement, surprisingly quite unknown to my mother. She was so innocent in her pursuit of Christianity that she became almost oblivious to what was happening around her. Still, to be on the safe side, I adopted my nickname "Wagio" (which I later changed to "Msaja"), so that my real name would not filter back and connect me with Mau Mau activities.

32 ◆ The Freedom Charter (1955)

Unlike Anton Lembede, Nelson Mandela did not embrace the Africanist philosophy. He believed that South Africa belonged to all who lived within its boundaries and that it should be a multiracial state in which all of the residents would receive equal access to the political process and equal treatment before the law. The fullest expression of this point of view was developed at the Congress of the People held in 1955, a mass meeting of representatives of all South Africans opposed to apartheid. On June 26, 1955, those gathered adopted a "freedom charter" for all South Africans (reproduced here in its entirety). The National Party government responded to this show of unity with police raids on the congress and interrogations of all of the participants. Eighteenth months later, in December 1956, the government ordered the arrest of more than 150 people, most of them participants at the meeting of the congress, and put them on trial for high treason (a death penalty charge). The core of the government's case was that the congress members, by calling for racial equality, demonstrated "hostile intent," which was, under South African law, a treasonable offense. After a very lengthy trial that prevented most of those accused from engaging in political action for almost half a decade, the courts in 1960 found the defendants not guilty on the grounds that the prosecution had failed, despite its promises to the contrary, to prove that the ANC had ever adopted a policy of violence.[4]

4. Http://www.anc.org.za/ancdocs/history/charter.html.

PREAMBLE

We, the people of South Africa, declare for all our country and the world to know:

That South Africa belongs to all who live in it, black and white, and that no government can justly claim authority unless it is based on the will of the people;

That our people have been robbed of their birthright to land, liberty and peace by a form of government founded on injustice and inequality;

That our country will never be prosperous or free until all our people live in brotherhood, enjoying equal rights and opportunities;

That only a democratic state, based on the will of the people, can secure to all their birthright without distinction of colour, race, sex or belief;

And therefore, we the people of South Africa, black and white, together—equals, countrymen and brothers—adopt this FREEDOM CHARTER. And we pledge ourselves to strive together, sparing nothing of our strength and courage, until the democratic changes here set out have been won.

THE PEOPLE SHALL GOVERN!

Every man and woman shall have the right to vote for and stand as a candidate for all bodies which make laws;

All the people shall be entitled to take part in the administration of the country;

The rights of the people shall be the same regardless of race, colour or sex;

All bodies of minority rule, advisory boards, councils and authorities shall be replaced by democratic organs of self-government.

ALL NATIONAL GROUPS SHALL HAVE EQUAL RIGHTS!

There shall be equal status in the bodies of the state, in the courts and in the schools for all national groups and races;

All national groups shall be protected by law against insults to their race and national pride;

All people shall have equal rights to use their own language and to develop their own folk culture and customs;

The preaching and practice of national, race or colour discrimination and contempt shall be a punishable crime;

All apartheid laws and practices shall be set aside.

THE PEOPLE SHALL SHARE IN THE COUNTRY'S WEALTH!

The national wealth of our country, the heritage of all South Africans, shall be restored to the people;

The mineral wealth beneath the soil, the banks and monopoly industry shall be transferred to the ownership of the people as a whole;

All other industries and trades shall be controlled to assist the well-being of the people;

All people shall have equal rights to trade where they choose, to manufacture and to enter all trades, crafts and professions.

THE LAND SHALL BE SHARED AMONG THOSE WHO WORK IT!

Restriction of land ownership on a racial basis shall be ended, and all the land re-divided amongst those who work it, to banish famine and land hunger;

The state shall help the peasants with implements, seed, tractors and dams to save the soil and assist the tillers;

Freedom of movement shall be guaranteed to all who work on the land;

All shall have the right to occupy land wherever they choose;

People shall not be robbed of their cattle, and forced labour and farm prisons shall be abolished.

ALL SHALL BE EQUAL BEFORE THE LAW!

No one shall be imprisoned, deported or restricted without fair trial;

No one shall be condemned by the order of any Government official;

The courts shall be representative of all the people;

Imprisonment shall be only for serious crimes against the people, and shall aim at re-education, not vengeance;

The police force and army shall be open to all on an equal basis and shall be the helpers and protectors of the people;

All laws which discriminate on the grounds of race, colour or belief shall be repealed.

ALL SHALL ENJOY HUMAN RIGHTS!

The law shall guarantee to all their right to speak, to organise, to meet together, to publish, to preach, to worship and to educate their children;

The privacy of the house from police raids shall be protected by law;

All shall be free to travel without restriction from countryside to town, from province to province, and from South Africa abroad;

Pass laws, permits and all other laws restricting these freedoms shall be abolished.

THERE SHALL BE WORK AND SECURITY!

All who work shall be free to form trade unions, to elect their officers and to make wage agreements with their employers;

The state shall recognise the right and duty of all to work, and to draw full, unemployment benefits;

Men and women of all races shall receive equal pay for equal work;

There shall be a forty-hour working week, a national minimum wage, paid annual leave, and sick leave for all workers, and maternity leave on full pay for all working mothers;

Miners, domestic workers, farm workers and civil servants shall have the same rights as all others who work;

Child labour, compound labour, the tot system and contract labour shall be abolished.

THE DOORS OF LEARNING AND OF CULTURE SHALL BE OPENED!

The government shall discover, develop and encourage national talent for the enhancement of our cultural life;

All the cultural treasures of mankind shall be open to all, by free exchange of books, ideas and contact with other lands;

The aim of education shall be to teach the youth to love their people and their culture, to honour human brotherhood, liberty and peace;

Education shall be free, compulsory, universal and equal for all children;

Higher education and technical training shall be opened to all by means of state allowances and scholarships awarded on the basis of merit;

Adult illiteracy shall be ended by a mass state education plan;

Teachers shall have all the rights of other citizens;

The colour bar in cultural life, in sport and in education shall be abolished.

THERE SHALL BE HOUSES, SECURITY AND COMFORT!

All people shall have the right to live where they choose, to be decently housed, and to bring up their families in comfort and security;

Unused housing space to be made available to the people;

Rent and prices shall be lowered, food plentiful and no one shall go hungry;

A preventive health scheme shall be run by the state;

Free medical care and hospitalisation shall be provided for all, with special care for mothers and young children;

Slums shall be demolished and new suburbs built where all shall have transport, roads, lighting, playing fields, crèches and social centres;

The aged, the orphans, the disabled and the sick shall be cared for by the state;

Rest, leisure and recreation shall be the right of all;

Fenced locations and ghettos shall be abolished, and laws which break up families shall be repealed.

THERE SHALL BE PEACE AND FRIENDSHIP!

South Africa shall be a fully independent state, which respects the rights and sovereignty of all nations;

South Africa shall strive to maintain world peace and the settlement of all international disputes by negotiation—not war;

Peace and friendship amongst all our people shall be secured by upholding the equal rights, opportunities and status of all;

The people of the protectorates—Basutoland, Bechuanaland and Swaziland—shall be free to decide for themselves their own future;

The right of all the peoples of Africa to independence and self-government shall be recognised, and shall be the basis of close cooperation.

Let all who love their people and their country now say, as we say here: "THESE FREE-DOMS WE WILL FIGHT FOR, SIDE BY SIDE, THROUGHOUT OUR LIVES, UNTIL WE HAVE WON OUR LIBERTY."

33 • A balance sheet of empire (1957)

Eighteen days after being elected prime minister of Great Britain, Harold Macmillan asked his colonial officials to provide him with an estimate of the "probable course of constitutional develop-ment in the Colonies over the years ahead," together with a "profit and loss account" for each colony. Three years later Macmillan became famous in Africa—and infamous in South Africa—for mak-ing a speech, first given in Accra in January 1960, then in Pretoria in February, in which he stated that "The wind of change is blowing through this continent. Whether we like it or not, this growth of national consciousness is a political fact."[5]

5. "Future constitutional development in the colonies," minute by Mr. Macmillan (prime minister) to Lord Salisbury (chairman of the Cabinet Colonial Policy Committee), Jan. 28, 1957, CAB 134/1555, CPC(57)6,

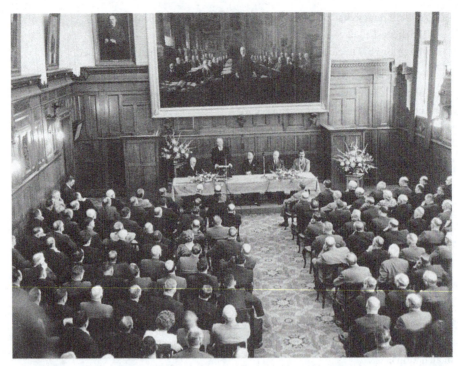

FIGURE 13 Harold Macmillan, prime minister of Great Britain, addresses a joint meeting of 250 members of the all-white South African parliament during his "Wind of Change" speech in Cape Town on February 3, 1960. He told the South African MPs, "As a fellow member of the Commonwealth it is our earnest desire to give South Africa our support and encouragement, but I hope you won't mind my saying frankly that there are some aspects of your policies which make it impossible for us to do this without being false to our own deep convictions about the political destinies of free men to which in our own territories we are trying to give effect." During Macmillan's administration, Britain granted independence to its major colonies, Ghana (1957), Nigeria (1960), and Kenya (1963). AP Photo.

Harold Macmillan, minute to Lord Salisbury (chairman of the Cabinet Colonial Policy Committee), January 28, 1957

It would be helpful if the Colonial Policy Committee could submit to the Cabinet their estimate of the probable course of constitutional development in the Colonies over the years ahead.

It would be good if Ministers could know more clearly which territories are likely to become ripe for independence over the next few years—or, even if they are not really ready for it, will demand it so insistently that their claims cannot be denied—and at what date that stage is likely to be reached in each case.

---

in Ronald Hyam and Wm. Roger Louis, eds., *The Conservative Government and the End of Empire 1957–1964* (London: Stationery Office, 2000), *Part 1: High Policy, Political and Constitutional Change*, 1–3.

It would also be helpful if this study would distinguish those Colonies which would qualify for full membership of the Commonwealth, and would indicate what constitutional future there is for the others which may attain independence but cannot aspire to full Commonwealth membership.

I should also like to see something like a profit and loss account for each of our Colonial possessions, so that we may be better able to gauge whether, from the financial and economic point of view, we are likely to gain or lose by its departure. This would need, of course, to be weighed against the political and strategic considerations involved in each case. And it might perhaps be better to attempt an estimate of the balance of advantage, taking all these considerations into account, of losing or keeping each particular territory.

There are presumably places where it is of vital interest to us that we should maintain our influence, and others where there is no United Kingdom interest in resisting constitutional change even if it seems likely to lead eventually to secession from the Commonwealth.

If your Committee will produce a report on these lines, the Cabinet might well devote the whole of a session to it without other business.

Skeleton Plan (to be followed in the consideration of each territory or area)

1. *Political and constitutional*
   (a) Outline of the present constitutional system;
   (b) Brief description of the internal and external political pressures;
   (c) The way in which these pressures will be reflected in demands for constitutional changes.
2. *Strategic*
   (a) An estimate of the strategic importance of a territory;
   (b) A statement of Her Majesty's Government's strategic requirements;
   (c) An estimate of the extent to which retention of these strategic requirements is dependent upon Her Majesty's Government's retaining jurisdiction.
3. *Economic*
   (a) The effect of independence upon the interests of the United Kingdom in terms of:
      (i) direct effect on the Exchequer;
      (ii) the effect on the sterling area;
      (iii) trade between the territory concerned and the United Kingdom.
4. *Obligations and repercussions*
   (a) An estimate of the effect upon the political, economic and social development of the territory of the withdrawal of United Kingdom jurisdiction, including the effect upon racial and tribal minorities;
   (b) The effect of the change of status in the territory upon the prestige and influence of the United Kingdom;
   (c) Whether the premature withdrawal of United Kingdom jurisdiction would leave a vacuum which would be filled by a country hostile to the United Kingdom and her Allies.
5. *Conclusions*

34 • **Freedom! Freedom! Freedom!** (1957)

On March 6, 1957, Ghana became the first colony in Africa to win its independence. The leader of the successful movement to end colonial rule was Kwame Nkrumah, a very different type of person from the sort of collaborator that the British had hoped would lead an independent Ghana. Nkrumah, like Azikiwe, had studied in the United States and graduated from Lincoln University. He was a strong proponent of the pan-African ideas of W. E. B. Du Bois and of Marcus Garvey (who had led a back-to-Africa movement in the United States during the 1920s). Despite subjecting him to lengthy periods of detention, the British were not able to undermine Nkrumah's leadership of the Ghanaian independence movement.

The most symbolic moment for the end of colonial rule always came at midnight on the eve of independence, as the flag of the old imperial power was lowered and that of the new state raised. This extract is from the speech that Nkrumah gave on March 6, 1957, to the people gathered at the flag ceremony, among them thousands of Ghanaians, representatives of many foreign nations, and numerous dignitaries from Britain, including Queen Elizabeth. For Nkrumah, this occasion symbolized the end of empire.[6]

At long last the battle has ended! And thus Ghana, your beloved country, is free for ever. And here again, I want to take the opportunity to thank the chiefs and people of this country, the youth, the farmers, the women, who have so nobly fought and won this battle. Also I want to thank the valiant ex-servicemen who have so co-operated with me in this mighty task of freeing our country from foreign rule and imperialism! And as I pointed out at our Party conference at Saltpond, I made it quite clear that from now on, today, we must change our attitudes, our minds. We must realise that from now on we are no more a colonial but a free and independent people! But also, as I pointed out, that entails hard work. I am depending upon the millions of the country, the chiefs and people to help me to reshape the destiny of this country. We are prepared to make it a nation that will be respected by any nation in the world. We know we are going to have a difficult beginning but again I am relying upon your support, I am relying upon your hard work, seeing you here in your thousands, however far my eye goes. My last warning to you is that you ought to stand firm behind us so that we can prove to the world that when the African is given a chance he can show the world that he is somebody. We are not waiting; we shall no more go back to sleep. Today, from now on, there is a new African in the world and that new African is ready to fight his own battle and show that after all the black man is capable of managing his own affairs. We are going to demonstrate to the world, to the other nations, young as we are, that we are prepared to lay our own foundation.

As I said in the Assembly just a few minutes ago, I made a point that we are going to see that we create our own African personality and identity; it is the only way in which we can show the world that we are masters of our own destiny. But today may I call upon you all; at this great day let us all remember that nothing in the world can be done unless it has the support of God. We have done with the battle and we again re-dedicate ourselves in the struggle to emancipate other countries in Africa, for our independence is meaningless unless it is linked up with the total liberation of the African continent.

6. Kwame Nkrumah, *I Speak of Freedom: A Statement of African Ideology* (New York: Praeger, 1961), 106–8.

Let us now, fellow Ghanaians, let us now ask for God's blessing, and in your tens of thousands, I want to ask you to pause for one minute, and give thanks to Almighty God for having led us through obstacles, difficulties, imprisonments, hardships and sufferings to have brought us to the end of our trouble today. One minute silence—Ghana is free forever! And here I will ask the band to play the Ghana national anthem.

Here the Ghana national anthem was played.

I want simply to thank those who have come from abroad to witness this occasion. Here I wish I could quote Marcus Garvey. Once upon a time, he said, he looked through the whole world to see if he could find a government of a black people. He looked around, he did not find one, and he said he was going to create one. Marcus Garvey did not succeed. But here today the work of Rousseau, the work of Marcus Garvey, the work of Aggrey, the work of Casely Hayford, the work of these illustrious men who have gone before us has come to reality at this present moment. And so we thank all of you and I am going to ask the band to play again, because it must sink in and make us realise that from today, we are no more a colonial people. This time, the national anthem is going to be played in honour of the foreign states who are here with us today to witness this occasion and I want you all, those who have hats on, to take off your hats and let the band play our national anthem. And from now on that national anthem is the national anthem of Ghana to be played on all occasions.

The national anthem was played, and played again amid cries of *Freedom! Freedom! Freedom!*

35 • Verwoerd reaffirms South Africa's commitment to white supremacy (1958)

While Nkrumah celebrated African independence in Ghana, Hendrik Verwoerd reflected on history as he spoke at Blood River on December 16, 1958, about the need for white South Africans to defend their ideals in a world increasingly hostile to the continuance of legalized racial discrimination. Verwoerd chose as the occasion for his reflections the 120th anniversary of the battle of Blood River, when on December 16, 1838, an armed force of Voortrekkers had avenged the death of their leader, Piet Retief, by massacring thousands of Dingane's Zulu subjects. For Verwoerd and for many other whites in South Africa, Blood River symbolized the triumph of civilization over savagery and the power of Europeans fighting with the Christian God on their side. Indeed, commemoration of the battle had become for whites an increasingly popular event in the twentieth century by providing an opportunity for stirring speeches about the need to stand together to face the forces of darkness. For Verwoerd and his followers, the move to independence in the rest of Africa made the struggle to maintain white rule in South Africa more difficult and more important than ever.[7]

Dear friends, I want to speak of then and now.

If we review the spirit of the world at the time of the Voortrekkers, we find that it was a period of commotion in the minds of men. A spiritual current was then flowing over the world which created a new atmosphere spreading its influence even as far as here in the southern

7. A. N. Pelzer, ed., *Verwoerd Speaks: Speeches 1948–1966* (Johannesburg: APB Publishers, 1966), 206–11.

FIGURE 14 South African police beat women with clubs in Durban in 1959 when the women protested the imposition of a government monopoly on the brewing and sale of beer. African women were restricted from most legal employment and relied on the sale of homemade beer to eke out a living in the cities. AP Photo.

part of Africa. We all know how a spirit of emancipation arose among humanity during the French Revolution, a spirit of freedom and brotherhood and equality of all people. It originated from the circumstances of the Europe of that time and was then wrongly applied to the outside world which was different.

The application of the idea of freedom, equality and fraternity of all people gave rise to violent disputes and strife and revealed the prevailing misconception regarding the life of people in other countries under different circumstances. In Europe they wrote about the "noble savage" while the human being among them, the European in his civilisation of that time, went unregarded. In that spirit the white men who were engaged in civilising countries and saving the savage from himself and from the oppressor among his own ranks, were described as oppressors.

The same happened to our own nation and the Voortrekkers. Gross misrepresentations were prevalent in Europe regarding our people and the deeds performed here. From those countries' foreign missionaries, the Phillips and the Van der Kemps, animated by the spirit which had spread over Europe, came to an area which they did not know. They brought not only the Gospel, but also the disturbance of misunderstanding. They rendered a disservice not only to the white man who at that time was penetrating the interior with the Bible in the hand, but also to the heathens by inciting them against the white man with all his goodwill and his knowledge of conditions here. They complicated matters and much of the blood

FIGURE 15 The ground was littered with the bodies of the dead and wounded in Sharpeville, South Africa, following a massacre by the police on March 21, 1960. What had started as a peaceful protest in which Africans burned the passbooks that restricted them from going into certain areas soon became violent when the South African police opened fire on the black civilians. At least 69 people were killed and 178 wounded during the violence. AP Photo.

which was spilt, and the strife engendered were the result of well-intentioned but misplaced transmission of a spirit which, in the circumstances of that time, did not fit here.

That spirit was not directed against the Afrikaner forefathers only but against all white men. The English-speaking people also realised that the christianising [sic] [?]process was necessary for Africa and that the supremacy of the white man was necessary in order to bring and extend civilisation and Christianity here in South Africa.

In the midst of all this the conduct of the Voortrekkers was characterised by three definite mental attitudes. The one was symbolised by the readiness of Piet Retief even when his people had found an unclaimed area, nevertheless to acquire it by proper negotiations. Piet Retief was prepared to enter into an agreement with Dingaan. He was prepared to trust and co-operate. He placed the lives of his small group of companions at the mercy of the barbarian. The white man's trust, the white man's honest sincerity, the white man's preparedness to negotiate, the readiness to grant suitable rights, each in its kind and place, were all symbolised in that act of Piet Retief. From the events at Murder Hill we also see that the people gathered there were not prepared to have a part in the suicide of a nation. They were not prepared to give way or to mix. They were prepared to remain or to trek to the Transvaal if necessary, but wherever they went, they were prepared to fight until victory was won, to struggle in order to help in building a nation. Whether the Voortrekker was journeying or fighting and whether he put his hand to the plough when left in peace, he was always busy building his nation. He was never prepared to break up, to destroy or to lose.

It was characteristic of that struggle that the Voortrekker always had his wife and child with him. It was not a struggle of men only. It was a struggle of the whole family—man, woman and child—side by side to safeguard the future of their posterity and to preserve the purity of the blood of the nation. Had only men surged into a country, there would perhaps not have been a white nation today. Because it was a family trek and because the unity of the family was the basic bond of the democratic government of the states established, order and peace could soon be found there. It was the family that trekked, the family that fought, the family that built.

That is what happened then. What is the position today?

There is a remarkable similarity. Is it not so that today a liberalistic current very similar to that of 120 years ago is again moving across the world? A spirit which originates from World War II, perhaps even from World War I; a spirit engendered by the experience of the people elsewhere and by their self-interest; a spirit of liberalism which causes the white states to become so divided among themselves that each, with a view to the success of its aims, tries to obtain the support of the non-white world—whether in Asia or in Africa; a spirit not born from the highest moral considerations, as it is frequently represented to be. If it were, then it would not look down so damningly upon the fellow white man in other parts of the world but could be as equally understanding towards him as it is towards the black man.

It is peculiar that the world spirit, just like then, is not directed against the Afrikaner, but against all whites. That spirit is permeated with glorification of the noble savage. Everything that the non-white says or does, is good or is glossed over. If he acts roughly or foolishly it is described as merely characteristic of the transition period. But if the white man by standing firm has to ensure that civilisation is preserved, then it is oppression and he is maligned. The world spirit is also directed at all the colonial powers in Africa, whether it be the Portuguese or the British or the Belgians or the French, and whether it be the South Africans. Whoever brought civilisation here, whoever saved the people from mutual extinction, whoever provided shelter and food to greater masses than the country could carry previously goes unthanked for the life, for the prosperity, for the knowledge, and for the Divine enrichment of Primitive minds. It is also peculiar that once more foreign preachers have come to carry the misconceptions further—the Huddlestons, the Collins, the Scotts, the De Blanks—people perhaps with good intentions, people infused with the spirit of Europe which has been imbibed by them, some even animated by a spirit proceeding from the abject Communism. In this country where we as a Christian nation with knowledge of our history and of the nature of the Bantu people and the level of their development try to do what is right and good and Christianlike, we are condemned by mouths which should have come and learned before they talked.

They do not observe that, just like 120 years ago, there are the clearest evidences of our preparedness to let fairness and justice prevail. I have referred to the manner in which Piet Retief was prepared to enter into an agreement. I add thereto that after that Murder Hill episode, Andries Pretorius, who had come to mete out punishment for the misdeed, while on the way still sent a message to Dingaan saying that if he should show repentance the Voortrekkers would yet be forgiving and not carry the warfare to extremes. Because the message was regarded with contempt, the battle at Blood River had to take place.

Even so the white man is today prepared in all kinds of ways to have justice done to the Bantu. It is the policy of South Africa to grant rights to the non-white in his own community and in his own area where it is fitting.

Again it is the white people of South Africa, who know the conditions, who have designed and now follow the only method which can bring peace and do justice to all. But they are not supported therein by those who come from outside and do not understand it. These have already accepted as unavoidable the disappearance of the white race. When it is said in Europe and also by some in our own country that the solution of this struggle is to be found in the merger of all people—so-called integration—it is not realised that this is not unification. All that will happen is the destruction of the white race. Not integration, but disintegration—disintegration of the white race, of the civilisation and of the religion which we inherited, will be the only result. Therefore, even though we cannot trek any more, we say like the Voortrekker of yore, "we can still struggle." And we shall fight even though we have to perish. We shall keep on fighting for the survival of the white man at the southern tip of Africa and the religion which has been given to him to spread here. And we shall do it just as they did! Man, woman and child. We shall fight for our existence and the world must know it. We cannot do otherwise. Like Luther during the Reformation we are standing with our backs to the wall. We are not fighting for money or possessions. We are fighting for the life of our people.

But we are not fighting for our people only. I am deeply convinced in my soul that we are fighting for the survival of white civilisation. If ever a struggle between East and West were to come, if Africa ever were to throw in its weight somewhere—and it would be a decisive weight—then the weight of Africa would be on the side of the white man and the Western nations only if the idea for which we as a nation stand can remain victorious. The white man at the southern point of Africa is an outpost of white civilisation and as such the advance-guard of its forces, located where the first attacks are to come. We know that we are a small nation but we also know that we have in us the steel and the strength which resulted in the triumph of Blood River. When you are in the forward lines and see the danger coming, you are entitled to send messages to the armies in the rear who are still sheltering behind you. Hence we send this message to the outside world and say to them once again that there is but one way of saving the white races of the world. And that is for the white and the non-white in Africa each to exercise his rights within his own areas.

We are fighting with all that is within us because we know that we are a nation in the making. We know that we are not yet halfway up the mast. We know that we are still foundation layers just like the heroes of Blood River. We also know that we are ordinary people with many weaknesses. But we know that those who are making history, like they did and we are doing now, are doing so with a young nation still in the spring-time of its life. If the foundations are laid right, the walls can be built strongly. And the foundations that we lay we are endeavouring to lay solidly and securely. We are trying to dig down through the clay to the gravel and bed-rock so that the nation of South Africa may exist to remote times in the future. That is why we are not allowing ourselves to be driven to rashness or to panic. That is why we are building on the only rock of nations, namely the faith and the same helping hand which gave our forefathers the victory of Blood River. We are building in faith, we are building with power because we know that we have not been planted here aimlessly. Why should Whites have been led to the southern tip of Africa three hundred years ago? Why was half of the country unoccupied, why could small numbers of people increase so much and become spread over the whole country? Why could they, in spite of their Moordkrans and Italeni [two battlefield defeats], also gain their Blood River? Why could they go through their wars of independence and, win or lose, yet survive as a nation? Why was this all given to us if there is no purpose in it? And I believe this to be the purpose—that we should be an anchor and a stay for Western civilisation and for the Christian religion. Western civilisation and the white races are also going through a crisis, even though they do not notice it. Never before in history, at any rate the history of the past two thousand years, has the position of the white races been so perilous. They are in danger not because of their lack of knowledge or power, but on account of that which is going on in their own spirit: their inner weakening and wrong conception of what their task is on earth. And there sometimes have to be small groups that offer resistance; a resistance that can be extended until it embraces the whole pattern of nations.

Perhaps it was intended that we should have been planted here at the southern point within the crisis area so that from this resistance group might emanate the victory whereby all that has been built up since the days of Christ may be maintained for the good of all mankind. May you have the strength, people of South Africa, to serve the purpose for which you have been placed here!

36 • The Cold War begins in earnest (1960)

During World War II, a Brookings Institute study challenged the then influential geopolitical argument that whoever "controlled the great land masses of Eurasia and Africa, with adjacent islands, called the World Island, would ... control the seas and thus the world."[8] This argument had been developed by, among others, the English geographer Halford Mackinder, had been discussed by Adolf Hitler in Mein Kampf, and was understood by the Brookings authors as having "influenced his [Hitler's] campaign" in World War II.

The authors of the Brookings report argued that minerals, not land masses, were the key to world control. "The geopolitical thesis of the present book is that potential world control is not necessarily afforded by control of any of the great land masses, but that it lies in the control of mineral resources, wherever they are, backed up by control of the land and the sea. It further emphasizes the fact that the combined mineral resources controlled by the United States and the British Empire far outweigh the mineral resources of the World Island as envisaged in the German geopolitical concept, and afford a much broader and more powerful base for world control, both for peace and war."

Outside Russia, the Brookings study demonstrated, Africa was the most important and often the only source for the West of increasingly significant strategic minerals (defined as minerals that would be needed to supply the military, industrial, and essential civilian needs of the United States during a national emergency). Such strategic minerals included chromite (Africa had nearly 100 percent of the world's reserves), cobalt (more than 50 percent), manganese (more than 75 percent), and platinum (73 percent). Africa also supplied other minerals needed for war production, includ-

8. C. K. Leith, J. W. Furness, and Cleona Lewis, *World Minerals and World Peace* (Washington, D.C.: The Brookings Institution, 1943), ii.

ing copper, bauxite, zinc, vanadium, antimony, beryllium, graphite, mica, talc, fluorspar, uranium, and industrial diamonds, as well as the world's largest supplies of gold.

Within Africa, one of the richest sources of minerals was the Belgian Congo, and just as the Portuguese had been drawn to that area's wealth in the mid-fifteenth century and Henry Morton Stanley in the mid-nineteenth century, so too was the United States in the mid-twentieth century concerned that the mineral resources of the Congo basin—so important for control of the world—not fall into the hands of the Russians through the person assumed to be their puppet, Patrice Lumumba.

Belgium pulled out of the Congo in 1960, moving in the course of a few months from a claim that it would continue to rule the country for the foreseeable future to complete abandonment of its formerly prized possession. Growing demonstrations and the refusal of the bulk of the population to accept the Belgians' attempts to identify a collaborationist group propelled the colonialists out of the country, but not before they had attempted to secure their economic interests in the mineral-rich southeastern province of Katanga. Belgian and South African investors encouraged the regional leader of Katanga, Moise Tshombe, to organize a secessionist movement. At the same time, the Congo became swept up in the Cold War as Russian and U.S. diplomats competed to incorporate this potentially rich and strategically situated country into their respective spheres of influence.

Patrice Lumumba was caught up in these contradictory forces. He had led the movement for independence and became the first president of an independent Congo. Perceived as anti-Belgium by the Belgians, as prosocialist by South African businessmen (who feared nationalization of their Katangan mining companies), as pro-Communist by the United States, and as too intransigent in his opposition to Katangan secession by the leaders of the United Nations, Lumumba became increasingly isolated internationally and viewed by Americans as a potentially dangerous enemy in independent Africa. According to sworn testimony by CIA agents to a congressional committee, the director of the CIA from 1953 to 1961, Allen Dulles, under orders from President Eisenhower, plotted Lumumba's assassination. The cables and testimony reproduced below come from a congressional investigation organized by Senator Frank Church in 1975 that investigated covert operations and assassination attempts on foreign leaders undertaken by the United States during the presidencies of Eisenhower, Kennedy, and Nixon.[9]

Chronology

June 30, 1960:	Patrice Lumumba declares the Congo independent of Belgium.
August 26, 1960:	Allen Dulles, director of the CIA, orders removal of Lumumba.
September 6, 1960:	Joseph Kasa-Vubu, president of the Congo, dismisses Lumumba as prime minister.

9. The Church Committee, *Alleged Assassination Plots Involving Foreign Leaders: An Interim Report of the Select Committee to Study Governmental Operations with Respect to Intelligence Activities [chaired by Senator Frank Church], United States Senate . . . November 20, 1975* (Washington, D.C.: U.S. Government Printing Office, 1975), Section III, Assassination Planning and the Plots. A. Congo, 14, 15, 17, 20, 21, 23, 24, 25, 26, 68, 70.

September 14, 1960:   Joseph Mobutu, chief of staff of the Congolese armed forces, announces on the radio that he is "neutralizing" politicians until December 31, 1960.

September 27, 1960:   CIA agent Joseph Scheider arrives in Leopoldville with poison to assassinate Lumumba.

October 10, 1960:   Lumumba is placed under house arrest, "protected" or guarded by a double cordon of soldiers, first from the UN, then from Mobutu.

December 2, 1960:   UN transfers Lumumba to Mobutu's troops.

January 17, 1961:   Mobutu's forces transfer Lumumba, together with Maurice Mpolo (minister of youth) and Joseph Okito (vice president of the Congo Senate), to the secessionist forces of Moise Tshombe in Katanga.

February 10, 1961:   Radio Katanga announces that Lumumba, Mpolo, and Okito are on the run.

February 13, 1961:   Katanga interior minister announces that Lumumba, Mpolo, and Okito have been killed by "bush villagers."

November 11, 1961:   UN official investigation concludes that Lumumba, Mpolo, and Okito were killed on January 17, 1961.

A. Cables sent between CIA agents in the Congo and CIA headquarters in Washington D.C., August–September 1960

CIA CABLE, LEOPOLDVILLE STATION OFFICER VICTOR HEDGMAN TO DIRECTOR ALLEN DULLES, AUGUST 18, 1960

EMBASSY AND STATION BELIEVE CONGO EXPERIENCING CLASSIC COMMUNIST EFFORT TAKEOVER GOVERNMENT. MANY FORCES AT WORK HERE: SOVIETS . . . COMMUNIST PARTY, ETC. ALTHOUGH DIFFICULT DETERMINE MAJOR INFLUENCING FACTORS TO PREDICT OUTCOME STRUGGLE FOR POWER, DECISIVE PERIOD NOT FAR OFF. WHETHER OR NOT LUMUMBA ACTUALLY COMMIE OR JUST PLAYING COMMIE GAME TO ASSIST HIS SOLIDIFYING POWER, ANTI-WEST FORCES RAPIDLY INCREASING POWER CONGO AND THERE MAY BE LITTLE TIME LEFT IN WHICH TAKE ACTION TO AVOID ANOTHER CUBA.

CIA CABLE, DIRECTOR DULLES TO LEOPOLDVILLE STATION OFFICER HEDGMAN, AUGUST 26, 1960

IN HIGH QUARTERS HERE IT IS THE CLEAR-CUT CONCLUSION THAT IF (LUMUMBA) CONTINUES TO HOLD HIGH OFFICE, THE INEVITABLE RESULT WILL AT BEST BE CHAOS AND AT WORST PAVE THE WAY TO COMMUNIST TAKEOVER OF THE CONGO WITH DISASTROUS CONSEQUENCES FOR THE PRESTIGE OF THE UN AND FOR THE INTERESTS OF THE FREE WORLD GENERALLY. CONSEQUENTLY WE CONCLUDE THAT HIS REMOVAL MUST BE AN URGENT AND PRIME OBJECTIVE AND THAT UNDER EXISTING CONDITIONS THAT SHOULD BE A HIGH PRIORITY OF OUR COVERT ACTION.

FIGURE 16 Belgian paratroopers arrive at the Leopoldville airport in the Congo on July 13, 1960. The Congo had received its independence only thirteen days earlier, followed by the mutiny of the Congolese army against the continuing control of the army by Belgian officers and the secession of the mineral-rich province of Katanga. The paratroopers were flown in to clear the airport of Congolese troops in order to allow Belgium to reintroduce its troops into the country to protect its citizens and economic interests. AP Photo/Jean-Jacques Levy.

CIA CABLE, LEOPOLDVILLE STATION OFFICER HEDGMAN TO DIRECTOR DULLES, SEPTEMBER 7, 1960

TO [STATION OFFICER] COMMENT THAT LUMUMBA IN OPPOSITION IS ALMOST AS DANGEROUS AS IN OFFICE [THE CONGOLESE POLITICIAN] INDICATED UNDERSTOOD AND IMPLIED MIGHT PHYSICALLY ELIMINATE LUMUMBA.

CIA CABLE, DIRECTOR DULLES TO LEOPOLDVILLE STATION OFFICER HEDGMAN, SEPTEMBER 13, 1960

LUMUMBA TALENTS AND DYNAMISM APPEAR OVERRIDING FACTOR IN REESTABLISHING HIS POSITION EACH TIME IT SEEMS HALF LOST. IN OTHER WORDS EACH TIME LUMUMBA HAS OPPORTUNITY HAVE LAST WORD HE CAN SWAY EVENTS TO HIS ADVANTAGE.

CIA CABLE, BISSELL, TWEEDY TO LEOPOLDVILLE STATION OFFICER HEDGMAN, SEPTEMBER 19, 1960

["JOE"] SHOULD ARRIVE APPROX 27 SEPT . . . WILL ANNOUNCE HIMSELF AS "JOE FROM PARIS" . . . IT IS URGENT YOU SHOULD SEE ["JOE"] SOONEST POSSIBLE

AFTER HE PHONES YOU. HE WILL FULLY IDENTIFY HIMSELF AND EXPLAIN HIS AS-
SIGNMENT TO YOU.

CIA CABLE, TWEEDY TO LEOPOLDVILLE STATION OFFICER HEDGMAN, SEPTEMBER 22, 1960

YOU AND COLLEAGUE [Scheider] UNDERSTAND WE CANNOT READ OVER YOUR
SHOULDER AS YOU PLAN AND ASSESS OPPORTUNITIES. OUR PRIMARY CONCERN
MUST BE CONCEALMENT (AMERICAN) ROLE. UNLESS OUTSTANDING OPPORTU-
NITY EMERGES WHICH MAKE CALCULATED RISK FIRST CLASS BET. READY ENTER-
TAIN ANY SERIOUS PROPOSALS YOU MAKE BASED OUR HIGH REGARD BOTH YOUR
PROFESSIONAL JUDGMENTS.

CIA CABLE, DIRECTOR DULLES TO LEOPOLDVILLE STATION OFFICER HEDGMAN, SEPTEMBER 24, 1960

WE WISH GIVE EVERY POSSIBLE SUPPORT IN ELIMINATING LUMUMBA FROM
ANY POSSIBILITY RESUMING GOVERNMENTAL POSITION OR IF HE FAILS IN LEO-
POLDVILLE, SETTING HIMSELF UP IN STANLEYVILE OR ELSEWHERE.

B. Testimony given by CIA agents to the Church Committee, 1975

BRONSON TWEEDY, CHIEF OF THE AFRICA DIVISION, CIA, TESTIMONY GIVEN UNDER OATH TO THE CHURCH COMMITTEE, OCTOBER 9, 1975

"What Mr. [Richard] Bissell [deputy director of plans (DPP) and head of clandestine
operations for the CIA] was saying to me [shortly before or shortly after Dulles's telegram of
August 26, 1960,] was that there was agreement, policy agreement, in Washington that Lumumba must be removed from the position of control and influence in the Congo . . . and
that among the possibilities of that elimination was indeed assassination. . . . The purpose of
his conversation with me was to initiate correspondence with the Station for them to explore
with Headquarters the possibility of . . . assassination, or indeed any other means of removing Lumumba from power . . . to have the Station start reviewing possibilities, assets, and discussing them with Headquarters in detail in the same way we would with any operation."

JOSEPH SCHEIDER, SPECIAL ASSISTANT TO THE DDP (BISSELL) FOR SCIENTIFIC MATTERS, TESTIMONY GIVEN UNDER OATH TO THE CHURCH COMMITTEE, OCTOBER 7 AND 9, 1975

[Bissell told him in late summer or early fall, 1960 that] "he [Bissell] had direction from
the highest authority . . . for getting into that kind of operation . . ." Scheider stated that the
reference to "highest authority" by Bissell "signified to me that he meant the President . . ."
After the meeting . . . Scheider reviewed a list of biological materials available at the Army
Chemical Corps installation at Fort Detrick, Maryland, that would produce diseases that
would "either kill the individual or incapacitate him so severely that he would be out of action . . ." Scheider selected one material from the list which "was supposed to produce a disease that was . . . indigenous to that area (of Africa) and that could be fatal." . . . We had to get
it bottled and packaged in a way that it could pass for something else and I needed to have a
second material that could absolutely inactivate it in case that is what I desired to do for some

contingency ... [Scheider also] prepared a packet of ... accessory materials [such as hypodermic needles, rubber gloves, and gauze masks] that would be used in the handling of this pretty dangerous material ... [Tweedy and his deputy asked Scheider to take the toxic materials to the Congo and deliver instructions from headquarters to the station officer] "to mount an operation, if he could do it securely ... to either seriously incapacitate or eliminate Lumumba."

VICTOR HEDGMAN, CIA STATION OFFICER IN LEOPOLDVILLE, TESTIMONY GIVEN UNDER OATH TO THE CHURCH COMMITTEE, AUGUST 21, 1975

Hedgman: It is my recollection that he [Scheider] advised me, or my instructions were, to eliminate Lumumba.

Q: By eliminate, do you mean assassinate?

Hedgman: Yes, I would say that was ... my understanding of the primary means. I don't think it was probably limited to that, if there was some other way of ... removing him from a position of political threat.

Hedgman said that the means of assassination was not restricted to use of the toxic material provided by Scheider ... He testified that he may have "suggested" shooting Lumumba to Scheider as an alternative to poisoning.

Hedgman: I must have ... pointed out that this was not a common or usual Agency tactic ... never in my training or previous work in the Agency had I ever heard any references to such methods. And it is my recollection I asked on whose authority these instructions were issued.

Q: And what did Mr. Scheider reply?

Hedgman: It is my recollection that he identified the President ... and I cannot recall whether he said "the President" or whether he identified him by name.

Hedgman: ... I doubt that I thought the President had said, you use this system. But my understanding is the President had made a decision that an act should take place, but then put that into the hands of the Agency to carry out his decision.

Q: Whatever that act was to be, it was clearly to be assassination or the death of the foreign political leader?

Hedgman: Yes.

Hedgman: I looked upon the Agency as an executive arm of the Presidency ... Therefore, I suppose I thought that it was an order issued in due form from an authorized authority. On the other hand, I looked at it as a kind of operation that I could do without, that I thought that probably the Agency and the U.S. government could get along without. I didn't regard Lumumba as the kind of person who was going to bring on World War III. I might have had a somewhat different attitude if I thought that one man could bring on World War III and result in the deaths of millions of people or something, but I didn't see him in that light. I saw him as a danger to the political position of the United States in Africa, but nothing more than that.

37 ♦ Patrice Lumumba writes his last letter to his wife (1961)

In November 1960, Patrice Lumumba was arrested by soldiers loyal to then Colonel Mobutu (later the dictator of Zaire for nearly forty years, Mobutu Sese Seko) and in January 1961 was secretly handed over, along with two members of his cabinet, Maurice Mpolo and Joseph Okito, to Moise Tshombe and flown to Katanga. Lumumba and his companions were never again seen alive. The Katangans officially announced his death on February 13, 1961.

Before he was handed over to Tshombe, Lumumba wrote this letter to his wife not knowing whether or not she would receive it.[10]

My dear wife,

I am writing these words not knowing whether they will reach you, when they will reach you, and whether I shall still be alive when you read them. All through my struggle for the independence of my country, I have never doubted for a single instant the final triumph of the sacred cause to which my companions and I have devoted all our lives. But what we wished for our country, its right to an honourable life, to unstained dignity, to independence without restrictions, was never desired by the Belgian imperialists and their Western allies, who found direct and indirect support, both deliberate and unintentional, amongst certain high officials of the United Nations, that organisation in which we placed all our trust when we called on its assistance.

They have corrupted some of our compatriots and bribed others. They have helped to distort the truth and bring our independence into dishonour. How could I speak otherwise? Dead or alive, free or in prison by order of the imperialists, it is not I myself who count. It is the Congo, it is our poor people for whom independence has been transformed into a cage from beyond whose confines the outside world looks on us, sometimes with kindly sympathy, but at other times with joy and pleasure. But my faith will remain unshakeable. I know and I feel in my heart that sooner or later my people will rid themselves of all their enemies, both internal and external, and that they will rise as one man to say No to the degradation and shame of colonialism, and regain their dignity in the clear light of the sun.

We are not alone. Africa, Asia and the free liberated people from all corners of the world will always be found at the side of the millions of Congolese who will not abandon the struggle until the day when there are no longer any colonialists and their mercenaries in our country. As to my children, whom I leave and whom I may never see again, I should like them to be told that it is for them, as is it for every Congolese, to accomplish the sacred task of reconstructing our independence and our sovereignty: for without dignity there is no liberty, without justice there is no dignity, and without independence there are no free men.

Neither brutality, nor cruelty nor torture will ever bring me to ask for mercy, for I prefer to die with my head unbowed, my faith unshakeable and with profound trust in the destiny of my country, rather than live under subjection and disregarding sacred principles. History will one day have its say, but it will not be the history that is taught in Brussels, Paris, Washington

10. Patrice Lumumba, with a foreword and notes by Colin Legum, trans. Graham Heath, *Congo, My Country* (London: Pall Mall with Barrie and Rockliff, 1962; first published in French in 1961 as *Le Congo—terre d'avenir—est-il menacé?*), xxiii–xxiv.

or in the United Nations, but the history which will be taught in the countries freed from imperialism and its puppets. Africa will write her own history, and to the north and south of the Sahara, it will be a glorious and dignified history.

Do not weep for me, my dear wife. I know that my country, which is suffering so much, will know how to defend its independence and its liberty. Long live the Congo! Long live Africa!

Patrice

38 • The final hours of Patrice Lumumba, Maurice Mpolo, and Joseph Okito (1961)

The details of Lumumba's, Mpolo's, and Okito's last hours long remained a secret, especially so long as Mobutu remained dictator of Zaire, and that remained the case until the end of 1997. The fullest story to date was published in 1999 by Belgian author Ludo de Witte. His research was exhaustive, and his story compelling.[11]

10 PM, January 17, 1961, Katanga

. . . the prisoners were taken out of the car. They were barefoot, and dressed only in their trousers and vests. [Commissioner Frans] Verscheure [Belgian advisor to the Katangan police] removed the handcuffs. He was walking behind Lumumba who asked him: "You're going to kill us, aren't you?" to which Verscheure simply answered "Yes" . . . According to Verscheure, Lumumba "took very well" the announcement of his imminent death. The prisoners stood on the path, surrounded by the policemen and soldiers. Verscheure said "they were still on their feet," implying that they bore the marks of the previous few hours' beatings. Verscheure told them they were going to be shot. According to [Captain Julien] Gat [Belgian military police], they were "given time to prepare, to pray." Verscheure said that Lumumba rejected the offer. Meanwhile, the first firing squad of two soldiers and two policemen got ready. The police had Vigneron sten guns, the [three Belgian] soldiers FAL rifles. Someone apparently intoned a native oath. Verscheure took Joseph Okito to a tree. According to Verscheure, Okito said, "I want my wife and children in Léopoldville to be taken care of." Somebody answered: "We're in Katanga, not in Léo!" Okito leaned against the tree, his face turned towards the firing squad already in position 4 metres away. A short hail of bullets, and the former vice president of the Senate was dead; his body was immediately thrown into the grave. After "the little one," it was the turn of "the big one," as Verscheure said later. The commissioner placed Maurice Mpolo against the tree; a round of bullets from another squad mowed him down. Finally a third firing squad faced Lumumba. Verscheure, who had taken him to the big tree, later said that Lumumba trembled when led to the edge of the grave, but "mute, completely dazed, his eyes misty, he put up no resistance." An enormous hail of bullets riddled the former prime minister's body. "After execution, we picked up half a kilo of cartridges," the police commissioner said . . .

11. Ludo de Witte, trans. Ann Wright and Renée Fenby, *The Assassination of Lumumba* (London: Verso, 2001; published originally as *De moord op Lumumba*, 1999), 120–21, 140–41.

FIGURE 17 Patrice Lumumba (right), the first elected prime minister of the independent Congo, under arrest with two of his colleagues, Maurice Mpolo (far left) and Joseph Okito (center). Lumumba had been deposed by a military coup carried out by Colonel Joseph Mobutu with the support of the Belgian government. Lumumba had sought Soviet aid to fend off continuing Belgian interference in the country's affairs in the first weeks of independence. Lumumba, Mpolo, and Okito were later murdered by Belgian troops. This is the last picture of Lumumba alive (December 1960). AP Photo.

Shortly before nightfall on 18 January . . . a convoy left [Elisabethville] for the scene of the execution. It was almost dark when Police Commissioners [Gerard] Soete, Verscheure and [Pius] Sapwe and the nine policemen who took part in the assassination arrived. Exhuming the corpses from the sandy soil did not take much effort. The bodies were rolled up in mortuary cloths and put in the back of a lorry . . . Not far from Kasenga [220 kilometers northeast of Elisabethville], the lorry stopped and the bodies were interred in a hastily dug grave behind an ant-hill, a few paces from the road . . .

Lumumba, Mpolo and Okito were not to stay in their new grave in Kasenga for long. A definitive solution was planned over the next two days. Early in the afternoon of 21 January, two Europeans in uniform and a few black assistants left [Elisabethville] for Kasenga in a lorry belonging to the public works department and containing road signs, geometrical instruments, two demijohns filled with sulphuric acid, an empty 200-litre petrol barrel and a hacksaw . . . the equipment was provided by the public works department . . . the sulphuric acid came from the Union Minière. On their arrival, they unloaded the road signs and a theodolite to make passers-by think they were doing a land survey. But they could not find the grave, and had to stop searching at nightfall. Not until the evening of the next day did they find the grave and start their lugubrious task. The corpses were dug up, cut into pieces with knives and the hacksaw, then thrown into the barrel of sulphuric acid. The operation took hours and only ended the next morning, on 23 January. At first the two Belgians wore masks over their mouths but took them off when they became uncomfortable. Their only protection against the stench was whiskey, so . . . they got drunk. One of the black assistants spilt acid on his foot and burned it badly. They discovered that they did not have enough acid and only burned part of the bodies. According to Verscheure, the skulls were ground up, and the bones and teeth (that neither acid nor fire can destroy) were scattered on the way back. The same occurred with the ashes. Nothing was left of the three nationalist leaders; nowhere could their remains, even the most minute trace of them, be found.

PART II

The Emergence of Independent Africa (1961–2008)

INTRODUCTION

At the outset of the independence period, African leaders assessed the obstacles they would face in creating nations from colonies and fashioned goals and strategies that could help Africans to realize their continent's wealth and potential after centuries of exploitation. The problems were grave, for despite colonial administrative policies that used some traditional authorities to implement colonial rule, few of the newly independent states inherited national networks of administration, communication, or transportation. Those that did were left with an administrative structure superimposed on an artificially constructed "nation" and ruled from above through authoritarian, not democratic, procedures. Trade with the former colonial powers continued, however, in most cases still under the control of privately owned European companies. And even when the local companies were nationalized in states that adopted socialism, the cash crops (luxury or industrial, not food crops) to which people had been required to devote their land and labor still had to be sold in a world market where prices fluctuated greatly. African leaders found themselves faced with the remnants of a colonial system of administration, geared to rule from the top down without regard for the needs or opinions of the ruled. Moreover, fragile export economies—cocoa in Ghana, coffee in Rwanda (accounting for 75 percent of the country's foreign earnings), even gold in South Africa—made political stability difficult to achieve. A fall in world prices could easily precipitate violence, as the collapse in cocoa prices did in the mid-1960s for Ghana, the decline in the price of gold in the 1980s for South Africa, and the fall in coffee prices in the late 1980s for Rwanda. At the same time, such revenue was crucial to building the social and industrial infrastructure necessary for true independence without incurring massive debts. Unfortunately, democracy, economic self-sufficiency, adequate living conditions, health and relative peace would all prove elusive as the task of rebuilding Africa proceeded in the wake of the colonial experience.

As Frantz Fanon observed even before the advent of independence, the colonial system created serious economic, political, and social problems that continued well into the independence period; was independent Africa to be a place where freedom reigned, or was its dependence on the West to continue? Kwame Nkrumah believed that only the unification of all of the countries on the African continent into a federally unified state would enable Africans to channel the continent's enormous economic resources into rebuilding societies for the benefit of their members rather than the profit of multinational corporations. Julius Nyerere argued that Africans should aim for self-sufficiency by developing indigenous models of socialism and creating their own forms of democracy different from those of the West. Yet, in the postcolonial situation, or under "neocolonialism" as Fanon and others called the psychological and political twilight zone between oppression and freedom, only the middle classes or petty bourgeoisie would likely reap the benefits of independence as they had under colonialism, trained to serve an exploitative system. Indeed, Amilcar Cabral argued that the petty bourgeoisie would necessarily have to commit class "suicide" in order to break the bonds of colonialism before Africans could really free themselves politically.

However, in the early 1960s not all were yet free. The Portuguese remained firmly entrenched in their colonial possessions, arguing that they were better able to bring about reform than their African subjects. White settlers in South Africa and Southern Rhodesia likewise claimed that continued policies of racial separation and white supremacy were necessary for the upliftment of Africans and for the defense of democracy in Africa against the predatory aims of the Soviet Union. Such hypocrisy was rejected by people like Cabral, Eduardo Mondlane, and Nelson Mandela, who, in light of the fact that Africans were neither permitted any political rights (certainly not the right to vote) within the states that remained under European rule nor allowed to protest peacefully without risk of arrest and banning, adopted policies of armed struggle. Thus, armed struggle began in the Portuguese colonies, in South Africa, and in Southern Rhodesia and continued throughout the 1970s. For Southern Rhodesia/Zimbabwe it ended with the negotiated victory in 1980 of Robert Mugabe's revolutionary forces. For South Africa it continued until the release of Nelson Mandela and the unbanning of the ANC in 1990. For Angola and Mozambique, war brought about the fall of the Portuguese dictatorship in 1974, but internecine struggles have continued to ravage the countryside, especially in Angola, where, after almost forty years of fighting, peace seems almost unimaginable.

The states that had become independent around 1960, faced with immediate and overwhelming problems of national cohesion and economic instability, entered a destructive cycle of civil wars and armed conflict that in many cases continues unabated into the twenty-first century. Ghana, one of the richest former colonies, saw the military overthrow of the charismatic Nkrumah, while Nigeria, the most populous former colony, fell apart in coups and civil war and was brought together only at the expense of democracy. Deploring the premature death of such high hopes, African writers watched and recorded as the tragedies unfolded. Chinua Achebe, Africa's foremost novelist, chronicled the unraveling of Nigeria in a brilliant series of novels that detail the transformation of colonial bureaucrats into successful power brokers, confirming Cabral's worst fears about the petty bourgeoisie during independence. Throughout Africa, ordinary people suffered under autocratic rule in Ethiopia and Malawi, as well as Angola and South Africa.

Outside intervention added to political instability. This was especially a problem in southern Africa, where, in order to uphold white supremacy, the apartheid government sent invasion forces and bomb and assassination squads (all the while denying that it was doing so) into Mozambique, Angola, Zimbabwe, and Zambia, while continuing to militarily occupy Namibia in defiance of the United Nations, which, in international law, had final authority for administering the former German colony. Seldom hesitating to interfere in the politics of their former colonies, the French sent expeditionary forces to help those they deemed the "legitimate" authorities—usually former colonial collaborators—who so long as they favored French strategic and economic interests could reign as despots with metropolitan approval. More often the outside interference was less obvious—and all the more pernicious for being so disguised— in the form of underhanded business relations between European and South African business investors and dictators like Mobutu Sese Seko of Zaire.

However, despite all of these impediments to freedom and democracy, people continued to struggle for liberation, against white rule, and against the legacy of colonialism. The leaders of the "black consciousness" movement in South Africa, particularly Steve Biko, argued that Africans first had to break the psychological bonds of colonialism in order to free themselves completely. Though Biko was beaten to death in police custody, his message was taken up by thousands of young people who rose in protest against apartheid in Soweto in 1976 and, despite suffering torture and often death, continued to resist with support from throughout the black community of South Africa. In Malawi the poet Jack Mapanje would take up the torch carried by John Chilembwe and fight against the dictatorship of Hastings Banda and, though subjected to lengthy imprisonment, found the answer scratched in the walls of Mikuyu prison: Resistance would never cease so long as people lived.

Nonetheless, the end of the twentieth century and the beginning of the twenty-first witnessed the repeated recurrence of some of colonialism's most brutal methods of control over "nations" that have known nothing else. In Rwanda, for example, where in the course of a few months in 1994 a million people were killed by their immediate neighbors, a genocide that had ethnic dimensions but that arose, more than from any other causes, as a result of the familiar residue of colonialism: divide-and-rule policies favored by the Belgians during the colonial era, French interference in the postcolonial period, and the dependence of the country's economy on a single export crop for its stability (or lack thereof). In Sierra Leone in 1999, where civil war has all but destroyed the country, "rebels" fought the government for control of the diamond industry, and children, their parents killed by the rebels in order to acquire and train a force of barely teenage soldiers, cut off the hands of people to dissuade them from supporting the duly elected government. Such dismemberment for a supposedly precious stone is reminiscent of the atrocity photographs collected by Roger Casement to illustrate how King Leopold made Africans collect rubber faster and reminds us of how the scramble for Africa really took off only after the first discovery of diamonds within South Africa 130 years ago. In Darfur, Sudan, a bloody civil war between various government militias and Muslims has claimed thousands of victims, reminding us again of the problems of building a nation-state from communities that did not necessarily have anything in common either politically, economically, or socially at the time of conquest, with the added component of lucrative wealth in the form of massive oil reserves linked to the Sudan's Red Sea port. Ethnic divisions, valuable resources, and a dose of massive brutality have combined to create a familiar scenario in independent Africa.

A new generation of leaders has emerged in Africa, many raised under independence without the experience of colonialism and others reemergent after years of exile or imprisonment. Younger leaders like Jerry Rawlings in Ghana (out of office since 2001) or Yoweri Museveni in Uganda (president since 1986) place much of the blame for Africa's problems on the shoulders of their African predecessors, accusing them of corruption and pointing out the need for bigger and better systems of rule throughout Africa. Yet there is often little new in their pronouncements despite their assertions to the contrary. While rejecting the generation of the 1960s, these new leaders often echo the analyses of Cabral and Nkrumah, with the difference that they now blame Africans rather than Europeans for creating Africa's problems and see in the "free market" a better solution for economic development than the socialism so favored by their predecessors.

Older leaders, nearly returned from the dead, have struck a different chord. Nelson Mandela, for instance, became the first president of postapartheid South Africa after spending twenty-seven years in prison, and Olesegun Obasanjo was elected president of Nigeria in 1999 after almost four decades of military rule (a period of which Obasanjo himself administered in the 1970s). They strive to remind Africans that theirs is a continent and a culture worth saving, building, and sharing. Although both are now out of office, Mandela is still celebrated in his own country and worldwide, but Obasanjo is being investigated for corruption in 2009.

Younger leaders such as Thabo Mbeki and Jacob Zuma have insisted more recently that we must accept the realities: that no matter how noble or villainous Africa's leaders, they face a monumental task in reversing the patterns of the past in forging new African nations. Still seeking uniquely African solutions, these statesmen ask Africans to look within their own societies for answers, not blame, and for the strength to rebuild African communities not only to imitate the past but to move into a future of progress.

CHAPTER FIVE

African Ideologies of Independence (1961–71)

39 • Frantz Fanon discusses the
limits of African independence (1961)

*As independence approached for most African countries, an important question was what rela-
tionship these sovereign nations should have with their former colonizers. Was it wise to sever all
ties, and was it even possible to do so? Was it possible to develop a new cooperative relationship
given the economic exploitation common to colonialism? Did continued contact and economic interaction threaten the viability of the new states? As the expansion and intensification of the Cold
War threatened to draw Africa into the calculations of global strategists, African politicians had to
face these crucial issues immediately upon independence. The former colonizers, such as England,
France, Belgium, and Portugal, wanted to foster close economic association and to keep their former colonial possessions within their sphere of influence. However, this form of continued colonialism, known as "neocolonialism" in Africa, provided little advantage for the inhabitants of the newly
independent states. Only politicians and the small middle-class were able to secure much (and often
considerable) profit from continued dependence on the West. Thus, within each country conflicting
interests battled for control of these new states and their attendant resources, too often leading to
military coups, popular resistance, and civil war—conflicts that continue to the present day.*

*Frantz Fanon (1925–1961) was Africa's most prominent theoretician of revolution and in-
dependence and its attendant difficulties. Born in Martinique (Caribbean), he studied medicine in
France and specialized in psychiatry. He accepted a position as psychiatric physician at a hospital
just outside Algiers, Algeria, in a country just commencing a mass-based, anticolonial war. In this
position, Fanon observed the psychological effects of colonialism and revolution. In this selection
from his numerous works, Fanon deals with the questions mentioned earlier concerning African independence and the relationship between former colonizer and former colonized. He examines the
demands that Western countries have made on Africa and the compromises that the leaders of the
new states will inevitably have to make. Such compromises, he notes, would lead to further friction
within those societies that had just—as in Nkrumah's words—celebrated their entry into a new era
of "freedom."*[1]

1. Frantz Fanon, *Toward the African Revolution*, trans. Haakon Chevalier (New York: Grove, 1964), 121–26.

FIGURE 18 A bust of former Belgian king Leopold lies on the ground at Stanleyville on May 6, 1961, after it was removed from its base by Congolese workers. This bust, along with those of former Belgian king Albert and explorer Henry Stanley, symbols of brutal colonial rule under the Belgians, were taken down following Congolese independence and were replaced with statues of the slain leader Patrice Lumumba. AP Photo.

First Truths on the Colonial Problem

The twentieth century, when the future looks back on it, will not only be remembered as the era of atomic discoveries and interplanetary explorations. The second upheaval of this period, unquestionably, is the conquest by the peoples of the lands that belong to them.

Jostled by the claims for national independence by immense regions, the colonialists have had to loosen their stranglehold. Nevertheless, this phenomenon of liberation, of triumph of national independence, of retreat of colonialism, does not manifest itself in a unique manner. Every former colony has a particular way of achieving independence. Every new sovereign state finds itself practically under the obligation of maintaining definite and deferential relations with the former oppressor.

The parties that lead the struggle against colonialist oppression, at a certain phase of the combat, decide for practical reasons to accept a fragment of independence with the firm intention of arousing the people again within the framework of the fundamental strategy of the total evacuation of the territory and of the effective seizure of all national resources. This style, which has taken form on a succession of occasions, is today well known. On the other hand, there is a whole opposite dialectic which, it seems, has not received sufficient attention.

A FIRST CONDITION: "THE RIGHTS" OF THE FORMER OCCUPANT

Some decades ago, the colonialist rulers could indefinitely propound the highly civilizing intentions of their countries. The concessions, the expropriations, the exploitation of the workers, the great wretchedness of the peoples, were traditionally conjured away and denied. Afterwards, when the time came to withdraw from the territory, the colonialists were forced to discard their masks. In the negotiations on independence, the first matters at issue were the economic interests: banks, monetary areas, research permits, commercial concessions, inviolability of properties stolen from the peasants at the time of the conquest, etc . . . Of civilizing, religious, or cultural works, there was no longer any question. The time had come for serious things, and trivialities had to be left behind. Such attitudes were to open the eyes of men struggling in other regions of the world.

The actual rights of the occupant were then perfectly identified. The minority that came from the mother country, the university missions, technical assistance, the friendship affirmed and reaffirmed, were all relegated to a secondary level. The important thing was obviously the real rights that the occupant meant to wrench from the people, as the price for a piece of independence.

The acceptance of a nominal sovereignty and the absolute refusal of real independence —such is the typical reaction of colonialist nations with respect to their former colonies. Neo-colonialism is impregnated with a few ideas which both constitute its force and at the same time prepare its necessary decline.

In the course of the struggle for liberation, things are not clear in the consciousness of the fighting people. Since it is a refusal, at one and the same time, of political non-existence, of wretchedness, of illiteracy, of the inferiority complex so subtly instilled by oppression, its battle is for a long time undifferentiated. Neo-colonialism takes advantage of this indetermination. Armed with a revolutionary and spectacular good will, it grants the former colony everything. But in so doing, it wrings from it an economic dependence which becomes an aid and assistance program.

We have seen that this operation usually triumphs. The novelty of this phase is that it is necessarily brief. This is because it takes the people little time to realize that nothing fundamental has changed. Once the hours of effusion and enthusiasm before the spectacle of the national flag floating in the wind are past, the people rediscovers the first dimension of its requirement: bread, clothing, shelter.

Neo-colonialism, because it proposes to do justice to human dignity in general, addresses itself essentially to the middle class and to the intellectuals of the colonial country.

Today, the peoples no longer feel their bellies at peace when the colonial country has recognized the value of its elites. The people want things really to change and right away. Thus it is that the struggle resumes with renewed violence.

In this second phase, the occupant bristles and unleashes all his forces. What was wrested by bombardments is reconverted into results of free negotiations. The former occupant intervenes, in the name of duty, and once again establishes his war in an independent country.

All the former colonies, from Indonesia to Egypt, without forgetting Panama, which have tried to denounce the agreements wrung from them by force, have found themselves obliged to undergo a new war and sometimes to see their sovereignty again violated and amputated.

The notorious "rights" of the occupant, the false appeal to a common past, the persistence of a rejuvenated colonial pact, are the permanent bases of an attack directed against national sovereignty.

A SECOND OBSTACLE: THE ZONES OF INFLUENCE

The concern to maintain the former colony in the yoke of economic oppression is obviously not sadism. It is not out of wickedness or ill-will that such an attitude is adopted. It is because the handling of their national riches by the colonized peoples compromises the economic equilibrium of the former occupant. The reconversion of the colonial economy, the industries engaged in processing raw materials from the underdeveloped territories, the disappearance of the colonial pact, competition with foreign capital, constitute a mortal danger for imperialism.

For countries like Great Britain and France there arises the important question of zones of influence. Unanimous in their decision to stifle the national aspirations of the colonial peoples, these countries wage a titanic struggle for the seizure of world markets. The economic battles between France, England, and the United States, in the Middle East, in the Far East, and now in Africa, give the measure of imperialist voracity and bestiality. And it is not an exaggeration to say that these battles are the direct cause of the strategies which, still today, shake the newly independent states. In exceptional circumstances, the zones of influence of the pound sterling, of the dollar, and of the franc, are converted and become, by a conjurer's trick, the Western world. Today in Lebanon and in Iraq, if we are to believe Mr. [Andre] Malraux, it is *homo occidentalis* who is threatened.

The oil of Iraq has removed all prohibitions and made concrete the true problems. We have only to remember the violent interventions in the West Indian archipelago or in Latin America every time the dictatorships supported by American policy were in danger. The Marines who today are being landed in Beirut are the brothers of those who, periodically, are sent to reestablish "order" in Haiti, in Costa Rica, in Panama. The United States considers that the two Americas constitute a world governed by the Monroe Doctrine whose application is entrusted to the American forces. The single article of this doctrine stipulates that America belongs to the Americans, in other words, to the State Department.

Its outlets having proved insufficient, it was inevitable that America would turn to other regions, namely the Far East, the Middle East, and Africa. There ensued a competition between beasts of prey; its creations are: the Eisenhower doctrine against England in the Middle East; support for Ngo Dinh Diem against France in Indochina; Economic Aid Commission in Africa announced by the presidential voyage of Mr. [Richard] Nixon, against France, England, and Belgium.

Every struggle for national liberation must take zones of influence into account.

THE COLD WAR

This competitive strategy of Western nations, moreover, enters into the vaster framework of the policy of the two blocs, which for ten years has held a definite menace of atomic disintegration suspended over the world. And it is surely not purely by chance that the hand or the eye of Moscow is discovered, in an almost stereotyped way, behind each demand for national independence, put forth by a colonial people. This is because any difficulty that is put in the way of the supremacy of the West in any given section of the world is a concrete threat to its economic power, to the range of its military strategic bases, and represents a limiting of its potential.

Every challenge to the rights of the West over a colonial country is experienced both as a weakening of the Western world and as a strengthening of the Communist world.

Today an island like Cyprus, which has almost no resources of its own and which has a population of barely half a million people, is the object of violent rivalries. And even NATO, an organization designed to parry a Soviet invasion, is being endangered by the problem to which the isle of Cyprus gives rise.

THE THIRD BLOC

The position taken by a few newly independent countries, which are determined to re-main outside the policy of the coalitions, has introduced a new dimension into the balance of forces in the world. Adopting the so-called policy of positive neutralism, of non-dependence, of non-commitment, of the third force, the underdeveloped countries that are awakening from a long slumber of slavery and of oppression, have considered it their duty to remain out-side of any warlike involvement, in order to devote themselves to the urgent economic tasks, to staving off hunger, to the improvement of man's lot.

And what the West has in truth not understood is that today a new humanism, a new theory of man is coming into being, which has its root in man. It is easy to regard President [Jawaharlal] Nehru as indecisive because he refuses to harness himself to Western imperial-ism, and Presidents [Gamal Abdel] Nasser or Sukarno as violent when they nationalize their companies or demand the fragments of their territories that are still under foreign domina-tion. What no one sees is that the 350 million Hindus, who have known the hunger of British imperialism, are now demanding bread, peace, and well-being. The fact is that the Egyptian *fellahs* and the Indonesian boys, whom Western writers like to feature in their exotic novels, insist on taking their own destiny into their hands and refuse to play the role of an inert panorama that had been reserved for them.

THE PRESTIGE OF THE WEST

And we here touch upon a psychological problem which is perhaps not fundamental but which enters into the framework of the dialectics that is now developing. The West, whose economic system is the standard (and by virtue of that fact oppressive), also prides itself on its humanist supremacy. The Western "model" is being attacked in its essence and in its fi-nality. The Orientals, the Arabs, and the Negroes, today, want to present their plans, want to affirm their values, want to define their relations with the world. The negation of political *beni-oui-ouism* [yes-man-ism] is linked to the refusal of economic *beni-oui-ouism* and of cultural *beni-oui-ouism*. It is no longer true that the promotion of values passes through the screen of the West. It is not true that we must constantly trail behind, follow, depend on someone or other. All the colonial countries that are waging the struggle today must know that the polit-ical independence that they will wring from the enemy in exchange for the maintenance of an economic dependency is only a snare and a delusion, that the second phase of total liberation is necessary because required by the popular masses, that this second phase, because it is a capital one, is bound to be hard and waged with iron determination, that, finally, at that stage, it will be necessary to take the world strategy of coalition into account, for the West simultaneously faces a double problem: the communist danger and the coming into being of a third neutral coalition, represented essentially by the underdeveloped countries.

The future of every man today has a relation of close dependency on the rest of the universe. That is why the colonial peoples must redouble their vigilance and their vigor. A new humanism can be achieved only at this price. The wolves must no longer find isolated lambs to prey upon. Imperialism must be blocked in all its attempts to strengthen itself. The peoples demand this; the historic process requires it.

40 • Nkrumah on pan-Africanism as an answer to neocolonialism (1961)

In 1957, Kwame Nkrumah had been the first African politician to lead his country to independence and freedom from colonialism. However, four years later, as he argued in his 1961 book, I Speak of Freedom: A Statement of African Ideology, *independence did not come unencumbered by continuing links to the West. Though Africa as a continent was rich in minerals and agricultural products, most of its people lived in poverty, producing goods for sale to the West at prices usually too low to sustain local development. Though the United States provided in many ways a model of democracy, Cold War politics meant that it, like the former colonial powers, intervened in African politics (though through its aid policies rather than the military means still adopted on occasion by the French).*

Nkrumah believed that the solution to these economic and political problems lay in African unity—in a practical realization of the pan-African ideals to which he had always held. Such ideals engendered considerable opposition within Ghana and from the outside world. He survived several assassination attempts and was routinely condemned by the West, especially the United States, for appearing to be too close to the camp of the Soviet Union. Becoming increasingly withdrawn while pursuing a cult of the personality in which his image appeared in public places throughout Ghana, he was overthrown in February 1966 by a coup led by members of the armed forces. The following document reprints in full the preface to I Speak of Freedom.[2]

The movement for independence in Africa which gained momentum after the Second World War has spread like a prairie fire throughout the length and breadth of Africa. The clear, ringing call for freedom which the eight independent states of Africa sounded in Accra in April 1958, followed by the All-African People's Conference in December of that year, stirred up the demand for independence from Conakry to Mogadishu, from Fort Lamy to Leopoldville. The "wind of change" has become a raging hurricane, sweeping away the old colonialist Africa. The year 1960 was Africa's year. In that year alone, seventeen African States emerged as proud and independent sovereign nations. Now the ultimate freedom of the whole of Africa can no more be in doubt.

2. Kwame Nkrumah, *I Speak of Freedom: A Statement of African Ideology* (New York: Praeger, 1961), ix–xii.

FIGURE 19 Kwame Nkrumah (second from right), the first president of Ghana, greets African American scholar W. E. B. Du Bois (second from left) at the World Peace Conference in Accra, Ghana, in 1962. Du Bois was one of the first leaders to advocate a pan-Africanist approach to the liberation of blacks everywhere, an ideology that Nkrumah championed across the continent in the 1950s and 1960s. Du Bois left the United States in 1963 to become a citizen of Ghana. AP Photo.

For centuries, Europeans dominated the African continent. The white man arrogated to himself the right to rule and to be obeyed by the non-white; his mission, he claimed was to "civilise" Africa. Under this cloak, the Europeans robbed the continent of vast riches and inflicted unimaginable suffering on the African people.

All this makes a sad story, but now we must be prepared to bury the past with its unpleasant memories and look to the future. All we ask of the former colonial powers is their goodwill and co-operation to remedy past mistakes and injustices and to grant independence to the colonies in Africa.

The new African nations from the very nature of things cannot but be economically weak at the early stages of nationhood as compared with the older and long established nations of the world. The long dependence on European and American financial and technical expertise has prevented the growth of local capital and the requisite technical knowledge to develop their resources. They need economic help, but in seeking outside aid they lay themselves open to a grave new danger which not merely threatens but could even destroy their hard-won freedom.

It is unreasonable to suppose that any foreign power, affluent enough to give aid to an African state, would not expect some measure of consideration or favour from the state receiving the aid. History has shown how one colonial empire in liquidation can easily be replaced by another, more insidious, because it is a disguised form of colonialism. The fate of those territories in Europe and North Africa which once formed the Turkish Empire is a warning to Africa today. It would be a tragedy if the initial weakness of the emergent African nations should lead to a new foreign domination of Africa brought about by economic forces.

It may be argued that the existence of the United Nations Organisation offers a guarantee for the independence and the territorial integrity of all states, whether big or small. In actual fact, however, the UN is just as reliable an instrument for world order and peace as the Great Powers are prepared to allow it to be. The present division of the world into rival blocs, and the dictates of power politics, offer little hope that this international body will ever become an effective instrument for world peace. Recent events in the Congo have not helped to foster confidence in the UN in the face of Great Power interests. Patrice Lumumba, democratically elected Prime Minister of the Congo Republic, who himself invited the UN to the Congo, was murdered along with two of his Ministers because the UN failed in its mission to maintain law and order.

It is clear that we must find an African solution to our problems, and that this can only be found in African unity. Divided we are weak; united, Africa could become one of the greatest forces for good in the world. Although most Africans are poor, our continent is potentially extremely rich. Our mineral resources, which are being exploited with foreign capital only to enrich foreign investors, range from gold and diamonds to uranium and petroleum. Our forests contain some of the finest woods to be grown anywhere. Our cash crops include cocoa, coffee, rubber, tobacco and cotton. As for power, which is an important factor in any economic development, Africa contains over 40% of the total potential water power of the world, as compared with about 10% in Europe and 13% in North America. Yet so far, less than 1% has been developed. This is one of the reasons why we have in Africa the paradox of poverty in the midst of plenty, and scarcity in the midst of abundance.

Never before have a people had within their grasp so great an opportunity for developing a continent endowed with so much wealth. Individually, the independent states of Africa, some of them potentially rich, others poor, can do little for their people. Together, by mutual help, they can achieve much. But the economic development of the continent must be planned and pursued as a whole. A loose confederation designed only for economic co-operation would not provide the necessary unity of purpose. Only a strong political union can bring about full and effective development of our natural resources for the benefit of our people.

The political situation in Africa today is heartening and at the same time disturbing. It is heartening to see so many new flags hoisted in place of the old; it is disturbing to see so many countries of varying sizes and at different levels of development, weak and, in some cases, almost helpless. If this terrible state of fragmentation is allowed to continue it may well be disastrous for us all.

There are at present some 28 states in Africa, excluding the Union of South Africa, and those countries not yet free. No less than nine of these states have a population of less than three million. Can we seriously believe that the colonial powers meant these countries to be independent, viable states? The example of South America, which has as much wealth, if not more than North America, and yet remains weak and dependent on outside interests, is one which every African would do well to study.

Critics of African unity often refer to the wide differences in culture, language and ideas in various parts of Africa. This is true, but the essential fact remains that we are all Africans, and have a common interest in the independence of Africa. The difficulties presented by questions of language, culture and different political systems are not insuperable. If the need for political union is agreed by us all, then the will to create it is born; and where there's a will there's a way.

The present leaders of Africa have already shown a remarkable willingness to consult and seek advice among themselves. Africans have, indeed, begun to think continentally. They realise that they have much in common, both in their past history, in their present problems and in their future hopes. To suggest that the time is not yet ripe for considering a political union of Africa is to evade the facts and ignore realities in Africa today. The greatest contribution that Africa can make to the peace of the world is to avoid all the dangers inherent in disunity, by creating a political union which will also by its success, stand as an example to a divided world. A union of African states will project more effectively the African personality. It will command respect from a world that has regard only for size and influence. The scant attention paid to African opposition to the French atomic tests in the Sahara, and the ignominious spectacle of the UN in the Congo quibbling about constitutional niceties while the Republic was tottering into anarchy, are evidence of the callous disregard of African Independence by the Great Powers.

We have to prove that greatness is not to be measured in stock piles of atom bombs. I believe strongly and sincerely that with the deep-rooted wisdom and dignity, the innate respect for human lives, the intense humanity that is our heritage, the African race, united under one federal government, will emerge not as just another world bloc to flaunt its wealth and strength, but as a Great Power whose greatness is indestructible because it is built not on fear, envy and suspicion, nor won at the expense of others, but founded on hope, trust, friendship and directed to the good of all mankind.

The emergence of such a mighty stabilising force in this strife-worn world should be regarded not as the shadowy dream of a visionary, but as a practical proposition, which the peoples of Africa can, and should, translate into reality. There is a tide in the affairs of every people when the moment strikes for political action. Such was the moment in the history of the United States of America when the Founding Fathers saw beyond the petty wranglings of the separate states and created a Union. This is our chance. We must act now. Tomorrow may be too late and the opportunity will have passed, and with it the hope of free Africa's survival.

41 • Julius Nyerere argues for African democracy, self-reliance, and socialism (1967)

While Kwame Nkrumah was the most prominent spokesman for pan-Africanism in the early 1960s, Julius Nyerere (1922–99), who in 1961 became the first prime minister of Tanganyika (and in 1964 the first president of Tanzania when Tanganyika joined with Zanzibar to form a republic), articulated a vision of a socialist Africa, one that did not follow foreign models but was distinctly indigenous, in which all commercial enterprises would be nationalized and active steps taken by the state to reduce inequalities of income between the poor and the rest of society. Tanzania, he argued, could be self-reliant economically, should develop a special form of African socialism rather than borrow foreign models, and was inherently democratic. In the following selections, Nyerere argues that African democracy could flourish without an "official opposition" (as the West constantly demanded in its evaluation of whether democracy had been achieved in Africa). Africa, he contended, did not have to follow Western models because Africans were, within their small-scale village communities, traditionally—and indeed naturally—democratic. The second selection recounts Nyerere's own discussion of the significance of his Arusha declaration of February 5, 1967. The declaration was regarded by many at the time as a blueprint for the development of African independence under socialism. At a teach-in held at Dar es Salaam University College in August 1967, after explaining that Arusha was "a declaration of intent; no more than that," Nyerere goes on to describe in plain language how he believed the intentions of the declaration could be achieved.[3]

A. The African and democracy

By the end of this present decade the whole of the African continent will have freed itself from colonial rule. The African nationalist claims that the end of colonialism will mean the establishment of democracy. His present rulers, who have themselves shown little respect for democracy, are equally convinced that the African is incapable of maintaining a democratic form of government. They prophesy that the end of colonialism will lead to the establishment of dictatorships all over the African continent. This debate over the ability or inability of the African to be a democrat rages whenever the words "Africa" and "Democracy" are mentioned together.

I have chosen to join the debate, in this article, not because I want to take sides but, because I believe the debaters have not bothered to define their terms. If they had done so, and particularly if they had cared to analyse the term "democracy," they would probably have discovered that their conceptions of democracy were totally different; that they were, in fact, wasting their time by arguing at cross purposes.

I think one of the first things one should beware of, in thinking of "democracy," is the tendency to confuse one's own personal picture of it—a picture which, if examined, will usually be found to include the "machinery" and symbols of democracy peculiar to the society with which one happens to be familiar—with democracy itself.

More than one attempt has been made to define democracy; probably the best, and certainly the most widely quoted, is that of Abraham Lincoln: "Government of the People, by the People, for the People." But I think the easiest way to eliminate the inessentials is to start by ignoring all such definitions and simply remember that the word means no more than "Government by the People." Now, if the ruling of a country is to be in the hands of the people of the country, the people must have some means of making their voice heard. It is obvious that not all of them can take a personal part in the actual legislation and policy-making,

3. A, Julius Nyerere, "The African and Democracy," in James Duffy and Robert A. Manners, eds., *Africa Speaks* (Princeton: Van Nostrand, 1961), 28–34; B, Mwalimu Julius K. Nyerere, "The Arusha Declaration Teach-in" (Dar es Salaam: Information Services; n.d. [1967]), 4–11.

FIGURE 20   President John F. Kennedy welcomes Julius Nyerere to the White House in 1961. Nyerere was the first prime minister of independent Tanganyika (later called Tanzania) and later served as its first president from 1964 to 1985. He promoted a variant of socialist agrarian policies that he called "Ujamaa," or "familyhood" in Swahili. Throughout the Cold War, Nyerere maintained a strictly neutral foreign policy for Tanzania, and although he was never able to dramatically improve Tanzania's economic situation, he is widely revered as one of the continent's ablest leaders. AP Photo.

so it is necessary for them to choose from among themselves a certain number of individuals who will "represent" them, and who will act as their spokesmen within the government. This may seem so elementary as to need no such elaborate explanation as I have given it here; but is it? If it is, why do so many people claim that "Africans cannot maintain democratic government in their own countries once they become independent"? And why do they always explain their doubts by saying that "Of course no African government will tolerate an Opposition"?

I do not think anybody, at this stage of our history, can possibly have any valid reason for claiming that the existence of an Opposition is impossible in an independent African state; but, even supposing this were true, where did the idea of an organization opposition as an essential part of democratic government come from? If one starts, as I have suggested, from the purely etymological definition of democracy it becomes clear that this idea of "for" and "against," this obsession with "Government" balanced by "Official Opposition," is in fact something which, though it *may* exist in a democracy, or *may not* exist in a democracy, is not essential to it, although it happens to have become so familiar to the Western world that its absence immediately raises the cry "Dictatorship."

To the Ancient Greeks, "democracy" meant simply government by discussion. The people discussed, and the result was a "people's government." But not all the people assembled for these discussions, as the textbooks tell us; those who took part in them were "equals" and this excluded the women and the slaves.

The two factors of democracy which I want to bring out here are "discussion" and "equality." Both are essential to it, and both contain a third element, "freedom." There can be no true discussion without freedom, and "equals" must be equal in freedom, without which there is no equality. A small village in which the villagers are equals who make their own laws and conduct their own affairs by free discussion is the nearest thing to pure democracy. That is why the small Greek state (if one excludes the women and slaves) is so often pointed out to us as "democracy par excellence."

These three, then, I consider to be essential to democratic government: discussion, equality, and freedom—the last being implied by the other two. Those who doubt the African's ability to establish a democratic society cannot seriously be doubting the African's ability to "discuss." That is the one thing which is as African as the tropical sun. Neither can they be doubting the African's sense of equality, for aristocracy is something foreign to Africa. Even where there is a fairly distinct African aristocracy-by-birth, it can be traced historically to sources outside this continent. Traditionally the African knows no "class." I doubt if there is a word in any African language which is equivalent to "class" or "caste"; not even in those few societies where foreign infiltration has left behind some form of aristocracy is there such a word in the local languages. These aristocrats-by-birth are usually referred to as "the great" or "the clever ones." In my own country, the only two tribes which have a distinct aristocracy are the Bahaya in Buboka, and the Baha in the Buha districts. In both areas the "aristocrats" are historically foreigners, and they belong to the same stock.

The traditional African society, whether it had a chief or not and many, like my own, did not, was a society of equals and it conducted its business through discussion. Recently I was reading a delightful little book on Nyasaland by Mr. Clutton-Brock; in one passage he describes the life of traditional Nyasa, and when he comes to the Elders he uses a very significant phrase: "They talk till they agree."

"They talk till they agree." That gives you the very essence of traditional African democracy. It is rather a clumsy way of conducting affairs, especially in a world as impatient for results as this of the twentieth century, but discussion is one essential factor of any democracy; and the African is expert at it.

If democracy, then, is a form of government freely established by the people themselves; and if its essentials are free discussion and equality, there is nothing in traditional African society which unfits the African for it. On the contrary, there is everything in his tradition which fits the African to be just what he claims he is, a natural democrat.

It was possible for the ancient Greeks to boast of "democracy" when more than half the population had no say at all in the conduct of the affairs of the State. It was possible for the framers of the Declaration of Independence to talk about "the inalienable rights of Man" although they believed in exceptions; it was possible for Abraham Lincoln to bequeath to us a perfect definition of democracy although he spoke in a slave-owning society; it was possible for my friends the British to brag about "democracy" and still build a great Empire for the glory of the Britons.

These people were not hypocrites. They believed in democracy. It was "government by discussion" which they advocated, and it was discussion by equals; but they lived in a world which excluded masses of human beings from its idea of "equality" and felt few scruples in doing so. Today, in the twentieth century, this is impossible. Today the Hungarys, the Little Rocks, the Tibets, the Nyasalands, and the Bantustans must be explained away somehow. They are embarrassing in this century of the Universal Declaration of Human Rights. Man, the ordinary man and woman in the street or in the "bush," has never had such a high regard for himself; and the demi-gods who try to treat him as their inferior are conscious of his power—this power frightens them, and they are forced to try to explain away their crimes. Today the "people," whose right it is to govern themselves, cannot exclude any sane, law-abiding adult person.

There is no continent which has taken up the fight for the dignity of the common man more vigorously than Africa. In other countries men may shout "One Man, One Vote" with their tongues in their cheeks; in Africa the nationalist leaders believe in it as a fundamental principle, and the masses they lead would accept nothing less. "Equal Pay for Equal Work" is a catch-phrase in many countries which practise nothing of the kind; in Africa the leaders believe sincerely in the basic justice of this, and again their followers expect nothing less. In many countries which claim to be democracies the leaders come from an aristocracy either of wealth or of birth; in Africa they are of the common people, for if ever there was a continent where no real aristocracy has been built, whether of birth or of wealth, that continent is Africa. Tradition has failed to create it, and the spirit of the twentieth century will make it almost impossible for it to grow now. Indeed, it is one way of discovering the widely different conceptions we may have of "democracy" to listen to those people who would like to build a middle class in Africa "as a safeguard for Democracy!" To them, democracy is government by the middle class, albeit the masses may play their part in electing that government.

Add, then, to the African tradition her lack of an aristocracy and the presence of a moral concept of human dignity on which she is waging her struggle for independence, and place these in the setting of this century of the Declaration of Human Rights, and it becomes difficult to see how anybody can seriously doubt the African's fitness for democracy.

I referred earlier in this article to the "machinery" and the symbols of democratic government. Many of the critics of African democracy are to be found in countries like Britain or the United States of America. These critics, when they challenge our ability to maintain a democratic form of government, really have in mind not democracy but the particular form it has taken in their own countries, the two-party system, and the debate conducted between the Government party and the opposition party within the parliament buildings. In effect, they are saying: "Can you imagine an African Parliament with at least two political parties holding a free debate, one party being 'for' and one 'against' the motion?"

Ghana and Nigeria would be understandably annoyed with me if I were to answer such critics by saying that I *can* "imagine" such countries; for they exist, and they are not figments of my "imagination."

But let us suppose they did not exist. To the Anglo-Saxon in particular, or to countries with an Anglo-Saxon tradition, the two-party system has become the very essence of democracy. It is no use telling an Anglo-Saxon that when a village of a hundred people have sat and talked together until they agreed where a well should be dug they have practiced democracy.

The Anglo-Saxon will want to know whether the talking was properly organized. He will want to know whether there was an organized group "for" the motion, and an equally well organized group "against" the motion. He will also want to know whether, in the next debate, the same group will be "for" and the same group "against" the next motion. In other words, he will want to know whether the opposition was organized and therefore *automatic,* or whether it was spontaneous and therefore *free.* Only if it was automatic will he concede that it was democracy!

In spite of its existence in Ghana and Nigeria, however, I must say that I also have my own doubts about the suitability for Africa of the Anglo-Saxon form of democracy. Let me explain:

In his own traditional society the African has always been a free individual, very much a member of his community, but seeing no conflict between his own interests and those of his community. This is because the structure of his society was, in fact, a direct extension of the family. First you had the small family unit; this merged into a larger "blood" family which, in its turn, merged into the tribe. The affairs of the community, as I have shown, were conducted by free and equal discussion, but nevertheless the African's mental conception of "government" was personal—not institutional. When the word government was mentioned, the African thought of the chief; he did not, as does the Briton, think of a grand building in which a debate was taking place.

In colonial Africa this "personal" conception of government was unchanged, except that the average person hearing government mentioned now thought of the District Commissioner, the Provincial Commissioner, or the Governor.

When, later, the idea of government as an institution began to take hold of some African "agitators" such as myself, who had been reading Abraham Lincoln and John Stuart Mill, and we began demanding institutional government for our own countries, it was the very people who had now come to symbolize "Government" in their persons who resisted our demands—the District Commissioners, the Provincial Commissioners, and the Governors. Not until the eleventh hour did they give way; and free elections have taken place in most of our countries almost on the eve of independence.

The new nations of the African continent are emerging today as the result of their struggle for independence. This struggle for freedom from foreign domination is a patriotic one which necessarily leaves no room for difference. It unites all elements in the country so that, not only in Africa but in any other part of the world facing a similar challenge, these countries are led by a nationalist movement rather than by a political party or parties. The same nationalist movement, having united the people and led them to independence, must inevitably form the first government of the new state; it could hardly be expected that a united country should halt in mid-stream and voluntarily divide itself into opposing political groups just for the sake of conforming to what I have called the "Anglo-Saxon form of democracy" at the moment of independence. Indeed, why should it? Surely, if a government is freely elected by the people, there can be nothing undemocratic about it simply because nearly all the people rather than merely a section of them have chosen to vote it into power.

In these circumstances, it would be surprising if the pattern of democracy in Africa were to take—at any rate for the first few years—the shape familiar to Anglo-Saxon countries. It would be illogical to expect it to; but it is unjust to African democrats to assume, therefore, that their own pattern of democratic government is less dedicated to the preservation of the rights and freedom of the individual, an assumption too often made by the very people who have delayed the establishment of democratic institutions on this continent.

I have already suggested that the nearest thing to pure democracy would be a self-governing village in which all affairs were conducted by free discussion. But I have also said that the government of a nation must necessarily be government by "representation"; therefore there must be elections and discussion-houses or parliaments. As a matter of fact, in Africa the actual parliament buildings are necessary rather for reasons of prestige than for protection against the weather. (Our weather is quite predictable!)

The two essentials for "representative" democracy are the freedom of the individual, and the regular opportunity for him to join with his fellows in replacing, or reinstating, the government of his country by means of the ballot-box and without recourse to assassination. An organized opposition is *not* an essential element, although a society which has no room and no time for the harmless eccentric can hardly be called "democratic." Where you have those two essentials, and the affairs of the country are conducted by free discussion, you have democracy. An organized opposition may arise, or it may not; but whether it does or it does not depends entirely upon the choice of the people themselves and makes little difference to free discussion and equality in freedom.

B. "The Arusha Declaration Teach-in," August 5, 1967

MEANING OF SELF-RELIANCE

What, then, is the meaning of self-reliance, and what are its implications for our future policies? First and foremost, it means that for our development we have to depend upon ourselves and our own resources. These resources are land, and people. Certainly we have a few factories, we have a small diamond mine, and so on. But it is important to realise that when measured in 1960 prices out of a gross domestic product estimated at Shs. 4,646 million in 1966, some Shs. 2,669 million—that is, more than 57%—was the direct result of agricultural activities. Only Shs. 321 million was the combined result of mining and manufacturing; that is to say that all the mining and manufacturing of Tanzania produced last year less than 7% of the gross domestic product.

The only thing we certainly do not have is money searching for investment opportunities. The per capita income in terms of 1966 prices, was about Shs. 525/- last year. That does not allow very much to be withdrawn from current consumption and invested in development. Indeed, we did very well last year to find Shs. 135 million (that is, about Shs. 14/- per person) from internal resources for development.

But to provide one job in a highly mechanised industry can cost Shs. 40,000/- or more. To build the oil refinery cost more than Shs. 110 million. To build a modern steel mill would cost rather more than that.

AGRICULTURE MAIN STAY

On the other hand, it is possible to double the output of cotton on a particular acre by spending Shs. 130/- on fertiliser and insecticide; it is possible to double a farmer's acreage under crops by the provision of ox-plough at a cost of Shs. 250/- or less, and so on. In other words, whereas it is possible to find the sort of investment capital which can bring great increases in agricultural output from our present resources, it is not possible for us to envisage establishing heavy industries, or even very much in the way of light industries, in the near future.

To be realistic, therefore, we must stop dreaming of developing Tanzania through the establishment of large, modern industries. For such things we have neither the money nor the skilled man-power required to make them efficient and economic. We would even be making a mistake if we think in terms of covering Tanzania with mechanised farms, using tractors and combine-harvesters.

Once again, we have neither the money, nor the skilled man-power, nor in this case the social organisation which could make such investment possible and economic. This is not to say that there will be no new modern industries and no mechanised farms. But they will be the exception, not the rule, and they will be entered upon to meet particular problems. They are not the answer to the basic development needs of Tanzania.

FUTURE IN AGRICULTURE

This is what the Arusha Declaration makes clear in both economic and social terms. Our future lies in the development of our agriculture, and in the development of our rural areas. But because we are seeking to grow from our own roots and to preserve that which is valuable in our traditional past, we have also to stop thinking in terms of massive agricultural mechanisation and the proletarianisation of our rural population.

We have, instead, to think in terms of development through the improvement of the tools we now use, and through the growth of co-operative systems of production. Instead of aiming at large farms using tractors and other modern equipment and employing agricultural labourers, we should be aiming at having ox-ploughs all over the country.

The jembe will have to be eliminated by the ox-plough before the latter can be eliminated by the tractor. We cannot hope to eliminate the jembe by the tractor. Instead of thinking about providing each farmer with his own lorry, we should consider the usefulness of oxen-drawn carts, which could be made within the country and which are appropriate both to our roads and to the loads which each farmer is likely to have.

Instead of the aerial spreading of crops with insecticide, we should use hand-operated pumps, and so on. In other words, we have to think in terms of what is available, or can be made available, at comparatively small cost, and which can be operated by the people. By moving into the future along this path, we can avoid massive social disruption and human suffering.

SMALL INDUSTRIES

At the same time we can develop small industries and service stations in the rural areas where the people live, and thus help to diversify the rural economy. By this method we can achieve a widespread increase in the general level of people's income, instead of concentrating any economic improvement in the hands of a few people.

Such capital as we do have will make the widest possible impact by being invested in fertilisers, in credit for better breeding stock, in improved instruments of production, and other similar things. These, although small in themselves, can bring a great proportionate increase in the farmers' income.

This does not mean that there will be no new investment in towns, or that there will be no new factories. When you have large numbers of people living together, certain public services are essential for public health and security reasons. It would be absurd to pretend that we can forget the towns, which are in any case often a service centre for the surrounding rural areas.

FACTORY SITES

Factories which serve the whole country also have to be sited in places which are convenient for transport and communications. For example, if we had put the Friendship Textile Mill in a rural area, we would have had to invest in special road, building etc. for it to be of any use, and in any case the number of its workers would soon mean that a new town had grown up in that place.

But even when we are building factories which serve the whole nation, we have to consider whether it is necessary for us to use the most modern machinery which exists in the world. We have to consider whether some older equipment which demands more labour, but labour which is less highly skilled, is not better suited to our needs, as well as being more within our capacity to build.

There are, however, two respects in which our call for self-reliance has been widely misunderstood or deliberately misinterpreted. The doctrine of self-reliance does not imply isolationism, either politically or economically. It means that we shall depend on ourselves, not on others.

TRADE WITH OTHERS

But this is not the same thing as saying we shall not trade with other people or co-operate with them when it is to mutual benefit. Obviously we shall do so. We shall have to continue to sell enough of our goods abroad to pay for the things we have to acquire. Up to now Tanzania has always done this; indeed, we have had a surplus of our balance of payment for many years. But the things we sell are the products of our agriculture, and this is likely to continue to be the case despite the problem of commodity prices in the world.

The things we import will increasingly have to be the things which are essential for our development, and which we cannot produce ourselves. Up to now we have been importing many things which a little effort would enable us to provide for ourselves, such as food, as well as luxury items which simply arouse desires among our people which could never be satisfied for more than a tiny minority.

Self-reliance, in other words, is unlikely to reduce our participation in international trade, but it should over time, change its character to some extent. We should be exporting commodities after at least some preliminary processing, and we should be importing the things which we cannot produce and which are necessary for the development and the welfare of our whole people.

TANZANIA WANTS CAPITAL ASSISTANCE

The other thing which is necessary to understand about self-reliance is that Tanzania has not said it does not want international assistance in its development. We shall continue to seek capital from abroad for particular projects or as a contribution to general development. It is clear, for example, that if we are to achieve our ambition of getting a railway which links

Tanzania and Zambia, we shall have to obtain most of the capital and the technical skill from overseas.

Overseas capital will also be welcome for any project where it can make our own efforts more effective—where it acts as a catalyst for Tanzanian activity. It is for this reason that the Government has made it clear that we shall welcome outside participation—whether private or Government—in establishment of many different kinds of factories, especially those which produce consumption goods or process our crops and raw materials.

Capital assistance for education of all kinds is another of the many fields in which outside assistance can be valuable, provided it is linked to our capacity to meet the recurrent costs. The important thing, however, is that we in Tanzania should not adopt an attitude that nothing can be done until someone else agrees to give us money.

There are many things we can do by ourselves, and we must plan to do them. There are other things which can become easier if we get assistance, but these we should reckon on doing the hard way, by ourselves, only being thankful if assistance is forthcoming.

EXPATRIATES AS WELL

But it is not only capital which we must welcome from outside, it is also men. Few things make me more angry than a refusal to accept and to work with people from other countries whose participation can make all the difference between our plans succeeding or failing. It is not being self-reliant to refuse to carry out the directions of a foreign engineer, a foreign doctor, or a foreign manager; it is just being stupid. It is absolutely vital that Tanzanians should determine policy; but if the implementation of a particular policy requires someone with good educational qualifications or long experience, it is not very sensible to allow that policy to fail through pride.

We must look at this question of employing expatriates scientifically and without prejudice; we must assess the interests of our development as a whole, not the interests of a particular person who feels that he would like the high post concerned but is neither ready for it nor prepared to go on learning from someone else.

NO FALSE PRIDE IN THIS MATTER

Let us take note of the fact that the developed countries have no false pride in this matter. Western Europe and North America recruit trained people from countries like India and Pakistan, and West European countries complain bitterly about what they call the "brain drain" caused by the richer United States offering high incomes to educated and skilled people.

It has been alleged that the United States has saved itself billions of dollars by attracting workers on whose education it has not spent one cent. Yet while wealthy and developed countries adopt this kind of attitude, we in Tanzania appear to rejoice when we lose a trained person to Europe or North America.

We rejoice on the grounds that it provides us with an opportunity for Africanisation, or for self-reliance! Anyone would think that we have a problem of unemployed experts. It is time that we outgrew this childishness; and we must do so quickly if we intend to tackle this problem of modern development really seriously.

SOCIALISM

What, then, of socialism—the other aspect of the Arusha Declaration? First, it is important to be clear that nationalisation of existing industries and commercial undertakings is only a very small part of the socialism which we have adopted. The important thing for us is the extent to which we succeed in preventing the exploitation of one man by another and in spreading the concept of working together co-operatively for the common good instead of competitively for individual private gain. And the truth is that our economy is now so under-developed that it is in growth that we shall succeed or fail in these things.

The nationalisation of the banks, of insurance, and of the few industries affected, was important; but much more important is whether we succeed in expanding our economy without expanding the opportunities and the incentives for human exploitation.

Once again this really means that socialism has to spread in the rural areas where our people live. In this we have an advantage over many other countries, just because of our lack of development. Up to now exploitation in agriculture is very limited; the greater part of our farming is still individual peasant farming, or family farming. But although this is not capital-ist, neither is it very efficient or productive in comparison with what it could be.

Indeed, it is true that where people work together in groups—and that is mostly in those restricted sectors of capitalist farming—there is often a greater output per worker and per acre. Our objective must be to develop in such a manner as to ensure that the advantages of modern knowledge and modern methods are achieved, but without the spread of capitalism.

HUMAN EQUALITY—THE ESSENCE OF SOCIALISM

Socialism, however, is not simply a matter of methods of production. They are part of it but not all of it. The essence of socialism is the practical acceptance of human equality. That is to say, man's equal rights to a decent life before any individual has a surplus above his needs; his equal right to participate in Government; and his equal responsibility to work and con-tribute to the society to the limit of his ability.

In Tanzania this means that we must safeguard and strengthen our democratic proce-dures; we must get to the position where every citizen plays an active and direct role in the government of his local community, at the same time as he plays a full role in the government of his own country. It also means that we have to correct the glaring income differentials which we inherited from colonialism, and ensure that the international imbalance between the wages of factory and service workers on the one hand, and of agricultural workers on the other, is not reproduced within our own nation. We have, in other words, to ensure that every person gets a return commensurate with the contribution he makes to the society.

But at the same time we have to make dignified provision for those whose age or disabil-ity prevents them from playing a full role in the economy. We have also to spread—although it can only be done gradually—equality of opportunity for all citizens, until every person is able to make the kind of contribution to our needs which is most within his capacity and his desires. But, most of all, we have to reactivate the philosophy of co-operation in production and sharing in distribution which was an essential part of traditional African society.

42 • The African National Congress (ANC) adopts a policy of violence (1961)

After the Sharpeville massacre of March 21, 1960, when members of the South African police shot dead (mostly in the back) sixty-nine Pan-Africanist Congress (PAC) members demonstrating peacefully against the pass laws, Hendrik Verwoerd's government declared both the PAC and the ANC illegal organizations and sentenced their leaders to terms of imprisonment (Robert Sobukwe of the PAC received three years of hard labor, later extended administratively to another nine years; Albert Luthuli, president of the ANC, went to prison for a year and was banned from speaking in public until his death). Nelson Mandela went underground and formed a new militant wing of the ANC, Umkhonto we Sizwe (Spear of the Nation). Having fought against segregation and apartheid by nonviolent means ever since its formation in 1912, the ANC believed that it had been forced into a corner. It adopted a policy of armed struggle and pursued this policy throughout the 1960s, 1970s, and 1980s. In a pamphlet issued on December 16, 1961 (the same day Verwoerd had chosen three years earlier to make his speech in defense of white supremacy), Umkhonto we Sizwe announced that it was beginning a campaign of sabotage directed at strategically significant targets (police stations, prisons, railways, power transmission lines, etc.).[4]

Units of Umkhonto we Sizwe today carried out planned attacks against Government installations, particularly those connected with the policy of apartheid and race discrimination.

Umkhonto we Sizwe is a new, independent body, formed by Africans. It includes in its ranks South Africans of all races. It is not connected in any way with a so-called "Committee for National Liberation" whose existence has been announced in the press. Umkhonto we Sizwe will carry on the struggle for freedom and democracy by new methods, which are necessary to complement the actions of the established national liberation organizations. Umkhonto we Sizwe fully supports the national liberation movement, and our members, jointly and individually, place themselves under the overall political guidance of that movement.

It is, however, well known that the main national liberation organizations in this country have consistently followed a policy of non-violence. They have conducted themselves peaceably at all times, regardless of Government attacks and persecutions upon them, and despite all Government-inspired attempts to provoke them to violence. They have done so because the people prefer peaceful methods of change to achieve their aspirations without the suffering and bitterness of civil war. But the people's patience is not endless.

The time comes in the life of any nation when there remain only two choices: submit or fight. That time has now come to South Africa. We shall not submit and we have no choice but to hit back by all means within our power in defence of our people, our future and our freedom.

The Government has interpreted the peacefulness of the movement as weakness; the people's non-violent policies have been taken as a green light for Government violence. Refusal to resort to force has been interpreted by the Government as an invitation to use armed force against the people without any fear of reprisals. The methods of Umkhonto we Sizwe mark a break with that past.

We are striking out along a new road for the liberation of the people of this country. The Government policy of force, repression and violence will no longer be met with nonviolent resistance only! The choice is not ours; it has been made by the Nationalist Government which has rejected every peaceable demand by the people for rights and freedom and answered every such demand with force and yet more force! Twice in the past 18 months,

4. Http://www.anc.org.za/ancdocs/history/manifesto-mk.html.

FIGURE 21 African women demonstrate on the steps of the Johannesburg City Hall in August 1961 demanding the release of Nelson Mandela, who was appearing in court on a charge of incitement. The women, joined by Mandela's wife, Winnie, chanted "down with Verwoerd." AP Photo/Dennis Lee Royle.

FIGURE 22 Nelson Mandela in 1961, following the acquittal of more than 150 political activists accused of treason for protesting the government's apartheid policies. At this time, Mandela secretly began planning armed resistance to the government, a course of action that led to his imprisonment from 1964 to 1990 for sabotage. AP Photo.

FIGURE 23 South African prime minister Hendrik Verwoerd is rushed to an ambulance following a fatal stabbing in Parliament in 1966. Verwoerd's assassin, Dimitri Tsafendas, was a parliamentary messenger whose mixed racial heritage—born in Maputo, Mozambique, of a Greek father and a Mozambican mother—caused him endless problems in race-conscious South Africa. Tsafendas was incarcerated in a mental hospital until his death in 1999. Verwoerd is credited with implementing most of the apartheid legislation as minister of native affairs and later prime minister. His administration (1958–66) oversaw the Sharpeville massacre, the banning of all African political groups, and South Africa's withdrawal from the British Commonwealth and its establishment as a republic. Despite his fervent support of Afrikaner nationalism, Verwoerd was born in Holland and was not an Afrikaner himself. AP Photo.

virtual martial law has been imposed in order to beat down peaceful, non-violent strike action of the people in support of their rights. It is now preparing its forces—enlarging and rearming its armed forces and drawing white civilian population into commandos and pistol clubs—for full-scale military actions against the people. The Nationalist Government has chosen the course of force and massacre, now, deliberately, as it did at Sharpeville [March 21, 1960].

Umkhonto we Sizwe will be at the front line of the people's defence. It will be the fighting arm of the people against the Government and its policies of race oppression. It will be the striking force of the people for liberty, for rights and for their final liberation! Let the Government, its supporters who put it into power, and those whose passive toleration of reaction keeps it in power, take note of where the Nationalist Government is leading the country!

We of Umkhonto we Sizwe have always sought—as the liberation movement has sought—to achieve liberation, without bloodshed and civil clash. We do so still. We hope—even at this late hour—that our first actions will awaken everyone to a realization of the disastrous situation to which the Nationalist policy is leading. We hope that we will bring the Government and its supporters to their senses before it is too late, so that both Government and its policies can be changed before matters reach the desperate stage of civil war. We believe our actions to be a blow against the Nationalist preparations for civil war and military rule.

In these actions, we are working in the best interests of all the people of this country— black, brown and white—whose future happiness and well-being cannot be attained without the overthrow of the Nationalist Government, the abolition of white supremacy and the winning of liberty, democracy and full national rights and equality for all the people of this country.

We appeal for the support and encouragement of all those South Africans who seek the happiness and freedom of the people of this country.

Afrika Mayibuye!

Issued by command of Umkhonto we Sizwe.

43 • "The Civilized Man's Burden" (1963)

Unlike the other colonial powers in Africa, Portugal, ruled by the dictator António de Oliveira Salazar from 1932 until his death in 1968, saw no benefit for colonizer or colonized in ending its empire. Africans needed, according to Salazar, leadership and expertise in order to develop to their full capacity. It did not need to be white leadership and expertise, but it did have to be civilized, and while a few Africans met Salazar's measure of "civilized," it was not nearly enough to govern their own societies. Pursuing continent-wide unity as proposed by Kwame Nkrumah would, in Salazar's view, only lead to the domination of sub-Saharan Africa by the "Arab" north, while attempts to forge a distinctly African path as described by Nyerere would inevitably lead to "black racism." With most of Africa either independent or on the verge of becoming so, and with armed struggle beginning in South Africa, Salazar spoke in 1963 of the determination of the Portuguese to retain their empire, while stressing at the same time that Portuguese colonialism was unlike that of the other European powers in that it was a multiracial enterprise in which qualified Africans could work side by side with Europeans. In a line often adopted by supporters of continued colonial and/or white rule in the latter half of the twentieth century, Salazar argued that those who were demanding immediate independence in Portuguese territories were not true patriots but were really the pawns of outside provocateurs, especially of the Soviet Union.[5]

The Civilized Man's Burden

The aspirations of the African peoples do not differ from those of the majority of communities spread throughout the world, which even today yearn for liberation from the cycle of underdevelopment in which they find themselves. Their objectives thus coincide with the

---

5. Ronald H. Chilcote, *Emerging Nationalism in Portuguese Africa: Documents* (Stanford: Hoover Institution Press, 1972), 2–4.

problems of governance in their respective countries or territories. And, as is the case every-where, when such problems are not solved, or when the pace of their solution fails to attain the rhythm desired by the people, governments immediately are faced with a political crisis because doubts are cast upon the effectiveness of the institutions and the competence of the bureaucracy. This phenomenon is all the more frequent the lower the technical level of the particular community, and this level, in turn, derives essentially from the degree of auton-omous economic development that has been reached, since instruction and education are not to be extracted from the soil or plucked from trees, like fruit growing spontaneously. They are acquired by work. It seems, therefore, that there is no way out from the cycle of under-development other than through the toil of the peoples concerned, since programs of mass culture imposed by aliens and, offered as gifts to boot, will fail to overcome the material ob-stacles which such programs encounter and which prevent the attainment of spectacular results. If this notion is true—and I cannot see that anywhere on the globe or at any time in history it has been proved otherwise—it would seem that the criterion for African develop-ment ought not to ignore the need for entrusting the responsibilities of administration to those best qualified to assume them, and for ensuring the active support of a political sover-eignty whose interest is to foster the progress of all.

This, however, has not been the general opinion. Rather, has it been held that the solu-tion to the problems will be better and will be found if the responsibilities of government in all the African territories are transferred to the local inhabitants, the contention being that human societies completely fulfill themselves only when they become arbitrary mistresses of their own destinies. This theory has been given the name of self-determination, and the move-ment directed to its achievement has come to be regarded as a natural force described as "the Tide of History."

I do not propose to raise certain doubts, the first of which would be whether this doc-trine, in practice, has sufficiently taken into account what to our mind should have been its chief justification—that is, the welfare of the interested parties. Nor will I seek answers to cer-tain queries, such as who has been gaining most from the "wind of change," and whether the doctrine is at all times being applied; or whether, on the contrary, the international community has been apathetically witnessing flagrant derogations of its principle. I shall confine myself to stating our opinion.

Through a long tradition of association, we have come to know the virtues and the ca-pacities of some outstanding African tribes. Hence we do not doubt their leaders' being fit for command, which in the Portuguese case they share and have always shared during our com-mon history. But we do not consider—and experience is confirming our conviction—that these elites exist in sufficient numbers in all fields and at all levels. It is so in the administra-tion of government as well as in private enterprise, without which the official administration would be pointless. Now the aforementioned insufficiency prevents them from assuming en-tirely on their own the complex management of public affairs under modern conditions. This seems to be proved by the fact that, in certain lands, an experiment is being carried out which appears to us to militate against the real autonomy of the peoples concerned. Thus, while sovereign power is made over to local inhabitants, basic economic enterprises and initiatives remain—and this under the most favorable circumstances—in the hands of men who, be-cause of remaining nationals of the former colonial power, have now become aliens in the country in which they serve. We are inclined to think that, when things are stripped of their veils and reduced to their essentials, these new states run the risk of finding themselves in the throes of a subjection graver than that from which they claim to have emancipated themselves. On the other hand . . . we have been witnessing, and I fear we shall be witnessing with growing frequency, a process of retrogression in economic and social life and a return to certain practices which are incompatible with the desired prosperity and progress . . .

The independence of African nations has, in general, been based on two erroneous premises that will work to those nations' detriment: anti-white racism and the alleged unity of the peoples of that continent. This latter supposition will tend to subordinate the Negro to the Arab; black racism will tend to bring about the rejection of all that the more progressive white men had brought in capital, labor, and culture. It would be wiser to replace clear-cut segregation with the working together which we have considered to be indispensable. For this reason we hold that the economic, social, and political advancement of those territories will only be possible on a multiracial basis in which the responsibilities of leadership in all fields fall to the most qualified, irrespective of their color.

I know we are accused of trying, by taking this stand, to ensure domination by the white race in Africa, the basis for this accusation being the fact that our multiracialism has not yet been implemented widely enough in the distribution of responsibilities throughout the Portuguese provinces in Africa. It is true that we are still far from attaining the point at which we might be fully satisfied with our achievements. However, it cannot be denied that not only is the road we are following the surest, but also the progress of the various Portuguese territories tends to spread to the whole of their population and not merely to the many groups already benefitted. It is impossible to deny this progress, since what has been achieved can, in many instances, be favorably compared with that of other African countries. And if our critics are so convinced that such is not the case, it is difficult to understand why they did not accept the suggestion that a trip for the purpose of studying overseas in Portugal be undertaken by prominent foreign personalities, under the auspices of the United Nations. Unfortunately, harangues were preferred to a dispassionate study of the realities under debate—a project to which we gave our support.

A word about Angola. We are being subjected there to attacks which, at first, were presented as an uprising of people anxious not to continue integrated in the Portuguese nation. However, the enthusiasm of the liberators of Africa did not allow them, except for a short time, to hide their intervention in the recruitment, financing and training of the foreign persons who infiltrate into Angola from neighboring states. Today, therefore, it is no longer possible to claim that what is happening in Angola is a revolt of a more or less nationalistic character. In point of fact, a war is being conducted by several states against Portugal in one of Portugal's overseas territories. Under the circumstances, two things must be considered certain. The first is that in such aggression, it is not only the Portuguese who are being attacked: one of the aggressors' aims is to weaken the positions—and not only the strategic positions—of the entire Western world. The second is that those who attack us, those who support the aggressors, and those who assist them by their indifference are acting against the real interest of the tribes in Angola simply by delaying their peaceful self-improvement and by attempting to sow there the seed of racial antagonism, which did not exist among us and which is today, as I specified above, the principal obstacle to progress and well-being in the African continent.

44 • Eduardo Mondlane rejects Portuguese apologetics (1969)

Supporters of independence in the Portuguese colonies, such as Eduardo Mondlane in Mozambique, rejected Salazar's defense of colonialism as a fraud. How, he argued, could anyone take seriously the claim that the Portuguese would encourage democratic change and economic development in Africa when the country itself had been a dictatorship for most of the twentieth century (and a monarchy before that) and the poorest country in Europe to boot? Like Mandela and Umkhonto we Sizwe, Mondlane argues that with no opportunity given to Africans to express their views publicly without becoming victims of the Portuguese secret police (the dreaded PIDE—Polícia Internacional e de Defesa do Estado), the only option open was to use violence to overthrow the colonial regime.[6]

The need for armed struggle

Although determined to do everything in our power to try to gain independence by peaceful means, we were already convinced . . . that a war would be necessary. People more familiar with the policies of other colonial powers have accused us of resorting to violence without due cause. This is partly refuted by the fate met by every type of legal, democratic and reformist activity tried over the preceding forty years.

The character of the government in Portugal itself makes a peaceful solution inherently unlikely. Within Portugal the government has promoted neither sound economic growth nor social well-being, and has gained little international respect. The possession of colonies has helped to conceal these failures: the colonies contribute to the economy; they add to Portugal's consequence in the world, particularly the world of finance; they have provided a national myth of empire which helps discourage any grumbling by a fundamentally dissatisfied population. The government knows how ill it can afford to lose the colonies. For similar reasons it cannot afford to liberalize its control of them. The colonies contribute to the metropolitan economy only because labour is exploited and resources are not ploughed back into local development; the colonies ease the discontent of the Portuguese population only because immigration offers to the poor and uneducated a position of special privilege. Not least, since the fascist government has eliminated democracy within Portugal itself, it can scarcely allow a greater measure of freedom to the supposedly more backward people of its colonies.

Despite all this, attempts were made to use persuasion, encouraged by the acceptance elsewhere of the principle of self-determination. But such efforts were never rewarded with any kind of "dialogue." The only reaction to them was prison, censorship, and the strengthening of the PIDE, the secret police. The character of the PIDE is itself an important factor. For it has a strong tradition of violence—its officers were trained by the Gestapo—and it enjoys a considerable measure of autonomy, allowing it to act outside the control of the official law.

This is why political activity in Mozambique has called for the techniques of the "underground," for secrecy and exile. On the only recent occasion when an open approach was made, what happened is instructive. It was the incident . . . at Mueda in 1960, when some 500

6. Eduardo Mondlane, *The Struggle for Mozambique* (Harmondsworth: Penguin, 1969), 123–26.

Africans were killed. It had been planned as a peaceful demonstration and to some extent owed its origin to police provocation: the authorities knew that there was political agitation in the region, much of it clandestine, and they had given out that the governor would attend a public meeting on 16 June where he would grant independence to the Makonde people. The police thus brought the disaffection into the open and immediately killed or arrested as many as they could of those involved. They had hoped to remove the leaders, intimidate the population and set an example to other regions. But despite its ferocity, the action was only partially and temporarily successful. It eliminated some of the leaders, but others remained; while, far from being intimidated, the population became more determined than ever to resist.

Some of the exiles and those involved in clandestine opposition hoped at first that, even if Portugal was impervious to peaceful demands from the people of her colonies, she might listen to international organizations and the great nations of the world, if these would intervene on our behalf. Stemming from the Goan issue, some international pressure was brought to bear on Portugal during the fifties. But Portugal's only response was the legislation of the early sixties, which supposedly introduced reforms but made no concession to the principle of self-determination. Since then Portugal has ignored or rejected all appeals from other states or international bodies made on behalf of the people in her colonies. Besides this, not all the major states support us. Since 1961 most Western powers, including the United States, have not cooperated with United Nations resolutions urging Portugal to give the right of self-determination to the people of her non-self-governing territories.

By 1961 two conclusions were obvious. First, Portugal would not admit the principle of self-determination and independence, or allow for any extension of democracy under her own rule, although by then it was clear that her own "Portuguese" solutions to our oppressed condition, such as assimilation by multi-racial *colonatos,* multi-racial schools, local elections etc., had proved a meaningless fraud. Secondly, moderate political action such as strikes, demonstrations and petitions, would result only in the destruction of those who took part in them. We were, therefore, left with these alternatives: to continue indefinitely living under a repressive imperial rule, or to find a means of using force against Portugal which would be effective enough to hurt Portugal without resulting in our own ruin.

This was why, to FRELIMO [Frente de Libertação de Moçambique] leaders, armed action appeared to be the only method. Indeed, the absence of any opposition to the use of force was one of the factors accounting for the very short period which elapsed between the formation of FRELIMO in 1962 and the beginning of the armed struggle on 25 September 1964.

45 • Black consciousness (1971)

With black opposition parties banned in South Africa (the apartheid regime viewed all Africans as aliens who were permitted residence in South Africa only so long as their services were needed as migrant workers) and Umkhonto we Sizwe crushed in the mid-1960s by police and military action, young African opponents of the apartheid regime looked back to the Africanist ideas of Anton Lembede, to the arguments of Kwame Nkrumah for "positive action," and to the developing black power movement in the United States to develop new ways of critiquing racism in South Africa. The founder of the black South African Students' Organization (SASO), Steve Biko (1946–77), argued that apartheid persisted in part because people allowed themselves to be colonized and that they should as a first step to revolution break the psychological bonds that bound them into subservience. Moreover, Biko argued, black consciousness should be a way of life, not just a political expedient. Through the development of a new self-awareness and pride and the adoption of peaceful means of organization, Africans would be able to bring about the end of apartheid. It did not mean hatred of whites. Looked upon favorably at first by the Afrikaner rulers of South Africa because his ideas seemed to support their aim of complete racial separation, Biko soon became viewed as a serious threat because of the popularity of his ideas among young people. Though Biko did argue for peaceful change, he also envisaged a future South Africa ruled by a black government. Proponents of white supremacy feared such a future, and in October 1977, a year after the Soweto uprising, white police officers killed Biko while he was in their custody. The following extract is from a paper that Biko presented to a meeting in Edendale, South Africa, in 1971.[7]

What are we talking about?

Here we are primarily concerned with SASO and its work. We talk glibly of "Black Consciousness" and yet we show that we hardly understand what we are talking about. In this regard it is essential for us to realise a few basic facts about "Black Consciousness."

"Black Consciousness" is essentially a slogan directing us away from the traditional political big talk to a new approach. This is an inward-looking movement calculated to make us look at ourselves and see ourselves, not in terms of what we have been taught through the absolute values of white society, but with new eyes. It is a call upon us to see the innate value in us, in our institutions, in our traditional outlook to life and in our own worth as people. The call of "Black Consciousness" is by no means a slogan driving people to think in a certain way politically. Rather it is a social slogan directed at each member of the black community calling upon him to discard the false mantle that he has been forced to wear for so many years and to think in terms of himself as he should. In this regard therefore Black Consciousness is a way of life that must permeate through the society and be adopted by all. The logic behind it is that if you see yourself as a person in your own right there are certain basic questions that you must ask about the conditions under which you live. To get to this stage there are three basic steps that have to be followed.

(i) We have to understand thoroughly what we are talking about and to impart it in the right context. This becomes especially necessary in a country like ours where such an approach lends itself easily to misinterpretation. For this reason we have made provision for a historical study of the theory of "black power" in this formation school.

(ii) We have to create channels for the adoption of the same approach by the black community at large. Here, again, one has to be realistic. An approach of this nature, to be successful, has to be adopted by as large a fraction of the population as possible in order to be effective. Whilst the student community may be instrumental in carrying the idea across to the people and remaining the force behind it, the approach will remain ineffective unless it gains

7. Hendrik van der Merwe, Nancy C. J. Charton, D. A. Kotzé, and Ake Magnusson, eds., *African Perspectives on South Africa: A Collection of Speeches, Articles, and Documents* (Stanford: Hoover Institution Press, 1978), 101–5.

FIGURE 24 Steve Biko, the founder of the black consciousness movement in South Africa, was beaten to death in police custody in 1977. Biko argued that all those discriminated against in South Africa on the basis of their skin color needed to become conscious of their own worth, reject South African racial discrimination, and stand up for their rights. He founded the South African Students Organization and later the black consciousness movement and inspired many of the students involved in the 1976 Soweto uprisings. AP Photo.

grass roots support. This is why it is necessary to create easily acceptable slogans and follow these up with in-depth explanations. Secondary institutions built up from members of the community and operating amongst the community have to be encouraged and these must be run by people who themselves understand what is involved in these institutions and in the approach we are adopting. One can expand and give many examples of such institutions but we expect this to come out of discussions at this formation school. Let it suffice to say that such institutions must cover all fields of activity of the black community—educational, social, economic, religious, etc.

(iii) People have to be taught to see the advantages of group action. Here one wonders whether a second look should not be taken at the government-instituted bodies like Urban Bantu Councils and bantustans. It is a universal fact that you cannot politicise people and hope to limit their natural and legitimate aspirations. If the people demand something and get it because they have an Urban Bantu Council or "territorial authority" to talk for them, then they shall begin to realise the power they wield as a group. Political modernisation of the black people may well find good expression in these institutions which at present are repugnant to us. In contrasting the approach adopted in the United States by the black people and our own approach here, it will be interesting to know what this formation school thinks of the various "territorial authorities" in our various "own areas."

There are some dangers that we have to guard against as we make progress in the direction we are pursuing. The first and foremost is that we must not make the mistake of wishing to get into the white man's boots. Traditional indigenous values tell us of a society where poverty was foreign and extreme richness unknown except for the rulers of our society. Sharing was at the heart of our culture. A system that tends to exploit *many* and favour a few is as foreign to us as hair which is not kinky or a skin which is not dark. Where poverty reigned, it affected the whole community simply because of weather conditions beyond our control. Hence even in our aspirations basic truth will find expression. We must guard against the danger of creating a black middle class whose blackness will only be literally skin-deep . . .

Secondly we must not be limited in our outlook. There is a mile of difference between preaching Black Consciousness and preaching hatred of whites. Telling people to hate whites is an outward and reactionary type of preaching which, though understandable, is undesirable and self-destructive. It makes one think in negative terms and preoccupies one with peripheral issues. In a society like ours it is a "positive feet-forward" approach that leads one into a vicious circle and ultimately to self-destruction through ill-advised and impetuous action. In fact it is usually an extreme form of inferiority complex where the sufferer has lost hope of "making it" because of conditions imposed upon him. His actual aspirations are to be like the white man and the hatred arises out of frustration.

On the other hand Black Consciousness is an inward-looking process. It takes cognisance of one's dignity and leads to positive action. It makes you seek to assert yourself and to rise to majestic heights as determined by you. No doubt you resent all forces that seek to thwart your progress but you meet them with strength, resilience and determination because in your heart of hearts you are convinced you will get where you want to get to. In the end you are a much more worthy victor because you do not seek to revenge but to implement the truth for which you have stood all along during your struggle. You were no less angry than the man who hated whites but your anger was channelled to positive action. Because you had a vision detached from the situation you worked hard regardless of immediate setbacks. White hatred leads to precipitate and short-run methods whereas we are involved in an essentially long-term struggle where cool-headedness must take precedence over everything else.

The third point is that we must not make the mistake of trying to categorise whites. Essentially all whites are the same and must be viewed with suspicion. This may apparently sound contradictory to what I have been saying but it is not in actual fact. A study of the history of South Africa shows that at almost all times whites have been involved in black struggles and in almost all instances led to the death or confusion of what they were involved in. This may not have been calculated sometimes but it arises out of genuine differences in approach and commitments. That blacks are deciding to go it alone is not an accident but a result of years of history behind black-white co-operation. Black-white co-operation in this country leads to limitations being imposed on the programme adopted. We must by all means encourage "sympathetic whites" to stand firm in their fight but this must be away from us. In many ways this is dealt with adequately in an article that appears in the August SASO Newsletter, "Black Souls in White Skins." The fact that "sympathetic whites" have in the past made themselves the traditional pace-setters in the black man's struggle has led to the black man's taking a backseat in a struggle essentially his own. Hence excluding whites tends to activate black people and in the ultimate analysis gives proper direction to whatever is being done. This is a fact that overseas observers visiting the country find hard to accept but it remains very true. Racial prejudice in this country has gone beyond all proportions and has subconsciously affected the minds of some of the most well-known liberals.

Where are we today?

SASO stands today at a very important stage of its life. The establishment of the organisation has had a very great impact in three major directions.

Firstly we have created a mood on the black campuses, which has set the stage for a complete revision of thinking. Our "blacks only" attitude has infused a sense of pride and self-reliance on almost all black campuses. Where originally one met with stiff opposition to all exclusive talk, it is now generally accepted that blacks must go it alone. This attitude is welcome to us but has to be guided very carefully and steadily least it falls prey to some of the dangers we have already mentioned. It is hoped that we shall translate all the intellectual talk about "black is beautiful" into some kind of meaningful practical language.

Secondly we have given impetus to meaningful thinking outside the campus. Suddenly black people are beginning to appreciate the value of their own efforts, unpolluted by half-hearted support from the white world. Though this kind of thinking is still limited to the black "intelligentsia" at present, there are all the signs that it will spread to the rest of the community.

Thirdly we have dealt an almost fatal blow at all black-white movements. One does not know whether to take pride in this or not, but definitely it is obvious that we have wasted a lot of valuable time in the so-called non-racial organisations trying to cheat ourselves into believing we were making progress while in fact by the very nature of these bodies we liquidated ourselves into inactivity. The more radical whites have in fact rejoiced at the emergence of SASO and some of them have even come up with useful support in terms of valuable contacts etc., but radical whites are very rare creatures in this country.

Our strength has been difficult to assess because of the battle we were waging for members. With the latest affiliations by Fort Hare and Ngoye we now stand in a position to get down to practical stuff.

Whither are we going?

At all costs we must make sure that we are marching to the same tune as the rest of the community. At no stage must we view ourselves as a group endowed with special characteristics. While we may be playing the tune, it is the rhythmic beating of the community's boots that spurs us to march on and at no stage should that rhythm be disturbed. As the group grows larger and more boots join the rhythmic march, let us not allow the beating of the boots to drown the pure tones of our tune for the tune is necessary and essential to the rhythm.

46 • Is neocolonialism rationalized imperialism? (1964)

Even before Eduardo Mondlane and FRELIMO embarked on armed struggle in Mozambique, the proponents of African independence in Portuguese Guinea (present-day Guinea and Cape Verde), the Partido Africano da Independência da Guiné e Cabo Verde (PAIGC) had begun to fight a liberation war that did not end until Portuguese troops themselves, weary of an endless colonial struggle that they did not believe they could win, overthrew the Portuguese dictatorship of Marcelo Caetano in 1974 and gave up the wars being fought throughout Africa (in Guinea, Angola, and Mozambique).

The founder and leader of the PAIGC, Amílcar Cabral (1921–73), trained as an agronomist in Portugal and worked in the colonial service in Guinea before voluntarily going into exile to pursue his political goals. Cabral led an insurgency movement in Guinea and was assassinated in the capital city, Conakry, in 1973. Here he speaks at the beginning of the liberation war of the even greater struggles that he foresees once liberation has been achieved. Speaking in May 1964 to European opponents of colonialism gathered for a seminar on revolution and the future at the symbolically named Frantz Fanon Centre in Milan, Italy, Cabral poses a number of questions. Is the national liberation struggle itself an imperialist initiative? Is neocolonialism really just a form of rationalized imperialism? In a society such as that of Guinea and of most colonies in Africa, in which no middle-class equivalent to that of the West existed because colonialism prevented its development, what role should the "stratum" of people who learned to manipulate the "apparatus of the state—the African petty bourgeoisie" (who are also the inheritors of state power in the postcolonial period) pursue? Should the petty bourgeoisie "commit suicide"? Is it likely to? And what happens if it does not?[8]

Our problem is to see who is capable of taking control of the state apparatus when the colonial power is destroyed. In Guinea the peasants cannot read or write, they have almost no relations with the colonial forces during the colonial period except for paying taxes, which is done indirectly. The working class hardly exists as a defined class, it is just an embryo. There is no *economically viable* bourgeoisie because imperialism prevented it being created. What there is is a stratum of people in the service of imperialism who have learned how to manipulate the apparatus of the state—the African petty bourgeoisie: this is the only stratum capable of controlling or even utilising the instruments which the colonial state used against our people. So we come to the conclusion that in colonial conditions it is the petty bourgeoisie which is the inheritor of state power (though I wish we could be wrong). The moment national liberation comes and the petty bourgeoisie takes power we enter, or rather return to history, and thus the internal contradictions break out again.

When this happens, and particularly as things are now, there will be powerful external contradictions conditioning the internal situation, and not just internal contradictions as before. What attitude can the petty bourgeoisie adopt? Obviously people on the left will call for the revolution; the right will call for the "non-revolution," i.e. a capitalist road or something like that. The petty bourgeoisie can either ally itself with imperialism and the reactionary strata in its own country to try and preserve itself as a petty bourgeoisie or ally itself with the workers and peasants, who must themselves take power or control to make the revolution. We must be very clear exactly what we are asking the petty bourgeoisie to do. Are we asking it to commit suicide? Because if there is a revolution, then the petty bourgeoisie will have to abandon power to the workers and the peasants and cease to exist qua petty bourgeoisie. For a revolution to take place depends on the nature of the party (and its size), the character of the struggle which led up to liberation, whether there was an armed struggle, what the nature of this armed struggle was and how it developed and, of course, on the nature of the state.

Here I would like to say something about the position of our friends on the left; if a petty bourgeoisie comes to power, they obviously demand of it that it carry out a revolution. But the important thing is whether they took the precaution of analysing the position of the petty

8. Richard Handyside, trans. and ed., *Revolution in Guinea: Selected Texts by Amilcar Cabral* (New York: Monthly Review Press, 1969), 69–75.

bourgeoisie during the struggle; did they examine its nature, see how it worked, see what instruments it used and see whether this bourgeoisie committed itself with the left to carrying out a revolution, before the liberation? As you can see, it is the struggle in the underdeveloped countries which endows the petty bourgeoisie with a function; in the capitalist countries the petty bourgeoisie is only a stratum which serves, it does not determine the historical orientation of the country; it merely allies itself with one group or another. So that to hope that the petty bourgeoisie will just carry out a revolution when it comes to power in an underdeveloped country is to hope for a miracle, although it is true that it *could* do this.

This connects with the problem of the true nature of the national liberation struggle. In Guinea, as in other countries, the implantation of imperialism by force and the presence of the colonial system considerably altered the historical conditions and aroused a response— the national liberation struggle—which is generally considered a revolutionary trend; but this is something which I think needs further examination. I should like to formulate this question: is the national liberation movement something which has simply emerged from within our country, is it a result of the internal contradictions created by the presence of colonialism, or are there external factors which have determined it? And here we have some reservations; in fact I would even go so far as to ask whether, given the advance of socialism in the world, the national liberation movement is not an imperialist initiative. Is the judicial institution which serves as a reference for the right of all peoples to struggle to free themselves a product of the peoples who are trying to liberate themselves? Was it created by the socialist countries who are our historical associates? It is signed by the imperialist countries, it is the imperialist countries who have recognised the right of all peoples to national independence, so I ask myself whether we may not be considering as an initiative of our people what is in fact an initiative of the enemy? Even Portugal, which is using napalm bombs against our people in Guinea, signed the declaration of the right of all peoples to independence. One may well ask oneself why they were so mad as to do something which goes against their own interests—and whether or not it was partly forced on them, the real point is that they signed it. This is where we think there is something wrong with the simple interpretation of the national liberation movement as a revolutionary trend. The objective of the imperialist countries was to prevent the enlargement of the socialist camp, to liberate the reactionary forces in our countries which were being stifled by colonialism and to enable these forces to ally themselves with the international bourgeoisie. The fundamental objective was to create a bourgeoisie where one did not exist, in order specifically to strengthen the imperialist and the capitalist camp. This rise of the bourgeoisie in the new countries, far from being at all surprising, should be considered absolutely normal, it is something that has to be faced by all those struggling against imperialism. We are therefore faced with the problem of deciding whether to engage in an out and out struggle against the bourgeoisie right from the start or whether to try and make an alliance with the national bourgeoisie, to try to deepen the absolutely necessary contradiction between the national bourgeoisie and the international bourgeoisie which has promoted the national bourgeoisie to the position it holds.

To return to the question of the nature of the petty bourgeoisie and the role it can play after the liberation, I should like to put a question to you. What would you have thought if Fidel Castro had come to terms with the Americans? Is this possible or not? Is it possible or impossible that the Cuban petty bourgeoisie, which set the Cuban people marching towards revolution, might have come to terms with the Americans? I think this helps to clarify the character of the revolutionary petty bourgeoisie. If I may put it this way, I think one thing that can be said is this: the revolutionary petty bourgeoisie is honest; i.e. in spite of all the hostile conditions, it remains identified with the fundamental interests of the popular masses. To do this it may have to commit suicide, but it will not lose, by sacrificing itself it can reincarnate itself, but in the condition of workers or peasants. In speaking of honesty I am not trying to establish moral criteria for judging the role of the petty bourgeoisie when it is in power; what I mean by honesty, in a political context, is total commitment and total identification with the toiling masses.

Again, the role of the petty bourgeoisie ties up with the possible social and political trans-formations that can be effected after liberation. We have heard a great deal about the state of national democracy, but although we have made every effort we have thus far been unable to understand what this means; even so, we should like to know what it is all about, as we want to know what we are going to do when we have driven out the Portuguese. Likewise, we have to face the question of whether or not socialism can be established immediately after the lib-eration. This depends on the instruments used to effect the transition to socialism; the es-sential factor is the nature of the state, bearing in mind that after the liberation there will be people controlling the police, the prisons, the army and so on, and a great deal depends on who they are and what they try to do with these instruments. Thus we return again to the problem of which class is the agent of history and who are the inheritors of the colonial state in our specific conditions ...

What really interests us here is neocolonialism. After the Second World War, imperial-ism entered on a new phase: on the one hand, it worked out the new policy of aid, i.e. granted independence to the occupied countries plus "aid" and, on the other hand, concentrated on preferential investment in the European countries; this was, above all, an attempt at rational-ising imperialism. Even if it has not yet provoked reactions of a nationalist kind in the Euro-pean countries, we are convinced that it will soon do so. As we see it, neocolonialism (which we may call rationalised imperialism) is more a defeat for the international working class than for the colonised peoples. Neocolonialism is at work on two fronts—in Europe as well as in the underdeveloped countries. Its current framework in the underdeveloped countries is the policy of aid, and one of the essential aims of this policy is to create a false bourgeoisie to put a brake on the revolution and to enlarge the possibilities of the petty bourgeoisie as a neu-traliser of the revolution; at the same time it invests capital in France, Italy, Belgium, England and so on. In our opinion the aim of this is to stimulate the growth of a workers' aristocracy, to enlarge the field of action of the petty bourgeoisie so as to block the revolution. In our opin-ion it is under this aspect that neocolonialism and the relations between the international working class movement and our movements must be analysed. If there have ever been any doubts about the close relations between our struggle and the struggle of the international working class movement, neocolonialism has proved that there need not be any. Obviously I don't think it is possible to forge closer relations between the peasantry in Guinea and the working class movement in Europe; what we must do first is try and forge closer links between the peasant movement and the wage-earners' movement in our own country. The example of Latin America gives you a good idea of the limits on closer relations; in Latin America you have an old neocolonial situation and a chance to see clearly the relations between the North

American proletariat and the Latin American masses. Other examples could be found nearer home.

There is, however, another aspect I should like to raise and that is that the European left has an intellectual responsibility to study the concrete conditions in our country and help us in this way, as we have very little documentation, very few intellectuals, very little chance to do this kind of work ourselves, and yet it is of key importance; this is a major contribution you can make. Another thing you can do is to support the really revolutionary national liberation movements by all possible means. You must analyse and study these movements and combat in Europe, by all possible means, everything which can be used to further the repression against our peoples. I refer especially to the sale of arms. I should like to say to our Italian friends that we have captured a lot of Italian arms from the Portuguese, not to mention French arms, of course. Moreover, you must unmask courageously all the national liberation movements which are under the thumb of imperialism. People whisper that so-and-so is an American agent, but nobody in the European left has taken a violent and open attitude against these people; it is we ourselves who have to try and denounce these people, who are sometimes even those accepted by the rest of Africa, and this creates a lot of trouble for us.

I think that the left and the international working class movement should confront those states which claim to be socialist with their responsibilities; this does not of course, mean cutting off all their possibilities of action, but it does mean denouncing all those states which are neocolonialists.

To end up with, I should just like to make one last point about solidarity between the international working class movement and our national liberation struggle. There are two alternatives: either we admit that there really is a struggle against imperialism which interests everybody, or we deny it. If, as would seem from all the evidence, imperialism exists and is trying simultaneously to dominate the working class in all the advanced countries and smother the national liberation movements in all the underdeveloped countries, then there is only one enemy against whom we are fighting. If we are fighting together, then I think the main aspect of our solidarity is extremely simple: it is to fight—I don't think there is any need to discuss this very much. We are struggling in Guinea with guns in our hands, you must struggle in your countries as well—I don't say with guns in your hands, I'm not going to tell you how to struggle, that's your business; but you must find the best means and the best forms of fighting against our common enemy: this is the best form of solidarity.

CHAPTER SIX

Colonial Legacies of Authoritarianism (1960–79)

47 • A man of the people

Chinua Achebe, whose novel Things Fall Apart, *about the impact of conquest on the Igbo people of southeastern Nigeria, has become a literary classic, takes up the problems of independent Nigeria in a less well known but equally penetrating account,* A Man of the People. *In the latter account, based on Achebe's reactions to developments in Nigeria in the early 1960s, politics in the ex-colony become an opportunity for the petty bourgeoisie feared by Cabral to exercise a self-seeking and corrupting influence on the new state. As these "new men" grasp after economic and political spoils for themselves they adopt an antiforeign rhetoric—easily transferred from the anticolonial struggle— as a means to disguise their own self-interest. Achebe's "man of the people," M. A. Nanga, is clearly a certain type of colonial product, schooled as British officials would have wished in Africa rather than overseas, a longtime member of Baden-Powell's scouting movement and, despite his pretensions to serving the needs of the community at large, fundamentally corrupt.*[1]

No one can deny that Chief the Honorable M. A. Nanga, M.P., was the most approachable politician in the country. Whether you asked in the city or in his home village, Anata, they would tell you he was a man of the people. I have to admit this from the outset or else the story I'm going to tell will make no sense.

That afternoon he was due to address the staff and students of the Anata Grammar School where I was teaching at the time. But as usual in those highly political times the villagers moved in and virtually took over. The Assembly Hall must have carried well over thrice its capacity. Many villagers sat on the floor, right up to the foot of the dais. I took one look and decided it was just as well we had to stay outside—at least for the moment.

Five or six dancing groups were performing at different points in the compound. The popular "Ego Women's Party" wore a new uniform of expensive accra cloth. In spite of the din you could still hear as clear as a bird the high-powered voice of their soloist, whom they admiringly nicknamed "Grammar-phone." Personally I don't care too much for our women's dancing but you just had to listen whenever Grammar-phone sang. She was now praising Micah's handsomeness, which she likened to the perfect, sculpted beauty of a carved eagle, and his popularity which would be the envy of the proverbial traveller-to-distant-places who must not cultivate enmity on his route. Micah was of course Chief the Honourable M. A. Nanga, M.P.

1. Chinua Achebe, *A Man of the People* (London: Heinemann, 1966), 1–6.

The arrival of the members of the hunters' guild in full regalia caused a great stir. Even Grammar-phone stopped—at least for a while. These people never came out except at the funeral of one of their number, or during some very special and outstanding event. I could not remember when I last saw them. They wielded their loaded guns as though they were playthings. Now and again two of them would meet in warriors' salute and knock the barrel of their guns together from left to right and again from right to left. Mothers grabbed their children and hurriedly dragged them away. Occasionally a hunter would take aim at a distant palm branch and break its mid-rib. The crowd applauded. But there were very few such shots. Most of the hunters reserved their precious powder to greet the Minister's arrival—the price of gunpowder like everything else having doubled again and again in the four years since this government took control.

As I stood in one corner of that vast tumult waiting for the arrival of the Minister I felt intense bitterness welling up in my mouth. Here were silly, ignorant villagers dancing themselves lame and waiting to blow off their gunpowder in honour of one of those who had started the country off down the slopes of inflation. I wished for a miracle, for a voice of thunder, to hush this ridiculous festival and tell the poor contemptible people one or two truths. But of course it would be quite useless. They were not only ignorant but cynical. Tell them that this man had used his position to enrich himself and they would ask you—as my father did—if you thought that a sensible man would spit out the juicy morsel that good fortune placed in his mouth.

I had not always disliked Mr. Nanga. Sixteen years or so ago he had been my teacher in standard three and I something like his favourite pupil. I remember him then as a popular, young and handsome teacher, most impressive in his uniform as scoutmaster. There was on one of the walls of the school a painting of a faultlessly handsome scoutmaster wearing an impeccable uniform. I am not sure that the art teacher who painted the picture had Mr. Nanga in mind. There was no facial resemblance; still we called it the picture of Mr. Nanga. It was enough that they were both handsome and that they were both impressive scoutmasters. This picture stood with arms folded across its chest and its raised right foot resting neatly and lightly on a perfectly cut tree stump. Bright red hibiscus flowers decorated the four corners of the frame, and below were inscribed the memorable words: *Not what I have but what I do is my kingdom.* That was in 1948.

Nanga must have gone into politics soon afterwards and then won a seat in Parliament. (It was easy in those days—before we knew its cash price.) I used to read about him in the papers some years later and even took something like pride in him. At that time I had just entered the University and was very active in the Students' branch of the People's Organization Party. Then in 1960 something disgraceful happened in the Party and I was completely disillusioned.

At that time Mr. Nanga was an unknown back-bencher in the governing P.O.P. A general election was imminent. The P.O.P. was riding high in the country and there was no fear of its not being returned. Its opponent, the Progressive Alliance Party, was weak and disorganized.

Then came the slump in the international coffee market. Overnight (or so it seemed to us) the Government had a dangerous financial crisis on its hands. Coffee was the prop of our economy just as coffee farmers were the bulwark of the P.O.P.

The Minister of Finance at the time was a first-rate economist with a Ph.D. in public finance. He presented to the Cabinet a complete plan for dealing with the situation.

The Prime Minister said "No" to the plan. He was not going to risk losing the election by cutting down the price paid to coffee planters at that critical moment; the National Bank should be instructed to print fifteen million pounds. Two-thirds of the Cabinet supported the Minister. The next morning the Prime Minister sacked them and in the evening he broadcast to the nation. He said the dismissed ministers were conspirators and traitors who had teamed up with foreign saboteurs to destroy the new nation.

I remember this broadcast very well. Of course no one knew the truth at that time. The newspapers and the radio carried the Prime Minister's version of the story. We were very indignant. Our Students' Union met in emergency session and passed a vote of confidence in the leader and called for a detention law to deal with the miscreants, The whole country was behind the leader. Protest marches and demonstrations were staged up and down the land.

It was at this point that I first noticed a new, dangerous and sinister note in the universal outcry.

The *Daily Chronicle*, an official organ of the P.O.P., had pointed out in an editorial that the Miscreant Gang, as the dismissed ministers were now called, were all university people and highly educated professional men. (I have preserved a cutting of that editorial.)

"Let us now and for all time extract from our body-politic as a dentist extracts a stinking tooth all those decadent stooges versed in text-book economics and aping the white man's mannerisms and way of speaking. We are proud to be Africans. Our true leaders are not those intoxicated with their Oxford, Cambridge or Harvard degrees but those who speak the language of the people. Away with the damnable and expensive university education which only alienates an African from his rich and ancient culture and puts him above his people. . . ."

This cry was taken up on all sides. Other newspapers pointed out that even in Britain where the Miscreant Gang got its "so-called education" a man need not be an economist to be Chancellor of the Exchequer or a doctor to be Minister of Health. What mattered was loyalty to the party.

I was in the public gallery the day the Prime Minister received his overwhelming vote of confidence. And that was the day the truth finally came out; only no one was listening. I remember the grief-stricken figure of the dismissed Minister of Finance as he led his team into the chamber and was loudly booed by members of the public. That week his car had been destroyed by angry mobs and his house stoned. Another dismissed minister had been pulled out of his car, beaten insensible, and dragged along the road for fifty yards, then tied hand and foot, gagged and left by the roadside. He was still in the orthopaedic hospital when the house met.

The Prime Minister spoke for three hours and his every other word was applauded. He was called the Tiger, the Lion, the One and Only, the Sky, the Ocean and many other names of praise. He said that the Miscreant Gang had been caught "red-handed in their nefarious plot to overthrow the Government of the people by the people and for the people with the help of enemies abroad."

"They deserve to be hanged," shouted Mr. Nanga from the back benches. This interruption was so loud and clear that it appeared later under his own name in the Hansard. Throughout the session he led the pack of back-bench hounds straining their leash to get at their victims. If any one had cared to sum up Mr. Nanga's interruptions they would have made a good hour's continuous yelp. Perspiration poured down his face as he sprang up to interrupt or sat back to share in the derisive laughter of the hungry hyena.

When the Prime Minister said that he had been stabbed in the back by the very ingrates he had pulled out of oblivion some members were in tears.

"They have bitten the finger with which their mother fed them," said Mr. Nanga. This too was entered in the Hansard, a copy of which I have before me. It is impossible, however, to convey in cold print the electric atmosphere of that day.

I cannot now recall exactly what my feelings were at that point. I suppose I thought the whole performance rather peculiar. You must remember that at that point no one had any reason to think there might be another side to the story. The Prime Minister was still talking. Then he made the now famous (or infamous) solemn declaration. "From today we must watch and guard our hard-won freedom jealously. Never again must we entrust our destiny and the destiny of Africa to the hybrid class of Western-educated and snobbish intellectuals who will not hesitate to sell their mothers for a mess of pottage . . ."

Mr. Nanga pronounced the death sentence at least twice more but this was not recorded, no doubt because his voice was lost in the general commotion.

I remember the figure of Dr Makinde the ex-Minister of Finance as he got up to speak— tall, calm, sorrowful and superior. I strained my ears to catch his words. The entire house, including the Prime Minister tried to shout him down. It was a most unedifying spectacle. The Speaker broke his mallet ostensibly trying to maintain order but you could see he was enjoying the commotion. The public gallery yelled down its abuses. "Traitor," "Coward," "Doctor of Fork your Mother." This last was contributed from the gallery by the editor of the *Daily Chronicle* who sat close to me. Encouraged, no doubt, by the volume of laughter this piece of witticism had earned him in the gallery he proceeded the next morning to print it in his paper. The spelling is his.

Although Dr Makinde read his speech, which was clearly prepared, the Hansard later carried a garbled version which made no sense at all. It said not a word about the plan to mint fifteen million pounds—which was perhaps to be expected—but why put into Dr Makinde's mouth words that he could not have spoken? In short the Hansard boys wrote a completely new speech suitable to the boastful villain the ex-minister had become. For instance they made him say he was a brilliant economist whose reputation was universally acclaimed in Europe. When I read this I was in tears—and I don't cry all that easily.

48 • Tearing things apart (1967)

The contradictions of postcolonial independence exploded in Africa's first coup—on January 15, 1966—when Nigerian military officers, most of them Igbo, assassinated Nigeria's prime minister, Abubakar Tafawa Balewa (a Muslim northerner), as well as the leaders of the western and northern regions of the country (Nnamdi Azikiwe, Nigeria's president, was in Britain seeking medical treatment at the time of the coup). The coup leaders stated that they had been forced to take action by the endemic corruption that was crippling the country, by the corrupt election that had taken place in October of the previous year, and by Nigeria's need for a strong and efficient central government rather than the federal system that Britain had put in place.

Aside from opposition to people like those represented by Achebe's semifictional M. A. Nanga, the Igbo officers were also concerned that the divide-and-rule policies left in place by Britain's transfer of power had privileged the north at the expense of the south. This imbalance, the coup leaders felt, had been further reinforced by the 1962 census, a highly suspect head count that had concluded that the north had almost two-thirds of Nigeria's population, an impossibly high proportion, and was therefore entitled to an equivalent share of the parliamentary seats. Northerners, most of them Muslim, for their part viewed the coup as an attempt by mainly Christian Igbo to impose themselves upon the country. The leaders of the rebellion were themselves deposed by army officers led by an Igbo general. However, rioting broke out, especially in northern Nigeria, where large numbers of Igbo were massacred, and thousands fled to their southeastern homeland, fearing genocide. As the country became enmeshed in violence, northern officers staged a coup of their own, which in turn increased Igbo fears of pogroms. In the following speech, made on May 30, 1967, proclaiming the establishment of the Republic of Biafra, C. Odumegwu Ojukwu, an Igbo military officer who led the Biafran secessionist movement from 1967 until its defeat in 1970 (with between one and three million people dead from hostilities, disease, and starvation), explains why he and his supporters (who included Chinua Achebe) felt it necessary to try to withdraw from the Nigerian federation.[2]

It is right and just that we of this generation of Eastern Nigeria should record for the benefit of posterity some of the reasons for the momentous decision we have taken at this crucial time in the history of our people.

The military government of Eastern Nigeria has, in a series of publications, traced the evils and injustices of the Nigerian political association through the decades, stating also the case and standpoint of Eastern Nigeria in the recent crisis.

Throughout the period of Nigeria's precarious existence as a single political entity, Eastern Nigerians have always believed in fundamental human rights and principles as they are accepted and enjoyed in civilized communities. Impelled by their belief in these rights and principles and in their common citizenship with other Nigerians after Amalgamation, Eastern Nigerians employed their ideas and skills, their resourcefulness and dynamism, in the development of areas of Nigeria outside the East. Eastern Nigerians opened up avenues of trade and industry throughout the country; overlooked the neglect of their homeland in the disposition of national institutions, projects, and utilities; made available their own natural resources to the rest of the country; and confidently invested in the general economic and social development of Nigeria. Politically, Eastern Nigerians advocated a strong, united Nigeria: for ONE COUNTRY, ONE CONSTITUTION, ONE DESTINY. Eastern Nigerians were in the vanguard of the struggle for national independence and made sacrifices and concessions for the cause of national unity. They conceded the inauguration of a federal instead of a unitary system of government in Nigeria.

Leaders of Northern Nigeria have told us several times that what our former colonial masters made into "Nigeria" consisted of an agglomeration of people, distinct in every way except in the color of their skins, and organized as a unit for their own commercial interests

---

2. C. Odumegwu Ojukwu, *Biafra: Selected Speeches and Random Thoughts of C. Odumegwu Ojukwu, General of the People's Army, with Diaries of Events* (New York: Harper and Row, 1969), 177–84.

and administrative convenience. The name "Nigeria" was regarded by many as a mere "geo-graphical expression."

In course of time, the peoples of the other parts of Southern Nigeria found that they possessed many things in common with those of Eastern Nigeria, and while the colonial master made adjustments to accommodate these common ties between the Southern inhabitants, the peoples of the North insisted on maintaining their separateness.

On October 1, 1960, independence was granted to the people of Nigeria in a form of "federation," based on artificially made units. The Nigerian Constitution installed the North in perpetual dominance over Nigeria. The Federation was predicated on the perpetual rule by one unit over the others. The Constitution itself contained provisions which negated the fundamental human freedoms which it purported to guarantee for the citizens. Thus were sown, by design or by default, the seeds of factionalism and hate, of struggle for power at the center, and of the worst types of political chicanery and abuse of power. One of two situations was bound to result from that arrangement: either perpetual domination of the rest of the country by the North, not by consent but by force and fraud, or a dissolution of the federation bond. National independence was followed by successive crises, each leading to near-disintegration of the country. Some of the major events which are directly attributable to the defective and inadequate Constitution may here be mentioned.

In 1962, an emergency was imposed on Western Nigeria. Jurists agree that the imposition was unconstitutional; it was a ruse to remove certain elements in Western Nigeria known to have taken a firm stand against the misuse of political power. A puppet of the North was maneuvered into power in Western Nigeria.

Also in 1962, and again in 1963, Nigerians tried for the first time to count themselves. What should ordinarily be a statistical and dull exercise was, because of the nature of the Constitution, turned into a fierce political struggle. The official figures established by these censuses have been discredited.

Federal elections followed in December, 1964—elections which have been described as the most farcical in our history. Candidates were kidnapped, killed, or forced to withdraw from the elections. Results announced were in direct opposition to the actual facts. The Southern parties had boycotted the election, and the deadlock which followed brought the country near to dissolution. The situation was patched up; the conflagration was brought under control, but its embers lay smoldering.

On October 11, 1965, elections were held to the Western House of Assembly. The puppet government of that region existed not by the will of the people of Western Nigeria but because of the combined power of the federal government and the Northern Nigeria government which installed it. The electorate of Western Nigeria was not permitted to declare its will in the elections. Fraud, foul play, and murder were committed with impunity. The smoldering embers of the recent past erupted with unquenchable virulence. The irate electorate showed its resentment in its own way. Complete disorder followed. Yet the federal government dominated by the North fiddled with the issue and even refused to recognize what the whole world had known, namely, that Nigeria was on the brink of disaster.

Only the armed forces remained politically uncommitted and nonpartisan. Some of their officers and men revolted against the injustices which were perpetrated before their very eyes and attempted to overthrow the federal government and regional governments. In desperation, the ministers of the federal government handed over power to the armed forces under the supreme command of Major General J. T. U. Aguiyi-Ironsi.

The military administration under Major General Aguiyi-Ironsi made the first real attempt to unite the country and its peoples. The Northerners saw in his efforts the possibility of losing their control of the affairs of the country. So while its leaders paid lip service to unity, they laid plans for making sure that it could never be achieved. Major General Aguiyi-Ironsi was, of course, an Easterner, but the majority of the individuals at the head of affairs were not. At no time under the civilian rule did Eastern Nigerians hold a dominating position in the government of the Federation.

On May 24, 1966, the military government issued a decree designed to provide a more unified administration in keeping with the military command. The people of Northern Nigeria protested against the decree, and on May 29, 1966, thousands of Easterners residing in the North were massacred by Northern civilians. They looted their property. The Supreme Military Council set up a tribunal to look into the causes of those unprovoked acts of murder and pillage and determine what compensations might be paid to the victims. The Northern emirs declared their intention to pull Northern Nigeria out of the Federation rather than face the tribunal. But the Supreme Military Council justly decided that the tribunal must do its duty.

Then, on July 29, 1966, two months after the May murders and despoliation, and four days before the tribunal was due to commence its sitting, the real pogrom against Eastern Nigerians residing in the Federation began. Major General Aguiyi-Ironsi and his host, Lieutenant Colonel Francis Fajuyi, were kidnapped at Ibadan and murdered. This time Northern soldiers acted in concert with Northern civilians. Defenseless men, women, and children were shot down or hacked to death; some were burned, and some buried alive. Women and young girls were ravished with unprecedented bestiality; unborn children were torn out of the womb of their mothers.

Again, on September 29, 1966, the pogrom was resumed. Thirty thousand Eastern Nigerians are known to have been killed by Northerners. They were killed in the North, in Western Nigeria, in Lagos; some Eastern soldiers in detention at Benin were forcibly removed from prison by Northern soldiers and murdered.

At the time of the incident, millions of Eastern Nigerians resided outside the East, and persons from other parts of the country lived in this region. While Eastern Nigerians who assembled at Northern airports, railway stations, and motor parks were set upon by Northern soldiers and civilians armed with machine guns, rifles, daggers, and poisoned arrows, the army and police in the East were specifically instructed to shoot at sight any Eastern Nigerian found molesting non-Easterners living in the region. By early October the sight of mutilated refugees, orphaned children, widowed mothers, and decapitated corpses of Eastern Nigerians arriving at our airports and railway stations inflamed passions to such an extent that it was found necessary to ask all non-Easterners to leave the region in their own interest. Since the events of July, 1966, there has been a mass movement of population in this country. Nigerian society has undergone a fundamental change; it is no longer possible for Eastern Nigerians to live outside their region without fear of loss of life or of property.

Two facts emerge from the events described above. The widespread nature of the massacre and its periodicity—May 29, July 29, and September 29—show first, that they were premeditated and planned, and second, that Eastern Nigerians are no longer wanted as equal partners in the Federation of Nigeria. It must be recalled that this was the fourth in a series of massacres of Eastern Nigerians in the last two decades.

At the early stages of the crisis, the world was told that it was a conflict between the North and the East. That pretense collapsed when it became clear that Northern soldiers moved into Western Nigeria and Lagos as another step in Northern Nigeria's bid to continue her so-called conquest to the sea. Belatedly, it was generally accepted that the fundamental issue was not a struggle between the East and the North, but one involving the very existence of Nigeria as one political entity.

Throughout the Nigerian crises, some of the indigenous judges have been found quite unequal to their calling by reason of their involvement in partisan politics. People soon lost faith in them and would not go to their courts for redress. In some measure, they were responsible for the collapse of the rule of law in certain parts of Nigeria. Providence has spared us in the East from this terrible calamity.

It is now necessary to summarize the attempt of the government and people of Eastern Nigeria to solve the crisis, and the bad faith with which these attempts have been received.

On August 9, 1966, representatives of the military governors meeting in Lagos made decisions for restoring peace and for clearing the way for constitutional talks, notably the decision that troops be all repatriated to their region of origin. These decisions were not fully implemented.

On September 12, the Ad Hoc Constitutional Conference, consisting of delegates representing all the governments of the Federation, met in Lagos and for three weeks sought to discover a form of association best suited to Nigeria, having regard to the prevailing circumstances and their causes, and future possibilities. This conference was unilaterally dismissed by Lieutenant Colonel Gowon, the head of the Lagos government.

It had become then impossible for the Supreme Military Council, the highest governing body in the Federation, to meet on Nigerian soil. As long as Northern troops were in Lagos and the West, no venue could be found acceptable to all the military governors for a meeting of the Supreme Military Council in Nigeria. It met at Aburi in Ghana, January 4–5, 1967, on the basis of an agenda previously determined by the officials of the governments of the country and adopted by the Supreme Military Council. Decisions reached at the meeting were ignored by Lieutenant Colonel Gowon and the North. In the interest of this region and of the whole country, the East stood firmly by those decisions and warned that they would be applied to Eastern Nigeria if steps were not taken by the Lagos government to apply them generally. The East rejected all measures which did not reflect the decisions at Aburi.

The Aburi Accord was not implemented by the Lagos government. All the meetings of military leaders held since Aburi were held without the East. All the decisions taken by Lagos were taken without comment and concurrence from the East.

It became evident that each time Nigerians came close to a realistic solution to the current crisis by moving toward a loose form of association or confederation, Lieutenant Colonel Gowon unilaterally frustrated their efforts. When the representatives of the military governors decided on August 9, 1966, that troops be repatriated to their regions of origin, and it appeared to him that this would lead to confederation, he unilaterally refused to fully implement that decision. When in September, 1967, the Ad Hoc Constitutional Conference appeared near to agreement on a loose federation, he unilaterally dismissed them indefinitely. When in January, 1967, the military leaders agreed at Aburi on what the federal permanent secretaries correctly interpreted as confederation, he unilaterally rejected the agreement to which he had voluntarily subscribed. When in May, 1967, all the Southern military governors and the Leaders of Thought of their regions spoke out in favor of confederation, he dismissed the Supreme Military Council and proclaimed himself the dictator of Nigeria—an act which, to say the least, is treasonable.

Following the pogrom of 1966, some 7,000,000 Eastern Nigerians have returned from other regions, refugees in their own country. Money was needed to care for them—not to give them mere relief but to rehabilitate them and, in time, restore their outraged feelings. The Lagos government was urged to give the Eastern Nigeria government its share of the statutory revenues. Lieutenant Colonel Gowon refused to do so in the hope that the weight of the burden would lead to the economic collapse of Eastern Nigeria.

49 • An emperor and his court (1970s)

There was no more famous autocrat in Africa than Haile Selassie ("Might of the Trinity") (1892–1975), born Tafari Makonnen at the end of the nineteenth century. Educated by French missionaries, as a young man he was considered representative of a new generation of Ethiopian leaders who were determined to strengthen national independence (Ethiopia was the only African country— apart from the two states set up as refuges for freed slaves, Sierra Leone and Liberia—to successfully resist European imperialism) by encouraging economic and political reform. He successfully negotiated Ethiopia's admission to the League of Nations in 1923 and traveled widely in Europe. However, over time he became more and more of an autocrat. Crowned emperor in 1930, he devoted much of his attention to developing the power of Ethiopia's central government, aiming especially to concentrate power in his own hands. He gained even greater fame by leading Ethiopia's unsuccessful resistance against the invasion by Italy in 1935 and returned a hero in 1941, when the British reestablished him as emperor. Though his reputation in the West was that of a slightly romanticized and quaint African monarch, in Africa he was one of the leading figures of the Organization of African Unity (OAU). Moreover, in the Americas, Selassie was the symbolic head of the Rastafarian movement. However, in Ethiopia, where he brooked no opposition, his image was much less glowing. In particular, people complained of his aloofness, his reliance on a coterie of sycophants, and his refusal to support any fundamental change to improve the difficult economic and political conditions under which most Ethiopians lived.

Ryszard Kapúscínski, a Polish author who has based his account on interviews conducted in Ethiopia after the overthrow of the emperor, here paints a devastating portrait of Selassie shuffling around his palace while continually listening to stories brought to him by the spies that he had placed in every part of his domain. In this account, all the emperor cares about is his hold on power, and he will do whatever it takes to maintain it. Yet autocracy had its limits. Though Haile Selassie ruled Ethiopia for almost half a century, his power waned in the 1970s in the face of famine and starvation. Marxist-inspired army officers mutinied in 1974 and placed him under arrest. He was dead within a year, either from natural causes as publicly reported or strangled by the coup leaders as rumored. The leader of the coup, Haile Mariam Mengistu, buried Selassie's body under his office floor in order that his grave not become a symbol of opposition to the new regime.[3]

The Emperor began his day by listening to informers' reports. The night breeds dangerous conspiracies, and Haile Selassie knew that what happens at night is more important than what happens during the day. During the day he kept his eye on everyone; at night that was impossible. For that reason, he attached great importance to the morning reports. And here I would like to make one thing clear: His Venerable Majesty was no reader. For him, neither the written nor the printed word existed; everything had to be relayed by word of mouth. His Majesty had had no schooling. His sole teacher—and that only during his childhood—was a French Jesuit, Monsignor Jerome, later Bishop of Harar and a friend of the poet Arthur Rimbaud. This cleric had no chance to inculcate the habit of reading in the Emperor, a task made all the more difficult, by the way, because Haile Selassie occupied responsible administrative positions from his boyhood and had no time for regular reading.

But I think there was more to it than a lack of time and habit. The custom of relating things by word of mouth had this advantage: if need be, the Emperor could say that a given dignitary had told him something quite different from what had really been said, and the latter could not defend himself, having no written proof. Thus the Emperor heard from his subordinates not what they told him, but what he thought should be said. His Venerable Highness had his ideas, and he would adjust to them all the signals that came from his surroundings. It was the same with writing, for our monarch not only never used his ability to read, but he also never wrote anything and never signed anything in his own hand. Though he ruled for half a century, not even those closest to him knew what his signature looked like.

During the Emperor's hours of official functions, the Minister of the Pen always stood at hand and took down all the Emperor's orders and instructions. Let me say that during working audiences His Majesty spoke very softly, barely moving his lips. The Minister of the Pen, standing half a step from the throne, had to bend his ear close to the Imperial lips in order to hear and write down the Imperial decisions. Furthermore, the Emperor's words were usually unclear and ambiguous, especially when he did not want to take a definite stand on a matter that required his opinion. One had to admire the Emperor's dexterity. When asked by a dignitary for the Imperial decision, he would not answer straight out, but would rather speak in a voice so quiet that it reached only the Minister of the Pen, who moved his ear as close as a microphone. The minister transcribed his ruler's scant and foggy mutterings. All the rest was interpretation, and that was a matter for the minister, who passed down the decision in writing.

The Minister of the Pen was the Emperor's closest confidant and enjoyed enormous power. From the secret cabala of the monarch's words he could construct any decision that he wished. If a move by the Emperor dazzled everyone with its accuracy and wisdom, it was one more proof that God's Chosen One was infallible. On the other hand, if from some corner the breeze carried rumors of discontent to the monarch's ear, he could blame it all on the minister's stupidity. And so the minister was the most hated personality in the court. Public opinion, convinced of His Venerable Highness's wisdom and goodness, blamed the minister for any thoughtless or malicious decisions, of which there were many. True, the servants

3. Ryszard Kapúscínski, *The Emperor: Downfall of an Autocrat* (New York: Vintage, 1983), 7–12, 28–34.

whispered about why Haile Selassie didn't replace the minister, but in the Palace questions were always asked from top to bottom, and never vice versa. When the first question was asked in a direction opposite to the customary one, it was a signal that the revolution had begun.

But I'm getting ahead of myself and must go back to the moment when the Emperor appears on the Palace steps in the morning and sets out for his early walk. He enters the park. This is when Solomon Kedir, the head of the Palace spies, approaches and gives his report. The Emperor walks along the avenue and Kedir stays a step behind him, talking all the while. Who met whom, where, and what they talked about. Against whom they are forming alliances. Whether or not one could call it a conspiracy. Kedir also reports on the work of the military cryptography department. This department, part of Kedir's office, decodes the communications that pass among the divisions; it's good to be sure that no subversive thoughts are hatching there. His Distinguished Highness asks no questions, makes no comments. He walks and listens. Sometimes he stops before the lions' cage to throw them a leg of veal that a servant has handed to him. He watches the lions' rapacity and smiles. Then he approaches the leopards, which are chained, and gives them ribs of beef. His Majesty has to be careful as he approaches the unpredictable beasts of prey. Finally he moves on, with Kedir behind continuing his report. At a certain moment His Highness bows his head, which is a signal for Kedir to move away. He bows and disappears down the avenue, never turning his back on the Emperor.

At this moment the waiting Minister of Industry and Commerce, Makonen Habte-Wald, emerges from behind a tree. He falls in, a step behind the Emperor, and delivers his report. Makonen Habte-Wald keeps his own network of informers, both to satisfy a consuming passion for intrigue and to ingratiate himself with His Venerable Highness. On the basis of his information, he now briefs the Emperor on what happened last night. Again, His Majesty walks on, listening without questions or comments, keeping his hands behind his back. He approaches a flock of flamingos, but the shy birds scatter when he comes near. The Emperor smiles at the sight of creatures that refuse to obey him. At last, still walking, he nods his head; Habte-Wald falls silent and retreats backward, disappearing down the avenue.

Next, as if springing up from the ground, rises the hunched silhouette of the devoted confidant Asha WaldeMikael. This dignitary supervises the government political police. He competes with Solomon Kedir's Palace intelligence service and battles fiercely against private informer networks like the one that Makonen Habte-Wald has at his disposal.

The occupation to which these people devoted themselves was hard and dangerous. They lived in fear of not reporting something in time and falling into disgrace, or of a competitor's reporting it better so that the Emperor would think, "Why did Solomon give me a feast today and Makonen only bring me leftovers? Did he say nothing because he didn't know, or did he hold his tongue because he belongs to the conspiracy?" Hadn't His Distinguished Highness often experienced, at cost to himself, betrayal by his most trusted allies? That's why the Emperor punished silence. On the other hand, incoherent streams of words tired and irritated the Imperial ear, so nervous loquaciousness was also a poor solution. Even the way these people looked told of the threat under which they lived. Tired, looking as if they hadn't slept, they acted under feverish stress, pursuing their victims in the stale air of hatred and fear that surrounded them all: They had no shield but the Emperor, and the Emperor could undo them with one wave of his hand. No, His Benevolent Majesty did not make their lives easy.

As I've mentioned, Haile Selassie never commented on or questioned the reports he received, during his morning walks, about the state of conspiracy in the Empire. But he knew what he was doing, as I shall show you. His Highness wanted to receive the reports in a pure state, because if he asked questions or expressed opinions the informant would obligingly adjust his report to meet the Emperor's expectations. Then the whole system of informing would collapse into subjectivity and fall prey to anyone's willfulness. The monarch would not know what was going on in the country and the Palace.

Finishing his walk, the Emperor listens to what was reported last night by Asha's people. He feeds the dogs and the black panther, and then he admires the anteater that he recently received as a gift from the president of Uganda. He nods his head and Asha walks away, bent over, wondering whether he said more or less than what was reported by his most fervent enemies: Solomon, the enemy of Makonen and Asha; and Makonen, the enemy of Asha and Solomon.

Haile Selassie finishes his walk alone. It grows light in the park; the fog thins out, and reflected sunlight glimmers on the lawns. The Emperor ponders. Now is the time to lay out strategies and tactics, to solve the puzzles of personality, to plan his next move on the chessboard of power. He thinks deeply about what was contained in the informants' reports. Little of importance; they usually report on each other. His Majesty has made mental notes of everything. His mind is a computer that retains every detail; even the smallest datum will be remembered. There was no personnel office in the Palace, no dossiers full of personal information. All this the Emperor carried in his mind, all the most important files about the elite. I see him now as he walks, stops, walks again, lifts his head upward as though absorbed in prayer. O God, save me from those who, crawling on their knees, hide a knife that they would like to sink into my back. But how can God help? All the people surrounding the Emperor are just like that, on their knees, and with knives. It's never comfortable on the summits. An icy wind always blows, and everyone crouches, watchful lest his neighbor hurl him down the precipice.

50 ◆ Who will start another fire? (1970s)

Many of the first-generation leaders of independent African nations did not take criticism very well. They often tended to be autocratic, paranoid about any form of criticism, and violently opposed to losing their positions of power. Some declared themselves presidents for life, and one named himself an emperor. Freedom of speech was rare in independent Africa, especially for writers who pointed out the shortcomings of those who governed the new states. Malawi, where John Chilembwe had led his revolt against British colonialism and which had been ruled since independence by Hastings Kamuzu Banda, was one of the most restrictive states when it came to such criticism. Banda had spent much of his life as a medical doctor in Britain, but he returned home to become Malawi's first prime minister in 1964. Over time he became increasingly dictatorial, naming himself president for life, banning opposition parties, and arresting anyone who spoke against his regime. One of Banda's most eloquent critics was Jack Mapanje, who sought in verse "a way of preserving sanity" in an oth-erwise oppressively insane society. In "Before Chilembwe Tree" Mapanje looks to the great martyr figure as a model for resistance to repression and wonders who will take up the call. Because of this poem and other scathing depictions of corruption and self-seeking in independent Malawi, Banda banned Mapanje's volume of poems and imprisoned the author.[4]

Before Chilembwe Tree

1

Didn't you say we should trace
your footprints unmindful of
quagmires, thickets and rivers
until we reached your *nsolo* tree?

Now, here I seat my gourd of beer
on my little fire throw my millet
flour and my smoked meat
while I await the second coming.

2

Why does your mind boggle:
Who will offer another gourd
Who will force another step
To hide our shame?

The goat blood on the rocks
The smoke that issued
The drums you danced to
And the rains hoped for

You've chanted yourselves hoarse
Chilembwe is gone in your dust
Stop lingering then:
Who will start another fire?

51 • The fate of political dissidents (1975)

The methods that Africa's new dictators used to silence their critics were often brutal. One of the favored treatments was to "detain" people as political prisoners—though without ever calling them such, for that implied a lack of respect for freedom of speech—and keep them in prison for an in-definite period. What one had to do to earn this punishment was usually arbitrary; one could even be a party supporter and be detained if the leader was concerned about losing his power base. Pres-

4. Jack Mapanje, *Of Chameleons and Gods* (London: Heinemann, 1981), 18–19.

ident for life Hastings Kamuzu Banda of Malawi threw numerous people into prison for views that they expressed and, as the following case shows, for those that they did not necessarily espouse. Sam Mpasu, later a member of parliament, was imprisoned by Banda in 1975. A civil servant at the time, Mpasu was working on a major financial project for the government when members of the Special Branch escorted him from his workplace to Mikuyu Maximum Security Prison, where he remained for two years, even though he was never formally charged or brought to trial. His interrogation upon his incarceration follows, capturing both the ordeals that Mpasu went through as a political prisoner and the precarious nature of existence endured by members of Africa's postcolonial elite, who often found themselves either prisoner or prison guard without any apparent action on their own part.[5]

When the large, metal door of Zomba Central Prison closed with a bang behind me, I came face to face with the prison warders [guards]. They seemed too busy to attend to me so I sat down on a form. It seemed to me that good manners were out of place.

"Sit down on the floor!" one of them shouted at me very angrily. "A prisoner does not sit on a chair!" he added.

It did not make sense to me that I should sit down on the floor while there were unoccupied chairs in the office. Nevertheless, although dressed in a suit, I sat down on the floor. I was simmering with rage at my humiliation and helplessness.

At last one of them took out a blank, red folder and started to take down my personal details of name, village, date of birth, next of kin and so forth. Then I was ordered to empty all my pockets, take off my wrist-watch and wedding-ring. I surrendered all to him. Then he demanded my tie, belt, shoes and socks as well. He shoved all of these into a cloth bag which he tossed at the comer of the office. He was through with me.

I was taken out of the administration block into the courtyard. We immediately turned right. The next block served as a clinic on top but underneath were three cells. The prison warder opened the middle cell and pushed me in. He closed the door and bolted it from outside. It was a bare, empty cell. A few minutes later, the door opened again. The guard tossed an old threadbare blanket at me. I caught it with my hands before it could fall on the floor. He looked at me with contempt as if I was not worth speaking to. As far as he was concerned, I was probably less than human or an animal.

He walked away without saying a word. His colleague, who carried a gun, closed the door and then stood guard outside. He used a peep-hole to check on me regularly. I wondered if they would spare the life of that warder if by any chance I escaped. It seemed to me that they, too, were prisoners of a sort. They had to do what they were doing even if they hated it.

The thought of escape was utterly unrealistic. The walls were very thick. The door itself was thick and made of hardwood. There was a tiny window at the top but it was full of thick, steel bars. Besides, the window itself was so high that one would need a ladder to reach it. And it was on the same side where the guard stood. The ceiling was the concrete floor of the upper storey. There was no lighting. Digging the floor was impossible with bare hands. It was concrete.

My threadbare blanket was more than a blanket. It was a bed, a mattress, a bedsheet and a blanket, all rolled into one. It was the only thing between me and the bare concrete floor. I

5. Sam Mpasu, *Political Prisoner 3/75* (Harare, Zimbabwe: African Publishing Group, 1995), 30–40.

was so bewildered that I could not believe or understand what was happening to me. Luckily, the weather in January was fairly warm, but I dreaded what it was like in June when the temperatures dropped.

I spread the blanket on the bare floor. I lay down. I folded my jacket to use it as a pillow. I blinked wide awake for a good part of the night wondering what was happening to me. I was very worried about my wife and her delicate condition. I had not eaten anything the whole day yet they had locked me up for the night without giving me a glass of water or a morsel of food.

It was a long, long night. Morning broke in the end. I heard the sound of keys in the padlock and then the bolt being pulled back. The door was opened to check if I was still in. For some strange reason they kept the door open this time. Later on they allowed me to step outside if I wanted to, but not much farther than the doorstep. The armed guard was trying to be friendly as soon as he ensured that none of his colleagues was looking at him. I sat on the doorstep.

"Is it possible for me to go to the toilet, wherever it is?" I asked him.

"Let us go. I will escort you," he replied. "But you must not speak with anyone."

With his gun on the shoulder he came behind me. He stood by as I faced the urinal. The thought of walking barefoot in that busy toilet, which was hardly clean, filled me with fear about contracting all sorts of diseases.

On return to my cell we found an old prisoner with a wizened, weather-beaten face and a head which was entirely covered with grey hair, waiting for me. He had brought me an old, badly dented, aluminium plate, half-full of porridge. He looked at me with understanding. He shook his head in dismay.

"Eat!" he said. "Prison food is not anything like home food, but that is the only way to stay alive here."

"Where is the spoon and the sugar?" I asked him in all sincerity.

"Sugar and a spoon, in prison?" he asked me, in total disbelief over my naivety.

He laughed a little. He then demonstrated how I could eat the porridge. Eating on a table while sitting on a chair was a luxury that was not available. I sat on the floor.

I lifted the plate to my lips with both hands. I sucked the porridge into my mouth a little at a time. He watched me excitedly as if he was watching a child who was beginning to walk. He displayed a big smile after I had finished.

"Do not be disheartened, this is what men must sometimes go through in life," he told me encouragingly.

"Why am I not allowed to speak to you or to anyone?" I asked.

"That is nonsense. Do not bother about them," he said nonchalantly. "They are trying to intimidate you."

I was really glad to have someone to talk to. At least someone who was not afraid of the arbitrary rules. Apparently, they had appointed him to look after me as a way of preventing me from meeting the other prisoners. He brought me food from the kitchen every day and took back the plate. They did not want me to move away from my cell.

"What are you in prison for?" I asked him. "Theft," he said quite happily, as if theft was something to be proud of.

"How long have you been here and when are you getting released?" I asked him again.

He laughed a bellyful.

"You see," he said, "they built this prison in 1938 and that was the first time I came in. I built it. I have been here ever since."

This was 1975. I could not believe that the man had been in this horrible place for 37 years.

"Are you here for murder perhaps?" I asked him.

"No, no. The only crime I know is theft," he replied honestly.

"You see, when they first locked me up, I was young. After my sentence I went home but I felt out of place. I had no family and no friends. They all felt ashamed of me. They kept away from me. So I stole again in order to come back. This is my home now. I will die here. Whenever my sentence is over, I reserve my place in the cell. I get back the same day. All I do is pick somebody's pocket at the bus station in full view of a policeman. Sometimes I just snatch a banana from a baby's hand and if it cries then that is it; I run a little to allow the people to catch me. When they take me to the police station, I know I am back in prison. The only regret I have is that such small thefts do not get me many years of imprisonment," he said with a straight face.

I could not believe what this old man was saying. One day in that place was too long for me. Yet he wanted to spend the rest of his life there.

"When they let you out, why don't you get a job?" I asked him.

"And look after myself?" he asked me as an answer. Then he laughed. "I tried that once but got bored with waiting for my pay-day. I stole my employer's wrist-watch in order to come back here."

"Don't you feel like having a wife and children? Having a family you can really be proud of?" I asked him.

"What can I give to a family?" he replied.

I got the impression that life had no real meaning to the man. His permanent stay in prison was all that life meant to him.

He disappeared at two o'clock in the afternoon and brought me a plate of badly cooked *nsima* and a metal mug half-full of badly cooked pigeon peas. That was both my lunch and dinner. The food was very unpalatable, but he encouraged me to eat it in order to preserve my life. At four o'clock in the afternoon I was ordered back into my cell. The door was bolted from outside and locked.

When they opened my cell again in the morning I was surprised to see a white man sitting on the doorsteps of the next cell. He, too, was completely bewildered. I gathered a little bit of courage to defy the orders. I greeted the white man in the presence of the prison guard. We got talking. The guard ignored us. The only thing the white man could not stomach was the terrible food. He refused to touch it. He told them that he was prepared to die from starvation. They buckled down and brought him half a loaf of bread and a small can of sardines. His problem was how to eat that bounty without the aid of a table knife, a fork or a spoon. But he soon overcame that by using his unwashed fingers.

Apparently his crime was that he had made some remarks about the political situation in the country when one of his employees was picked up by the Special Branch. Without checking out the veracity of the allegation he was pulled out of his car and rushed to Zomba prison in a police car. That was his arrest, trial, conviction and sentence. That morning he was making a great deal of fuss about the need to see his ambassador urgently. He was a South African and a General Manager of a company in Blantyre. In the afternoon his ambassador, accompanied by his wife, arrived to see him. Later in the evening the police came to take him out. I learnt that he was deported out of the country on twenty-four hours' notice.

On Friday morning, I was on my way to the common toilet when a sick man called my name out from the balcony of the upper storey which served as a clinic.

"Hey Sam, it's me, Richard. Richard Sembereka!" The name did not fit the appearance of the man. I was horrified with what I saw. I had known Richard Sembereka for many years. The last time I had seen him he was the Minister of Labour, a plump and well-dressed man. That was several years before but here was a pathetic-looking skeleton of a man, completely disfigured and destroyed by his long imprisonment. My eyes welled up with tears as I desperately tried to take in the entire picture. The unanswered question I asked myself in my mind was, if this cruel and beastly government could do that to its own Cabinet Minister, then how much more would it do to me, a humble civil servant.

According to the story which circulated at the time Mr. Richard Sembereka disappeared, he had been driving in his ministerial black Mercedes Benz car from Zomba to Blantyre, with the pennant flying on the bonnet, when the police stopped the car at a road-block. Without much ceremony the police pulled him out of the ministerial car and shoved him into a waiting police vehicle. He was then driven straight to Zomba prison for his long, indefinite imprisonment without charge or trial. Five or so years on, he had been reduced to this pathetic skeleton in front of my eyes. I think he saw the distress in my eyes and read my mind.

"Steel yourself up," he said, "it is a very tough world!"

I waved my hand feebly at him, but the prison guard pushed me on. We continued to the public toilet.

On return from the toilet, I was called out to the administration block. Charles Ngwata had come for me. I was led out of the prison to a waiting small van. I was told to go into the back of that van. He closed the door from outside and turned to join the driver in the cab. There were no seats in the van. I sat on the floor.

On arrival at Zomba Police Headquarters, I was led to the Special Branch offices which were in a two-storey block on its own. We climbed stairs to the upper storey where the office of Focus Gwede was. He was not in. I was made to wait in an adjoining office. What I immediately noticed was the atmosphere of fear and trepidation which pervaded the whole place. The policemen could not even mention the name of Focus Gwede but referred to him reverently as "Bwana." He was obviously something of a small god around there. On the grass lawn outside sat small groups of men, women and children, waiting fearfully for this small god to give them permits to visit their relatives in Zomba and Mikuyu prisons.

Focus Gwede was Deputy Head of the Special Branch at the time but he behaved very much as if he owned the place entirely. His close association with Albert Muwalo, who was both the Secretary General and Administrative Secretary of the Malawi Congress Party, ensured that he wielded a lot of power. Mr. Muwalo was virtually Home Affairs Minister, although none of that was reflected in his job title. Pretty soon, the Head of the Special Branch, Mr. Kumpukwe, was appointed into the Diplomatic Service and posted to Britain. Focus Gwede then formally took over as Head of the Special Branch.

A poor messenger was getting out of Gwede's office where he had gone to leave files. He was spotted by none other than Gwede himself. Gwede came up the stairs seething and trembling with rage. He went straight for the poor messenger. Gwede repeatedly and threateningly jabbed his right-hand forefinger on the messenger's chest.

"You do not enter my office when I am not there! Do you understand?" shouted Gwede repeatedly in his rage.

"Yes, sir! No, sir! I am sorry, sir! I will not do it again, sir!" whined the poor messenger subserviently.

He was expecting the whole world to explode in his face any moment.

I watched the whole incident with disgust. I do not know if the incident was stage-managed by Gwede for effect on me and the others. If it was, then it certainly lowered my opinion of Gwede in my mind. I had known Gwede before for some years. I had never known him or even imagined him to be such a mean-spirited terror. If a messenger in full police uniform could not enter Gwede's office, then why on earth was the office left open and why didn't Gwede clean his own office?

Anyway, Gwede cooled down. The poor messenger gratefully walked away, thankful that his explanations and apologies had been accepted. The fact that he had been humiliated in public counted for nothing. I could not understand why he did not stand up for his own human dignity and tell Gwede to piss off. Maybe the job meant much to him or maybe he could have been locked up summarily as well.

It was my turn. Gwede sat me on a chair in his office, opposite his. Between us was his large wooden desk. The desk was totally bare except for an old tape recorder and a horse-whip. Charles Ngwata sat on another chair but on Gwede's side.

"Yes, my friend! Why are you here?" Gwede asked me.

"You called for me," I replied.

He then pulled out the drawer of the desk and laid a sheath of blank paper on the desk. He pulled out another drawer, pulled out a revolver for me to see and then put it back. From his jacket he pulled out a BIC pen and got himself ready to write.

"Who appointed you to go into the Diplomatic Service?" he bellowed at me.

"You should know!" I said to him.

"I am asking you!" he retorted angrily.

"Listen," I said, "I never applied for the job. Nobody applies for that kind of job. I was just told that the President had appointed me to go into the Diplomatic Service. How the hell would I know who had recommended my name?"

Gwede tore up whatever he had been writing and tossed the pieces of paper into a waste-paper basket by his side.

"Alright, let us start again," he said getting another blank sheet of paper ready.

"Who did you meet while you were in the Diplomatic Service?" he asked.

I really thought it was an asinine question.

"You meet and see thousands of people everyday. And you ask me who I met in a period of over two years?" I replied.

"Okay, did you meet any of the rebels?" he asked me.

"Look," I said, "even if I met any of them now, I could not recognize them. I saw both Mr. Kanyama Chiume and Mr. Henry Chipembere, here on Malawi soil, when I was a young boy in secondary school and they were cabinet ministers."

"We know that. If you had met any of them we would have known immediately," replied Gwede boastfully.

"So, why did you ask me?" I said angrily as I stood up.

I leaned on his desk with my left hand and attempted to reach out for his shirt-collar with my right hand. Gun or no gun, I was going to punch his face. He drew back out of my reach.

"Alright, let us start again," he said when he realised that my temper was not as long as he thought it was. "Sit down. Do you want a cup of coffee?" he asked.

"I do not want your coffee!" I replied as I sat down.

He tore up the piece of paper he had been scribbling on and threw the bits into the waste-paper basket again.

"You came back from the Diplomatic Service over a year ago. Why were you still using a diplomatic passport? We found a diplomatic passport in your house!" he started again.

"Every time I go out of the country or come in, I pass through the Immigration. Are you suggesting that the Immigration Officers of Malawi do not recognize a Malawi diplomatic passport?" I asked him.

"Answer the question!" he demanded.

"For your information, I went to the Immigration Office immediately after my return from the Diplomatic Service. I gave them my diplomatic passport and asked for my ordinary passport, but they refused. They said that I should hang on to my diplomatic passport because they are wasting a lot of money. They exchange an ordinary passport for a diplomatic passport and a few months later the same person is appointed into the diplomatic service again. Ask them! Ring them now!" I said to him.

Gwede tore up the sheet he had been writing on and threw the pieces into the waste-paper basket.

"Alright, let us begin again," he said. "You wrote a book about the President. You said that he has no friends."

"Have you read the book?" I asked him.

"Answer me!" he demanded.

"*Nobody's Friend* is the title of the small novel I wrote. It has absolutely nothing to do with Dr Banda or anyone else. It is a book about ordinary people. It is fiction. You should have read it," I told him.

"But there is a passage about a president being assassinated in that book," he said triumphantly.

"That is rubbish!" I said. "Have you read Hamlet, Macbeth or King Lear, all by William Shakespeare? There are passages in all those books about Kings being assassinated. Have you banned those books because they mention the assassination of Kings? Have you banned the Holy Bible because it mentions that Jesus was killed?"

"Let us begin again," Gwede said as he tore up the sheet of paper he had been writing on. He threw the pieces into the waste-paper basket. This time he did not bother to write again.

"Listen to me, my friend! You are finished, finished, finished! I am the last word on detention in Malawi. No one else is above me. As you sit there I have three options for you. Firstly, I can release you now. Yes, you can go home to your wife and back to your job. Secondly, I can take you to court for trial where you will get many years of imprisonment. Lastly, I can send you to Mikuyu Maximum Security Prison, without trial, where you will count the hair on your head. You will never come out. I have decided to send you to Mikuyu where others like you are rotting," he said chillingly. "As long as I sit on this chair, you will never come out. You will rot there!"

He said all this emphatically as he banged the top of the desk with his right-hand fist. I looked at him very defiantly.

"Gwede," I said, "last year, you were not sitting on that chair. Next year, you do not know if you will still be sitting on that chair. Only the Almighty God knows. If God has made it for me to live the rest of my life and die in Mikuyu prison, so be it. It is not you who has done it. You are just an instrument used by God. But I assure you that if God has not made it for me to die in Mikuyu, I shall come out alive and well. And much earlier than you think."

What I said unnerved him a bit. He had played his last card. He had failed to reduce me to a cowering, tearful coward, crying for mercy at his feet. The degree of my defiance shook his self-confidence thoroughly.

"You go for lunch. We shall meet again this afternoon," he said to me as he terminated the interrogation.

Charles Ngwata took me outside. Gwede closed the door of his office. A police constable brought me a plate of rice and red beans. What was strange was that they gave me a spoon as well. That was on Friday, 25 January 1975. My interrogation had taken Gwede's entire morning.

52 • The rebellion begins, South Africa, June 1976

A major turning point occurred in South African history on Wednesday, June 16, 1976, when armed police in Soweto fired on a peaceful demonstration of school children. The children were participating in a march to protest the recently decreed Bantu education amendment, which required African schools to teach much of their curriculum in Afrikaans, viewed by most Africans as the language of their oppressors. They were also objecting to the continued implementation of apartheid, then a three-decade-old policy and one that had long come to be viewed (other than in the public pronouncements of its proponents) as impossible—in its theoretical goal of total racial separation—to achieve. The police shooting, reminiscent of the killing of protestors at Sharpeville a decade and a half earlier, caused international outrage and alerted the world to the tragedy of racism in South Africa. More important, it galvanized another generation of young people in South Africa (much like World War II had influenced Nelson Mandela's generation) to resist with physical force the violence of the apartheid state.

Mark Mathabane was born in 1961 and raised in Alexandra township, a teeming ghetto that supplied cheap labor for white industries near Johannesburg. His parents came from different ethnic groups, but his life was quite disconnected from the rural base of either culture. He was very much a product of the township. In this selection from his hugely popular book, Kaffir Boy, Mathabane describes the events that took place in Alexandra after people heard of the massacre in Soweto. In particular, he captures the process by which mass protest developed in a situation in which all of the prominent leaders of African resistance (such as Nelson Mandela, Steve Biko, and others) were either imprisoned or forced into exile. Revolution did not need to be led; it could take off from the massive discontent of the people.[6]

6. Mark Mathabane, *Kaffir Boy: Growing Out of Apartheid* (London: Pan Books, 1986), 259–68.

FIGURE 25 Students hold a banner protesting apartheid at the funeral of Dumisani Mbatha in Soweto. Mbatha was one of hundreds of students arrested during the Soweto uprising in 1976 and one of at least six hundred dead by the end of the year. AP Photo.

No one thought it would happen, yet everyone knew it had to happen. All the hate, bitterness, frustration and anger that had crystallized into a powder keg in the minds of black students, waiting for a single, igniting spark, found that spark when the Department of Bantu Education suddenly decreed that all black schools had to teach courses in Afrikaans instead of English.

The first spontaneous explosion took place in Soweto on the afternoon of Wednesday, June 16, 1976, where about ten thousand students marched through the dirt streets of Soweto protesting the Afrikaans decree. The immense crowd was orderly and peaceful, and included six- and seven-year-olds, chanting along with older students, who waved placards reading: To Hell with Afrikaans, We Don't Want to Learn the Language of Our Oppressors, Stop Feeding Us a Poisonous Education and We Want Equal Education Not Slave Education.

Unknown to the marchers, along one of the streets leading to Phefeni High School, where a protest rally was to be held, hundreds of policemen, armed with tear gas canisters, rifles, shotguns and sjamboks, had formed a barricade across the street. When they reached the barricaded street the marchers stopped, but continued waving placards and chanting:

"*AMANDLA! AWETHU! AMANDLA! AWETHU!* (POWER IS OURS! POWER IS OURS!)"

While student leaders argued about what to do to diffuse the situation, the police suddenly opened fire. Momentarily the crowd stood dazed, thinking that the bullets were plastic and had been fired into the air. But when several small children began dropping down like swatted flies, their white uniforms soaked in red blood, pandemonium broke out.

The police continued firing into the crowd. Students fled into houses alongside the street; others tripped, fell and were trampled underfoot. Some were so shocked they didn't know what to do except scream and cry. Still others fought bullets with rocks and schoolbags. One youth saw a thirteen-year-old go down, a bullet having shattered his forehead. He picked the dying boy up, and carried him to a yard nearby. The photo of the two—the lifeless boy in the hands of a youth whose face blazed with anger, hate and defiance—made headlines around the world.

In the school bus from Tembisa, reading the gruesome accounts of what took place in Soweto in the late afternoon edition of the *World,* I felt hate and anger well up inside me. I cried. The entire edition of the *World* was devoted to the story. One of the pictures of the carnage showed a hacked white policeman near an overturned, burnt police car, surrounded by groups of students shouting defiant slogans, fists upraised in the black power salute. I gloated, and wished that more white people had been killed.

The bus was packed, yet silent. Heads were buried inside newspapers. Tears flowed freely down the cheeks of youths returning from school, and men and women returning from work. I again looked at the photo of the two boys, and then and there I knew that my life would never, could never, be the same again.

"They opened fire," mumbled David, who was sitting alongside me, shaking his head with disbelief. "They didn't give any warning. They simply opened fire. Just like that. Just like that," he repeated. "And small children, small defenseless children, dropped down like swatted flies. This is murder, cold-blooded murder."

There was nothing I could say in reply, except stare back. No words could possibly express what I felt. No words could express the hatred I felt for the white race.

"This is the beginning of something too ugly to contemplate," David said. "Our lives can, and should, never be the same after this."

I nodded.

At school assembly the next day, the mood was somber. There was tension in the air. There was a fire, a determination, in students that I had never seen before. The first thing the principal said was, "I guess you've all heard about the tragedy that took place in Soweto yesterday."

"Yes," the crowd of students roared.

"It is indeed a dark moment in our lives," the principal said. "But we here have to go on learning. The government has ordered all other schools to stay open. I'm sure things will settle down and will return to normal soon."

A murmur of disapproval surged through the crowd. One student in the back row shouted, "There can be no school while our brothers and sisters are being murdered in Soweto!"

"Yes, yes, no school, no school!" erupted the rest of the students.

"There will be no demonstrations in this school," the principal said authoritatively. "We've had enough bloodshed in Soweto already."

"The struggle in Soweto is our struggle too," some students clamored. "The Afrikaans decree applies to us as well. We too want an equal education. The bloody Boers should stop force-feeding us slave education. To hell with Afrikaans! To hell with Afrikaans!" The cry infected everybody. Students began organizing into groups to plot strategy for a peaceful rally in solidarity with our brothers and sisters in Soweto. The principal tried to restore order but was ignored. Most teachers helped us with the planning of the rally. "Be peaceful and orderly," one teacher said, "or else you'll have the whole Boer army down your necks in no time."

We painted placards that condemned Bantu Education, Afrikaans and apartheid. We demanded an equal education with whites. We urged the government to stop the killings in Soweto. Student leaders were chosen to lead the march to other schools in the area, where we planned to pick up more students for a rally at a nearby stadium. Within an hour we had filled the street and formed columns. We began marching.

"AMANDLA! AWETHU! AMANDLA! AWETHU!" we chanted and waved placards.

From government buildings nearby white people who headed the Tembisa city councils hurriedly stepped out, jumped into cars and zoomed off under police escort. Our ranks swelled with youths who didn't attend school. Black men and women cheered and exhorted us from yards alongside the streets. "TO HELL WITH A FOURTH-CLASS EDUCATION!" "STOP THE GENOCIDE IN SOWETO!" "AMANDLA! AWETHU! AMANDLA! AWETHU!" The cries reverberated through the air.

We picked up hundreds of students from other schools and then headed for the stadium. As the river of black faces coursed through the street leading to the stadium, a group of police vans and trucks suddenly appeared from nowhere and barricaded the street.

"Don't panic! Don't panic!" the student leaders yelled at the restless crowd. "Let's remain peaceful and orderly. They'll leave us alone if we don't provoke them."

Policemen with riot gear, rifles, tear gas canisters and sjamboks poured out of the trucks and formed a phalanx across the wide street. As in Soweto, most of them were black. From one of the trucks the husky voice of a white man suddenly boomed through a megaphone: "DISPERSE AND RETURN TO YOUR HOMES AND SCHOOLS! OR WE'LL BE FORCED TO USE FORCE!"

A few students started turning back, but the majority stood and waited, chanting defiantly with fists raised in the black power salute. We began singing, "Nkosi Sikelel'i Afrika" ("God Bless Africa"), the ANC's anthem:

> God bless Africa
> Raise up our descendants
> Hear our prayers.
> Come, holy spirit,
> Come, holy spirit,
> Lord bless us,
> Us, your children.

The police charged. Several shots rang out. Pandemonium broke out. Students fled for cover. It rained tear gas canisters. David and I managed to flee into one of the nearby yards, jumped its fence and ran all the way to school, where teachers told us to go home immediately, for police were raiding schools. The bus stop was a mile or so away. As we made our way through the matchbox-type Tembisa houses, we saw fires and palls of black smoke in the distance. Some beer halls and vehicles had been gutted.

"I hope there's still a bus out of this place," David panted.

We found what turned out to be one of the last buses out of Tembisa, for the police were quarantining the ghetto, barring all company vehicles and public transportation. On our way to Alexandra there was unusual traffic on the highway leading to the Jan Smuts Airport.

"White folks are fleeing by the droves," I remarked.

"They're afraid this whole thing may turn into a revolution," David replied.

Approaching Alexandra, we saw several armoured cars formed into roadblocks, sealing all the roads leading in and out of Alexandra. All vehicles were being stopped and searched. Our bus was stopped, and several soldiers in camouflage uniforms, carrying automatic weapons, ordered us out and lined us up alongside the body of the bus. I shook like a leaf. In the distance, Alexandra resembled a battlefield. Smoke and fire engulfed the area, and from time to time, the sound of gunfire reverberated through the clouds of smoke.

"You'll have to walk home," one of the white soldiers ordered us. "Buses can't go in there. You bloody Kaffirs are burning down everything."

We immediately headed homeward across the veld. From time to time, people glanced nervously over their shoulders, afraid of being shot in the back. When David and I entered Alexandra, we saw several burning government buildings, beer halls, schools, stores belonging to Indians and Chinamen. A bus had been overturned and set afire. People were looting all around, making off with drums of paraffin, bags of mealie meal, carcasses of beef still dripping blood, Primus stoves, boxes of canned goods, loaves of bread and so on. There were power and energy in men, women and children that I had never seen before.

The rebellion had begun in Alexandra.

53 • Torture under apartheid (1977)

Fearful of the challenge to white rule, the apartheid regime embarked on a massive campaign to crush the protest movement that had begun in Soweto on June 16, 1976, and that soon expanded enormously throughout the rest of South Africa. In the following six to nine months, the police arrested at least six thousand people, "detained" thousands more under the Terrorism Act (which permitted detention without charge, trial, or even the informing of the next of kin that an individual had been detained), and killed at least seven hundred individuals, the great majority of them under the age of twenty-five. One of the protestors arrested was Dan Montsisi, then a teenager, who in testimony that he was finally able to give in public in 1996, described the torture to which the police had subjected him two decades earlier.

Montsisi and his generation emerged from their ordeals even more committed to the struggle to end apartheid. Many sought refuge overseas and became soldiers in a renewed armed struggle that the ANC embarked upon in the late 1970s and the 1980s. In 1994, when South Africa elected its first postapartheid government, Montsisi won a seat in the new parliament as a representative of the ANC. The white electorate for its part also hardened in its attitudes. In the 1977 parliamentary election the National Party returned to power with its largest number of seats ever, supported by an overwhelming majority of both Afrikaans- and English-speaking white voters. The white electorate continued to return the National Party to power throughout the 1980s. The following text is from Montsisi's testimony to the Truth and Reconciliation Commission in July 1996.[7]

Mr. Montsisi: Ja [yes] I was subjected to torture. I was not the only one. It was quite a number of us and I have spoken to some of the officials about that issue. I mean like I said about the detention we got detained on the 10th in 1977. They started quite early. Probably they were eager on the 13th June we were taken to Protea Police Station where the torture actually started, and the type of questions they asked obviously they wanted to know if we are working for the ANC, and they wanted Paul Langa. They arrested Paul before me, so what they wanted to do was that I must testify and say that Paul did all these things and so on and so on. At that time I didn't know Paul, I mean that's what I said to them. So they were quite angry. They asked about Winnie Mandela, whether I have been to Winnie Mandela's place. And they asked also about activities in the demonstration, where I participated. I tried to cooperate with them concerning student activities because I was a student and even those demonstrations where I did not go I said I did, those meetings where students were, where I was not even there, I said I did, simply because I did not want them to press me on other issues. I was not a member of the suicide squad. I knew about the suicide squad but I denied it. So well they got fed up with me and they actually began in a sense, so there was this trolley and Van Roy, those who fetched me from John Vorster Square and we drove down to Protea Police Station, and they used the rubber truncheon to beat you all over the head and it was quite difficult because I was blindfolded and I couldn't see the direction from which the truncheon was coming from, so it was quite easy for them. It went on for quite some time. And then you could also be kicked and beaten with fists, stomach and so on. And there was also one other method they used, the rifle. They used the rifle to stamp on your toes. So every time you talk what they do not agree with they use the rifle on your toes. And one method they referred to as an airplane, I didn't know what they were talking about, but I was grabbed and they swung me and they threw me right into the air but when you land, fortunately it was a wooden floor so they did that several times. All along I mean they were like laughing and so on and so on, ridicule you and so on. And they were pulling the muscles on the back to put a strain on you so they come from behind and they pull the muscles with their own hands. And so they also forced me to squat. That time I was quite weak and I didn't have much power left in me. I could have collapsed any time but they still continued, so I had to squat against the wall and a brick was placed on my hands as I squatted against the wall. I don't know what happened because I think the brick fell and it hit me on the head and when I regained consciousness they had poured water all over me. So the first person I saw looking down at me was Visser, Captain Visser from Protea Police Station. So all I said to him when I saw him was that "Baas they are killing me," that is what I said to him. And I never thought I would say "baas" but I did. So they explained to him that—they used very strong language . . . so they were going to continue. That time they had removed the blindfold and he left the room, and then as soon as he left I could see the people who were instrumental in the torture. Although there were something like eight policemen inside there were two others Trollip and Van Rooyen,

---

7. The full transcript of Dan Montsisi's testimony to the Truth and Reconciliation Commission is available at http://www.doj.gov.za/trc/hrvtrans/soweto/montsisi.htm.

those were the ones who were the leaders and the senior was this Lieutenant van Rooyen. So they blindfolded me again and this time they took off my pants and my underpants and they used what we referred to later as we were talking about it as a USO, an unidentified squeezing object, but probably it was a plier to actually press my testes. They did that twice or thrice and when they do that it becomes very difficult for you to scream because you like choke. When they leave you then you are able to scream. So they did that twice, thrice. I don't know what happened and again they poured water all over me. And I was taken to John Vorster and ja I was dumped there. Later I saw a doctor, a district surgeon Williamson, so he was able to treat me. He wasn't supposed to see me, it was just a mistake on the part of the police, because in the cells in John Vorster Square when they were opening the cells they opened my own cell by mistake. Those who were tortured must not be seen by the doctor because they will be . . . (indistinct), so this policeman opened my door unaware and then I couldn't go on my own so I used the wall to walk towards the part of the cells [that] was a surgery where the doctor saw us, so I crawled and so on and so on. When the security police saw me they wanted to take me back to the cells so I screamed, so fortunately the doctor came out and he saw me, then he said I want to see that man. So our own political activists, the students who were tortured were there to see the doctor but fortunately if he doesn't . . . (indistinct) allow you. My whole body was swollen, there were stripes all over the body and so on. So the doctor was able to see me and he made a profile of a human being to indicate all areas of injury. My medical record was subsequently submitted in court so it's properly recorded. When I recovered this was some time in September they took me again. This time it was on the 10th Floor of John Vorster Square and there it was De Meyer, Sergeant de Meyer, Captain . . . (tape ends)

. . . they didn't touch the face and Stroewig was just concentrating on the head. He didn't hit anything except the head. So he just focused on the head and so on and so forth. For the whole day he did not hit anything except the head and I think I collapsed and again I was taken to hospital. So this time they took me to the Florence Nightingale Clinic in Hillbrow. It was a White hospital so no Africans can see one of the student activist casualties, unlike if you had to take him to an African clinic, quite a number of people could have seen him. So I was smuggled into an exclusive White clinic. There they did brain scanning and well they checked me and they wanted to do a lumbar puncture. At that time I didn't understand what a lumbar puncture was so they explained that they are going to stick a needle in my spine and extract the liquid. I refused because I wasn't quite sure whether I could trust them to do that to me. I knew the spine to be quite sensitive so I refused. So the security cops came again to try and talk to me to do the lumbar puncture, I refused. They promised that they would take me back to prison and beat me up and bring me . . . (indistinct) and so on and so on, but once I was with the doctor I was able to tell the doctor that he shouldn't, so fortunately the doctor did not do it. I recovered after some time. I was taken back to the cells. Later well we were tried I was sentenced to Robben Island and Mandela wanted a report about June 16 including Mr. Sisulu there and Govan Mbeki. So together with . . . (indistinct) we had liked to write a comprehensive report about the events. They also saw the truth, I mean the Cilliers Commission report [the official government report on the Soweto uprising] and we were able in fact to get a copy of that and actually criticise it.

But having said all this that I have said, I want to say that the students at that time they had a support base and members of the community whom even up to this point in time we hold very, very dear. People for instance like Fanyana Mazibuko, Tom Manthata and Ligau Matabata, those were teachers during that period with whom we worked very, very closely. And there was Dr Abu Asfad, Dr Massari and Dr Motlana, most of the casualties, those that we did not want to take to hospital we took to them and student activists who no longer had parents, who no longer had their homes were just wandering around, whenever they are sick these are the doctors who used to attend to them. There is one other doctor whom I have actually forgotten the name but somewhere in Molapo, those were some of the kind people who used to treat us when we are ill, whether it's flu, cold or that. And you had people like Beyers Naude for instance. From Beyers we could be able to like I said print pamphlets, get vehicles and also get financial resources from him. Beyers was banned that time but he was amongst some of the Whites who were able to come into the township of Soweto in the evening to be with the students. I remember at one stage when we were in town and we had seen him he had to drive all the way from town to actually bring us into the township.

When I started to read the Freedom Charter very early in the 70s and so on, later in the 80s I didn't understand what the ANC meant when they said South Africa belonged to all those who live in it, both Black and White, but immediately I saw practically a White man like Beyers Naude risking his own life to come into the township I knew that there were White South Africans in South Africa who were quite prepared to lend a hand and be part of this lovely country.

54 • A task which shook my whole being (1970s)

Torture was no more effective in crushing opposition in South Africa than it was in Banda's Malawi or elsewhere in Africa. Indeed, state repression became itself a further instigator of public protest, especially in South Africa, where opposition to apartheid grew massively in the late 1970s and throughout the 1980s. The basis of this opposition rested on ordinary people fighting racism daily. Ellen Kuzwayo, a prominent leader of this opposition, did much to promote awareness of the way in which women were ill-treated under apartheid. She was ready to risk her own life in order to speak out for what she believed was right. In the following extract, Kuzwayo explains why she agreed to testify at the trial of several youths whom she did not even know (they included Dan Montsisi). At the time Kuzwayo was approached by the defense lawyer, she had just been released from a banning order. Though speaking out in court risked further state sanction, Kuzwayo decided that she could not stand by and allow the courts to act without getting some understanding of what urban family life was like for young Africans growing up in Soweto, Alexandra, and other apartheid ghettos in the 1970s. Like Montsisi, Kuzwayo was elected to parliament in South Africa's first fully democratic election in 1994. She served until 1999, and died in 2006 at the age of ninety-two.[8]

[O]nce in my life I was called upon to do a task which shook my whole being as it involved me mentally, emotionally, physically and, I have no doubt, spiritually too.

It was on my release from detention, when there was very alarming talk that eleven students—ten boys and one girl—who had been arrested under the Terrorism Act were facing

8. Ellen Kuzwayo, *Call Me Woman* (San Francisco: Spinsters Ink, 1985), 222–27.

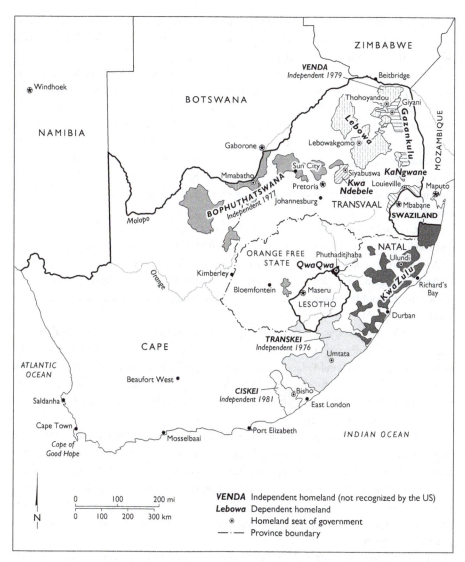

MAP 1 South Africa's homelands, which constituted less than 20 percent of the country's total land, were designated as the legal home of more than 80 percent of the country's population under apartheid. The homelands were designated for individual tribes, and the South African government tried to promote them as individual and independent countries for Africans. More than 3.5 million Africans were forcibly removed from South African cities and placed in the homelands during the 1970s and 1980s. The homelands did not officially cease to exist until 1994.

very serious charges which could lead to long prison sentences, or worse. I had only been out of detention myself about two months when I received a letter from Advocate Ernest Wentzel, a leading Johannesburg lawyer, well-known for dealing with political cases. He wanted me to see him in his office. When I delayed responding, he sent me a second letter expressing the urgency of the matter he wished to talk to me about. This weighed rather heavily on my mind, with the scar of detention still very fresh in my memory. But his letter, which should have clarified the issue and thus eased my mind, was vague as well as pressing and when I arrived in his office, I had numerous unanswered questions on my mind.

Advocate Wentzel started by outlining in detail the case of the eleven students, emphasising the gravity of the charges they faced, and expressing his fears of what the outcome could be. Genuinely puzzled by this story, as I had absolutely no contact with this case, I bluntly put a question to him, "What has all this to do with me, Mr. Wentzel?" It was only at this point that he disclosed to me in his gentle way the need to find a social worker of repute and an unimpeachable record of service in the black community, to plead in mitigation for those students. It was hoped in this way to reduce the possibility of heavy sentences—then estimated at nothing less than life imprisonment for some, without ruling out capital punishment for one of them.

But, I simply could not come to terms with why this lawyer was sharing this very delicate and challenging subject with me. Looking straight into his face, and very much agitated, I replied, "Why do you tell me all this? It has nothing to do with me." He continued to share with me his fears for the outcome of the case and revealed that after consideration he had concluded that he could not find anyone better qualified than myself to make the plea in mitigation for the students.

I frankly told him that the fact that I had just been released from detention alone disqualified me from carrying out that assignment, as it might have an adverse influence on the court; further that this would place me in jeopardy with the authorities, who already saw me as a troublemaker and might thus find good reason to put me back in prison. I completely turned down the request. No amount of persuasion would change my mind. I was too disoriented by my recent experiences to accept the challenge.

Yet Advocate Wentzel did not give up. He painted a picture of the judge expected to be on the Bench that day. He said he needed someone who would be able to get through to the humanity of the man. He needed in particular a social worker who would be able to describe in court some of the very oppressive conditions experienced by the majority of the young population in Soweto. Everyone had advised him to approach me. But my reaction to this was precise, simple and clear; that there were many of us with my training and experience in our practice in Soweto.

His last words to me were: "I approached you because I have great fears about the outcome of the sentence. I appealed to you in the firm belief that you are the only person who would bring home to the judge the truth about the conditions and circumstances which contribute to some of the seemingly negative behaviour of youth in Soweto. I am not saying your mitigation would have a favourable effect on the sentences of the day; on the other hand, I have a hope it might. If some of them end up with life imprisonment or capital punishment after your mitigation, then we shall say we tried, and our best was not good enough. Now that you say you cannot, when the worst comes to the worst, we shall have nothing to test what could have been our best performance against the sentence they will get."

It was at that point that something sparked a completely new feeling in me. Fear, doubt, hesitation, all three deserted me. I turned to Advocate Wentzel saying, "If I am the last and only person you placed your hopes on for this case, in the name of the black child, I have no choice but to plead in mitigation for their safety and for my conscience. If they get life imprisonment or capital punishment after I refused to assist, I will carry a guilt feeling to my dying day."

I had hardly left his office when I found my mind immersed in the decision I had made. Had I done the right thing? Would this involvement not have repercussions which would see me back in prison? Was there still a chance of backing out of this arrangement? But if I did that, what would happen to the students?

There was still about a month to go before the trial, and I passed a very tedious four weeks, endlessly reviewing the decision I had made. This was often accompanied by sleepless nights spent in an effort to reconcile myself to this very frightening commitment which left me frantic and quite isolated. I did not share my decision with my family and close friends, to avoid severe criticism and possible ridicule from them for making a martyr of myself.

The fateful day and hour finally arrived and found me still full of doubts, regrets, fears and completely withdrawn from any possible source of support, encouragement and understanding. On my arrival at court that morning I felt completely numb and cold. The unfamiliar location of the court and its surroundings in Kempton Park added to my bewilderment. I moved from one end of the corridor to the other in the hope of bumping into the defending counsel or someone I knew. Instead, the interior seemed to be full of black and white uniformed police who all appeared very unfriendly, or so I saw them. Here and there were intimate groups of ordinary people who I assumed were either relatives of the accused or their close friends. I finally collected myself and sat down in one place hoping to see the advocate or his colleague walk in. As I raised my eyes I saw Mathabo Pharase, one of the women I had been detained with. We were both so preoccupied with our own thoughts that we greeted each other very casually, just a "How do you do?," both cool and vacant.

At about eight fifty-five, I could not contain my panic, and at that point approached one of the court officials to find out the whereabouts of the lawyers' offices. I walked in after a distant "Come in," to find the gentlemen on their feet ready to go into court. They didn't dismiss me ungraciously, rather, as they walked out they left me with the impression of how much depended on me. But I still had not received the support I had so much hoped for.

Five minutes dragged by. I was experiencing hot and cold flushes. I was aware of the heavy thump of my heart, and my short intake of breath in between. As people moved into court, I mingled apologetically with them and found myself a protected seat amongst the spectators.

I fixed my eyes on the steps leading from somewhere under the building from where I expected the accused to emerge. I was very keen to see them as I knew nothing about them, yet, when they finally walked up the steps, I felt a cold chill run down my spine. They were so composed and very strong, a condition which strangely unsettled me. I suddenly felt altogether unequal to the task.

I listened with great interest to Mr. Montsisi, the father of Dan Montsisi, the first accused. He pleaded the case of his son with courage, composure and absolute conviction. He encouraged and inspired me. The priest who followed, on the other hand, sounded frightened when he was called to testify about Dan Montsisi as a member of his congregation.

When my name was called to enter the witness box, my mind was in complete turmoil. At that point, I turned to the long-standing, living practice of mine, which has seen me through some of the most awesome experiences in my life. I handed over the challenge which faced me to the "powers" which were fed to me by my mother in my early childhood, as the "foundations of living": "Nothing is too big or difficult for the Creator," and "Always turn to Him when you are in need." Those words came alive at that moment of reckoning.

I remember very clearly standing in the witness box with my hand up, saying, "So help me God" as I faced the judge, still in the grips of fear. When he started questioning me I was completely at a loss as I did not know how to address him. This was my very first experience in the witness box. The quick-thinking, supportive interpreter handed me a piece of paper on which he had scribbled: "Address the judge 'Your Lordship.'" You can be sure I still made mistakes, but I managed.

I did fairly well with the advocate. He asked for my name, established my profession and occupation, and asked me to say why, as a social worker, I saw the black children in the country as very deprived. My response to this was to highlight the complete absence of recreational facilities in the form of playgrounds and leisure equipment, to point to the overcrowding in homes where ten to fifteen people living in a three-roomed house was a common condition; to describe how the youth gathered on street corners at night; to explain that parents—mothers in particular—had to leave their young children sometimes as early as four o'clock in the morning and come back long after six or seven o'clock in the evening, in a desperate effort to augment their husbands' appallingly low wages.

It was against this background that I appealed to the judge to see and understand the life of the Soweto child. When I thought that I read doubt on his face, I supported all that I had said by outlining a very nasty and recent experience that the Orlando Home for Children had had. Thugs had walked into the children's Home at night, ignoring the staff on duty there, and had removed the TV set donated to the Home by some well-wishers. The children, all aged less than twelve years, were left shaken with fright, puzzled and robbed of the best, last and only instrument of joy and entertainment they cherished in their lives. This offence the police, perhaps for reasons beyond their control, failed to investigate to the fullest, and it was left to the staff to discover the stolen TV set, which they brought back, reporting their find to the police.

In his amazement the judge wanted to know whether what I had just related was true. I reminded him that I was giving my evidence under oath. That was sufficient. There was no doubt he was puzzled beyond all understanding, but believed my story, which was true in all respects.

Unfamiliar with court procedure, and accepting my first evidence as final, I was taken aback when the prosecutor took over from the defence advocate, displaying an attitude of impatience and superiority. After reminding me that he had heard that I was a social worker of standing in Soweto with long dealings with youth, he wanted to know if I had any knowledge of Black Consciousness, and what my opinion of it was; further, if I believed in it. A very loaded question by any standard. I was rather disturbed by his arrogant manner, but I felt the need to give him an unflinching and convincing reply. "Yes, I know something about 'Black Consciousness,'" I said. I went on to tell the court, interrupted by the prosecutor's retorts and unsettling interjections, that I saw it as a very significant period in the history and life of the black people in South Africa; a stage when they had been compelled to pause, stunned by the overwhelming impact of political events, and assess who they were, where they came from and where they were going. The prosecutor's irritating interjections were undoubtedly affecting my speech and disposition at this stage.

Unexpectedly, the judge, seeing my predicament, I suppose, addressed me by name. I raised my head from the gradual droop it was taking and looked up startled. "I am the only person in this court you should address yourself to and be conscious of. Be free to express your convictions and beliefs without any inhibition." I took in the message, resumed my courage and followed his guidance to the letter with confidence. I ended up saying that, to me, Black Consciousness was an institution, a process whereby blacks in South Africa were beginning to take a serious took at themselves against the perilous political plight of a history of close on 350 years, and to find a way of redeeming themselves from that crippling situation. "This is our dilemma," I finished. "I believe in Black Consciousness."

By now I was very tired, having spent two hours in the witness box, and dry from my non-stop presentation. I appealed to the judge saying, "My Lord, am I allowed to drink water in your court?" His subtle support and protection from the haughty prosecutor had fully restored my confidence. With a wry smile, he then ordered that I be given a glass of water and let me drink it at my leisure. I recognised a clear and unspoken expression of justice and felt good.

I had hardly taken my seat with the rest of those who had come to court when suddenly someone took me in his arms and crushed me, almost squeezing the very last breath out of me. As I turned to see who this very brave person was, I saw a man who looked beside himself, as if under some strange influence. All he said to me was, "You are not an ordinary woman, you pleaded like a man, only a man could speak the way you did." Before I could respond or ask a question, he was kissing me and thanking me. He was one of the parents of the eleven appearing in court that morning. I was just overwhelmed both by the mill I had been through in the witness box and the unexpected response of this parent. I sat huddled in my seat as if nailed to it.

When sentence was passed, four were found guilty including Dan Montsisi, who was sentenced to four years; the other three received shorter sentences. The remaining seven were given a warning and discharged.

55 • Another coup in Ghana (1979)

Africa had undergone its second coup in February 1966 when army officers overthrew Kwame Nkrumah while he was out of the country. Discontent was fueled by a disastrous drop in the international price of Ghana's major export, cocoa, coupled with the extravagant cost of Nkrumah's development projects. Nevertheless, the coup leaders justified their action as necessitated by a combination of authoritarian rule and corruption. Their aim, they argued, was to restore democracy in Ghana. Thirteen years and another coup later, junior officers led by Flight Lieutenant Jerry Rawlings attempted a rebellion in May 1979 against senior officers who, they argued, had become as antidemocratic and as corrupt as the politicians they had overthrown. Rawlings and his coconspirators were not successful and were imprisoned. A few weeks later, however, other junior officers sympathetic to Rawlings's aims removed the senior generals who had ruled Ghana since the country's second coup in January 1972 and released Rawlings from prison. The generals were later executed. The following speech, in which he explains the aims of the coup leaders, was broadcast by Rawlings two weeks after he came to power on June 4, 1979. Rawlings has been one of the more charismatic and successful politicians in postcolonial Africa. He returned Ghana to civilian rule in September 1979 but again led a coup—based on the argument that the new government was unable to cope with economic crises (often arising from the falling price of cocoa)—in December 1981. Rawlings introduced the structural adjustment program in Ghana in 1983, often used authoritarian rule to enforce implementation of unpopular polices, and remained head of state until 2001. The text is from a radio broadcast made by Rawlings on June 17, 1979.[9]

I came to the studio tonight to talk to you about the crucial presidential and parliamentary elections scheduled for tomorrow, Monday, 18 June 1979. In my maiden broadcast to the nation I made it abundantly clear that the elections would go on as planned, and the Armed Forces Revolutionary Council would not do anything that would disrupt the programme for the election. In fulfilment of this promise, the Armed Forces Revolutionary Council has had consultations with the Electoral Commissioner and has been offered all the necessary assistance needed to accomplish it.

The Council has issued directives to all government departments to release (? the people) to assist the Electoral Commission. Aircraft have been made available to the Commission to distribute their election material and equipment. A communications network has been set up for the collation and relaying of election results. (? Twenty thousand police) officers are going to be deployed and attached to the country's (? 20,000) polling booths, and security coverage is to be provided for the security of all its papers and other electorally sensitive material.

Let me at this juncture refer briefly to some of the glaring injustices of the society which made the Armed Forces Revolutionary Council take over the reins of government of this country in the course of this month. These injustices are in the main due to the unfair distribution of the national cake; there are two aspects to this: in the first instance, we have our fellow countrymen and women using their connections to lay their hands on certain portions of [words indistinct] national resources, they then come round and use this position and the factor of [word indistinct] to exploit their fellow countrymen by manipulations of various types. In this category of nation wreckers are the hoarders and profiteers as well as Shylock landlords and transport owners. Another group of thieves are those who refuse to return to the national coffer what they know to be legitimately due from them. The result of this is that the national coffers are absolutely empty. This group, no less than the first—though by different means—exploits the ordinary Ghanaian and must bear their full share of the blame for the intolerable plight that is the lot of the majority. By their action, they have reduced the vital resources which would otherwise be available to improve the lot of the ordinary man, by their rationing these same resources to themselves, their families, and their friends, by illegally keeping for themselves what is not theirs, they deprive others of what should be a fair share of the national resources.

The activities of these groups of Ghanaians—including some non-Ghanaians—who have used the safety from detection and punishment provided them by their connection with those in power, have led to a situation of a widening divergence between productive effort and reward. The nation is full of numerous stories and examples of the non-productive but

9. Barbara E. Okeke, *4 June: A Revolution Betrayed* (Enugu, Nigeria: Ikenga, 1982), 135–38. The text in parentheses in the speech is by Okeke.

well-connected individual getting increasingly and openly wealthy, while the hard-working but lowly, get increasingly impoverished.

We intend, in the short period at our disposal, to wage a relentless war against these social injustices. We intend to ensure that whatever resources we have should be used to improve the living conditions of Ghanaians as a whole, and not for any privileged minority. We intend to ensure that only those living within the law and selling at the official prices will remain within the distributive trade. We do not promise the impossible; we recognize that while Ghana is potentially rich, we have problems. We are, at present, a developing country, and hence poor. All we ask is that all those connected with the distribution system to desist forthwith from any act which leads to the unnecessary exploitation of the common man . . .

The basic task is that together we must try to use all the resources at our disposal to increase the overall supply of goods in the system and ensure that the goods thus produced are fairly distributed.

I wish to avail myself of this opportunity to emphasize once again our resolve not to entrench ourselves in office; we are professional soldiers, and we want to return to the line. It was for the resuscitation and the preservation of the traditions of our profession, and the correction of injustices in the society to which we all belong [? that led us] to overthrow the Supreme Military Council. We are in for house-cleaning, and not for the government of this country. In this situation, we would like to assure the nation that we do not favour or support any of the political parties or presidential candidates contesting the election. Let the people choose freely, honestly and wisely for themselves the people they want to rule them. As soldiers, we are prepared to cooperate with, and be loyal to, any democratically and popularly elected government . . .

Since our assumption of office we have had several proposals on the return of the country to civilian rule. After careful consideration of all the proposals, the Armed Forces Revolutionary Council has decided that Monday, 1st October 1979, should be the target date for the return of the country to civilian rule.

CHAPTER SEVEN

Colonial Legacies of Exploitation (1980–2008)

56 • The problem with Africa (1980)

By the end of the 1970s, it was clear that there was not going to be an easy path to either political stability or economic growth in Africa. Although Portugal had withdrawn from its African possessions, in southern Africa war expanded as South Africa sought to destabilize the new independent socialist governments of Angola and Mozambique. It came about by covert invasion in Angola and by military raids and the use of proxies in Mozambique. Robert Mugabe and his allies had fought the white settler government of Ian Smith to a standstill in 1980, and when independence came to southern Rhodesia as the new state of Zimbabwe, the social and economic costs of two decades of war were enormous. Elsewhere in Africa, economic decline was evident, especially as international prices fell for the raw materials exported from the continent. In 1980, the World Bank, established in 1945 to rebuild Europe after World War II, turned its focus to poverty reduction in Africa with a report that attempted to assess the causes of economic distress on the continent (in the course of which the bank provided a brief assessment of the legacy of colonialism) and to develop a program of what would be termed "structural adjustment."[1]

The Present Economic Crisis

During the past two decades economic development has been slow in most of the countries of Sub-Saharan Africa. When, in the mid-1970s, the world economy experienced inflation and recession, nowhere did the crisis hit with greater impact than in this region.

The picture is not uniformly bleak. There are signs of progress throughout the continent. Vastly more Africans are in schools, and most are living longer. Roads, ports and new cities have been built and new industries developed. Technical and managerial positions, formerly occupied by foreigners, are now held by Africans. Of the 45 countries in the region, nine posted annual growth rates of over 2.5 percent per capita between 1960 and 1979.

But for most African countries, and for a majority of the African population, the record is grim and it is no exaggeration to talk of crisis. Slow overall economic growth, sluggish agricultural performance coupled with rapid rates of population increase, and balance-of-payments and fiscal crises—these are dramatic indicators of economic trouble.

Between 1960 and 1979, per capita income in 19 countries grew by less than 1 percent per year, while during the last decade, 15 countries recorded a *negative* rate of growth of in-

---

1. World Bank, *Accelerated Development in Sub-Saharan Africa: An Agenda for Action* (Washington, D.C.: World Bank, 1981), 2–5, 9–12.

come per capita. And by the end of the 1970s, economic crises were battering even high-growth countries like Kenya, Malawi, and Ivory Coast—where annual per capita GNP growth had averaged an annual 2.7 percent between 1960 and 1979—compelling them to design programs, supported by the Bank, to restructure their economies. Output per person rose more slowly in Sub-Saharan Africa than in any other part of the world, particularly in the 1970s, and it rose more slowly in the 1970s than in the 1960s.

The tragedy of this slow growth in the African setting is that incomes are so low and access to basic services so limited. Per capita income was $329 in 1979 (excluding Nigeria) and $411 when Nigeria is included. Death rates are the highest in the world and life expectancy is the lowest (47 years). Fifteen to twenty percent of the children die by their first birthday, and only 25 percent of the population have access to safe water. Of the 30 countries classified by the United Nations Conference on Trade and Development (UNCTAD) as the poorest in the world, 20 are African. Of the 36 countries listed in the World Bank's World Development Report 1981 as "low income" (a per capita income of less than $370), almost two thirds are African.

The economic crisis is especially evident in agriculture, and is reflected in output figures. Export crop production stagnated over the past two decades. A 20-percent increase in production registered during the 1960s was wiped out by a decline of similar proportions in the 1970s. Consequently, Africa's share of the world market dwindled. As for food crops, while data are uncertain, they leave no doubt about general tendencies. Total food production rose by 1.5 percent per year in the 1970s, down from 2 percent in the previous decade. But since population was rising rapidly—by an annual average of 2.5 percent in the 1960s and 2.7 percent in the 1970s—food production per person was stagnant in the first decade and actually declined in the second. Imports of food grains (wheat, rice, and maize) soared—by 9 percent per year since the early 1960s—reinforcing food dependency. Food aid also increased substantially. Since 70 to 90 percent of the population earns its income from agriculture, the drop in production in this sector spelled a real income loss for many of the poorest.

The deterioration in agriculture and other internal and global factors led to widespread balance-of-payments crises in the 1970s. Current account deficits in the region as a whole rose from a modest $1.5 billion in 1970 to $8 billion in 1980. External indebtedness climbed from $6 billion to $32 billion between 1970 and 1979, and debt service increased from 6 percent to 12 percent of export earnings in the same period ... Fiscal pressures also intensified in many countries, as indicated by declining real budgetary allocations for supplies and maintenance, growing imbalances between salary and nonsalary spending, and difficulties in financing local and recurrent costs of externally funded development projects.

The crises that evolved in much of the region are particularly disturbing since, during the period from 1960 to 1974, world trade and the world economy in general expanded rapidly, and many less-developed countries elsewhere experienced relatively high growth rates ...

In sum, past trends in African economic performance and continued global recession together explain the pessimistic projections for African economic growth in the 1980s. The *World Development Report 1981,* under its most optimistic set of assumptions about the expansion of the world economy, forecasts virtually no growth in per capita income for the continent in this decade; under less favorable assumptions, a negative rate of growth (–1.0 percent per year) is projected for the poorest nations in the region.

These prospects and their political, social and economic implications are not acceptable either to the countries concerned or to the international economy. There is an urgent need to understand what has gone wrong and what must be done—by African governments themselves and the concerned international community—to assure a better future for Africa's people.

Sources of Lagging Growth

Africa's disappointing economic performance during the past two decades reflects, in part, internal constraints based on "structural" factors that evolved from historical circumstances or from the physical environment. These include underdeveloped human resources, the economic disruption that accompanied decolonization and postcolonial consolidation, climatic and geographic factors hostile to development, and rapidly growing population ...

UNDERDEVELOPED HUMAN RESOURCES. One of the most critical problems of the past 20 years has been the scarcity of trained manpower ... In most Sub-Saharan countries, over three quarters of this cadre [university trained] were foreign. Senior executive and technical jobs in government were dominated by expatriates. Zaire, which was left without a single African doctor, lawyer, engineer, or army officer at independence was an extreme case, but foreigners occupied many positions of skill and responsibility even in the countries with the most advanced education systems; in Nigeria, Africans held fewer than 700 of the 3,000 senior posts in the civil service until the mid-1950s, and in Senegal, 1,500 French technical personnel occupied almost all the top jobs in 1961. And where there were large numbers of settlers, even fewer Africans were trained in modern skills. In Kenya and Tanzania, for example, fewer than 20 percent of high-level civil service posts were in African hands in the early 1960s.

Throughout the region, trade and industry were almost entirely owned and managed by foreigners. As recently as 1975 there were only 80 African-owned shops in the Mozambican capital of Maputo, and after sixty years of colonial rule, African-owned and operated enterprises with more than ten employees were extremely rare, even in the relatively advanced economies of Kenya, Uganda, and Zimbabwe. In the wage sector, the foreign presence extended even to first-level supervisory positions: in 1960, for example, 300 of Ghana's 900 foremen were expatriates.

This pattern of underdeveloped human resources is partially explained by the fact that even by the end of the 1950s, advanced education was still largely unavailable to most Africans: local facilities did not exist or, where they did, African enrollment was often restricted. Thus, in 1958, less than 10,000 African students were attending universities at home or abroad (one student per 20,000 population), some 6,500 of whom were from Ghana and Nigeria ...

The number of people educated at the secondary level was also limited. In the late 1950s, the entire region produced only 8,000 secondary school graduates per year, 40 percent of whom were in Ghana and Nigeria. In fact, only 3 percent of high-school-age students were being educated at the secondary level in Africa in 1960, compared with over 25 percent in the Philippines, 20 percent in India, and 10 percent in Burma.

The severe shortage of skilled labor and entrepreneurs was also the result of the immigration policies in the colonial period. Foreign workers at all skill levels were sought to meet specific labor shortages and later came to occupy dominant positions as traders and merchants, building contractors and artisans, industrial entrepreneurs, and skilled manual and clerical workers ... it was often cheaper to import and train foreign labor than to recruit locally. Moreover, because of colonial social conventions, Africans were rarely allowed to supervise non-Africans. As a result, the local population was prevented from moving up the skill ladder or assuming entrepreneurial roles.

Just as educational and training needs were not being met, so too were health needs neglected. In 1960, for example, there was just one physician for every 50,000 people in Sub-Saharan Africa as compared to one per 12,000 in other low-income countries ... Life expectancy was lower than the average for all low-income countries (39 years compared with 42), and child death rates (deaths of children from one to four years of age) were substantially higher (39 per thousand compared with 23). Colonial governments made valiant attempts to control endemic diseases in many parts of the region, but the majority of rural people were not affected; systematic efforts at malaria control, for example, were largely restricted to major urban centers.

The scarcity of managerial and technical cadres at the time of independence had strong adverse effects on public administration, industrial development, wage levels, and costs. Furthermore, the lack of education among the population reduced the stimuli for progressive change generally experienced where education is more widespread. Finally, the debilitating effects of disease and sickness lowered the productivity of the labor force and the propensity to innovate.

POLITICAL FRAGILITY ... In the wake of independence, violent internal conflict burst forth in many of the new nations, stemming from the pluralism of African societies and the difficulties of postcolonial political consolidation ...

Civil and military strife and the political fragility which it reflected had several negative economic effects. First, it forced the postindependence leadership to give especially high priority to short-term political objectives. Second, it triggered large-scale displacement of people. In the 1970s, the number of people who fled across national frontiers in Africa rose from 750,000 to over 5 million, accounting for about half of all refugees worldwide ... Third, civil strife induced a diversion of resources to military spending. While the share of GNP devoted to military purposes remained fairly constant for the region as a whole (2.9 percent), the proportion nearly doubled among the poorest group (the low-income semiarid countries), rising from 2.3 to 4.3 percent of GNP.

INSTITUTIONAL ADAPTATION ... Two sets of problems were particularly relevant. First, colonial governments had created many subregional organizations that did not prove to be viable after independence. Some were functional groups, such as the West African Cocoa Research Institute, the West African Examination Council, the East African Railway and Harbour Authority, and the East African Airways. Others, more important, were supranational groupings—the Federation of French West and Equatorial Africa, the Central African Federation, and the East African Common Market. All proved no longer suitable to the new national realities and were disbanded. But the reorganization which this required imposed heavy costs on the newly independent governments.

The second and related problem was that of adapting existing national institutions, which had been closely patterned on those of the colonial power, to African needs. Systems of local government, general administration, health care, and education had to be restructured; the fashioning of "appropriate" institutions proved to be a mammoth undertaking, one that remains unfinished.

THE ECONOMIC INHERITANCE. Modern economic growth has a relatively brief history in Sub-Saharan Africa. Colonial administration established itself in most cases in the last two decades of the nineteenth century. Economic expansion came quickly in a few countries —Ghana, Senegal, Uganda, and Zaire, for example—and spread elsewhere later, with interruptions during World Wars I and II and the depression of the 1930s. However, general and sustained development came only after World War II in most of the countries of the region.

In part because of this time factor, the African economies at independence were unevenly developed and dualistic, more so than most other developing regions. For example, in West Africa, where peasant production of export crops was the primary motor of development, modern economic activity took place mainly in the forest and coastal zones extending 200 kilometers inland from the sea. In the vast interior, where most of the population was (and still is), evidence of economic change was barely visible, with the exception of groundnut production in Nigeria and Senegal. In Central, East, and Southern Africa, dualism was even more marked; the modern economy consisted largely of European-run mining enclaves and islands of settler agricultural activity. In the mineral-producing countries which had significant settler communities, the "native areas" were neglected and usually targets of discrimination. African farmers, therefore, produced little for the market.

Thus, as the postcolonial period began, most Africans were outside the modern economy . . . over 70 percent of the land under cultivation was devoted to subsistence crops, while less than 10 percent was planted for export. African labor was overwhelmingly concentrated in subsistence-oriented farming. In 1960, there were probably no more than 10 million African wage earners during any part of the year; only in Southern Africa was as much as 10 percent of the population engaged in paid employment in the modern sector. Moreover, "circular" migration (the practice of workers returning to their villages more or less regularly) was still quite common throughout the continent.

The dominance of subsistence production presented special obstacles to agricultural development. Farmers had to be induced to produce for the market, adopt new crops, and undertake new risks. Established farming systems, which had evolved over centuries and were well adapted to the local environment, had to be revamped if production was to increase. Little was known about new crops, new methods of crop rotation, seed protection, or more productive farming techniques. Agricultural research and experimentation were lacking, but so too was most basic information about rainfall, river flow, soil quality, farming systems, and patterns of land use. Accordingly, the experimental and intellectual raw material necessary for progress in agriculture was very sparse. The fragility of African soils, the irregularity of rainfall, and the ecological diversity that characterizes even small subregions in this part of the world make location-specific, detailed knowledge especially necessary; its absence presented an usually severe obstacle to effective agricultural development.

Moreover, basic infrastructure was, in some areas, almost nonexistent: roads, railroads, ports, buildings, and communications systems were scant and did not penetrate the hinterland. Public capital investment had initially been limited by the shortage of local resources, as well as by the doctrine of "colonial self-sufficiency" that prevailed until World War II, its central tenet being that colonies should not be subsidized by metropoles. In addition, private capital flows into most African countries were much smaller than in other developing regions, and even that which went to Africa was very unevenly distributed. According to a classic study [Frankel, *Capital Investment in Africa*, 1938], 40 percent of the total private foreign investment in Africa south of the Sahara between 1880 and 1936 went to South Africa; Zambia and Zimbabwe together received 18 percent; Zaire 11 percent; and Kenya and Uganda together received 4 percent. Elsewhere, investment was negligible . . .

Growth was also affected by a set of external factors—notably adverse trends in the international economy, particularly since 1974. These include "stagflation" in the industrialized countries, higher energy prices, the relatively slow growth of trade in primary products, and—for copper and iron-ore exporters—adverse terms of trade . . .

The internal "structural" problems and the external factors impeding African economic growth have been exacerbated by domestic policy inadequacies, of which three are critical. First, trade and exchange-rate policies have overprotected industry, held back agriculture, and absorbed much administrative capacity. Second, too little attention has been paid to administrative constraints in mobilizing and managing resources for development; given the widespread weakness of planning, decision making, and management capacities, public sectors frequently become overextended. Third, there has been a consistent bias against agriculture in price, tax, and exchange-rate policies.

New Priorities and Adjustments in Policy

A reordering of postindependence priorities is essential if economic growth is to accelerate. During the past two decades most African governments rightly focused on political consolidation, on the laying down of basic infrastructure (much of it tied to the goal of political integration), and on the development of human resources. Relatively less attention was paid to production. Now it is essential to give production a higher priority—without neglecting these other goals. Without a faster rate of production increase, other objectives cannot be achieved, nor can past achievements be sustained. Three major policy actions are central to any growth-oriented program: (1) more suitable trade and exchange-rate policies; (2) increased efficiency of resource use in the public sector; and (3) improvement in agricultural policies.

57 • Structural adjustment in Ghana (1983–89)

Gold had first attracted Europeans to Ghana (the "Gold Coast" in colonial parlance) in the fourteenth century, and cocoa added to the economic attraction of the area in the nineteenth and twentieth centuries. However, by 1980 the country was in difficult straits economically and politically, and this situation had led to a continuing series of coups. Jerry Rawlings adopted the recommendations of the World Bank in instituting an economic recovery program (ERP) in 1983 and implementing structural adjustment throughout the 1980s and 1990s and into the twenty-first century. Structural adjustment in Ghana has often been viewed, especially by the World Bank, as a success story for the program in Africa.

Nonetheless, the program has had a checkered history, as these documents show. When first introduced, the ERP for 1984–86 budgeted less than 5 percent of estimated expenditures on "social sectors" (education, health, etc.), while the bulk of funds were allocated to the export sector (cocoa, mining, timber), other market-oriented parts of the economy (agriculture and manufacturing), and development of the physical infrastructure of the economy (fuel and power production and the building of roads). Imports were encouraged, leading to an undercutting of local producers; a value-added tax (VAT) was introduced, further increasing prices for consumer goods; and state enterprises were sold off to build the private sector rather than the public. Often such sales meant the acquisition of significant sectors of the economy by foreign investors, such as the takeover of the largest Ghanaian gold company, Ashanti Goldfields, by the South African Anglo American Corporation in 1992.

The impact of these policies on the poor was so harsh that the Ghanaian government introduced policies to "mitigate" the impact of structural adjustment. The mitigation efforts did not succeed. The World Bank reported in 1990 "that PAMSCAD [Programme of Actions to Mitigate the Social Costs of Adjustment] had not shown significant benefits in terms of mitigating the social cost of adjustment," that the majority of the poor were food crop and export crop farmers, and that "the poor have so far gained very little from social spending."

Such results led to considerable internal criticism of structural adjustment and of the authoritarian ways in which it was being forcibly introduced by Rawlings's regime. Albert Adu Boahen, a distinguished historian of Africa, was the most eloquent critic. He pointed out that the social consequences of structural adjustment were so great that revolution might well result. He also cautioned that the huge debt that Ghana incurred also raised the potential of a new imperialist rush for Africa if the Western lenders became concerned about their investments and the ability of an independent Ghana to keep paying.

The following sections from the ERP plans use the exact spelling of the original, official publications. It is notable that the first ERP of 1983, with its expectations of quick and great success for that year, uses American spelling; the subsequent reports, which document the problems arising from structural adjustment, use primarily (though not exclusively) English spelling.[2]

A. Official reasons for the introduction of structural adjustment (1983)

ECONOMIC DEVELOPMENTS SINCE 1970

The performance of the economy in the last decade [1970s] has been characterized by declining output of key sectors, persistently high rate of inflation, balance of payments difficulties, large Government budgetary deficits, and excess liquidity. The combined effects of these adverse developments resulted in a sharp reduction in the standard of living of the av-

2. A, *Republic of Ghana Economic Recovery Program 1984–1986* (Accra: Government of the Republic of Ghana, October 1983), vol. 1, Report prepared by the Government of Ghana for the Meeting of the Consultative Group for Ghana, Paris, November 1983, 7–8, 15–16, 33; B, *Republic of Ghana Economic Recovery Program 1984–1986* (Accra: Government of the Republic of Ghana, November 1984), Report prepared by the Government of Ghana for the Meeting of the Consultative Group for Ghana, Paris, December 1984, v, ix, x, 30; C, *Republic of Ghana Programme of Actions to Mitigate the Social Costs of Adjustment* (Accra: Government of the Republic of Ghana, November 1987), 3, 5–6, 8–9; D, Albert Adu Boahen, *The Ghanaian Sphinx: Reflections on the Contemporary History of Ghana 1972–1987* (Accra: Ghana Academy of Arts and Sciences, 1989), 69–71, 72, 75.

erage Ghanaian, rising cost of living and depreciation of the value of the currency. Between 1974 and 1981, per capita income declined by over 20 per cent. Cocoa production has fallen to less than half its 1974 level, and inflation has averaged 50 per cent per year.

The reasons for this poor performance are of both internal and external origin. A series of past policy decisions and actions had a cumulative adverse effect on the economy. These included:

- the maintenance of a fixed and highly overvalued exchange rate that discouraged exports and produced huge profits for traders of imported goods;
- large deficits in the Government's budgets which resulted in inflationary pressures which further distorted the effective exchange rate;
- the imposition of price controls at the manufacturing stage which discouraged production, while giving excessive profits to the unregulated small-scale trading sector;
- misallocation and use of import licences which created further inefficiencies and denied critical inputs and equipment in high priority areas.

There have also been several adverse external factors. Adverse weather in 1978–79 and 1982–83 seriously reduced agricultural output, creating major food shortages. In addition, the sharp increases in petroleum prices in 1979, followed by a world recession and declining export prices, created a major deterioration in the terms of trade. Another adverse factor has been the recent expulsion of over one million Ghanaians from Nigeria.

These factors interacted to produce a major secular decline in the economy. As export earnings fell, there was inadequate foreign exchange for raw materials, spares, and investment in the export sectors and other critical areas of the economy. As a result, critically needed infrastructure in transport and communications and public utilities declined. The decline in the transport sector became so severe that export goods could often not be moved to the ports for shipment. Declining imports and exports limited the Government's revenues, while a growing population increased the demand for services, resulting in huge deficits. Declining output and expanded money supply combined to accelerate inflation. The inflationary forces induced the Government to react by extending price controls, but these only further discouraged production, which in turn further added to inflation. Inflationary pressures, together with low nominal interest rates, also discouraged private savings. The public sector meanwhile became a net dissaver. As performance deteriorated, aid donors withdrew their support which further reduced the ability of the country to invest and import. At the present time, bilateral and multilateral aid commitments to Ghana are among the lowest in the world for a country of Ghana's size and income level . . .

ECONOMIC RECOVERY PROGRAM . . .

The economic recovery program is set within a four-year time frame. The first year, calendar year 1983, is devoted to stabilization and consolidation and the preparation of the economic, social and political conditions for the launching of a three-year Medium-Term Plan in 1984.

The main objectives of the economic recovery program are:

1. to restore incentives for production of food, industrial raw materials and export commodities and thereby increase their output to modest but realistic levels;

2. to increase the availability of essential consumer goods and improve the distribution system;

3. to increase the overall availability of foreign exchange in the country, improve its allocation mechanism and channel it into selected high priority areas;

4. to lower the rate of inflation by pursuing prudent fiscal, monetary and trade policies;

5. to rehabilitate the physical infrastructure of the country in support of directly productive activities, and;

6. to undertake systematic analyses and studies leading towards a major restructuring of economic institutions in the country . . .

INVESTMENT POLICY

Foreign investment will be welcome and actively encouraged in petroleum exploration and production, mining and mineral processing, timber logging, wood processing, quarrying, deep sea fishing, food processing, and domestic-resource based manufacturing industries. To achieve this objective, the new mineral code will streamline, centralize and remove bottlenecks in the processing of applications for prospecting and exploitation. External account status will be granted to new projects as well as existing projects which are able to self-finance their foreign exchange requirements. These accounts are intended to guarantee free transferability of dividends and debt service payments and to ensure the regular and uninterrupted availability of imported inputs and raw materials.

At the same time the existing foreign investors have been assured that they would be allowed to operate freely within the confines of their obligations and responsibilities and the general laws of the country. The socially conscious investors who are interested in re-investment in productive ventures using domestic raw materials and labor intensive techniques will be given all possible assistance. As the foreign exchange problem eases, the Bank of Ghana will make endeavors to assist such investors in clearing their payment arrears . . .

It should be noted that Ghana's debt servicing obligations are modest at present, amounting to less than 13 per cent of total export earnings. If its present requirements for assistance can be met on concessionary terms, the debt service ratio will decline further, to about 7 per cent of exports by 1990. Thus, if the economy and economic management continue to improve, Ghana could conceivably become credit-worthy for greater lending on non-concessionary terms.

B. Report on the first year of structural adjustment (1984)

Despite fairly active support from multilateral and bilateral sources, the Programme ran into unforeseen hurdles from the start. To begin with, the nation had to cope with the staggering burden of a million returnees in 1983; suddenly, every sixth member of the labour force was a returnee . . . Additionally the country faced yet another season of devastating drought in 1983–84 . . . Furthermore, the actual damage to the rail and road systems proved to be substantially greater than the consultants' earlier estimates . . .

Indebtedness. Debt service payments are pre-empting an unusually high proportion of export earnings. Amortization and interest payments in 1984, largely accounted for by old debts and oil credits, are estimated at $251 million or 43 per cent of total exports. For 1985, these payments rise to $423 million. Therefore, new doses of aid will need to be larger and on highly concessional terms because until exports pick up the Government can ill-afford to borrow on commercial terms . . .

Ghana is a resource rich country, bled, weakened and run down over the years. Its engine of growth must be the recovery of its productive base . . . The economy needs a potent stimulant, a catalytic agent to liberate its growth potential. In particular, an immediate boost in imports is needed to stimulate the key sectors of the economy. In addition, the increase in imports will have useful side effects on the economy. Import taxes will enable the Government to increase the development budget. There would also need to be less borrowing from banking sources. This would permit a corresponding freeing of funds for the private sector, and a relaxation of the credit squeeze currently faced by productive enterprises.

C. The social costs of adjustment (1987)

The reversal of more than a decade of national economic decline has been a major preoccupation of the Government of the Provisional National Defence Council of Ghana since its accession to office on 31st December 1981 . . .

The Economic Recovery Program (ERP), initiated in 1983, has managed to reverse this downward trend and place the economy once again on the growth path. But despite medium-to-long term growth prospects, the economy is characterized by widespread poverty and economic hardship. Moreover, the ERP will not be able to alleviate the economic hardship of many of the poor and vulnerable groups in the short run. Indeed, some components of the ERP have and will exacerbate the economic problems of certain vulnerable groups in the short run, and this may impede the sustainability of the recovery program itself . . .

SHORT-TERM EFFECT OF THE ERP ON THE POOR

While there is little doubt that a large proportion of the population is likely to be better off with the ERP in the medium to long term, and while the economy has grown at a healthy rate over the past four years, it is unlikely that without specific programmes, the economic hardship of marginal, poor and vulnerable groups will be alleviated in the short term through the ERP . . . the precarious condition of these groups inherited from the period of economic decline is unlikely to be altered much in the short run . . . Indeed, certain groups, including at least some of the poor, will have to bear the costs of adjustment in the short term . . .

THE VULNERABLE GROUPS

Based on general knowledge about the incidence of poverty, the following groups have been identified as being the most vulnerable, and hence as the target groups for PAMSCAD: (1) rural households especially in the Northern and Upper Regions, who have low productivity, poor access to social services and income increasing opportunities, and who suffer particularly from unemployment and hunger during the lean season; (2) low income un- or under-employed urban households, who lack productive economic opportunities and have suffered from the increase in prices of essential commodities; and (3) retrenched workers from the civil service, state enterprises and private enterprises, who lack productive employment opportunities.

D. A local critic of adjustment: Albert Adu Boahen (1989)

My dear friends, the trouble with us in Ghana and indeed in the whole of our benighted continent, is not lack of ideas, plans and programmes for the solution of our problems. There are innumerable such plans in this country beginning with the excellent and practicable one drawn up for us by Professor Arthur Lewis [*Report on Industrialization and the Gold Coast*] as far back as 1953 ... What has been lacking are, as far as Ghana is concerned, not effective machinery and the appropriate manpower and expertise for their implementation, but the resolve and integrity to implement them and above all the priorities to be accorded ...

Surely, given the fact that about seventy percent of our population live in the rural areas, that we still cannot feed ourselves, that we do not have adequate foreign exchange to import raw materials to feed our factories, that 80% of our exports are or can be obtained from the rural areas and that the rural-urban migration and contrast have been assuming alarming proportions, our priorities should be on agricultural and age-based and cottage industries and not on import substitution industries, on increased agricultural productivity and not on industrial productivity, on rural electrification and feeder roads and not on urban housing and four-lane streets, on reducing illiteracy especially in the rural areas and not on JSS [junior secondary school], on an appropriate technology for rural farmers and peasants and not on armoured vehicles, on credit and incentives and subsidies to cocoa, cash-crop and foodcrop farmers and not on the reduction of income tax, on better pricing for food and cash crops and not on the free importation of all vehicles below 1600cc, and so on ... The 1988 Budget Statement indeed reads like a budget drawn up for a predominantly industrialized and urban-based community or country and not for a predominantly agricultural and rural based one. For a government with all its populist mass rhetoric dedicated to improving the lot of the workers, the masses, peasants, farmers and the down-trodden and whose slogan is "Power to the People" about 80% of whom live in the rural areas and are involved in agriculture, this is simply incomprehensible ...

My solution ... is to advise, first that we go straight back to Arthur Lewis and give priority attention to agriculture and make it so much more lucrative than the selling of dog chains, hair creams and imported gods; secondly the standard of living in the rural areas should be raised in such a way that people will be attracted back there from the urban areas. Herein lies the economic salvation not only of this country but indeed of the whole of Africa ...

And may I be permitted at this juncture to caution this and all African and Third World governments that if we do not put an end to this reckless accumulation of foreign debts, we stand a great risk of being recolonised by the industrialized countries and their agencies in the near future. It should never be forgotten that one of the reasons for the scramble for and the partition of Africa was the need felt by the imperial countries to safeguard their investments and loans. It was definitely this consideration that led to the British occupation of Egypt in 1882 which touched off the scramble in that region. Already Liberia has now been virtually recolonised or put into receivership by the United States. And how many IMF and World Bank experts do we have in both advisory and managerial positions in this country at this very moment? We are warned! ...

Our country is one of the best endowed countries in Africa in terms of both human and material resources, and there is therefore no real reason why we should be confronted by such a sphinx riddle [pp. 1–2: for Ghana does pose a riddle: the riddle being why is it that a country which is so well endowed by Nature has failed so dismally to develop and progress?]. I hope the features of that riddle have been accurately delineated and some of the measures towards its solution have been proposed. It is up to you and me, to all of us, and in particular to the PNDC [Provincial National Defense Council], to add to these solutions and above all to see that they are implemented. If we do not, to borrow the phrase of the late James Baldwin, it may be fire next time!

58 • Thabo Mbeki on AIDS and poverty in Africa (2000)

In 2000, South Africa hosted the Thirteenth International AIDS Conference, the first time that the event had taken place in Africa, the continent with the greatest number of cases (70 percent) of the disease in the world, and in a country in which it was then estimated that, because of AIDS, one-third of the children under age fifteen would not reach adulthood. Thabo Mbeki, Nelson Mandela's successor as president of South Africa, made a speech at the opening session of the conference that has haunted him ever since, particularly because of the controversial stances that he has taken— questioning medical evidence of the links between HIV and AIDS and being slow in the eyes of many in implementing policies to combat AIDS in South Africa. Leaving aside for the moment the more controversial aspects of Mbeki's arguments, his speech warrants a close reading, especially with regard to the importance that he gives to poverty as being the fundamental cause of ill health— physical, and, by extension, social, and economic—in Africa.[3]

Chairperson, Participants at the 13th International AIDS Conference; Comrades, ladies and gentlemen:

On behalf of our government and the people of South Africa, I am happy to welcome you to Durban and to our country.

You are in Africa for the first time in the history of the International AIDS Conferences.

We are pleased that you are here because we count you as a critical component part of the global forces mobilised to engage in struggle against the AIDS epidemic confronting our Continent.

The peoples of our Continent will therefore be closely interested in your work. They expect that out of this extraordinary gathering will come a message and a programme of action that will assist them to disperse the menacing and frightening clouds that hang over all of us as a result of the AIDS epidemic.

You meet in a country to whose citizens' freedom and democracy are but very new gifts. For us, freedom and democracy are only six years old.

The certainty that we will achieve a better life for all our people, whatever the difficulties, is only half-a-dozen years old.

Because the possibility to determine our own future together, both black and white, is such a fresh and vibrant reality, perhaps we often overestimate what can be achieved within each passing day.

3. *Issued by the Office of the Presidency, 9 July 2000,* http://www.anc.org.za/show.php?doc=ancdocs/history/ mbeki/2000/tm0709.html.

FIGURE 26 Between 1990 and 2004, despite or perhaps as a result of international policies of structural adjustment, poverty in sub-Saharan Africa dramatically increased in every category. According to the definitions adopted by Western analysts, the subjacent poor are those who live on less than $1 a day, the medial poor on less than 75 cents daily, and the ultrapoor (a group now composed almost entirely of people living in Africa) on less than 50 cents a day. Akhter U. Ahmed, Ruth V. Hill, Lisa C. Smith, Doris M. Wiesmann, and Tim Frankenberger, *The World's Most Deprived: Characteristics and Causes of Extreme Poverty and Hunger*, 2007.

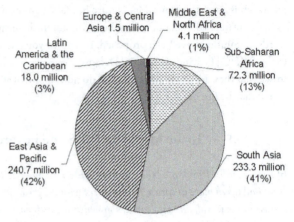

Subjacent poor in 1990: 670 million

Europe & Central Asia 1.5 million

Middle East & North Africa 4.1 million (1%)

Latin America & the Caribbean 18.0 million (3%)

Sub-Saharan Africa 72.3 million (13%)

East Asia & Pacific 240.7 million (42%)

South Asia 233.3 million (41%)

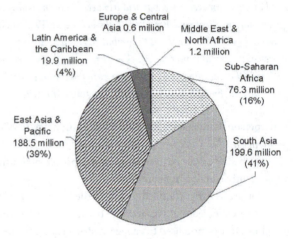

Medial poor in 1990: 486 million

Europe & Central Asia 0.6 million

Middle East & North Africa 1.2 million

Latin America & the Caribbean 19.9 million (4%)

Sub-Saharan Africa 76.3 million (16%)

East Asia & Pacific 188.5 million (39%)

South Asia 199.6 million (41%)

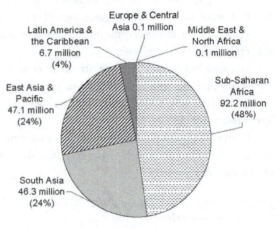

Ultra poor in 1990: 193 million

Europe & Central Asia 0.1 million

Latin America & the Caribbean 6.7 million (4%)

Middle East & North Africa 0.1 million

East Asia & Pacific 47.1 million (24%)

Sub-Saharan Africa 92.2 million (48%)

South Asia 46.3 million (24%)

Subjacent poor in 2004: 485 million

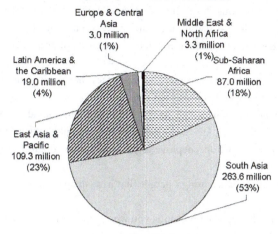

Europe & Central Asia 3.0 million (1%)
Middle East & North Africa 3.3 million (1%)
Latin America & the Caribbean 19.0 million (4%)
Sub-Saharan Africa 87.0 million (18%)
East Asia & Pacific 109.3 million (23%)
South Asia 263.6 million (53%)

Medial poor in 2004: 323 million

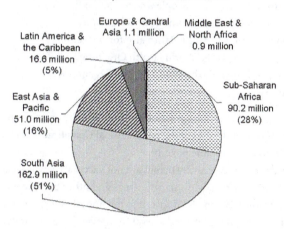

Europe & Central Asia 1.1 million
Middle East & North Africa 0.9 million
Latin America & the Caribbean 16.6 million (5%)
East Asia & Pacific 51.0 million (16%)
Sub-Saharan Africa 90.2 million (28%)
South Asia 162.9 million (51%)

Ultra poor in 2004: 162 million

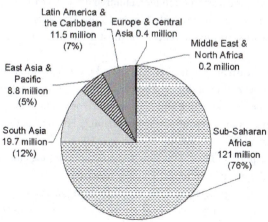

Latin America & the Caribbean 11.5 million (7%)
Europe & Central Asia 0.4 million
Middle East & North Africa 0.2 million
East Asia & Pacific 8.8 million (5%)
South Asia 19.7 million (12%)
Sub-Saharan Africa 121 million (76%)

Perhaps, in thinking that your Conference will help us to overcome our problems as Africans, we overestimate what the 13th International AIDS Conference can do.

Nevertheless, that overestimation must also convey a message to you. That message is that we are a country and a Continent driven by hope, and not despair and resignation to a cruel fate.

Those who have nothing would perish if the forces that govern our universe deprived them of the capacity to hope for a better tomorrow.

Once more I welcome you all, delegates at the 13th International AIDS Conference, to Durban, to South Africa and to Africa, convinced that you would not have come here, unless you were to us, messengers of hope, deployed against the spectre of the death of millions from disease.

You will spend a few days among a people that has a deep understanding of human and international solidarity.

I am certain that there are many among you who joined in the international struggle for the destruction of the anti-human apartheid system.

You are therefore as much midwives of the new, democratic, non-racial and non-sexist South Africa as are the millions of our people who fought for the emancipation of all humanity from the racist yoke of the apartheid crime against humanity.

We welcome you warmly to South Africa also for this reason.

Let me tell you a story that the World Health Organisation told the world in 1995. I will tell this story in the words used by the World Health Organisation.

This is the story:

> The world's biggest killer and the greatest cause of ill-health and suffering across the globe is listed almost at the end of the International Classification of Diseases. It is given the code Z59.5—extreme poverty.
>
> Poverty is the main reason why babies are not vaccinated, why clean water and sanitation are not provided, why curative drugs and other treatments are unavailable and why mothers die in childbirth. It is the underlying cause of reduced life expectancy, handicap, disability and starvation. Poverty is a major contributor to mental illness, stress, suicide, family disintegration and substance abuse. Every year in the developing world 12.2 million children under 5 years die, most of them from causes which could be prevented for just a few US cents per child. They die largely because of world indifference, but most of all they die because they are poor . . .
>
> Beneath the heartening facts about decreased mortality and increasing life expectancy, and many other undoubted health advances, lie unacceptable disparities in wealth. The gaps between rich and poor, between one population group and another, between ages and between sexes, are widening. For most people in the world today every step of life, from infancy to old age, is taken under the twin shadows of poverty and inequity, and under the double burden of suffering and disease.
>
> For many, the prospect of longer life may seem more like a punishment than a gift. Yet by the end of the century we could be living in a world without poliomyelitis, a world without new cases of leprosy, a world without deaths from neo-

natal tetanus and measles. But today the money that some developing countries have to spend per person on health care over an entire year is just US $4—less than the amount of small change carried in the pockets and purses of many people in the developed countries.

A person in one of the least developed countries in the world has a life expectancy of 43 years according to 1993 calculations. A person in one of the most developed countries has a life expectancy of 78—a difference of more than a third of a century. This means a rich, healthy man can live twice as long as a poor, sick man.

That inequity alone should stir the conscience of the world—but in some of the poorest countries the life expectancy picture is getting worse. In five countries life expectancy at birth is expected to decrease by the year 2000, whereas everywhere else it is increasing. In the richest countries life expectancy in the year 2000 will reach 79 years. In some of the poorest it will go backwards to 42 years. Thus the gap continues to widen between rich and poor, and by the year 2000 at least 45 countries are expected to have a life expectancy at birth of under 60 years.

In the space of a day passengers flying from Japan to Uganda leave the country with the world's highest life expectancy—almost 79 years—and land in one with the world's lowest—barely 42 years. A day away by plane, but half a lifetime's difference on the ground. A flight between France and Cote d'Ivoire takes only a few hours, but it spans almost 26 years of life expectancy. A short air trip between Florida in the USA and Haiti represents a life expectancy gap of over 19 years . . .

HIV and AIDS are having a devastating effect on young people. In many countries in the developing world, up to two-thirds of all new infections are among people aged 15–24. Overall it is estimated that half the global HIV infections have been in people under 25 years—with 60% of infections of females occurring by the age of 20. Thus the hopes and lives of a generation, the breadwinners, providers and parents of the future, are in jeopardy. Many of the most talented and industrious citizens, who could build a better world and shape the destinies of the countries they live in, face tragically early death as a result of HIV infection. (World Health Report 1995: Executive Summary, WHO)

This is part of the story that the World Health Organisation told in its World Health Report in 1995. Five years later, the essential elements of this story have not changed. In some cases, the situation will have become worse.

You will have noticed that when the WHO used air travel to illustrate the import of the message of the story it told, it spoke of a journey from Japan to Uganda, another from France to the Cote d'Ivoire and yet another from the United States to Haiti.

From developed Asia, Europe and North America, two of these journeys were to Africa and the third to the African Diaspora.

Once again, I welcome you to Africa, recognising the fact that the majority of the delegates to the 13th International AIDS Conference come from outside our Continent.

Because of your heavy programme and the limited time you will spend with us, what you will see of this city, and therefore of our country, is the more developed world of which the WHO spoke when it told the story of world health in 1995.

You will not see the South African and African world of the poverty of which the WHO spoke, in which AIDS thrives—a partner with poverty, suffering, social disadvantage and inequity.

As an African, speaking at a Conference such as this, convened to discuss a grave human problem such as the acquired human deficiency syndrome, I believe that we should speak to one another honestly and frankly, with sufficient tolerance to respect everybody's point of view, with sufficient tolerance to allow all voices to be heard.

Had we, as a people, turned our backs on these basic civilised precepts, we would never have achieved the much-acclaimed South African miracle of which all humanity is justly proud.

Some in our common world consider the questions I and the rest of our government have raised around the HIV-AIDS issue, the subject of the Conference you are attending, as akin to grave criminal and genocidal misconduct.

What I hear being said repeatedly, stridently, angrily, is—do not ask any questions!

The particular twists of South African history and the will of the great majority of our people, freely expressed, have placed me in the situation in which I carry the title of President of the Republic of South Africa.

As I sat in this position, I listened attentively to the story that was told by the World Health Organisation.

What I heard as that story was told, was that extreme poverty is the world's biggest killer and the greatest cause of ill health and suffering across the globe.

As I listened longer, I heard stories being told about malaria, tuberculosis, hepatitis B, HIV-AIDS and other diseases.

I heard also about micro-nutrient malnutrition, iodine and vitamin A deficiency. I heard of syphilis, gonorrhoea, genital herpes and other sexually transmitted diseases as well as teenage pregnancies.

I also heard of cholera, respiratory infections, anaemia, bilharzia, river blindness, guinea worms and other illnesses with complicated Latin names.

As I listened even longer to this tale of human woe, I heard the name recur with frightening frequency—Africa, Africa, Africa!

And so, in the end, I came to the conclusion that as Africans we are confronted by a health crisis of enormous proportions.

One of the consequences of this crisis is the deeply disturbing phenomenon of the collapse of immune systems among millions of our people, such that their bodies have no natural defence against attack by many viruses and bacteria.

Clearly, if we, as African countries, had the level of development to enable us to gather accurate statistics about our own countries, our morbidity and mortality figures would tell a story that would truly be too frightening to contemplate.

As I listened and heard the whole story told about our own country, it seemed to me that we could not blame everything on a single virus.

It seemed to me also that every living African, whether in good or ill health, is prey to many enemies of health that would interact one upon the other in many ways, within one human body.

And thus I came to conclude that we have a desperate and pressing need to wage a war on all fronts to guarantee and realise the human right of all our people to good health.

And so, being insufficiently educated, and therefore ill prepared to answer this question, I started to ask the question, expecting an answer from others—what is to be done, particularly about HIV-AIDS!

One of the questions I have asked is—are safe sex, condoms and anti-retroviral drugs a sufficient response to the health catastrophe we face!

I am pleased to inform you that some eminent scientists decided to respond to our humble request to use their expertise to provide us with answers to certain questions.

Some of these have specialised on the issue of HIV-AIDS for many years and differed bitterly among themselves about various matters. Yet, they graciously agreed to join together to help us find answers to some outstanding questions.

I thank them most sincerely for their positive response, inspired by a common resolve more effectively to confront the AIDS epidemic.

They have agreed to report back by the end of this year having worked together, among other things, on the reliability of and the information communicated by our current HIV tests and the improvement of our disease surveillance system.

We look forward to the results of this important work, which will help us to ensure that we achieve better results in terms of saving the lives of our people and improving the lives of millions.

In the meantime, we will continue to intensify our own campaign against AIDS, including:

- a sustained public awareness campaign encouraging safe sex and the use of condoms;
- a better focused programme targeted at the reduction and elimination of poverty and the improvement of the nutritional standards of our people;
- a concerted fight against the so-called opportunistic diseases, including TB and all sexually transmitted diseases;
- a humane response to people living with HIV and AIDS as well as the orphans in our society;
- contributing to the international effort to develop an AIDS vaccine; and,
- further research on anti-retroviral drugs.

You will find all of this in our country's AIDS action plan which I hope has been or will be distributed among you.

You will see from that plan, together with the work that has been going on, that there is no substance to the allegation that there is any hesitation on the part of our government to confront the challenge of HIV-AIDS.

However, we remain convinced of the need for us better to understand the essence of what would constitute a comprehensive response in a context such as ours which is characterised by the high levels of poverty and disease to which I have referred.

As I visit the areas of this city and country that most of you will not see because of your heavy programme and your time limitations, areas that are representative of the conditions of life of the overwhelming majority of the people of our common world, the story told by the World Health Organisation always forces itself back into my consciousness.

The world's biggest killer and the greatest cause of ill health and suffering across the globe, including South Africa, is extreme poverty.

Is there more that all of us should do together, assuming that in a world driven by a value system based on financial profit and individual material reward, the notion of human solidarity remains a valid precept governing human behaviour!

On behalf of our government and people, I wish the 13th International AIDS Conference success, confident that you have come to these African shores as messengers of hope and hopeful that when you conclude your important work, we, as Africans, will be able to say that you who came to this city, which occupies a fond place in our hearts, came here because you care. Thank you for your attention.

59 • Africa's debt crisis (2004)

In 1989, Albert Adu Boahen cautioned his fellow citizens on the dangers of taking on so much debt that their country would forever be in the control of foreign investors. Mbeki in 2000 drew attention to the terrible impact of poverty on the health of Africa's native inhabitants. In 2004 the United Nations Conference on Trade and Development (UNCTAD) issued a report that suggested that Africa had indeed become so beholden to its Western creditors that it was almost impossible for it to escape from a continuing cycle of debt and debt payments that would forever keep its people in poverty despite the fact that they were producing enormous amounts of wealth for these same creditors. Whereas in 1970 the long-term official debt of the continent was $6,967,000,000, in 1980 it was $47,349,000,000; in 1990, $158,082,000,000; and by 2000, $194,337,000,000. One of the report's many findings really stands out. During the period 1970–2002, sub-Saharan African countries received $294 billion in loans (most of this as a result of structural adjustment), and during the same period they paid back $268 billion in debt service, yet in 2002 they still had a debt to the West of $210 billion. Thus, UCNTAD concluded that this process amounted to "a reverse transfer of resources from the world's poorest continent" to the world's richest countries in the West.

During the same period in which Africa's debt increased, the rate of poverty on the continent increased enormously. Whereas in 1990, 241 million people in Africa lived on less than $1 a day (one commonly accepted measure of poverty), by 2004, 298 million Africans lived at that level of income, and they had gone from composing 19 to 31 percent of the world's poor. More disturbingly, the number of Africans among the "ultrapoor," a new definition developed for a world in which poverty was growing and which described those living on less than 50 cents a day, grew from 92 million in 1990 to 121 million in 2004. Indeed, by the latter date Africans constituted 76 percent of the world's ultrapoor.[4]

One of the major consequences of such levels of poverty was an extraordinarily low life expectancy rate, even without the additional impact of AIDS. Africans have a life expectancy at birth approximately half that of people living in the West. A girl born in Zambia today can expect on average to live to 38, a boy to 39; in South Africa 44 and 45, respectively; in Nigeria 43 and 44; in the Democratic Republic of the Congo 43 and 45; and in Ghana, best of all, 57 and 58. Life expectancy in sub-Saharan Africa as a whole is 46 for men and 47 for women; in the West it is 76 for men and

4. Akhter U. Ahmed, Ruth Vargas Hill, Lisa C. Smith, Doris M. Wiesmann, and Tim Frankenberger, *The World's Most Deprived: Characteristics and Causes of Extreme Poverty and Hunger* (Washington, D.C.: International Food Policy Research Institute, 2007); http://www.ifpri.org/sites/default/files/publications/vp43.pdf.

82 for women.[5] *The following text is taken from the 2004 UNCTAD report on "debt sustainability" and economic development in Africa.*[6]

In the context of the Millennium Development Goals (MDGs), the international community has set itself a target of reducing poverty by half by the year 2015. Many observers have now come to the conclusion that, on present trends, there is very little likelihood that this objective can be achieved at any time close to that date in the poorer countries, including in Africa . . .

Debt sustainability is basically a relative concept. The questions that beg for a response are: what level of debt is sustainable for countries in which the vast majority of the population lives on under $1 a day per person? Have debt sustainability criteria been based on internationally recognized benchmarks such as those of the MDGs, or on objectively and theoretically verifiable criteria? What is the relationship between Africa's total external debt stocks and the actual amount of debt serviced? Is complete debt write-off a moral hazard or a "moral imperative"? . . .

The debt relief mechanisms launched in the late 1980s in the wake of the Latin American debt crisis addressed the commercial bank debt of middle income developing countries. At the same time, in 1980, 56 per cent of Africa's total public and publicly guaranteed debt was official, and by 1995 the figure had increased to about 77 per cent. Corresponding ratios for multilateral debts were 14 per cent (1980) and 27 per cent (1995). Between 2000 and 2002, more than 80 per cent of Africa's public and publicly guaranteed debt was official, and about one third of it was multilateral debt. Debt owed to multilateral financial institutions (MFIs) was considered immutable because of concerns with respect to the preferred creditor status of these institutions . . .

While private commercial bank lending accounts for much of the external debt of middle-income developing countries, most low-income African countries have borrowed more from multilateral financial institutions and official bilateral creditors. Such loans were directly contracted from other Governments or their export credit agencies (ECAs), and private loans were insured for payment by ECAs. Indeed, in 1995 more than three-quarters of Africa's public and publicly guaranteed debt was official, and the continent's external debt crisis is therefore more of an "official" than a "commercial bank debt" crisis.

Africa's external debt burden increased significantly between 1970 and 1999. From just over $11 billion in 1970, Africa had accumulated over $120 billion of external debt in the midst of the external shocks of the early 1980s. Total external debt then worsened significantly during the period of structural adjustment in the 1980s and early 1990s, reaching a peak of about $340 billion in 1995, the year immediately preceding the launch of the original HIPC [heavily indebted poor countries]. Overall, Africa's external debt averaged $39 billion during the 1970s, before ballooning to just over $317 billion in the late 1990s. Over the same

5. World Bank, *World Development Report 2007: Development and the Next Generation,* 2006; http://econ
.worldbank.org.

6. United Nations Conference on Trade and Development, *Economic Development in Africa: Debt Sustainability: Oasis or Mirage?* (New York: United Nations, 2004), 1, 2, 3, 5, 7–9, 11, 77; http://www.unctad
.org/Templates/WebFlyer.asp?intItemID=3246.

period, total debt service paid by the continent increased from about $3.5 billion to a peak of $26 billion.

A major observation is that the continent's worsening external debt crisis was underscored by the ever-increasing levels of arrears, an indicator of the inability to service debt obligations on time. In 1995, for example, accumulated arrears on principal repayments had exceeded $41 billion, with countries in sub-Saharan Africa (SSA) owing almost all of this and arrears representing one fifth of the total debt stock of SSA. Secondly, there was a significant increase in the multilateral and official debt components of total outstanding debt during the 1980s and 1990s.

A significant factor in the debt crisis of African countries was the two oil price shocks of 1973–1974 and 1979–1980, the latter leading to a deterioration in the external environment that lasted until 1982. The rise in oil prices not only had an adverse impact on the trade balance of oil-importing countries, but also caused fiscal crises in most of these countries, thereby undermining domestic investment. The second shock occurred at a most inauspicious period, as it coincided with sharp rises in real interest rates. Within the context of the global recession of 1981–1982, which depressed demand for developing countries' exports, and deteriorating terms of trade, the balance of payments crisis that afflicted developing countries was exacerbated, not only for oil importers but also for oil exporters. However, based on the assumption that the global recession would be short-lived and that prices of non-fuel commodities would recover quickly, most of these countries resorted to external borrowing to finance fiscal and external imbalances.

Some Asian countries with a strong manufacturing base chose to restrict the increase in their debt indicators by expanding export volume via a variety of export promotion measures and industrial policies. Many other developing countries did not adjust in this way, either because their economies were not sufficiently diversified or because they deliberately chose not to at the time. For many African countries, there was little room for manoeuvre not only because of their non-diversified economies, but mostly because of the steep decline in non-fuel primary commodity prices during the global recession of 1981–82. In sub-Saharan Africa, between 1980 and 1987, debt to GDP ratio rose from 38 per cent to 70 per cent, while the debt to export ratio rose from 150 per cent to 325 per cent. Per capita incomes fell by 14 per cent during the period. Lending to low-income countries, particularly those in Africa, by bilateral and multilateral creditors was predicated on economic reforms being undertaken in the context of structural adjustment programmes, and total long-term outstanding debt increased by about 200 per cent between 1980 and 1995, the year before the HIPC initiative was launched. The multilateral and official debt components increased by more than 500 per cent and 300 per cent respectively over the same period. The fact that these programmes failed to deliver on the promise of growth and development meant that the debt situation of many African countries continued to deteriorate.

Overall, the debt crisis in low-income developing countries . . . could be traced to a combination of the following factors:

1. Exogenous shocks (e.g., adverse terms of trade or bad weather), which affected highly commodity-dependent countries;
2. Lack of appropriate macroeconomic and structural policy response to such shocks;

3. Lending and refinancing by creditors, initially mostly on non-concessional terms (i.e., on commercial terms with short repayment periods), but from the 1980s shifting to concessional assistance and grants;

4. Imprudent debt management policies by borrowing countries, and use of loans on projects of doubtful viability, which undermined the capacity of countries to repay loans; and,

5. Political factors such as wars and social strife in some borrowing countries.

A part of Africa's debt, particularly that of countries of geopolitical or strategic interest, is regarded by many as "odious," which raises the issue of the appropriate way to deal with the continent's debt crisis. For example, estimates show that, including imputed interest earnings, the accumulated stock of flight capital of Zaire (now the Democratic Republic of Congo) amounted to nearly $18 billion. The country's public external debt build-up thus appears to have been matched or exceeded by the accumulation of private external assets. Some evidence has been presented to the effect that the official and private creditors of the Mobutu regime knew, or should have known, that there was a high risk that their loans, or a substantial part of them, would not be used to benefit the Congolese people. A cursory glance at Africa's debt profile shows that the continent received some $540 billion in loans and paid back some $550 billion in principal and interest between 1970 and 2002. Yet Africa remained with a debt stock of $295 billion. For its part, SSA received $294 billion in disbursements and paid $268 billion in debt service, but remains with a debt stock of some $210 billion. Discounting interest and interest on arrears, further payment of outstanding debt would represent a reverse transfer of resources.

That Africa's debt burden has been a major obstacle to the region's prospects for increased savings and investment, economic growth and poverty reduction cannot be denied. The continent's debt overhang has inhibited public investment in physical and social infrastructure. It has also hampered private investment, as investors could not be assured of policy continuity in an environment marked by severe external imbalances. And by undermining critical investments in health and human resource development, the debt overhang has compromised some of the essential conditions for sustainable economic growth, development, and poverty reduction. There is now a consensus that a permanent solution to the external debt crisis, along with increased official development assistance (ODA) and enhanced trade based on a level playing field, are critical to sustainable growth and development and to meeting the development challenges facing the African continent, including the Millennium Development Goals (MDGs), in particular that of halving poverty by 2015. Indeed, it is now generally agreed that the continent would need to at least double its rate of economic growth to some 7–8 per cent per annum and sustain this for about a decade in order to meet the MDGs . . .

That Africa's debt burden has been a major obstacle to the region's prospects for economic growth and investment and poverty reduction is not in doubt. The continent's debt overhang has frustrated public investment in physical and social infrastructure, and therefore deterred private investment. And by undermining critical investments in health and human resource development, the debt overhang has compromised some of the essential conditions for sustainable economic growth and development and poverty reduction. There is now a consensus that, for a permanent solution to the external debt crisis, African countries would need to pursue policies of prudent debt management, economic diversification and sustained economic growth, which would require greater policy space. Equally, there is a consensus that the international community has to support these national policies with concerted and coherent actions in the areas of trade and finance through increased market access and major reductions, and eventually elimination, of agricultural subsidies, combined with international action on commodities, and increased ODA. It is only through this partnership that African countries would be able to achieve sustained high growth rates and development, implement the poverty reduction strategies necessary to meet the development challenges facing the continent, and attain the MDGs, in particular that of halving poverty by 2015.

CHAPTER EIGHT

The Continuing Transition
to Freedom (1990–2008)

60 • The crisis of the state in Africa (1990)

Yoweri Museveni (b. 1944), the president of Uganda, is considered one of a new generation of leaders, coming of age in independent rather than colonial Africa. In the 1960s Museveni studied in Tanzania, where he imbibed the socialism of Julius Nyerere and viewed the working out of FRELIMO's socialist policies in northern Mozambique in the 1970s. An opponent of Idi Amin, the dictatorial ruler of Uganda in the 1970s, Museveni first supported the return to Uganda of Milton Obote, who had led the country to independence. However, when Obote won election to the presidency in a process marked by widespread fraud, Museveni formed the National Resistance Movement. He eventually succeeded in winning power by armed struggle, forcing Obote to flee Uganda and appointing himself president in 1986. His position as president was confirmed by popular vote in 1996.

Despite his disavowal of earlier ideologues, Museveni echoes the analyses of Frantz Fanon, who stated that the petty bourgeoisie is trained to serve power; of Chinua Achebe, who maintained that technocrats are necessary to solve Africa's problems; and of Kwame Nkrumah, who believed that African unity is the path to success. Though Museveni sees the answer to Africa's problems in the free market rather than socialism, he recognizes, like his predecessors, the difficulty of attaining political stability on a continent where the monocrop export economies inherited from colonialism remain fundamentally unstable.[1]

The crisis of the state in Africa, May 13, 1990

The lack of ideological independence in Africa has been a very destabilising factor because it has generated wrong ideas. The regimes which said they were rightist are in a state of crisis; those which said they were leftist are also in a state of crisis. So what is the problem? How can they all be a crisis?

The main problem was that our leaders were besieged by advice and threats from East and West. If we do not solve this crisis, I think we shall remain in a lot of turmoil for a long time and keep jumping from one mistake to another. We can borrow ideas, but nobody should force us to adopt them if they are not suited to our conditions.

1. Yoweri Museveni, *What Is Africa's Problem? Speeches and Writings on Africa* (Kampala: NRM Publications, 1992), 185–95.

When I received the invitation to come and address this seminar, I tried to put some thoughts down but I shall not read the written speech. I shall summarise what I think are the salient points of this important subject: "The Crisis of the State in Africa."

Soon after the formal departure of colonial rulers at independence, the state in Africa was beset by many problems and I shall concentrate on the most crucial of them. The first problem was that the state was economically dependent on the former colonial powers, especially for technology. We often talk of economic dependence, but this dependence is coupled with and aggravated by an absence of technology: we do not have the technical and managerial skills to enable us to solve our own problems.

After a number of years of independence—more than 30 years in some countries—we have been able to train a few economists and some scientists, professional people like yourselves. If these people could have helped us, we would have got somewhere. But because we have not solved the problem of technological dependence and been able to participate in technological developments, we are not making much headway.

The only way we can participate at present is by someone giving us technology in the form of aid. The donor finances it and then his people come and build a factory in our country. Occasionally, we buy technology with our own money. Right here in this area, there is a salt factory but it is not producing anything because our people bought technology from Germany and found that it was the wrong kind of technology. They are completely dependent on the Germans or some other outsiders to come and put it right. This is a very big handicap indeed.

Since the modern Africa state cannot be independent, it becomes easy prey to manipulation. If our states can be so manipulated, how can they expect to solve the problems of the people except with the permission of the former colonial rulers? A state which does not have capacity to tell the colonial or neo-colonial rulers that it will act independently, in spite of what those rulers think, is completely handicapped. If you need ideas on how to solve problems, why must you borrow from or imitate somebody outside?

Ideological dependence

The problem of economic and technological dependence was aggravated by ideological dependence. If you want a microphone, like this one I am using now, you must import it because you do not have anyone in your country who can make it, which is bad enough. In addition to that, however, you are also ideologically dependent: you need ideas on how to solve problems and you must borrow from or imitate somebody outside.

In Africa's case, this problem was very serious because our states were born during a time of conflict between the Eastern and Western European countries which had their own arguments about how best to organise themselves. Some said that we should use market forces and others that we should have planned economies. Behind these ideological arguments was European nationalism and chauvinism. There were ideological and nationalist tussles and there was always the old quest for domination, more organised peoples dominating less organised ones.

Africa was thus dragged into European arguments. As soon as any country came to the fore—as soon as any country became independent—the question would come up: "Are you pro-East or pro-West? You must answer that question first before you can do any business with us. What is your ideological colour? You have to take a position." Some of our people did not have the capacity to be able to say: "This is not my argument or my quarrel. Or even if it is my quarrel, it is only partially so." Some countries tried to be pro-capitalist and others tried to be pro-Marxist, even when the conditions were not conducive to being either.

In Uganda for instance, in 1980 and earlier on, we had political groups which had existed since the days of colonial rule. These groups were artificially divided between those called "leftist" and others called "rightist." But when you examined them closely, there was no substance as to why one was called rightist and the other leftist. These were simply opportunistic groupings seeking platforms from which to seek external support. When some people want to get aid from the Russians, they say they are leftist; when they want to get aid from America, they say they are rightist. But when you examine the content of their programmes there is nothing that shows that they are either one thing or the other. They are just small élite groups seeking power, and in order to take political power, they need foreign support. In order to qualify for that support, therefore, they must sing the song of their benefactors.

We, in our [National Resistance] Movement, however, refused to join these opportunists. We refused even to recognise the so called leftist-rightist categorisation. We felt that the opportunistic groups should be got rid of altogether so that we could make a fresh start. We would not join them because they had no genuine platforms. The ideological debate in Africa was thus taken over by opportunists, and opportunism became their ideology: how to qualify for aid from so and so. Even the liberation movements were affected—both the Soviets and the Chinese supported liberation movements which had to declare whether they were pro-Soviet or pro-Chinese and this was very disruptive indeed.

I think the lack of ideological independence has been a very destablising factor because it has generated wrong ideas most of the time. This is why you see that the state in Africa is now in a crisis, as the theme of your conference states. The regimes which said they were rightist are in a state of crisis; those which said they were leftist are also in a state of crisis. So what is the problem? How can they all be in crisis? That means there is something fundamentally wrong. The main problem is that our leaders did not find time to define the issues confronting them. They borrowed foreign ideas and superimposed them on their countries: this could not, and did not, work.

If you examine the scene in Africa, it is quite difficult to find a model solution. Those who followed the planned economy system got into very serious problems with their economies; those who adopted the so-called market forces approach fared no better either. In very few cases was there real structural economic transformation to generate sustained growth. Those who adopted the planned economy approach over-extended the involvement of the state and went into all sorts of little ventures, which in itself undermined production. The economy was taken over by bureaucrats who had no interest in it and the consequence was that the population was not given a chance to take part in meaningful production. Economies which adopted the market forces approach concentrated on producing raw materials like coffee and tea but these were not integrated with the industrial sector. Therefore, whenever there is a price crisis, it is heavily reflected in the concerned country. Capitalist-oriented regimes were successful only for as long as commodity prices were high.

My personal view, therefore, is that we should have used a mixture of market force and planned economy approaches, depending on convenience and individual countries' circumstances. Above all, we should have aimed at integrating the various economic sectors: the industrial sector interacting with the agricultural sector; agriculture producing raw materials for industry; and industry transforming these into finished products for domestic consumption, leaving the surplus for export. Our industries should have been geared to producing inputs like tools and chemicals for agricultural use.

This, however, was not done and economies which were supposed to follow the capitalist approach were only concerned with producing raw materials and exporting them in an unprocessed, raw form. The prices of these raw materials are, however, very uncertain. The problem was that even where our people could have detected the impending crisis and done something about it, they were besieged by advice and threats from East and West. If we do not solve this crisis, I think we shall remain in a lot of turmoil for a long time and we shall keep jumping from one mistake to another. We must have ideological independence, we can borrow ideas but nobody should force us to adopt them if they are not suited to our conditions.

Africa's "big armies"

Another problem of the state in Africa is the inadequacy of its means to assert its independence. There is a belief, which I personally do not share, that the armies in Africa are too big, for instance. I often hear these opinions expressed on the radio that Africa is not developing because its big armies are consuming all the resources. But where are these big armies? Sudan, for instance, is 2.5 million square miles, without modern communication systems. How do you maintain the unity of such a country without a big army? Therefore, my view, which is contrary to what some people have been saying, is that one of the biggest problems in Africa is the weakness of the state apparatus, i.e., the armies, the police, etc. When the state tries to strengthen these institutions, however, it sometimes acquires equipment which is not suited to its circumstances. Sometimes a state may build up a wrong type of army, for example, a mechanised army instead of an adequately equipped infantry.

If we take the police, I am informed that in Europe the ratio of police to population is one policeman to every 500 people. But here in Uganda, at one time there was one policeman to every 100,000 people. The population was, therefore, left at the mercy of criminals. For instance, the law here says that you are not supposed to beat your wife because she has her citizen's rights like everybody else. But who will enforce this? Who will even detect that you have beaten your wife? Nobody!

Of course, I should be careful here: do not think that I am supporting the strengthening of every type of state. We must first of all define the character of the state. Is this state democratic or not? If it is undemocratic but strong, it will be very dangerous. But even if it is democratic but weak, the people will suffer as much as if it were not democratic.

Low cultural level

Another problem which beset [the] African state was the low cultural level of the people who took charge of our affairs. You must have heard of people like Idi Amin and [Emperor] Bokassa. If you examine the matter carefully and pose the question: "Who was Idi Amin?" you will find that Idi Amin was a sergeant in the British Army. A sergeant is ordinarily taught to manage 30 people under the supervision of an officer. He is not allowed to manage those 30 people on his own: he must do so under supervision of someone more cultured and better trained than himself.

But here we had a situation where suddenly people who were simply ignorant and hopelessly out of their depth were propelled into positions of very great power. This is a big problem. The endemic corruption in Africa is partly caused by this low level of culture. Culture first generates knowledge, then it generates ethics. How do you define right and wrong? How do you differentiate between what is acceptable and what is not acceptable in society?

In addition to the problems already discussed, the state in Africa also had a problem of the cultural slavery of the small élite groups. I am informed that at independence, Tanganyika only had 13 university graduates. How can you run a country with such a small number of graduates? We had very few educated people, but even the few we had were cultural slaves to foreign ideas. If you did not do things the way they were done in Europe you were not proper and our élites put pressure on governments to make wrong decisions. Even when they were not themselves in government, the élites exerted all kinds of pressure on governments. The ability to improvise and find solutions was thus completely impaired by cultural slavery.

Our élites do not have the capacity to educate our people to use the means which are within their reach: they are always hoping for things which they can never get. As a result, nothing useful is ever done. When you are a slave to certain ideas, you incapacitate yourself because you make yourself incapable of taking another route from that taken by people you regard as superior. Any initiative is stifled because you must do things the way they are done somewhere else.

Interrupted state formation

When the imperial powers started penetrating Africa, the process of state formation—the amalgamation of clans into tribes and of tribes into nations—was beginning to crystallise in different places throughout the continent, although it had not yet become consolidated. Some empires had emerged in west, central and east Africa but there was no urgency for the formation of centralised states. When you are living in the tropics with a small population, there is no great urge for one clan to go and conquer another in order to form an empire. The problems we face here are not so numerous. If you live in the Middle East, however, you have a lot of urge to conquer others because you need their resources. Here each clan can stay in its own area: once in a while they all go and raid cattle from another clan, but they will come back home. There is no great need to establish hegemony over other people.

Therefore, the urge to form states was not as strong as in other parts of the world. All the same, there was some linkage at various levels. The clans were linked culturally, although politically they were not centrally organised. Linguistic groupings like the Bantu and the Luo are a manifestation of cultural linkage. A few chiefs tried to unite these clans in order to control resources in their areas and put them under one authority. When colonialism came, however, this process was interrupted and frozen. The territories were channelled to deal with European powers so that horizontal contact between them was discouraged, or stopped altogether in many cases.

Instead, the colonialists encouraged vertical interaction: between the colonised and the colonising people. They also brought new contradictions like factional religious sectors.

Religions have played a prominently disruptive role in confusing and dividing our illiterate people and this added to the crisis of the state where you will find people killing one another in the name of religion. However, this sectarianism is sometimes over-stressed in writings on Africa which talk so much about tribes in Africa. People are not aware that the problems were caused by colonial and neo-colonial political organisation and that there is, in fact, a great deal of cultural homogeneity.

Africa is still pre-capitalist

Another problem confronting the state in Africa is the pre-capitalist nature of African societies today. African societies are still living either at clan or, in some cases, at feudal levels of organisation. Hardly any African state has reached the capitalist stage. The European capitalist class was very useful for integration. If you want pan-Africanists, you should look for capitalists because capitalists would be very good pan-Africanists. Why? Because a capitalist is a producer of wealth: he needs a market for his products and he needs labour in some cases. He cannot, therefore, afford to be parochial: he will work for integration and expansion and he will not support the splitting up of a country because this will split up his market.

It was the capitalist middle class which caused the unification of the German states. Until 1870, the Germans were living more or less as we were living here. People in Bavaria and Prussia spoke the same language but they were not politically united. It was the industrialists and capitalists who wanted a united market, and it was they who pushed Bismarck for German unification.

In Africa, this class does not exist. The middle classes in Africa are not producers of wealth; instead they are salesmen selling other people's products. Fanon said this middle class became senile before they were young. The African middle class is a caricature of the European middle class. Any resemblance between the African middle class and the European middle class is limited merely to the wearing of suits and ties, because in terms of their relationship with the means of production, they could hardly be more different.

In order to have integration, one must use one of the two things. You could use either vested economic interests or ideologically committed people who can work for integration if they are intellectually convinced that it is the right thing to do. The churches offer a good example. Although churches have economic interests, they also have evangelists who preach with conviction. Such people can advance the cause for which they are preaching—although they are often used for other, less laudable, purposes by some interest groups.

If you do not have ideologically committed people and you do not have people with vested interests who can push for integration and, therefore, the stability of the state, then you are in a crisis. You must have one or the other. For instance, the Tanzanians have pushed the process of integration a bit further than some of us, because the leaders who were in charge of state affairs from the very beginning, for instance, used the Swahili language to advance the integration of their country.

Lack of democracy and accountability

Another problem that has plagued the state in Africa has been the lack of democracy and accountability. When I talk of democracy, I should not be confused with those who are talking about multi-parties. The talk about multi-parties is about form, it is not about substance. Each country's circumstances should dictate what form of democratic expression should be used. There should be control of the top leadership by the population; there must be regular elections; leaders must submit themselves to elections and be thrown out if they are rejected by the electorate. As long as that is happening, I think there will be democracy and account-ability, although the exact form this democracy assumes is a different matter. I do not agree with those who are trying to push the idea of multi-parties down everybody's throats.

Having outlined all these crises, is the situation in Africa hopeless? Should we become despondent and give up? I would not myself agree with such a pessimistic view. In fact, the situation in Africa is very bright and it can be turned around very quickly because we have a lot of resources and manpower in many of our countries. There are a few countries, especially those in the Sahel belt, with real problems because they lack water and other resources, but in most cases, we can turn the situation around. I am firmly convinced of this.

What is the solution to the crisis?

How can we correct the present situation? These are some of the steps we need to take:

1. First of all, we must acquire ideological independence. We must stop ourselves being pushed around by exporters of ideas. We should be very adamant about doing what is good for our people. If we do not do this the crisis will continue.

2. Secondly, we must acquire technology. We must take deliberate steps to acquire access to the scientific know-how which can transform our natural products into finished goods. We should pay scientists handsomely, so that the few we have do not keep running to Europe and America. My own view is that these scientists should be bribed. If they are not committed to working for their countries, let us bribe them! They should be given very huge salaries, vehicles, and other incentives to make them stay here so that they can help us solve the problem of our technological dependence. We have tried to put this programme into ac-tion here in Uganda but I do not know why there are so many vested interests opposed to it. However, we shall soon sort it out. Ideological conviction is not a very common attribute, so we cannot rely on it. Let us instead rely on the mercenary instinct and bribe our scientists to make them stay here!

Let us also deliberately push the teaching of science in our schools and universities by providing laboratories and other scientific materials. I am sure these two methods will enable us to overcome this problem over the next 10 years or so. We should also open more techni-cal schools and institutions for artisans.

3. Thirdly, we should co-ordinate better among African countries because acting singly is not good enough. We are really not so weak as is generally assumed. For instance, Cuba, a small country, and Angola, were able to break the myth of the power of the South African army and change strategic thinking completely. I had occasion to tell Sir Geoffrey Howe in this very room—he was British Foreign Secretary at the time—that, in my view, the South Africans were making a mistake by thinking that their present superiority over African coun-tries was a perpetual phenomenon. We are disorganised, we are uncoordinated, we are not mobilised, so they seem superior, when actually that is not the case.

My view is that the South Africans should have looked for political solutions while there was still time to do so. The events in Angola were an example of what a sizeable force we can muster if we act together. Not only would better co-ordination make us strong, it would also minimise the conflicts between African states which sap the energy of the continent as a whole.

4. Fourthly, we should institute universal education. We must aim at providing universal education up to the twelfth year of school because we still have millions of people in Africa who are ignorant. Uganda for instance, has a population of 18 million, but of these, perhaps as many as 17 million are still ignorant, illiterate and superstitious. Because of lack of knowledge, these millions are either completely immobilised or only partly mobilised. If we had universal education, however, we would have a big strategic advantage.

5. Fifthly, we must encourage the African languages that can be easily spoken by a wide range of the African population. In East Africa, I would recommend Kiswahili. There are other languages in other regions, such as Lingala in Central Africa and Hausa in West Africa. Language can be a major factor in promoting integration and stability.

6. Finally, we must have democratisation. Without democracy things are bound to go wrong. You cannot manage states properly without democracy. We must have elections and democratic practices which ensure against sectarianism and opportunism. If you campaign on a sectarian platform, you should be automatically disqualified. If the political process is about real issues, they must be submitted to democratic debate and decision by the population.

I think that if we implemented some of these measures, we would resolve the situation on our continent. There are a lot of resources, although they are still untapped, and there is quite a lot of homogeneity on the continent in terms of culture and language. There is an impression that there is so much conflict in Africa that Africans cannot work together: this is not correct. We must stop highlighting our differences and instead highlight the many similarities which can unite and help us develop our continent.

61 • The elements of democracy in Africa (1992)

Olesegun Obasanjo has long been involved in the politics of Nigeria. In 1970 he led the forces that finally ended the Biafran secessionist movement. In 1976 he succeeded Murtala Muhammad as head of state when Murtala was assassinated in an abortive coup and led the military administration of the country until the return of civilian rule in 1979. Obasanjo became well known internationally during the 1980s, during which time he acted as an arbitrator in disputes between certain African countries and took a prominent role as a critic of apartheid. Though a military officer, he spoke of the importance of democracy and saw intervention by the armed forces in government matters as necessary only in exceptional circumstances and for short periods of time. In the early 1990s, he became especially associated with the Africa Leadership Forum, which he helped form and which aimed at bringing African leaders together to engage in dialogues about how to encourage democracy in Africa. In the following speech to a meeting of the forum, he argued that Africa was experiencing a "phenomenal spread of democracy" but that this democracy had to take a distinct African form, echoing Julius Nyerere's analysis from the 1960s. Western practices could not be imported "lock, stock, and barrel" with any real hope of success. While Obasanjo's views were much admired outside Nigeria, he did not find a receptive audience among those who governed the country. In 1995 he was imprisoned on the orders of Sani Abacha, then dictator of Nigeria, and remained in detention until Abacha's death in 1998. He ran for president in 1999 and won an overwhelming

victory. Obasanjo stepped down from the presidency in 2007, successfully supporting in the fol-
lowing election his hand-picked successor, Umaru Musa Yar'Adua, as the new leader of Nigeria.
In 2008, however, Obasanjo and members of his family came under investigation for corruption,
though some argued that he was the victim of a vendetta by political foes (now including Yar'Adua).
Obasanjo gave the following speech to members of the Africa Leadership Forum.[2]

There is an ongoing and ever-spreading wind of change in the air all over the world. Even in spite of its bewildering and sometimes confounding notation, the freshness of its appeal has neither grown stale nor become any less attractive. It is the concept and practice of democracy, which forms the focus of our gathering this weekend.

Democracy is an expression and expansion of man's freedom and has over time become synonymous with man's progress. Democracy is the option which the governed prefers but which is often denied them by the governor under one pretext and pretence or the other. Taken in its totality and at a more ecumenical level, the natural instinct of man as a governed animal is for democracy. I believe that the basic reason for the persistence and recent phenomenal spread of democracy is the ever-alluring appeal it has to man's finer instincts and ideas about the process of governance.

As a form of power, it is of course never ideal and it probably might not be ideal but more than any other form of power, it embodies an immanent tendency of man towards freedom and thereby remains the best and the most humane form of power.

Democracy is not a static phenomenon, it has an in-built dynamism which requires that it must be developed and consolidated. This is made all the more important because democracy releases the total energy of all citizens for development. On the other hand, restraint, curtailment, suppression and oppression associated with authoritarian regimes, breed resentment, apathy, and withdrawal syndrome which release negative thoughts and tendencies to the development process.

In the Nigerian situation, democracy is the only integrative glue that can bind different sub-national groups together into a nation with a common destiny, equal status and common identity on a permanent basis. The appeal of democracy when firmly established, also lies in its pragmatism and realism as a means of guaranteeing individual rights, interests and social justice. It preserves harmony within communities through consensus and agreement, it thereby integrates societies. It can be made to generate growth and development and distribute wealth more equitably. To admit that democracy is unworkable in a place is to imply that freedom is not cherished in that place.

Agreeably, the variegated nature of the Nigerian polity is an added dimension to the problems of institutionalising democratic process. More often than not, the democratic process has been touted as a destabilizing mechanism in Nigeria. I neither share nor appreciate this opinion. For me a true and genuine democratic process must make the game of politics a game of inclusion rather than exclusion. It must be a game of service rather than a game of cake sharing.

2. Olusegun Obasanjo and Akin Mabogunje, eds., *Elements of Democracy* (Abeokuta, Nigeria: Africa Leadership Forum Publications, 1992), 59–62.

The important point for us in Nigeria is the need to ensure that both the minority and the majority have adequate access to the institutions of governance. In other words the form and nature of our democratic structure and processes must be aimed at assisting us in allaying our hidden and explicit fears about the system.

Our two attempts at democratic governance have proved that democracy à la West, lock, stock, and barrel cannot resolve our problems. The inability of our structures and processes during these periods has bred and injected a disturbing modicum of cynicism among the citizenry. The important point to think of resolving this weekend is the need to visualize a modality capable of assisting us to expel the choking air of cynicism and its epi-phenomenon of apathy among the populace. Perhaps the first step would be the need to prevent the constant privatisation of the state by our power elites. This must be done in addition to a move to separate the business of governance from the business of economic transactions; it is time to move from the power state of *Ibn Khaldun* to the popular state. It is only in this regard that we can make the democratic process relevant to the daily existence of the people. One of the anchoring bases of this move is the need to embrace, integrate, imbibe and acculturate the spirit of mutual empowerment between the state and the people.

Democratic process must become a way of instituting cultural identity and promoting national unity. It must not be used to disintegrate as was the case in the past. Democratic process in a multi-nationality like ours must be anchored and premised on an order that guarantees justice and equity. We must seek a process that unifies law, morality and justice. It must, as a matter of necessity, be an order that conforms and agrees with our culture, with the will and nature of the humanity of our populace. It must not stultify or limit ambitions by practice, convention or constitution. It must give hope and inspiration to all.

Our process, as a multi-national society, must move to particularize the will of the varying sections of the society. The aim must be to make our society seek the well-being of its different sections by establishing good relationships among them. As a form of self government it must be self-creating, while ebbing away the tendency towards authoritarianism.

It is important that we must not allow our democratic process to be used as a legitimating influence for corruption and tyranny, be it of a group or a person. Genuine democratic process must have embodied in it safeguards against the possibility of its being hijacked by any group. Justice and its pursuit are essential ingredients in the democratic process. In addition to all of these let me say that some essential and vital ingredients for the proper institutionalization of a genuine democratic process include among others:

a). Trust creation and confidence building between the leaders and the populace.
b). Periodic election of political leadership through the secret ballot.
c). Creation of an appropriate political machinery.
d). Promotion and defence of human rights.
e). Political communication.
f). Decentralization of political power and authority.
g). Education and political education.

Democracy, as a game of inclusion rather than exclusion, requires and demands popular participation of all adults particularly in the election process. Freedom and choice are two cardinal pillars of democracy and the elections must be free and fair and allow for choice of programmes and personalities.

There must be orderly and periodic succession of leaders at all levels. The society must be open with an independent judiciary. Freedom of the press must include freedom of ownership. Other freedoms enshrined in the United Nations Charter on Human Rights including the OAU [Organization of African Unity] declaration on Human Rights and People's Rights including the Rights of the Child must be promoted and defended. Freedom also connotes obligations and duties which must neither be ignored nor abused. The point must be made, that without fundamental human rights, there can be no democracy. And sustenance of democracy can only be made on democratic culture and democratic spirit both of which have to be engendered and watered.

Democracy need not be too expensive as a form of government. And what is gained in unity, freedom, consensus, stability, commitment and development in a truly democratic society easily outweighs the cost of maintaining and sustaining the structures of democracy. Effective democratic process provides checks and balances which limit the abuses of power, corruption, oppression and dictatorial and authoritarian tendencies.

Democratic principles will only have their full effect if the democratic state operates in such a manner as to guarantee individual liberties through the observance of separation of powers, separation of the state and religious institutions and forces and separation of the state and political party/parties.

The suppression of national interest by tribal interest, favouritism, clientelism and nepotism accentuates social inequalities and undermines the ethics and practice of democracy. Democracy cannot operate successfully within a tribalistic society. Tribalism often stems from perceived or real frustrations assumed or caused by cultural contempt, the refusal to recognise the other in its specificity, the act of basing oneself on one's culture in order to practise discriminations of all sorts. Cultural pluralism is an effort to recognise the specificity of the different cultures or sub-cultures of one nation while avoiding ranking them and yet giving each an equal chance to develop. Without cultural pluralism in a multi-national society, political pluralism will be at risk.

Political authority must be institutionalised and it must not take a patrimonial character. Those who govern must not behave as if authority or power is their personal property and something they can hand down to their heirs. To institutionalize political authority is to compel rulers to conform to pre-established texts and to change them is to suit personal ambitions. They should be made to acknowledge that they are only representatives of the nation and not the owners or proprietors of sovereignty.

62 • Negotiating democracy in South Africa (1993)

Faced by ever-growing, mass-based opposition to its apartheid policies, the National Party government of South Africa in the late 1980s decided to adopt a policy of "reform." Why the government adopted that policy and what it hoped to achieve remain questions of considerable debate among scholars. What is indisputable is that the government did take certain key steps that in themselves set in motion an unstoppable process: It repealed most apartheid legislation during the late 1980s, it lifted the ban on the ANC and other previously illegal organizations, and it freed Nelson Mandela from prison (where he had been for almost thirty years) in 1990. It also began a process of negotiation to implement a new political structure for South Africa, one that would not recognize racial differences and that would permit all citizens the right to vote for the first time in the country's history. The negotiations were held under the auspices of the Convention for a Democratic South Africa (CODESA), an umbrella organization (including the ANC, the National Party, and several other political groups) that met for the first time in December 1991 and that continued negotiations—with occasional breaks—until the first nationwide election was held in 1994 (won by Mandela and the ANC). The pamphlet reproduced here in full lists the aims agreed upon by the members of CODESA.[3]

Declaration of intent

We, the duly authorized representatives of political parties, political organizations, administrations and the South African Government, coming together at this first meeting of the Convention for a Democratic South Africa, mindful of the awesome responsibility that rests on us at this moment in the history of our country, declare our solemn commitment:

1. to bring about an undivided South Africa with one nation sharing a common citizenship, patriotism and loyalty, pursuing amidst our diversity freedom, equality and security for all irrespective of race, colour, sex or creed; a country free from apartheid or any other form of discrimination or domination;

2. to work to heal the divisions of the past, to secure the advancement of all, and to establish a free and open society based on democratic values where the dignity, worth and rights of every South African are protected by law;

3. to strive to improve the quality of life of our people through policies that will promote economic growth and human development and ensure equal opportunities and social justice for all South Africans;

4. to create a climate conducive to peaceful constitutional change by eliminating violence, intimidation and destabilisation and by promoting free political participation, discussion and debate;

5. to set in motion the process of drawing up and establishing a constitution that will ensure, inter alia:

   a. that South Africa will be a united, democratic, nonracial and non-sexist state in which sovereign authority is exercised over the whole of its territory;

   b. that the Constitution will be the supreme law and that it will be guarded over by an independent, non-racial and impartial judiciary;

   c. that there will be a multiparty democracy with the right to form and join political parties and with regular elections on the basis of universal adult suffrage on a common voters roll; in general the basic electoral system shall be that of proportional representation;

   d. that there shall be a separation of powers between the legislature, executive and judiciary with appropriate checks and balances.

   e. that the diversity of languages, cultures and religions of the people of South Africa shall be acknowledged;

3. "Declaration of Intent," Convention for a Democratic South Africa (CODESA), 1991–1993.

f. that all shall enjoy universally accepted human rights, freedoms and civil liberties including freedom of religion, speech and assembly protected by an entrenched and justiciable Bill of Rights and a legal system that guarantees equality of all before the law.

We agree:

1. that the present and future participants shall be entitled to put forward freely to the Convention any proposal consistent with democracy.
2. that CODESA will establish a mechanism whose task it will be, in co-operation with administrations and the South African Government, to draft the text of all legislation required to give effect to the agreements reached in CODESA.

[Signatures attached of Mandela, de Klerk, and representatives of seventeen other political parties and/or homeland governments].

Addendum:

For the avoidance of doubt as to the interpretation of the Declaration of Intent, it is declared by its signatories that irrespective of their individual interpretive views thereof, no provisions of the Declaration, interpreted alone or in conjunction with any other provision thereof shall be construed as:

1. favouring or inhibiting or precluding the adoption of any particular constitutional model, whether unitary, federal, confederal, or otherwise, consistent with democracy;
2. preventing any participant from advocating the same or the separation, in terms of any constitutional model, of powers between a central government and the regions; during the proceedings of CODESA or any of its committees or Working Groups;
3. and that this Addendum shall be added to and form part of the Declaration.

63 • Scrubbing the furious walls of Mikuyu prison (1990s)

For his poetry, Jack Mapanje was imprisoned for three years, seven months, and sixteen days. No charges were ever brought against him. He was released from prison in May 1991 and sent into exile in Britain. Hastings Banda remained president for life of Malawi for another three years, not leaving office until 1994, when the growth of public protest forced him out. (He was then in his early nineties and of debatable mental capacity.) In poems that Mapanje wrote about his prison ordeal, one describes the evidence that he found in even the harshest of circumstances of the willingness of people to continue to resist their oppressors.[4]

Scrubbing the Furious Walls of Mikuyu

Is this where they dump those rebels,
these haggard cells stinking of bucket
shit and vomit and the acrid urine of

4. Jack Mapanje, *The Chattering Wagtails of Mikuyu Prison* (London: Heinemann, 1993), 53–54.

yesteryears? Who would have thought I
would be gazing at these dusty, cobweb
ceilings of Mikuyu Prison, scrubbing
briny walls and riddling out impetuous
scratches of another dung-beetle locked
up before me here? Violent human palms
wounded these blood-bloated mosquitoes
and bugs (to survive), leaving these vicious
red marks. Monstrous flying cockroaches
crashed here. Up there the cobwebs trapped
dead bumblebees. Where did black wasps
get clay to build nests in this corner?

But here, scratches, insolent scratches!
I have marvelled at the rock paintings
of Mphunzi Hills once but these grooves
and notches on the walls of Mikuyu Prison,
how furious, what barbarous squiggles!
How long did this anger languish without
charge without trial without visit here and
what justice committed? This is the moment
we dreaded; when we'd all descend into
the pit, alone; without a wife or a child
without mother; without paper or pencil
without a story (just three Bibles for
ninety men) without charge without trial.
This is the moment I never needed to see.

Shall I scrub these brave squiggles out
Of human memory then or should I perhaps
Superimpose my own, less caustic; dare I
Overwrite this precious scrawl? Who'd
Have known I'd find another prey without
Charge without trial (without bitterness)
In these otherwise blank walls of Mikuyu
Prison? No, I will throw my water and mop
Elsewhere. We have liquidated too many
Brave names out of the nation's memory;
I will not rub out another nor inscribe
My own, more ignoble, to consummate this
Moment of truth I have always feared!

64 • An intimate genocide (1994)

One of the terrible facts of the twentieth century is the periodic campaign of mass killing by various groups. The Nazis murdered Jews in Europe, the Serbian Christians killed Albanian Muslims in Kosovo, and the Hutu massacred thousands of Tutsis in Rwanda. In Europe, military technology and rapid transit helped facilitate the slaughter of millions of people, but in Africa the implementation of genocide has been an intimate affair. Much of the time it was personal and achieved with hand-held weapons, seldom firearms.

Rwanda, primarily home to two ethnic groups, the majority Hutu (89 percent) and the minority Tutsi (10 percent), lost close to a million people between April and July 1994, when supporters of the Hutu-dominated central government sought to exterminate all potential opponents in the country. In their divide-and-rule policies, the Belgians had long favored the Tutsi at the expense of the Hutu. Upon abandoning their colonial possessions in 1959, however, they did nothing to protect their former collaborators when the Hutu massacred tens of thousands of their Tutsi oppressors. Many Tutsi fled as refugees into Uganda, from which they began to plan their return to Rwanda. A collapse of world coffee prices in 1989—coffee accounted for 75 percent of Rwanda's export earnings—provided an opportunity for the refugees to invade, as well as the difficult economic conditions in which Hutu extremists in the Rwandan government began to demonize their opponents. In order to make pointless any military victory for the former refugees, the Hutu extremists planned genocide against the Tutsi still living within Rwanda.

The killing began in the middle of 1994. Precipitated by the mysterious assassination of the presidents of Rwanda and Burundi (when the plane carrying both was shot out of the sky as it was about to land in Rwanda's capital) and carried out by mobs incited by radio broadcasts in which government officials called on all "loyal" Rwandans to hunt down and kill every Tutsi they could find, the slaughter extended also to Hutu opponents of the ruling party. In this case, ethnicity served as a useful camouflage for political persecution. Despite calls for international intervention, the West did practically nothing. Minute in numbers, the few Belgian and UN "peacekeepers" stood by and watched as people were macheted to death in front of them. The genocide ended only when a rebel army of Tutsi-led soldiers infiltrated Rwanda from Uganda, defeated the Rwandan national army, and forced the Hutu terrorist gangs (the Interahamwe) to flee into neighboring countries (especially Zaire, where they have remained a destabilizing force ever since).

Fergal Keane is an award-winning BBC reporter who traveled to Rwanda just after the genocide to investigate its lingering effects. During that time he talked to many of the victims of the genocidal campaign, to members of the rebel army, to Hutu officials who had ordered the killings (and who have since sought refugee status themselves outside Rwanda), and to members of relief organizations. He also witnessed scenes of immense carnage since the perpetrators of the genocide left their victims' bodies to rot where they fell. In this account of his travels in Rwanda, Keane describes what he saw at Nyarubuye parish, site of an awful massacre in which hundreds were killed. His description evokes the intimacy required of the perpetrators to accomplish their goal and of the situation in which the individual victims were involved prior to their death. Near the beginning of his book he impresses upon the reader the following chilling fact: "Before you read this book and while you read it, remember the figures, never ever forget them: in one hundred days up to one million people were hacked, shot, strangled, clubbed and burned to death. Remember, carve this into your consciousness: one million."[5]

[Note: Keane shifts regularly between italic and regular text] *Begin with the river. From where I stand near the bridge it looks like a great soup. It is brown with upland silt and thick with elephant grass. It has come swirling down from the far reaches of the land and is fat with rain. I am arguing with Frank. "Marriage is for old men and idiots," says Frank. "You should try it first, you old cynic," I tell him. Frank believes in loving and leaving, or so he says. I think he had some kind of special feeling for Rose but he won't admit it. I think his talk about having girlfriends everywhere is just a front. Frank is quiet and shy around women. There is an exaggerated politeness about him, even when he is with women soldiers of the RPF [Rwandan Patriotic Front]. "How could I be married anyway doing this job?" he asks. Valence is standing behind us and polishing his rifle. Frank says something to him in Kinyarwanda and he laughs. "What was that?" I ask. "Oh, I just told him you were looking for a wife for me," he replies and we both laugh. The talk goes on like this for several more minutes. It is pleasantly distracting. So much so that at first I do not notice them. And then I turn around and for the first time I see two bodies bobbing along. Then three more. They nudge in and out of the grass and the leaves and are carried towards the falls. One swirls in towards the bank and I notice that it is a woman who has been chopped and hacked. But it is not the gash in her head, the gouges in her back and arms, that frighten and offend. Rather, I am shocked by her nakedness. Like the others she is bloated and her bare body turns and drops and turns and drops in the current. Near the bridge the current picks up and I watch her tumble down into the white water, disappearing fast. She comes up again, headfirst, and is bounced against the rocks.*

"Don't worry man. Don't be surprised," says Frank. "They've been coming through in their hundreds." I look down directly on to the falls and see that there are two bodies wedged tight into the rocks. One is that of a man wearing a pair of shorts. He appears to be white, but this is because the days in the water have changed his colour. Near by there is a baby, but I can only make out the head and an arm. The infant is tossed around by the falling water but is tangled in the weeds that cover the lower part of the rocks. The force of the water is unable to dislodge the baby and so it bounces up and down in the foam. At this I turn and walk away from the bridge and quietly take my place in the back of the car.

The aKagera River flows from the highlands of Rwanda, down through the country until it crosses the border into Tanzania and then Uganda, finally filtering out into the vastness of Lake Victoria. The river therefore became an ideal carriageway for the dispersal of evidence of Rwanda's genocide. People were routinely lined up beside the river for execution and then pushed into the flood. An alternative method of killing was to force people to jump into the fast running water. Most drowned within a few minutes. The Interahamwe gangs noted that this was a particularly efficient way of killing small children, who were more easily carried off in the current. The exhortations of the extremist leaders ... to send the Tutsis "back to the Ethiopia" were coming home with a terrible vengeance. Many of the illiterate peasants who were roused to acts of murder believed that the aKagera did actually flow to Ethiopia. But almost every other river and lake in the country also became dumping grounds for the dead.

5. Fergal Keane, *Season of Blood: A Rwandan Journey* (New York: Viking, 1995), 73–81.

There were so many bodies it seemed the earth could not hold them. When the dead finally reached Lake Victoria, Ugandan fishermen went out in their boats to recover them and give them a decent burial. Moses and Edward had heard of many men going out day after day without being paid, to gather in the corpses. Colleagues had seen the bodies of mothers and children who had been tied together and thrown into the water. There were thousands of corpses.

Driving down to the river, deeper into the heart of the killing grounds, I began to notice the first odours of death. As we drove along the road, the presence of corpses would be announced from a long distance, the rank smells reaching into the interior of our vehicles. I looked back and caught Glenn's eye. He shook his head and then buried his face in a small towel. But we could not see any dead people. They were lying out of view in the plantations and the storm drains, covered now by the thickly spreading vegetation of the summer. In this part of the country close to the border with Tanzania, there was nothing left. There were no people, no cattle, no cats and dogs. The militias had swept through the hills destroying everything before them in a plague of knives and spears.

That morning, as we were leaving Byumba, Frank told us about a massacre that had taken place in the townland of Nyarubuye near the Tanzanian border. An estimated 3,000 Tutsis had taken refuge in and around the parish church. Frank said that a handful of people had survived and were being looked after at a small camp in the offices of the former local administration. "We can get there by this afternoon, if you want to. The tar road is good as far as Rusomo Commune and then we have to leave and go into the bush." The journey passed in quietness and we half slept for several hours, until Frank directed the Land Rovers off the main road and on to a rough bush track.

This was always going to be the hardest part, this remembrance of what lay ahead in the dusk on that night in early June. My dreams are the fruit of this journey down the dirt road to Nyarubuye. How do I write this, how do I do justice to what awaits at the end of this road? As simply as possible. This is not a subject for fine words. We bounce and jolt along the rutted track on an evening of soft, golden light. The air is sweet with the smell of warm savannah grass. Clouds of midges hover around the cars, dancing through the windows. Although I can sense the nervousness of everybody in the car, we are exhausted and hungry from the long day's travelling, and we are too tired to bother fighting off the insects. Moses shifts down into first gear as we face into a long climb. The wheels begin to lose their grip and they spin in the loose sand of the incline. "Oh, shit," mutters Moses. We climb out and begin to shove and push, but the car rolls back down the hill and we have to jump out of the way. The countryside is vastly different to the deep green hills around Byumba. From the top of the hill we can see a great expanse of yellow savannah grass, dotted here and there with thornbush and acacia. Glenn says it reminds him of home. He is right. This could be the bushveld around Louis Trichardt in the far Northern Transvaal. After about fifteen minutes of manoeuvring Moses eventually gets the car going again and we move off. Frank has become very quiet and he is fingering the stock of his assault rifle. After about another fifteen minutes we come to a straight stretch of track, wider than before and with a line of tall trees on either side. Up ahead is the facade of a church built from red sandstone. "This is Nyarubuye," says Frank. Moses begins to slow the car down and Glenn is preparing his camera to film. As we drive closer the front porch of the church comes into view. There is a white marble statue of Christ above the door with hands outstretched. Below it is a banner proclaiming the celebration of Easter, and below that there is the body of a man lying across the steps, his knees buckled underneath his body and his arms cast behind his head. Moses stops the car but he stays hunched over the wheel and I notice that he is looking down at his feet.

I get out and start to follow Frank across the open ground in front of the church. Weeds and summer grasses have begun to cover the gravel. Immediately in front of us is a set of classrooms and next to that a gateway leading into the garden of the church complex. As I walk towards the gate, I must make a detour to avoid the bodies of several people. There is a child who has been decapitated and there are three other corpses splayed on the ground. Closer to the gate Frank lifts a handkerchief to his nose because there is a smell unlike anything I have ever experienced. I stop for a moment and pull out my own piece of cloth, pressing it to my face. Inside the gate the trail continues. The dead lie on either side of the pathway. A woman on her side, an expression of surprise on her face, her mouth open and a deep gash in her head. She is wearing a red cardigan and a blue dress but the clothes have begun to rot away, revealing the decaying body underneath. I must walk on, stepping over the corpse of a tall man who lies directly across the path, and, feeling the grass brush against my legs, I look down to my left and see a child who has been hacked almost into two pieces. The body is in a state of advanced decay and I cannot tell if it is a girl or a boy. I begin to pray to myself. "Our Father who art in heaven . . ." These are prayers I have not said since my childhood but I need them now. We come to an area of wildly overgrown vegetation where there are many flies in the air. The smell is unbearable here. I feel my stomach heave and my throat is completely dry. And then in front of me I see a group of corpses. They are young and old, men and women, and they are gathered in front of the door of the church offices. How many are there? I think perhaps a hundred, but it is hard to tell. The bodies seem to be melting away. Such terrible faces. Horror, fear, pain, abandonment. I cannot think of prayers now. Here the dead have no dignity. They are twisted and turned into grotesque shapes, and the rains have left pools of stagnant, stinking water all around them. They must have fled here in a group, crowded in next to the doorway, an easy target for the machetes and the grenades. I look around at my colleagues and there are tears in Tony's eyes. Glenn is filming, but he stops every few seconds to cough. Frank and Valence have wandered away from us into a clump of trees and the older man is explaining something to the boy. I do not know what he is saying, but Valence is looking at him intensely. I stay close to David because at this moment I need his age and strength and wisdom. He is very calm, whispering into Glenn's ear from time to time with suggestions, and moving quietly. The dead are everywhere. We pass a classroom and inside a mother is lying in the corner surrounded by four children. The chalk marks from the last lesson in mathematics are still on the board. But the desks have been upturned by the killers. It looks as if the woman and her children had tried to hide underneath the desks. We pass around the corner and I step over the remains of a small boy. Again he has been decapitated. To my immediate left is a large room filled with bodies. There is blood, rust coloured now with the passing weeks, smeared on the walls. I do not know what else to say about the bodies because I have already seen too much. As we pass back across the open ground in front of the church I notice Moses and Edward standing by the cars and I motion to them to switch on the headlights because it is growing dark. The sound of insects grows louder now filling in the churchyard silence. David and the crew have gone into the church and I follow them inside, passing a pile of bones and rags. There are other bodies between the pews and another pile of bones at the foot of the statue of the Virgin Mary. In a cloister, next to the holy water fountain, a man lies with his arms over his head. He must have died shielding himself from the machete

blows. "This is fucking unbelievable," whispers Tony into my ear. We are all whispering, as if some-
how we might wake the dead with our voices. "It is just fucking unbelievable. Can you imagine what
these poor bastards went through?" he continues. And I answer that no, I cannot imagine it because
my powers of visualization cannot possibly encompass the magnitude of the terror. David and
Glenn say nothing at all and Frank has also lapsed into silence. Valence has gone to join the driv-
ers. I do not know the things Valence has seen before this and he will not talk about them. I imag-
ine that the sight of these bodies is bringing back unwelcome memories. Outside the church the night
has come down thick and heavy. Tony shines a camera light to guide our way. Even with this and
the car lights I nearly trip on the corpse of a woman that is lying in the grass. Moths are dancing
around the lights as I reach the sanctuary of the car. While we are waiting for Glenn and Tony to
pack the equipment away, we hear a noise coming from one of the rooms of the dead. I turn to Moses
and Edward. "What is that? Did you hear that?" I ask. Edward notices the edge of fear in my voice
and strains his ear to listen. But there is no more sound. "It is only rats, only rats," says Moses. As
we turn to go I look back and in the darkness see the form of the marble Christ gazing down on the
dead. The rats scuttle in the classrooms again.

There was little talk on the way back to the main road. Tony produced one of our whisky bottles and we passed it around. I took several long draughts and lit a cigarette and noticed then that my hands were shaking. Frank watched the road ahead closely and told Moses to drive as quickly as he could. The men who had done the killing, the Interahamwe of Rusomo Commune and Nyarubuye itself, might have fled to Tanzania, but they crossed the border at night to stage guerrilla attacks and to kill any Tutsis who might have escaped the massacres. I should have felt fear at that moment but I had too much anger inside. After a long silence it was Moses who spoke. "How can they do that to people, to children? Just how can they do it?" he asked. Nobody answered him and he said nothing else. The journey back to the main road seemed to last an eternity. All along the way I could think only of the churchyard and the dead lying there in the dark. Although the sight of the massacre made me feel ill, I was not frightened of the dead. They were not the source of evil that filled the air at Nyarubuye and that now began to undermine my belief in life. Now that we had left, the killing ground would be quiet again. Perhaps the militiamen passed there from time to time as they crossed back and forth into Tanzania. Were they still able to pass the scene of their crimes without feeling guilt? Did the rotting dead frighten them? The killers must have moved in close to their victims. Close enough to touch their shaking bodies and smell their fear. Were there faces among the crowd that they recognized? After all, the militia men came from the same neighbourhood. Some of them must have been on speaking terms with the people who pleaded for mercy. I thought of Seamus Heaney's line about "each neighbourly murder" in the backroads of County Fermanagh. Back in the north of Ireland I had reported on numerous cases of people being murdered by men who worked with them or who bought cattle and land from them. In Rwanda that intimate slaughter was multiplied by tens of thousands.

65 • Nelson Mandela and a new Africa (1994)

Released from prison in 1990, Nelson Mandela—for years denounced by leaders of the apartheid
regime as a Communist, a terrorist, a traitor—was elected president in 1994, the first person to hold

that office on the basis of universal suffrage. He delivered his inaugural address (below) on May 10, 1994, in Pretoria, the administrative capital of South Africa, before a huge crowd of people. Despite his years of incarceration, he showed no bitterness toward his former captors but counseled reconciliation in the interest of society at large. At the beginning of the twenty-first century, Mandela is still the dominant figure in African politics. Though retired now from the presidency, he continues to symbolize the determination of people to struggle throughout their lives against oppression, their readiness to reconcile with their former enemies rather than treat them as they had been treated themselves, and the avoidance of the trappings of postcolonial majesty so favored by the dictators, supporters of one-party states, and other politicians no longer in power in most of the rest of Africa.[6]

Your Majesties, your Highnesses, Distinguished Guests, Comrades and Friends:

Today, all of us do, by our presence here, and by our celebrations in other parts of our country and the world, confer glory and hope to newborn liberty.

Out of the experience of an extraordinary human disaster that lasted too long must be born a society of which all humanity will be proud.

Our daily deeds as ordinary South Africans must produce an actual South African reality that will reinforce humanity's belief in justice, strengthen its confidence in the nobility of the human soul, and sustain all our hopes for a glorious life for all.

All this we owe both to ourselves and to the peoples of the world who are so well represented here today.

To my compatriots, I have no hesitation in saying that each one of us is as intimately attached to the soil of this beautiful country as are the famous jacaranda trees of Pretoria and the mimosa trees of the bushveld.

Each time one of us touches the soil of this land, we feel a sense of personal renewal. The national mood changes as the seasons change.

We are moved by a sense of joy and exhilaration when the grass turns green and the flowers bloom.

That spiritual and physical oneness we all share with this common homeland explains the depth of the pain we all carried in our hearts as we saw our country tear itself apart in terrible conflict, and as we saw it spurned, outlawed, and isolated by the peoples of the world, precisely because it has become the universal base of the pernicious ideology and practice of racism and racial oppression.

We, the people of South Africa, feel fulfilled that humanity has taken us back into its bosom, that we, who were outlaws not so long ago, have today been given the rare privilege to be host to the nations of the world on our own soil. We thank all our distinguished international guests for having come to take possession with the people of our country of what is, after all, a common victory for justice, for peace, for human dignity.

We trust that you will continue to stand by us as we tackle the challenges of building peace, prosperity, nonsexism, nonracialism, and democracy.

We deeply appreciate the role that the masses of our people and their democratic, religious, women, youth, business, traditional, and other leaders have played to bring about this

---

6. Http://www.anc.org.za/ancdocs/history/mandela/1994/inaugpta.html.

conclusion. Not least among them is my Second Deputy President, the Honorable F. W. de Klerk.

We would also like to pay tribute to our security forces, in all their ranks, for the distinguished role they have played in securing our first democratic elections and the transition to democracy, from bloodthirsty forces which still refuse to see the light.

The time for the healing of the wounds has come.

The moment to bridge the chasms that divide us has come.

The time to build is upon us.

We have, at last, achieved our political emancipation. We pledge ourselves to liberate all our people from the continuing bondage of poverty, deprivation, suffering, gender, and other discrimination.

We succeeded to take our last steps to freedom in conditions of relative peace. We commit ourselves to the construction of a complete, just, and lasting peace.

We have triumphed in the effort to implant hope in the breasts of the millions of our people. We enter into a covenant that we shall build the society in which all South Africans, both black and white, will be able to walk tall, without any fear in their hearts, assured of their inalienable right to human dignity—rainbow nation at peace with itself and the world.

As a token of its commitment to the renewal of our country, the new interim government of national unity will, as a matter of urgency, address the issue of amnesty for various categories of our people who are currently serving terms of imprisonment.

We dedicate this day to all the heroes and heroines in this country and the rest of the world who sacrificed in many ways and surrendered their lives so that we could be free.

Their dreams have become reality. Freedom is their reward.

We are both humbled and elevated by the honor and privilege that you, the people of South Africa, have bestowed on us, as the first president of a united, democratic, nonracial, and nonsexist government.

We understand it still that there is no easy road to freedom.

We know it well that none of us acting alone can achieve success.

We must therefore act together as a united people, for national reconciliation, for nation building, for the birth of a new world.

Let there be justice for all.

Let there be peace for all.

Let there be work, bread, water, and salt for all.

Let each know that for each the body, the mind, and the soul have been freed to fulfill themselves.

Never, never, and never again shall it be that this beautiful land will again experience the oppression of one by another and suffer the indignity of being the skunk of the world.

Let freedom reign.

The sun shall never set on so glorious a human achievement!

Let freedom reign.

God bless Africa!

Thank you.

66 • Growing conflict in Africa (1980–2008)

Contemporary Africa is often best known in the West because of images and reports of almost un-believable horror. Child soldiers as young as five in Sierra Leone and Liberia and the Congo and Uganda cutting off the limbs of their victims apparently without remorse. Reports of a new form of ethnic cleansing in Darfur, supposedly carried out by lighter-skinned Muslims against darker-hued Christians. Little wonder that in this context, a mass media publication like Time *magazine would carry a story in its February 14, 2008, issue headlined "Come Back Colonialism: All Is Forgiven," reporting on the basis of the views of one resident of the Congo how the colonial past is considered better by far than the independent present.[7]*

Although the Time *writer likely had no understanding of the history of colonialism in this reference to a rosy-hued past, the defense lawyers for Charles Taylor, on trial in 2008 for crimes against humanity, also reached into history to explain the present. When confronted with evidence of the use of child soldiers by Taylor and his forces, the defense attorneys argued that this was merely a modern-day example of traditional practices of the incorporation of young men into the adult world.*

Yet a historical examination of the use of African children as soldiers suggests that it is a more recent past that explains the horrific practices of the 1980s, the 1990s, and the first decade of this century. The many European reports of the wars of conquest in the late nineteenth and early twentieth centuries make no mention of the use of children as soldiers. Forced labor, however, as introduced by most European powers (see the discussion of Belgian and Portuguese practices in volume 2, part 1, chapters 1 [document 4] and 2 [document 14]) and incorporating not only adult men but also women and children, was a real change in daily life for most Africans.

Moreover, the first reported forcible incorporation of large numbers of children as young as five into armies took place not in "traditional" Africa but in the context of the struggle for liberation in southern Africa in the 1970s and 1980s. The Resistência Nacional Moçambicana (RENAMO) was established in 1975 by Ian Smith's white settler forces in Southern Rhodesia and made use of the services of Portuguese settlers and African mercenaries opposed to the independence of Mozambique and Angola. After the fall of white Rhodesia in 1980, the South African military took control of RENAMO. As shown (A) by a series of interviews carried out in the latter half of the 1980s, RENAMO utilized policies of terror in combating opposition and in particular used children as both soldiers and sex slaves.

The terror tactics of RENAMO were copied elsewhere in Africa (B), the greatest consequence of which was an appalling increase in civilian deaths. Whereas in World War I civilians accounted for less than 10 percent of war casualties and in World War II closer to 50 percent, in Africa at the end of the twentieth century civilians accounted for more than 90 percent of casualties, as evidenced (C) in the huge numbers who died from war-related consequences in the Congo.

Wars are always fought about something, and often that something is an item of value—diamonds in the case of Sierra Leone and Liberia, in societies that were otherwise marked by ever-increasing examples of extreme poverty (and conditions have not gotten better: in 2007, 82 percent of the people in Sierra Leone and 80 percent of those in Liberia lived in poverty). With the world

7. Http://www.time.com/time/world/article/0,8599,1713275,00.html.

becoming ever more dependent on scarce energy resources, covetous eyes are again looking at Africa, and oil is at the center of this attention. In the Sudan, though the Darfur issue "began" in 2004, increased levels of conflict date back especially to the discovery of oil in the 1980s and to the opening of an oil pipeline from the fields through Khartoum to the Red Sea in 1999. From the time of conquest at Omdurman in 1898 to 1946, Britain administered its colony in the Sudan as two separate entities, north and south. Conflict between northerners and southerners erupted in 1955, ostensibly about the failure of the north to share greater power with the south, but became most intense from the mid-1980s onward, especially over the oil fields that supply 70 percent of the Sudan's export earnings. Since 1989, a military dictatorship has ruled the Sudan and repressed all opposition with ferocity. By 2005, perhaps two million people have died as a result of half a century of armed conflict, the second highest death toll in Africa after that in the Congo. Some idea of the extent and impact of the wars can be gained from a diary (D) kept from 1992 to 1994 by a resident of El Obeid, the chief city of the Kordofan province, southwest of Omdurman and Khartoum.

Whereas in the early nineteenth century mapmakers believed that a river of gold (which turned out to be imaginary) lay under Darfur, at the end of the twentieth century a U.S. Geological Survey map (E) shows that there is indeed a lake of oil lying below Chad and the Sudan.[8]

A. Children and terror in southern Africa, 1980s

Tax areas [in Mozambique] tend to be rural areas in which the population resides in extremely dispersed patterns. Each family lives on the land it is farming, or in small extended family hamlets. RENAMO combatants move freely through such areas and routinely (weekly or monthly) visit the farmers. They demand a contribution of prepared and/or dry food (food grain or flour), chickens and goats, perhaps some clothes, a radio or other possession. They demand at will a young girl or married woman for sex.

To the degree that it is necessary to transport the resources which are extracted, the local people are obliged to serve as porters (RENAMO appears to have virtually no mechanized transport anywhere in Mozambique). But their trips tend to be of short duration (counted in hours, rather than days). As a general rule the porters are permitted to return to their homes when their service is completed. The journeys are short and not as harsh as those conducted in the other types of areas; reports of beatings of porters tend to be exceptions. If the family refuses to submit to these demands, they are likely to be severely beaten with heavy sticks or gun butts. It appears from refugee reports that local people are not permitted to flee the area.

8. A, Robert Gersony, consultant to the Bureau for Refugee Programs, "Summary of Mozambican Refugee Accounts of Principally Conflict-Related Experience in Mozambique," report submitted to Ambassador Jonathan Moore, director, Bureau for Refugee Programs, Dr. Chester A. Crocker, assistant secretary of state for African affairs, U.S. Department of State, April 1988, 16–17, 19, 20, 21, 24, 31, http://pdf.dec.org/pdf_docs/PCAAA945.pdf; B, Jessica Alexander, "Children Associated with Fighting Forces in the Conflict in Sierra Leone," May 4, 2007, from the transcript of the trial of Charles Taylor, Taylor case no. SCSL-2003-01-T, the *Prosecutor of the Special Court v. Charles Ghankay Taylor*, Monday, January 21, 2008, 9:30 A.M., trial chamber II, 1725–27, http://charlestaylortrial.org/; C, *Mortality in the Democratic Republic of Congo: An Ongoing Crisis* (New York: International Rescue Committee, 2007), ii–iii, http://www.theirc.org/resources/2007/2006-7_congomortalitysurvey.pdf; D, *Sudan: "In the Name of God": Repression Continues in Northern Sudan*, Human Rights Watch/Africa, vol. 6, no. 9, Nov. 1994, 12–17, http://www.hrw.org/reports/pdfs/c/crd/sudan94n.pdf; E, http://pubs.usgs.gov/fs/1997/fs053-97/Fig2.html.

But the burdens placed upon them are more moderate than those placed on the population of other areas. RENAMO's policy appears to be to maintain a level of taxation and abuse insufficient to motivate the population to risk the security dangers, economic perils, and social disruption represented by escape . . .

Combatant bases were described to be of two types: those reserved principally for permanent, resident combatants; and those reserved principally for combatants who are passing through an area or who are, for whatever reason, temporarily stationed there. Both areas are managed in roughly the same fashion. They are served by a staff of exclusively male captives who provide food, water, cleaning and other support services. Women are provided on demand from other sectors of the control areas.

Refugees who resided in "control" areas, as well as other refugees who had contact with RENAMO, said that its combatants represented indigenous language groups from all major regions of Mozambique. When they commented on recruitment in their own home villages, forced recruitment was said to be the principal method through which these men had been impressed into service. Two refugees provided detailed accounts of their own escapes from apparent forced recruitment roundups. One said that his group, awaiting disposition, had been locked in a guarded house without food and water for such a long time that four of the men had starved to death. A few refugees said that they witnessed either the recruitment of young (age ten and over) children or were themselves the victims of indiscriminate shootings or beatings by such young RENAMO combatants . . .

Second are permanent agricultural lands, significant expanses of RENAMO farms or plantations. The workers on these farms are captives who toil at a regular schedule, usually long hours during a six-day week. They do not benefit from the production of these fields. Their work is closely supervised, and physical punishment, in the form of beatings, is used to motivate those who take unauthorized rest or who refuse to continue. The worker population of these areas is reported to be principally older children of both sexes and adult males and females. In addition to its production tasks, this age group is also used as porters. Unlike porters in the tax areas, the marches undertaken by these porters tend to be of longer duration— sometimes a week or more roundtrip. While for some the portering is occasional, it appears that many of the porters perform this as a full-time service, making continuous rounds of arduous trips . . .

Another function of the young girls and adult women is to provide sex to the combatants. From refugee reports it appears that these women are required to submit to sexual demands, in effect to be raped, on a frequent, sustained basis. The rape may occur in field area residences. According to those who have served as porters, women are frequently raped along the transport routes . . .

The heart of the [surveillance] system are the RENAMO police, called *majuba* or *mujiba*. According to the refugees, these fall into two categories: (a) Former tax collectors and petty officials, some called *regulos*, associated with the previous Portuguese colonial administration, who were replaced by the FRELIMO [Frente de Libertação de Moçambique] government after independence from Portugal, and a small number of previous FRELIMO members who became disaffected; and (b) Captives identified by RENAMO and obliged to serve in this role. These captives may be motivated on the one hand by punishment should they either refuse the role or fail to effectively implement it, and on the other with some degree of preferential treatment. In general, the refugees indicate that these police tend to be armed with cutting instruments (machetes, knives, bayonets, axes) rather than with firearms ...

This type of attack causes several types of civilian casualties. As is normal in guerrilla warfare, some civilians are killed in crossfire between the two opposing forces, although this tends in the view of the refugees to account for only a minority of the deaths. A larger number of civilians in these attacks and other contexts were reported to be victims of purposeful shooting deaths and executions, of axing, knifing, bayoneting, burning to death, forced drowning and asphyxiation, and other forms of murder where no meaningful resistance or defense is present. Eyewitness accounts indicate that when civilians are killed in these indiscriminate attacks, whether against defended or undefended villages, children, often together with mothers and elderly people, are also killed.

B. Child soldiers in Sierra Leone, 1990s

In 1996 the Child Welfare Secretariat of Sierra Leone's Ministry of Social Welfare, Gender and Children's Affairs—began a Family Tracing and Reunification (FTR) program for all children separated during the conflict in Sierra Leone. In conjunction with UNICEF and other relevant stakeholders, the MSWGCA developed and administered forms in order to trace children and reunite them with their families. The forms, known as "Documentation and Registration Forms for Separated and Unaccompanied Children," gathered information on children's families, home villages, and the circumstances of their separations.

Using these forms housed at the MSWGCA in Freetown, the research team sought to:

(1) create an electronic database of the information on the forms for children who were abducted under the age of 15 years old (the Court's cut-off age to be considered a child).

(2) analyze the data and draw conclusions on the nature of the exploitation of children abducted during the civil conflict.

The research team entered into the database a total of 2,235 children who were abducted under the age of 15. The team also interviewed 36 social workers and stakeholders involved in the FTR and DDR process to further understand how information on the forms was collected, reported and verified. The database provides evidence of the abduction and use of children, both boys and girls, under the age of 15 during Sierra Leone's conflict. Key findings include:

Abduction: All warring factions were responsible for the abduction of children under 15. The RUF [Revolutionary United Front—the rebels] accounted for the most abductions/captures.

Age at Abduction: The median age at the time of abduction was 11 years old—4 years below the Court's cut-off age to be considered a child.

Military Training: Children were taken to a number of combat camps where they received various methods of military training.

Active Combat: Children as young as 5 years old at the time of their abduction were armed and took part in active combat. Twenty-five percent of children either took part in active combat or were intended to do so. The RUF and AFRC/RUF [Armed Forces Revolutionary Council] were the two groups most frequently cited for using children in active combat.

Sexual violence: Sexual violence and slavery took place, even to girls who were as young as 8 years old at the time of their capture/abduction.

Forced Labor: Outside of active fighting, children were subjected to forced labor and played a number of roles in assisting the operations of the armed groups.

Geography and Time Horizon: Children were abducted across a variety of districts and over a number of years.

Social workers who carried out interviews and were closely involved in the FTR process collected and recorded data from children as diligently as possible as accurate information was vital to the task of FTR. They used various methods to mitigate errors on the forms and had various ways of eliciting correct information from the children.

C. Civilian deaths in the Congo, 1998–2007

The Democratic Republic of Congo (DR Congo) has been mired in conflict for over a decade, with devastating effects on its civilian population. The most recent war of 1998–2002 was characterized by mass displacement, collapse of health systems and food shortages, all contributing to major elevations of mortality. Although a formal peace accord was signed in December 2002, the war has since given way to several smaller conflicts in the five eastern provinces that have continued to exact an enormous toll on the lives and livelihoods of local populations. Since 2000, the International Rescue Committee (IRC) has documented the humanitarian impact of war and conflict in DR Congo through a series of five mortality surveys. The first four studies, conducted between 2000 and 2004, estimated that 3.9 million people had died since 1998, arguably making DR Congo the world's deadliest crisis since World War II. Less than 10 percent of all deaths were due to violence, with most attributed to easily preventable and treatable conditions such as malaria, diarrhea, pneumonia and malnutrition. Recent political developments together with improvements in security and humanitarian funding have raised hope that DR Congo could emerge from years of crisis. A number of international agencies have expressed optimism that such progress would yield an early humanitarian dividend. But DR Congo faces many challenges on its road to recovery and development.

This fifth and latest survey, covering the period from January 2006 to April 2007, aims to evaluate the current humanitarian situation in DR Congo by providing an update on mortality. Investigators used a three-stage cluster sampling technique to survey 14,000 households in 35 health zones across all 11 provinces, resulting in wider geographic coverage than any of the previous IRC surveys.

The key findings and conclusions are:

1. Elevated mortality rates persist across DR Congo.

    More than four years after the signing of a formal peace agreement, the DR Congo's national crude mortality rate (CMR) of 2.2 deaths per 1,000 per month is 57 percent higher than the average rate for sub-Saharan Africa. This rate is unchanged since the previous IRC survey in 2004. These findings indicate that DR Congo remains in the midst of a major humanitarian crisis. As with previous surveys, mortality rates are significantly higher in the volatile eastern provinces than in the west of the country. In addition, mortality rates have risen significantly in the center of DR Congo (a region referred to as *Transition East* in the attached survey). Based on the results of the five IRC studies, we now estimate that 5.4 million excess deaths have occurred between August 1998 and April 2007. An estimated 2.1 million of those deaths have occurred since the formal end of war in 2002.

2. Modest, yet statistically significant improvements in mortality were documented in the eastern provinces.

For the period covered by the survey, the only region to record a significant reduction in mortality since 2004 was that encompassing the five eastern provinces . . . This improvement coincided with a reduction in the risk of violent death, as well as a more robust U.N. peacekeeping effort by MONUC [United Nations Organization Mission in the Democratic Republic of Congo], the international force in DR Congo. Nonetheless, the CMR in this region is still 2.6 deaths per 1,000 per month, a rate that is 85 percent higher than the sub-Saharan average. Ironically, it is these slight but notable improvements that are now being threatened by the current escalation of violence in North Kivu province.

3. Most deaths are due to preventable and treatable conditions.

While insecurity persists in the eastern provinces, only 0.4 percent of all deaths across DR Congo were attributed directly to violence. As with previous IRC studies in DR Congo, the majority of deaths have been due to infectious diseases, malnutrition and neonatal- and pregnancy-related conditions. Increased rates of disease are likely related to the social and economic disturbances caused by conflict, including disruption of health services, poor food security, deterioration of infrastructure and population displacement. Children, who are particularly susceptible to these easily preventable and treatable conditions, accounted for 47 percent of deaths, even though they constituted only 19 percent of the total population.

4. Recovery from conflict is a slow and protracted process.

The persistent elevation of mortality more than four years after the official end of the 1998–2002 war provides further evidence that recovery from conflict can take many years, especially when superimposed on decades of political and socioeconomic decline. These data are consistent with those from other conflict-impacted states. Sustained and measurable improvements in key indicators such as mortality will require committed national and international engagement for many years. The IRC survey overlaps only partially with the period since December 2006, during which there has been an escalation of violence in North Kivu province, resulting in the displacement of more than 400,000 persons. Recent political and humanitarian gains are in jeopardy and further escalation of the conflict could potentially destabilize the region beyond DR Congo's own borders. Steadfast international commitment to secure recent gains, prevent further deterioration and scale up assistance to other regions of the country is as necessary now in DR Congo as at any other recent period.

D. A year in the life of a Sudanese city (1992–93)

OCTOBER 1992: The [El Nahud] camp of the Nuba "returnees" (about 5,000) is closed, and the inmates moved to Rahmania and Sidra "to help in harvesting operations." They are practically only women, children, old people. In those areas, no church and no international organizations are allowed to operate; only Dawa Islamia and I.A.R.A. (Islamic African Relief Agency) are allowed.

NOVEMBER 1992: Truckloads of "returnees" from El Nahud start transiting through El Obeid, on their way to Rahmania and Sidra. They are unloaded in the outskirts and abandoned. They have no food, no money, ragged clothing—no means to fight the cold nights. They are a miserable sight: of hunger, of shame for their nakedness, of dejection at being kicked about like animals. The relief workers had taken along some tins of powdered milk for infants and searched through the various groups of about 2,000 people in all who camped under trees or along boundary walls. The people clasped to their chest their few possessions— some empty pots, some rags, rarely a straw mat—with the same empty, lost look on every face. The relief workers were forced to face the cruel, tragic reality: there are no children below the age of three or four years. Also, there are no boys beyond the age of ten or eleven. It is understood that older children and youth are forcibly taken up by the security and Popular Defense Force militias for military training and enrollment in a new militia called the "Nuba Friendly Forces." A certain Farouk, a former SPLA [Sudan People's Liberation Army] fighter, was captured in Kadugli in early 1992. In due time he resolved to cooperate with the government forces. He was entrusted to form and lead the new militias whose training camps are near Rashad and Dilling. In September 1992, two foreigners were sent away from this town: the security said that it was not an expulsion, but only "for the sake of their security." With the end of the rainy season, preparations are under way for a new offensive. Radio Kordofan proclaims that this offensive will be the "final blow to the rebellion." The largest secondary school in El Obeid, Khor Tagga, was closed and turned into a PDF [Popular Defence Forces] and Islamic training center. More training grounds were added and are now being filled with new recruits, in many cases collected from the nomadic Arab tribes. Special camel and horse-mounted battalions are being formed. Reports indicate that not all the new recruits are enthusiastic. Seven are said to have been killed in training and a good number to have run away. In late November security officers, escorted by heavily armed police, enter the church compound in Abu Gibeha and destroy it, an easy exercise since everything was made of straw: the kindergarten, classrooms, chapel and boundary fence. The security claimed that the order came from the Governor of El Obeid.

DECEMBER 1992: Several trucks of Timu and Kamda (Nuba Tulisci) arrive from Lagawa. The peace camp that was opened last year for about 5,000 "returnees" is being evacuated because the authorities are unwilling or unable to provide food. Some of those arriving in El Obeid speak of a handful of durra [sorghum] per day. At the beginning of December, Lagawa was heavily attacked by the SPLA from the Tulisci Mountains with heavy losses among the militia and mujahidin. The rebels made off with a large number of cattle, after having looted shops and stores. In late December about 200 women and children reach El Obeid. They had managed to walk out of the Tulisci Mountain range, helped by the SPLA. They speak of 700 deaths from hunger in the mountains during the past season. In El Obeid they are helped with food and blankets—temperature at night is down to five degrees—they are huddled in a small courtyard of a poor family. A police officer who requested absolute anonymity reports that the villages of Hamarat El Sheikh (northwest of Soderi in North Kordofan) is a gathering-place for children: Dinka mainly from Mujlad and Nuba from the Kadugli/Tulisci areas. The children are reportedly loaded onto trucks that proceed to Libya.

Another gathering place is Mohammed Gol, a small village on the Red Sea Coast where mainly Nuer and Shilluk children are dispatched by boat to Saudi Arabia but probably re-routed to Yemen and the Gulf countries. The police officer said the movement of children is administered by the PDF and that the normal police are never asked to take any action. Travel permits for foreigners to South Kordofan are denied by security, the military security, and the governor's office. From South Kordofan all reports indicate that intensive ethnic cleansing is being carried out. No witness is wanted.

JANUARY 1993: Reports from Abyei are not different from those of last year: steady flow of displaced people from northern Bahr El Ghazal and the oil field areas of Bentiu and Mayom. New arrivals are at a rate of 200–300 per day. Five fifteen-ton trucks arrived in Abyei with flour, milk, grain, sewing machines, and other items to establish a Dawa Islamia relief center while church relief efforts are impeded.

JANUARY 1993: The flow of displaced is uninterrupted. Today seven trucks arrive with over 300 Dinkas from Aweil/Abyei and four trucks with about 200 Nubas from Tulisci. They speak of a large and ruthless cleansing operation by the militia and mujahidin along the rail-way [south] to Wau to ensure the safe passage of a train from Babanusa, to refill the army stores in Wau. They say many people were killed and large herds of cattle seized and moved to Wau.

JANUARY 1993: A group of Southern University students arrive from Khartoum to Khor Tagga military and Islamic center for training.

JANUARY 1993: Lagawa again is attacked by the SPLA, it is called a major disaster among the militia and mujahidin.

JANUARY 1993: About 130 people arrive from Habila, a major agricultural area. They were seasonal workers in the durra cultivations. They were accused of helping the SPLA by the militia, who were called in by the Arab farmers for protection. One Dinka and one Nuer were killed while fleeing. All who fled lost their wages and have no way to make any claim.

JANUARY 1993: A big new offensive has been launched in the Tulisci and Habila areas by the army, the PDF and the mujahidin. A new larger wave of displaced (mainly women and children) has started arriving in El Obeid.

JANUARY 1993: The thirteen-year-old nephew of neighbors, and his friend, are missing. Their fathers went to look for them and were told by the police station to check with the army and the PDF. The following day they go to the army barracks where other people started gath-ering, also parents and wives of youth who have disappeared. Finally some trucks from the PDF training camps arrive and unload the new recruits, among them the boys who had dis-appeared. Their heads had already been neatly shaved. After some discussion, those who could prove to be students or married were released; all the others were returned to the camps. The day before, all buses were stopped by armed soldiers. The passengers were made to dismount and all boys were compelled to get into army trucks and were taken to enroll in the PDF. The same thing happened to all boys that were found along the roads and in the market places. The need is high for the PDF for new recruits to replace their heavy losses among their ranks. A relief convoy is sent from El Obeid to various Peace Camps in the Rahmania area. The Sudan Council of Churches is allowed to join the convoy with its trucks of food and some of their own monitors to make the correct distribution of food. Upon reaching Abu Gibeha, the security stops the Sudan Council of Churches officers. Only those of the Sudan Red Crescent and of the Islamic African Relief Agency are allowed to proceed. A relief worker is finally released from jail after accusations of SPLA collaboration. He is now free but must visit the security office every ten days and cannot leave town without permission from security.

FEBRUARY 1993: El Zubeir Mohamed Salih, the vice president, is in El Obeid to oversee the departure of a new contingent of PDF and mujahidin. There are reports of strong clashes around Dilling and of widespread destruction of villages and indiscriminate killing. Strong waves of displaced arrive from the Koalib, Mendi, Tima and Tulisci areas.

FEBRUARY 1993: Over fifty Bagarra-Missurya Arabs are taken to prison in El Obeid, accused of siding with the SPLA.

MARCH 1993: Seven trucks of PDF, all young boys, depart from the central mosque square to the battle areas.

MARCH 1993: A messenger from Abu Gibeha brings news that a church compound was demolished at the end of November 1992. The security forces are firm that a public meeting cannot be held on the grounds of the old church. They insist that in Abu Gibeha there cannot be any church unless a permit is obtained in Khartoum. A compromise is then reached: the security forces emphasize that there is full religious freedom, that Christians can pray whenever and wherever they want but not on that old place of the church because in Abu Gibeha there is no church. The next day a Catholic mass is celebrated under a large tree, very near to the old church, under the unobtrusive and quiet control of the security, with no disturbances.

MARCH 1993: Groups of displaced Nuba are taken to El Obeid from the Peace Camp of Rahamia to profess publicly their faith in Islam. They are all women. All boys beyond the age of twelve have been enrolled in a new militia. For the whole month of March there has been a steady flow of displaced from the Nuba Mountains and the south. Large military operations are under way in the Tulisci mountain range, particularly around Lagawa and Sellara, in the area between Dilling and Kadugli, and around Kadugli where massacres are rumored. Also heavy fighting is reported around the Miri mountains, in the Koalib area, around the oil areas of Bentiu, leaving masses of Nuer on the move, and in a large belt along the railway from Aweil to Wau. In two days, over 600 people arrive from Aweil and they speak of thousands brutally killed and 7,000 head of cattle stolen. In one day, over 200 Nuer arrive who tell of being harassed by the Arab militia between Abyei and Mujlad. Children are taken by force and adults that resist are simply shot. Several lost their lives.

APRIL 1993: The flow of displaced continues uninterrupted also for the month of April. Some who could be approached reported the following:

• All passengers from Aweil, Gogrial, Meiram, and Mayom are harassed and robbed of their belongings, sometimes just a handful of rags. One man was killed for refusing to hand over 58,000 Sudanese pounds (then about $200 U.S.). His friend who saw this gave up his 35,000 Sudanese pounds and survived.
• The Nuba Timu group that lived in the lower lands of the mountain range of Tulisci, near Lagawa, has been virtually eliminated. Only women and girls with children arrive in El Obeid. All the male population, down to boys of six or seven years, that could not reach the SPLA strongholds deep in the mountains, has been mercilessly massacred. All females from fourteen years and up are pregnant. These uneducated, simple people are too deeply wounded in their dignity to recount what they have passed through.

They are silent or evasive about certain inquiries. The word "rape" does not exist in their culture.

- A friendly soldier who was in a military convoy that took supplies to the military outpost of Heiban said that he entered the Peace Camp of about 5,000 on the outskirts of Rahmania, hoping to find someone he knew. He observed that all the inmates were women and girls, with children, from the Nuba Shatt tribal group. All the women were pregnant. For more than one year the only males in the camp were the PDF and the mujahidin, who are in charge of running it, backed by the Dawa Islamia. The only NGOs allowed in the area are Dawa Islamia and the Red Crescent. Some Sudan Council of Churches officers who were allowed to join a convoy with relief food for Rahamia were stopped in Abu Gibeha and not allowed to proceed.

- People arriving from the Gogrial, Aweil, Mayom regions speak of widespread famine, several saying they saw as many as eighty people die of hunger. The PDF and the mujahidin took advantage of the cease-fire with the SPLA to attack and destroy many villages left unprotected and to make off with the cattle.

- Reports of the murder of a sixteen-year-old girl by her master, Adam Mohammed El Daw. She had been working for him for three years, without salary. When she asked for some money to travel to El Obeid, he became furious and killed her.

- Other reports of a trick used by Arab farmers to avoid paying their seasonal employees who are almost exclusively displaced people from the south or the Nuba Mountains. When the harvesting is over, they spread the rumor that the SPLA is in the area. The PDF and the mujahidin rush in to protect the farmers and shoot at anybody who looks like a rebel. The displaced abandon the area, never to come back to claim their wages. Some of them lost their lives in such operations of "providing security to the farmers."

MAY 1993: At the beginning of the month, about ten trucks of PDF were dispatched into the Nuba Mountains. The flow of the displaced is still ongoing. They appear to be the wreckage and remnant of the Dinka, Nuer, and Nuba populations of vast areas where "cleansing" seems to be now well on its way or nearing completion. Some of their reports:

- In Gogrial and surrounding areas there is nothing left. A new, large military garrison has been established in the town in which the only inhabitants are soldiers, militia and mujahidin. Inexplicably, the rather large church is still untouched, but it stands alone, like a large grave tombstone. All women and children that could be rounded up are taken to Peace Camps where Khalwas (Islamic schools) have been erected. All the cattle have been taken away—nothing is left. Gogrial area used to be rich in cattle wealth and bustling in pastoral life. All food that arrives is stored for the army and the Khalwas, because all the children have "turned to Islam."

- New military garrisons also have been established in Meiram, Aweil and other larger towns. The situation is the same as for Gogrial.

- Many villages where the army has not yet arrived are dead. They are inhabited by shadows. "Nobody moves from the hut, nobody takes care of the cattle, they are all sick with strange infected wounds on their bodies." A young nurse working in Gogrial says there is a vast outbreak of plague, probably kalahazar. No doctors or medicines are available in these areas.

- Groups of youths and elderly men arrive from Abyei, Mujlad, Babanusa, and other agricultural areas of the Nuba region, covered only by a single, ragged piece of cloth. They and many others had been employed by Arab farmers and never paid. They were given only food, consisting of durra porridge and boiled vegetables. Very rarely could they get some meat and invariably it was entrails. They managed to slip away from their masters. But, they said, one must be very careful, because they are soon accused of belonging to the SPLA, and hunted down by the omnipresent militias and killed.
- Eyewitnesses from Kadugli (including friendly army officers) refer to harsh fighting still going on in the Nuba Mountains region. The army is trying to open the road to Talodi across the mountain range.
- Various groups of visitors from the U.N. and embassies were allowed to visit "South Kordofan" in May, and carefully guided to some selected towns, like Dilling, Kadugli, El Daein, up to Abyei. In all these towns, life is rather "normal," at least better than in operations areas, because it is under strict control of the army and militias. They were taken to Abyei by air, overflying the disaster below.

JUNE 1993: An educated man reports that near El Nahud the local Khalwa is freely selling Dinka children previously collected by the PDF at a rate of 13,000 pounds (U.S. $95 at the official rate of exchange) to anyone who asks. They are dressed in just one piece of cloth, a red jallabia, to be easily recognized if they attempt to escape. They are usually used to tend the cattle of the Bagarra and Rizeigat tribes whose youth have been enrolled in large numbers by the army and the various militias.

NOVEMBER 1993: By the end of November, a new wave of arrests is reported in El Obeid, Dilling, Kadugli. Large contingents of PDF and mujahidin are seen departing for the mountains. Unlike the previous years, their departure is without fanfare and fuss. Many of them are mere children of around fourteen, almost collapsing under the weight of their military gear. Word from Abyei is that the population now numbers about 200,000, including the displaced. The majority are non-Muslims and a good number of Muslims are "Fellata," immigrants from West Africa. The situation in the town is a strange mixture of war and peace. It is the headquarters of an important army garrison and large PDF and mujahidin camps, but is surrounded by the SPLA, who are only five to ten kilometers away. Rebels come to town half naked for shopping. Arabs are allowed to take their herds to pasture if unarmed. The most dangerous elements are the unruly militias, whose highest aspirations are robbery and rape. Water for the whole population is from three donkey-wells, all in the army barracks. Girls are normally in charge of fetching water. They must enter the barracks, and must first satisfy the whims of the soldiers by providing water for the soldiers' quarters and families, in a kind of forced water-for-labor exchange.

DECEMBER 1993: In the wake of the government campaign to counteract and deny the accusations of infringement of human rights and denying freedom of religion, festive Christmas celebrations are held without impediments. The Kordofan governor made it a point to attend the whole High Mass on Christmas morning in the Catholic Cathedral of El Obeid, with his ministers and high officers. After the mass he addressed the huge crowd assembled

Countries with the Highest Mortality Rates in Children Younger than Five Years, 2006

	Deaths*	Rank		Deaths*	Rank
Sierra Leone	270	1	Kenya	121	31
Angola	260	2	Ghana	120	32
Afghanistan	257	3	Malawi	120	32
Niger	253	4	Tanzania	118	34
Liberia	235	5	Senegal	116	35
Mali	217	6	Madagascar	115	36
Chad	209	7	Gambia	113	37
Equatorial Guinea	206	8	Togo	108	38
Congo, Democratic Republic	205	9	Zimbabwe	105	39
Burkina Faso	204	10	Myanmar	104	40
Guinea-Bissau	200	11	Yemen	100	41
Nigeria	191	12	Pakistan	97	42
Zambia	182	13	Sao Tome & Principe	96	43
Burundi	181	14	Gabon	91	44
Central African Republic	175	15	Sudan	89	45
Swaziland	164	16	Azerbaijan	88	46
Guinea	161	17	Cambodia	82	47
Rwanda	160	18	Haiti	80	48
Cameroon	149	19	India	76	49
Benin	148	20	Laos	75	50
Somalia	145	21	Eritrea	74	51
Mozambique	138	22	Papua New Guinea	73	52
Uganda	134	23	Solomon Islands	73	52
Lesotho	132	24	Bhutan	70	54
Djibouti	130	25	Bangladesh	69	55
Côte d'Ivoire	127	26	South Africa	69	55
Congo	126	27	Comoros	68	57
Mauritania	125	28	Tajikistan	68	57
Botswana	124	29	Kiribati	64	59
Ethiopia	123	30	Guyana	62	60
			Namibia	61	61

*Deaths per thousand live births by age five.

African countries predominate among those with the highest mortality rates of children under five years of age (U5MR), a measure that is considered a critical indicator of the well-being of children. As a measure of comparison, the U5MR for the United States is 8 deaths per thousand live births, for the United Kingdom, 6, for Germany, France, and Japan, 4, and for Singapore, 3.

Adapted from United Nations Children's Fund (UNICEF), *The State of the World's Children,* 2008 (New York: UNICEF, 2007), 113; http://www.unicef.org/sowc08/.

in front of the cathedral, with highly resounding words of peace. Kordofan TV highlighted the event in the nightly broadcast. Amid all the loud talk of peace and dialogue, large detachments of army, PDF, mujahidin are seen being dispatched almost daily to the Nuba Mountain areas where a new offensive is in full swing. Furious fighting and aerial bombardment are reported from the areas of Kadugli, Heiban, Buram, Talodi, Shatt, Tes.

E. A lake of oil beneath Africa (1997)

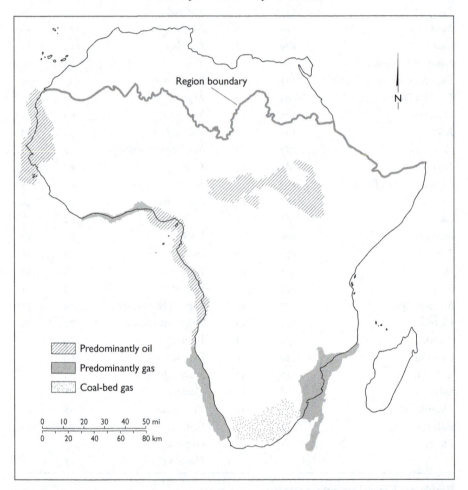

MAP 2 With more oil now imported into the United States from Africa than from the Middle East, a trend that is expected to increase in the future, the United States is paying much greater attention to the exploration of the African continent for fuel and mineral resources. This U.S. Geological Survey (USGS) map of African oil and gas reserves shows enormous resources in areas that have already captured America's interest: Nigeria, Chad, and the Sudan (Darfur especially), all of which sit on lakes of oil where once the West hunted for rivers of gold. United States Geological Survey.

67 • Holding someone responsible (2007–8)

Atrocities have perpetrators, and by the twenty-first century the world was ready to hold someone responsible for the genocide. As of the writing of this book, many of the individuals considered primarily responsible for the genocide in Rwanda and the killings in Sierra Leone and Liberia are on trial before international courts of justice. The crimes of these individuals are real, and the responsibility for so many deaths needs to be determined, but some cynics might note that no European colonial official has been held responsible for any of the atrocities committed in the name of colonialism. In addition, none of the rulers of apartheid South Africa have been prosecuted for the killings committed while defending white rule. Here is the final submission made by the prosecution in June 2007 in the case of the four military leaders—Theoneste Bagosora, Aloys Ntabakuze, Anatole Nsengiyumva, and Gratien Kabiligi—accused of genocide in Rwanda. The court in December 2008 found Bagosora, Ntabakuze, and Nsengiyumva guilty of genocide and sentenced all three to life in prison. Kabiligi was found not guilty on all charges.[9]

1. International Criminal Tribunal for Rwanda (ICTR) Prosecutor, Hassan B. Jallow, made his final submissions in the case against the military leaders charged with orchestrating the 1994 genocide in Rwanda. The submissions came at the end of 403 trial days in which Trial Chamber I heard testimony from 242 witnesses for both the prosecution and the defence and reviewed 459 prosecution exhibits.

2. The four accused, Theoneste Bagosora (Rtd. Colonel), Gratien Kabiligi (Rtd. Brigadier General and Chief of Military Operations at the General Staff of the Rwandan Army), Aloys Ntabakuze (Rtd. Mayor, Commander of the Paracommando battalion) and Anatole Nsengiyumva (Rtd. Lt. Colonel and Gisenyi Operational Secteur Commander) are charged with conspiracy to commit genocide, genocide, complicity in genocide, war crimes, including rape as crime against humanity, inhumane acts and outrages. Nsengiyumva is also charged with incitement to commit genocide. They all denied the charges. It will be recalled that during the Rwandan genocide, close to a million Tutsi civilians were murdered in one hundred days.

3. The Prosecutor argued on 28 May that all four men held immense power and authority during the Rwanda genocide and that all four used their power, control and influence, individually, and in their official capacities to prepare, plan, order, direct, incite, encourage and approve the killing of civilian Tutsi men, women and children, and others considered their accomplices.

4. Prosecutor Jallow told the Chamber that the evidence presented by the prosecution, including testimony from the UNIMIR [United Nations Assistance Mission for Rwanda] commander, General Romeo Dallaire, has established the guilt of the accused beyond reasonable doubt and that it was now up to the Chamber to hold them accountable for their criminal acts. Prosecutor Jallow stressed that no persons could be more culpable than the four accused for the success of the grisly campaign of slaughter.

9. The Web site for the trial of Theoneste Bagosora can be found at http://69.94.11.53/. The prosecution's final statement was made on June 1, 2007, and can be found at http://www.ictr.org/ENGLISH/cases/Bagosora/decisions/070601_pros_closing.pdf.

5. The Prosecutor highlighted salient points of his case against the accused. They included the assassination of significant political figures such as Prime Minister Agathe Uwilingiyimana. "Bagosora's hand was clearly visible in the murder of the Prime Minister. The evidence demonstrates that he instructed subordinate military soldiers to use all possible means to assassinate her."

6. The man in charge of the military on 6 and 7 April 1994 was Theoneste Bagosora. Bagosora ordered the execution of political opponents by extremist members of the Rwandan Armed Forces. They included the President of the Constitutional Court, Joseph Kavaruganda, Faustin Rucogoza, Minister of Information, Frederick Nzamurambaho, Minister of Agriculture and Chairman of the PSD [Social Democratic] Party, Landoald Ndasingwa, Minister of Labour and Community Affairs and Vice Chairman of the PL [Liberal] Party. Meanwhile, Ministers and key personalities belonging to the ruling MRND [Mouvement Révolutionnaire National pour le Développement] party and the extremist or power wings of the MDR [Mouvement Démocratique Républicain], PL and PSD party were protected at FAR [Rwandan Armed Forces] military bases or remained in their homes unharmed. No measures were taken by the military to intervene and protect the opposition politicians being targeted and killed. This was because the political killings were an essential element of the genocidal plot. These extremists also targeted and killed 10 Belgian UN peacekeepers at the Military Camp in Kigali.

7. Prosecutor Jallow stated that Bagosora and his co-accused in the trial planned the extermination of the Tutsi and that at dawn on 7 April 1994, Bagosora gave the order to the militia to begin the genocide. In Gisenyi, Nsengiyumva ordered a subordinate officer to begin the killings. Back in Kigali, Major Ntabakuze instructed his soldiers to avenge the death of President Habyarimana by killing Tutsi civilians whom he held responsible. Kabiligi also joined in the execution of the common plan to exterminate the Rwandan Tutsi population and their perceived accomplices. The message from the accused to the military and the militia according to Jallow was clear and consistent: systematically kill the Tutsi innocent civilians.

8. The Prosecutor told the Chamber that planning of these events began years in advance. The conspiracy began to show itself from around October 1990 after the RPA [Rwandan Patriotic Army] attack on Rwanda on 1 October 1990. "The accused conspired to create the right circumstances to ensure the successful execution of genocide. A fire was set waiting for a spark to ignite it. Once ignited, the four accused fuelled and stoked the fire of fear and hatred of the Tutsi." These four senior military officers, together with others, created the Rwanda Armed Forces Document which defined the "enemy" as the Tutsi ethnic group; through efforts of these accused, every member of the Rwandan military came to regard members of the Tutsi ethnic group—even civilian men and women, young and old, as legitimate targets. Hence the mass killings of such civilians by soldiers and militia alike.

9. Messages in the Rwandan media made constant references to the Tutsi as "inyenzi" and the "enemy" and served the purpose of de-humanizing this ethnic group in preparation for the execution of the genocide. The RTLM [Radio Télévision Libre des Mille Collines] assisted in this process, and all four accused, either as share-

holders or otherwise, supported the RTLM and its propaganda. Bagosora, for example, was one of RTLM's largest shareholders.

10. An integral part of this conspiracy was the creation, training, arming and commanding of the militia of the MRND, the then ruling party. The evidence demonstrates beyond reasonable doubt that the militia, or the civil defence forces, quickly became a vital component of the "genocide machine." The civil defence forces were the brain child of Bagosora. The forces were developed, nurtured, maintained and used by him and the other conspirators: Nsengiyumva, Ntabakuze and Kabiligi.

11. The four accused also authored, received and used lists of Tutsi and their accomplices, naming specific individuals to be targeted and massacred by the Rwandan Armed Forces in collaboration with militia and civil defence forces; all of this is a testament to the cold and calculated plan for a genocide.

12. Besides issuing orders, Bagosora and the other accused supervised the massacres of Tutsi civilians by the interahamwe in hospitals, in schools, in churches and at roadblocks where they watched and encouraged the killing. They distributed weapons and visited the notorious killings fields to ensure that the genocide was continuing according to plan. The four accused orchestrated the killings across the country. From Byumba to Gisenyi to Butare to Gitarama. Their acts touched the whole of Rwanda and lives of millions of Rwandans, close to a million of whom perished in the tragedy.

13. The four accused were also responsible for the commission of sexual crimes in Rwanda. These crimes were widespread and notorious. The four accused knew that acts of rape, disembowelment of pregnant women and other gruesome acts of sexual violence were being committed by their soldiers and by civilian militia. They did nothing to stop them. They took no steps to punish any one for these acts. They considered such acts as a part of their genocidal plan to wipe out the Tutsi ethnic group, to make them a matter of history.

14. The Prosecutor reminded the Chamber that the four accused have not accepted any responsibility for their role in the killings. They have instead chosen to blame others. Although he did not make a recommendation on sentencing, Mr. Jallow told the Chamber that it must now lay the blame where it belongs and find all four accused guilty of the crimes as charged. The maximum punishment under the Statute of the ICTR is imprisonment for life.

15. On March 1, 2007, the Prosecution team led by Barbara Mulvaney, Senior Trial Attorney, filed a closing brief of 954 pages outlining the case of the Prosecution. Prosecutor Jallow paid tribute to the prosecution team which includes Drew White, Gregory Townsend, Christine Graham, Rashid Rashid and Kartik Murukutla.

16. The Trial Chamber has not fixed a date for delivery of the judgment. However, due to the length of the case and the testimony, observers expect delivery of the judgment towards the end of 2007 or early in 2008.

68 • U.S. policy planning for Africa (2004)

With world sources of energy scarce, the demand for oil is increasing, especially as conflict in the Middle East puts supplies from that area in contention and so long as environmental concerns prevent the fullest exploitation of the energy reserves of the United States. Africa currently supplies the United States with more oil than it gets from the Middle East, and that situation will only continue. Africa has become a central part of U.S. discussions about energy resources, about the need to control strategic minerals for world dominance (much as forecast by the Brookings Institute in 1943), and about how to achieve these goals in a world in which it appears that global policymakers no longer look askance at small and disintegrating states. These issues arise in a paper prepared for the White House National Intelligence Council in 2004, in which, on the first page, the authors write that "there is no longer an assumption that big states are necessarily better states. In Africa, for example, the more important states are not necessarily the bigger ones. Indeed, Ghana, Uganda, Mauritius and Botswana have been steady if imperfect recent performers. States are no longer valued in terms of territorial or population size, but rather their economic health. Who, for example, would claim that the DRC is more important than Singapore? And indeed, it may well be that smaller is often better in Africa, in particular, given the difficulties in extending governance capacity and consolidating rule." The following projections for Africa are from a March 2004 National Intelligence Council estimate.[10]

[T]en emergent trends in terms of external engagement with Africa can be identified:

First, an increasing external concern with failed, failing, weak African states as sources of insecurity, and a related concern over the rise of Islamic fundamentalism given the large number (250m) of African Muslims and their living conditions.

Second, an increasing external willingness to listen to African assessments of their development and security challenge (such as at the G-8 meetings), but which is not matched by a concomitant increase in aid disbursements.

Third, a more focused aid regime on issue-specific areas (governance, HIV-Aids, capacity-building). Related to this, there remains a focus on debt relief in exchange for poverty-alleviation "good governance" strategies. Africa's external debt stands at US$300 billion. Over 80% of the heavily indebted poor countries (HIPC) are in the region, and the continent's total debt service ratio in 1999 (debt as a percentage of exports of goods and services) was 13.9%, uncomfortably close to the 15–20% mark that is considered unsustainable. Around US$40 billion in debt has already been forgiven under the HIPC initiative. Paradoxically, Africa has lost an estimated US$150 billion in capital flight, with around 40% of private wealth held outside the continent, a higher percentage than in any other region.

Fourth, increasing military engagement by external powers—partly driven by 9/11, partly by the Rwandan genocide, and partly (Sierra Leone) by personal and colonial (Cote d'Ivoire) connections.

Fifth, the increasing importance of the oil sector in especially but not exclusively US policy calculations on Africa. Importantly, most of Africa's oil producers are not OPEC members —notably Angola, Gabon, Equatorial Guinea, Congo-Brazzaville and Cameroon.

10. "External Relations and Africa," paper prepared for the NIC 2020 project, http://www.dni.gov/nic/ PDF_GIF_2020_Support/2004_03_16_papers/external_relations.pdf.

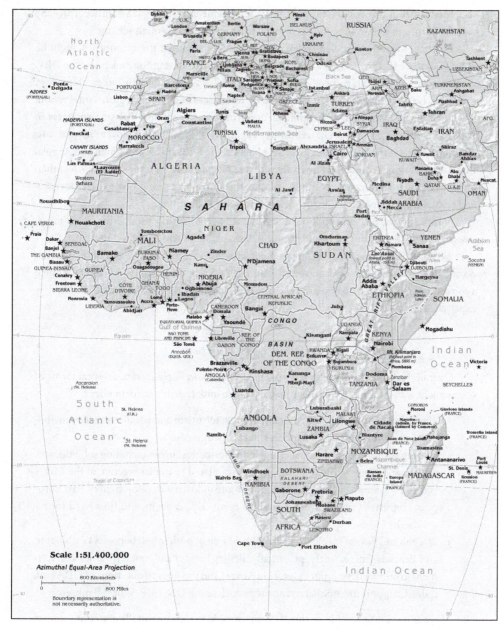

MAP 3 Political map of Africa, 2008. Central Intelligence Agency, *The World Factbook*, 2008.

Sixth, the rise of other powers such as China, which has both positive and negative implications for Africa in terms of the draw-card effect of China on global FDI and the impact of its manufacturing sector on Africa's, and more positively as a destination for African commodity exports.

Seventh, while trade access remains preferential and asymmetrical (i.e., that the developed world opens up faster than Africa is required to do so), there is a move towards greater reciprocity, such as through the various free trade agreements (EU-SA, US-Morocco, SA-US) and the European Union's regional economic partnership arrangement scheme.

Eighth, a focus on so-called "pivotal" states in the hope that these countries might be able to influence their regions in a positive manner. The need to stabilise Sudan and the DRC is often mentioned in this respect given their potential as African growth "poles." However, the reality is rather that these states, far from being sources of dynamic regional integration, have long been reasons for regional insulation from their problems. The smaller states in Africa have done comparatively well in per capita GDP growth terms over the past two decades, while it is the larger states including Nigeria, the DRC, Ethiopia, Sudan and Angola, that have performed comparatively badly with a per capita GDP of under US$200, less than half the continental average. In addition, despite their advantages for growth, their sheer size and related complexity has made the idea of intervention daunting.

Ninth, a focus, too, on support for and capacity-building in various African-led initiatives, notably the African Union and the New Partnership for Africa's Development.

Tenth, an increasing focus on engagement with the African diaspora. It is estimated that 60,000 doctors, engineers and university staff left Africa between 1985–90, and that since 1990 this figure has been 20,000 per year. The gap created by this loss has had to be filled by expatriates.

Conclusion: Likely Directions

Overall there are three major external factors that will likely dictate external terms of engagement with Africa and a number that are Africa initiated/driven/dependent.

1. The threat Africa poses in terms of migration, terrorism and social instability, including the ripeness for Islamic fundamentalism within Africa.
2. The intensification of a global struggle for scarce resources including oil, minerals, timber, and gems—this will likely intensify, related to the emergence of the PRC's "mega-economy" and expected economic and industrial development of East European countries (who will increase their productive capacity and thus need for resources).
3. The ebb and flow of ideological and political weight both in and between Washington and Brussels (increasingly, potentially, Beijing) and thus "concern" if not commitment to human development issues in Africa (and this goes to questions of ODA and, indeed, support for multilateral agencies such as the UN, IMF, World Bank, etc).

Africa does not face military threats from outside the continent. The security threats faced by African states are by-and-large internal. Where external grievances exist (i.e., from neighbouring countries), these are often a product of the failure of governments to extend their authority and governance to their legal geographic extremities. This reflects the core insecurity facing Africa today—a combination of weak and unresponsive government, limited resources, and political systems that centre on patronage and hierarchy rather than liberal free-market competition and bottom-up "people's power." Africa has also been blighted by poor leadership, reluctant until now of taking a firm stance against fellow leadership, this reflecting, at least, the personal and polity trauma of colonialism, the failure of post-colonial regimes and consequent collapse of expectations, and the damage done from Africa being a proxy playground for the excesses of Soviet Marxism and its ideological counterpart, US-led anti-communism. Taken together the resultant paradigm of much of Africa's leadership has been to simultaneously cock a snook at the West while turning to the external community for the answers to unlock its depressing cycle of poverty and instability. This schizophrenia is compounded by the West's hesitance sometimes to call things as they are in Africa, with policy positions too often influenced by direct interests, former colonial connections, or the need to excuse African leadership's excesses and failings given the understandable imperative instead to look towards the brighter whole of African development progress. But in so doing, it may be poisoning the very well it is trying to bring to life.

Yet a major hope for Africa lies paradoxically in a new generation of pragmatic, ideologically neutral, or broadly liberal democratic African leaders (such as Mbeki [forced out of office as president of South Africa in 2008], Mogae [stepped down as president of Botswana in 2008], Kufuor [born in 1938, president of Ghana], and Kibaki [born in 1931, president of Kenya]) who may be able to deepen democracy and enhance development. This generation compares favourably to the ideologues of Verwoerd [born in 1901, assassinated in 1966], Mengistu [born in 1937, living in Zimbabwe since 1991], Nkrumah [born in 1909, died in exile in 1972], Nyerere [born in 1922, died in 1999] and the last of their generation, Mugabe [born in 1924]. One issue critical to their success is, however, the degree to which Western democracies are prepared to invest in these countries and governments to enhance their chances of sustained reform and delivery.

In this regard, there will be nothing more powerful for African states, their leadership and indeed the populace (given the increasing power of telecommunications in Africa) than the "global and continental demonstration effect" of successful African economic "tigers" or, more accurately, "lions." If NEPAD [New Partnership for Africa's Development] is to achieve nothing else then it has to achieve—or help to achieve—successful case studies: here SA, Zimbabwe, Kenya, Egypt, Morocco, Ethiopia, Ghana, Botswana, Senegal, and Angola stand out as possibles.

69 · Jacob Zuma addresses the Solidarity Union National Congress (2008)

Jacob Zuma, elected president of the African National Congress in 2008, has often been perceived as more radical than Thabo Mbeki and more likely to respond to the demands of those who argue that not enough has been done to deal with the economic and social inequities left in place by apartheid. Zuma represents not a generation different from Mbeki's (they were both born in 1942) but an approach that may well be less responsive to the needs and demands of big business. This approach is signaled in a speech by Zuma given on March 6, 2008, at the closing dinner of the Solidarity Union National Congress, a group dissimilar to him in ethnicity—they are white Afrikaners— but with whom he identifies as fellow workers.[11]

11. Http://www.anc.org.za/ancdocs/history/zuma/2008/jz0306a.html.

General Secretary, Flip Buys,

Leadership of Solidarity,

Ladies and Gentlemen,

It is a great pleasure and honour to have been invited to address the closing dinner of your national Congress.

Being a former trade unionist, I feel at home in a gathering of workers such as this one. Solidarity has a good relationship with Cosatu trade unions. You also have a good track record in representing workers in the mining, metal, engineering, electrical and communications industries.

Most importantly, I am pleased to be addressing Afrikaner workers, who have a full commitment to this country and continent. You have no other home other than South Africa, and whatever issues you raise are aimed at making our country more successful, and to create a better future for your children.

I trust that the deliberations that have taken place over the course of this Congress will enable the union to better serve its members and contribute to the development of the South African economy and society.

We look forward to receiving a full report of the Congress outcomes and to engage on the many important issues that have no doubt been raised. I am aware that you seek further and more intensive engagement on issues, and we would certainly welcome that opportunity. Compatriots, occasions such as this congress provide an opportunity for us to celebrate the ushering of democracy in our country in 1994.

The advent of democracy produced a Constitution that enshrines various freedoms. This includes the freedom of workers to join trade unions of their choice. The rights of workers are protected in various pieces of legislation as you know, especially the Labour Relations Act. Being an activist union, you have taken full advantage of the legal environment, and are working hard to improve the lot of the Afrikaner worker and other members.

Barely two months ago, our organisation, the African National Congress, concluded our national conference in Polokwane.

We emerged from that conference united and more determined and ready to build a society in which all its people—black and white—can benefit from equal access to opportunities, decent jobs, safety and security, and an improving quality of life.

We produced a range of resolutions across a number of areas that are fundamental to advance the vision of a society that so many South Africans now share.

We know that we cannot build such a society alone. Only by working together as a nation—across boundaries of race, class, gender, history, culture and language—are we going to be able to realise the kind of future that we all seek.

Today's engagement provides a valuable opportunity to share our views and concerns, and together work to build the future we want for future generations.

I am encouraged to see that your work extends beyond shop floor issues, and that Solidarity actively works to alleviate poverty. Your Helping Hand Fund is a remarkable example of self-lessness and sacrifice, as it is financed by money deducted from ordinary workers, giving the union R500 000 a month.

You support 25 feeding schemes across the country, exclusively black. You distributed 2000 school cases and stationery packages to school children, more than 50% of whom were

FIGURE 27 Former South African president Nelson Mandela, flanked by ANC president Jacob Zuma (left) and South African president Thabo Mbeki (right), greets the crowds who gathered in Pretoria to celebrate his ninetieth birthday in August 2008. Mandela remains a revered figure of national unity in South Africa, and the ANC holds an overwhelming majority of political power. Nevertheless, Zuma and Mbeki represent differing ideologies, both of which emerged after fifteen years of majority rule. AP Photo/Jerome Delay.

poor grade 1 learners. We congratulate you for such patriotic duty, which is an example of nation building in practice.

There are various issues that concern your members, one of which is the scarcity of skills in the country, which we also share. To grow our economy we need to expand our skills base. One solution is for us to focus on our schools and educational institutions to ensure that they produce quality graduates that are up to the demands of a rapidly changing world.

We are willing to engage with Solidarity to know more about your project in which you will train about 5000 people this year, 450 of whom will be in scarce trades. We fully share your view that we should not ignore training our people just because it is cheaper to import skills.

We must examine where in our society rare skills can be found, that are currently not being utilised or which are being under-utilised. We see Solidarity playing a role in all of these areas.

Another issue of concern is no doubt affirmative action. We have legislation in our country that institutionalizes corrective action, because it is our view that the imbalances of the past should be addressed, for the sake of the sustainability of freedom and economic growth.

The majority of the population in any country would have to feature prominently in the economy to ensure long-term growth and sustainable development. I am sure that such issues are discussed vigorously on the shop floor amongst the employers and various labour unions, to ensure that the implementation of transformative legislation is understood by all the affected.

This is an important part of what we understand as affirmative action, bringing resources and opportunities to those who have never had it before. It also means taking steps to remove the remnants of minority privilege, so that all may compete on a level playing field.

As you will no doubt recognise, this is not an easy task. Some perceive the efforts to remove white or male privilege as an assault on the rights of white South Africans or on the rights of male South Africans. We need to answer such perceptions. And the only way we're going to do that is by sitting down and discussing such issues.

I know your concern that young white South Africans feel they cannot enter the labour market, and the fact that positions remain unfilled because the necessary affirmative action skills are not available.

You also state clearly that your position on affirmative action is not designed to protect the white elite which are guarding privileges, but to intercede on behalf of young people and ordinary workers who bear the brunt of affirmative action.

Let us find time to engage on these issues thoroughly and see how we can find common ground, for the common good of the country.

We all seek a society in which no person is privileged at the expense of another, and that no person is oppressed for the benefit of another.

That is why, among other things, the ANC welcomes increased interaction between the different formations of organised labour in this country.

The electricity crisis has affected all South African households, but in your case, it affects workers directly. I am disturbed to hear that some of your members are harassed by the public, even after hours, simply because they work for Eskom. They also have to work long overtime hours.

I trust that the union will, in its engagement with the employer, find an amicable solution very urgently. We cannot afford a situation where the low morale of workers affects the delivery of services.

Fellow South Africans, I know that you are concerned about the crime levels in our country. We have asked our branches all over the country to work with communities to assist law enforcement agencies to fight crime.

We congratulate members of Solidarity who already individually belong to various crime community forums and neighbourhood watches. That is the kind of community spirit that can assist us to reduce the hiding space for criminals. We are calling upon all communities to become actively involved and make our residential areas and business premises no go areas for criminals.

With regards to the economy in general, as a country we have made much progress in attending to the most basic needs of the poor—providing housing, water, electricity, sanitation, telecommunications and other infrastructure on a scale never before seen in this country.

We have improved access to schools and health care and have built a robust economy that has grown consistently, and has been creating jobs in greater numbers. But we still have a long way to go.

The levels of poverty amongst the majority of the population remain high. In addition, we share your concern about the rising poverty amongst white South Africans. We agree that the needs of the residents of 36 small white informal settlements in Pretoria need to be taken care of.

We trust that the relevant government agencies are aware of this situation. In our further engagements with Solidarity we can see how we take this matter forward with our government.

As a nation, we face a number of challenges. But we must face them united. This has been demonstrated in many examples, such as the current electricity crisis. South Africans have united behind government and other players to find a solution.

We must promote a common nationhood, as there is a lot that binds us as South Africans. Our unfortunate history and our respective experiences in it and the remarkable manner in which we were able to negotiate a settlement on our own and usher in a new order are some of the uniquely South African traits around which we can rally.

The Afrikaans-speaking South Africans have a role to play in building the country. We belong together and must work together to build a prosperous, democratic, non-racial and non-sexist South Africa.

There is no need for fear, despondency or low morale. Instead, there should be higher energy levels and high spirits as we work to build a better and more prosperous country. We should be working harder together to take care of the interests of the poor and marginalized.

South Africa is politically, economically and socially stable. We have a model constitution, a vibrant political climate, a very politically alert population that knows its rights, a growing economy and many other attributes which should make us expect a better tomorrow.

Let us put fear and anxiety aside. South Africa belongs to all, and South Africa is your home.

Thank you.

SELECTED BIBLIOGRAPHY

Bibliographic Guide

Norton, Mary Beth, and Pamela Gerardi, eds. *The American Historical Association's Guide to Historical Literature*, 3d ed. 2 vols. New York: Oxford University Press, 1995. The fullest bibliographic guide to world history, with comprehensive annotated entries.

Journals

African Affairs
Canadian Journal of African Studies
Imago Mundi: International Journal for the History of Cartography
International Journal of African Historical Studies
Journal of African History
Journal of Modern African Studies
Journal of Southern African Studies

Encyclopedias

Africana: The Encyclopedia of the African and African American Experience, ed. Kwame Anthony Appiah and Henry Louis Gates, 2d ed. 5 vols. New York: Oxford University Press, 2005.
New Encyclopedia of Africa, ed. John Middleton and Joseph Miller. 5 vols. Detroit: Thomson/Gale, 2008.

Maps

The most comprehensive published guides to historical maps of Africa are Oscar I. Norwich, *Norwich's Maps of Africa*, 2d ed. (Norwich, Vt.: Terra Nova, 1997); John MacIlwaine, *Maps and Mapping of Africa: A Resource Guide* (London: Hans Zell, 1997); and, especially, the definitive and beautifully illustrated volume by Richard L. Betz, *The Mapping of Africa: A Cartobibliography of Printed Maps of the African Continent to 1700* ('t Goy-Houten, the Netherlands: HES and De Graaf, 2007).

More dated but still the best sources of thematic maps of Africa are J. F. Ade. Ajayi and Michael Crowder, eds., *Historical Atlas of Africa* (New York: Cambridge University Press, 1985); J. D. Fage, *An Atlas of African History*, 2d ed. (London: Arnold, 1978); and Colin McEvedy, *The Penguin Atlas of African History*, rev ed. (New York: Penguin, 1996).

General Histories

The best one-volume histories of Africa are John Iliffe, *Africans: The History of a Continent*, 2d ed. (New York: Cambridge University Press, 2007), and Fred Cooper, *Africa since 1940: The Past of the Present*

(New York: Cambridge University Press, 2002). In addition, A. Adu Boahen, *African Perspectives on Colonialism* (Baltimore: Johns Hopkins University Press, 1989), is intellectually engaging.

Two older, multivolume series, the UNESCO and the Cambridge University Press histories of Africa, though not reflecting current scholarship, provide an enormous amount of information: UNESCO International Scientific Committee for the Drafting of a General History of Africa, *General History of Africa*, 8 vols. (Berkeley: University of California Press, 1981–93), and J. D. Fage and Roland Oliver, eds., *The Cambridge History of Africa*, 8 vols. (Cambridge: Cambridge University Press, 1982–86).

Books That We Use Regularly in Our Teaching

NOTE. This is not a comprehensive list but rather books that we find reflect high standards of scholarship, that are intellectually stimulating, and that students find useful and provocative in the classroom.

General

Appiah, Kwame Anthony. *In My Father's House: Africa in the Philosophy of Culture.* London: Methuen, 1992.

Birmingham, David, and Phyllis M. Martin, eds. *History of Central Africa.* 2 vols. New York: Longman, 1983.

Gilbert, Erik, and Jonathan T. Reynolds. *Africa in World History: From Prehistory to the Present,* 2d ed. Upper Saddle River, N.J.: Prentice Hall, 2007.

Hopkins, A. G. *An Economic History of West Africa.* London: Longman, 1973.

Meredith, Martin. *The Fate of Africa: From the Hopes of Freedom to the Heart of Despair: A History of Fifty Years of Independence.* New York: Public Affairs, 2005.

Africa in the Era of the Atlantic Slave Trade

Alpers, Edward. *Ivory and Slaves: Changing Patterns of International Trade in East Central Africa to the Later Nineteenth Century.* Berkeley: University of California Press, 1975.

Blackburn, Robin. *The Making of New World Slavery: From the Baroque to the Modern, 1492–1800.* New York: Verso, 1997.

Carney, Judith. *Black Rice: The African Origins of Rice Cultivation in the Americas.* Cambridge, Mass.: Harvard University Press, 2001.

Cooper, Frederick. *Plantation Slavery on the East Coast of Africa.* New Haven: Yale University Press, 1977.

Curtin, Philip. *The Atlantic Slave Trade: A Census.* Madison: University of Wisconsin Press, 1969.

Elphick, Richard. *Kraal and Castle: Khoikhoi and the Founding of White South Africa.* New Haven: Yale University Press, 1977.

Eltis, David. *The Rise of African Slavery in the Americas.* New York: Cambridge University Press, 2000.

Eltis, David, Stephen D. Behrendt, David Richardson, and Herbert S. Klein, eds. *The Trans-Atlantic Slave Trade: A Database on CD-ROM.* New York: Cambridge University Press, 2000.

Harms, Robert. *The Diligent: A Voyage through the Worlds of the Slave Trade.* New York: Basic Books, 2002.

Hawthorne, Walter. *Planting Rice and Harvesting Slaves: Transformations along the Guinea-Bissau Coast, 1400–1900.* Portsmouth, N.H.: Heinemann, 2003.

Hochschild, Adam. *Bury the Chains: Prophets and Rebels in the Fight to Free an Empire's Slaves.* Boston: Houghton Mifflin, 2005.

Isaacman, Allen F. *Mozambique: The Africanization of a European Institution: The Zambesi Prazos, 1750–1902.* Madison: University of Wisconsin Press, 1972.

Levtzion, Nehemia. *Ancient Ghana and Mali*. London: Methuen, 1973.

Lovejoy, Paul. *Transformations in Slavery: A History of Slavery in Africa*, 2d ed. New York: Cambridge University Press, 2000.

Miller, Joseph C. *Kings and Kinsmen: Early Mbundu States in Angola*. Oxford: Clarendon, 1976.

———. *Way of Death: Merchant Capitalism and the Angolan Slave Trade, 1730–1830*. Madison: University of Wisconsin Press, 1988.

Russell, Peter. *Prince Henry "the Navigator": A Life*. New Haven: Yale University Press, 2001.

Sheriff, Abdul. *Slaves, Spices and Ivory: Integration of an East African Commercial Empire into the World Economy, 1770–1873*. London: James Currey; Nairobi: Heinemann Kenya; Dar es Salaam: Tanzania Publishing House; Athens: Ohio University Press, 1987.

Thomas, Hugh. *The Slave Trade: The Story of the Atlantic Slave Trade, 1440–1870*. New York: Simon and Schuster, 1997.

Thornton, John K. *Africa and Africans in the Making of the Atlantic World, 1400–1800*, 2d ed. New York: Cambridge University Press, 1998.

Africa in the Era of Colonialism

Allman, Jean, Susan Geiger, and Nakanyise Musisi, eds. *Women in African Colonial Histories*. Bloomington: Indiana University Press, 2002.

Anderson, David. *Histories of the Hanged: The Dirty War in Kenya and the End of Empire*. New York: Norton, 2005.

Bender, Gerald J. *Angola under the Portuguese: The Myth and the Reality*. Berkeley: University of California Press, 1978.

Bonner, Philip, Peter Delius, and Deborah Posel, eds. *Apartheid's Genesis*. Johannesburg: Ravan, 1993.

Bundy, Colin. *The Rise and Fall of the South African Peasantry*. London: Heinemann, 1979.

Clark, Nancy L. *Manufacturing Apartheid: State Corporations in South Africa*. New Haven: Yale University Press, 1994.

Clark, Nancy L., and William H. Worger. *South Africa: The Rise and Fall of Apartheid*. New York: Pearson Longman, 2004.

Cooper, Frederick. *Decolonization and African Society: The Labor Question in French and British Africa*. New York: Cambridge University Press, 1996.

———. *From Slaves to Squatters: Plantation Labor and Agriculture in Zanzibar and Coastal Kenya, 1890–1925*. New Haven: Yale University Press, 1980.

Elphick, Richard, and Rodney Davenport, eds. *Christianity in South Africa: A Political, Social, and Cultural History*. Berkeley: University of California Press, 1997.

Human Rights Watch. *Leave None to Tell the Story: Genocide in Rwanda*. New York: Human Rights Watch, 1999.

Mamdani, Mahmood. *Citizen and Subject: Contemporary Africa and the Legacy of Late Colonialism*. Princeton: Princeton University Press, 1996.

Ranger, T. O. *Revolt in Southern Rhodesia, 1896–7: A Study in African Resistance*. London: Heinemann, 1967.

van Onselen, Charles. *Chibaro: African Mine Labour in Southern Rhodesia, 1900–1930*. London: Pluto, 1976.

Weiskel, Timothy C. *French Colonial Rule and the Baule Peoples: Resistance and Collaboration, 1889–1911*. New York: Oxford University Press, 1980.

White, Landeg. *Magomero: Portrait of an African Village*. New York: Cambridge University Press, 1987.

Worger, William H. *South Africa's City of Diamonds: Mine Workers and Monopoly Capitalism in Kimberley, 1867–1895*. New Haven: Yale University Press, 1987.

Wright, Donald R. *The World and a Very Small Place in Africa: A History of Globalization in Niumi, the Gambia,* 2d ed. Armonk, N.Y.: Sharpe, 2004.

Zwede, Bahru. *A History of Modern Ethiopia 1855–1991.* 2nd ed. Oxford: James Currey, 2001.

Autobiographical Works

Emecheta, Buchi. *Head above Water.* Portsmouth, N.H.: Heinemann, 1994.

Mandela, Nelson. *Long Walk to Freedom: The Autobiography of Nelson Mandela.* Boston: Little, Brown, 1994.

Oliver, Roland. *In the Realms of Gold: Pioneering in African History.* Madison: University of Wisconsin Press, 1997.

Vansina, Jan. *Living with Africa.* Madison: University of Wisconsin Press, 1994.

Fiction

Achebe, Chinua. *Things Fall Apart.* London: Heinemann, 1962.

Dangaremgba, Tsitsi. *Nervous Conditions: A Novel.* Seattle: Seal, 1988.

Emecheta, Buchi. *The Joys of Motherhood: A Novel.* Portsmouth, N.H.: Heinemann, 1988.

Laye, Camara. *The Dark Child.* New York: Farrar, Straus, and Giroux, 1954.

Matshoba, Mtutuzeli. *Call Me Not a Man.* London: Longman, 1987.

Mda, Zakes. *The Heart of Redness.* New York: Farrar, Straus, and Giroux, 2002.

Sources for Illustrations

Ahmed, Akhter U., Ruth V. Hill, Lisa C. Smith, Doris M. Wiesmann, and Tim Frankenberger. *The World's Most Deprived: Characteristics and Causes of Extreme Poverty and Hunger.* Washington, D.C.: International Food Policy Research Institute, 2007. Http://www.ifpri.org/sites/default/files/publications/vp43.pdf.

Baden-Powell, R. S. S. *The Downfall of Prempeh; a Diary of Life with the Native Levy in Ashanti.* London: Methuen, 1896.

Baikie, William Balfour. *Narrative of an Exploring Voyage up the Rivers Kwóra and Bínue, (Commonly Known as the Niger and Tsádda) in 1854.* London: Murray, 1856.

Bentley, W. Holman. *Pioneering on the Congo.* 2 vols. London: Religious Tract Society, 1900.

Bovill, E. W. *The Golden Trade of the Moors,* 2d ed. New York: Oxford University Press, 1970.

Brown, Robert. *The Story of Africa and Its Explorers.* London: Cassell, 1895.

Chambliss, J. E. *The Life and Labors of David Livingstone, Covering His Entire Career in Southern and Central Africa.* Philadelphia: Hubbard Bros, 1876.

Dapper, Olfert. *Umbständliche und eigentliche Beschreibung von Africa.* Amsterdam: Jacob von Meurs, 1670–71.

Great Britain, Naval Intelligence Division. *French West Africa.* London: Her Majesty's Stationary Office, 1943–44.

Laird, Macgregor, and R. A. K. Oldfield, *Narrative of an Expedition into the Interior of Africa, by the River Niger: in the Steam-vessels Quorra and Alburkah in 1832, 1833 and 1834.* 2 vols. London: Bentley, 1837.

Livingstone, David, and Charles Livingstone. *Narrative of an Expedition to the Zambesi and Its Tributaries: and of the Discovery of the Lakes Shirwa and Nyassa, 1858–1864.* Harper and Brothers, 1866.

Major, Richard Henry. *The Life of Prince Henry of Portugal, Surnamed the Navigator.* London: Asher, 1868.

Mayer, Brantz. *Captain Canot, or, Twenty years of an African slaver, Being an Account of his Career and Adventures on the Coast of the Interior, on Shipboard, and in the West Indies.* New York: Appleton, 1854.

Michell, Lewis. *The Life of the Rt. Hon. Cecil John Rhodes, 1853–1902.* London: Edward Arnold, 1910.

Park, Mungo. *Travels in the Interior Districts of Africa, Performed under the Direction and Patronage of the African Association, in the Years 1795, 1796, and 1797.* London: John Murray, 1816.

Schreiner, Olive. *Trooper Peter Halket of Mashonaland.* Boston: Roberts Brothers, 1897.

Southworth, Alvan S. *Four Thousand Miles of African Travel: A Personal Record of a Journey up the Nile and through the Soudan to the Confines of Central Africa, Embracing a Discussion on the Sources of the Nile, and an Examination of the Slave Trade.* New York: Baker, Pratt and Co., 1875.

Stanley, Henry M. *The Congo and the Founding of Its Free State: A Story of Work and Exploration.* London: Sampson Low, Marston, Searle and Rivington, 1886.

———. *In Darkest Africa, Or, the Quest, Rescue, and Retreat of Emin, Governor of Equatoria.* 2 vols. New York: Chas. Scribner's Sons, 1890.

Twain, Mark. *King Leopold's Soliloquy: A Defense of His Congo Rule.* Boston: P. R. Warren Company, 1905.

Weule, Karl. *Native Life in East Africa: The Results of an Ethnological Research Expedition.* Translated by Alice Werner. New York: D. Appleton and Company, 1909.

WEB SITES

A. General Guides to Information Available on the Web

AfricaFocus

www.africafocus.org/

Up-to-the-minute, comprehensive, and informed reporting and links about contemporary events in Africa. Run by William Minter, a highly respected specialist on Africa and the author of several well-regarded books on southern and Lusophone Africa.

Stanford University Guide to Internet Sources on Africa South of the Sahara

www-sul.stanford.edu/africa/guide.html

A huge, continually updated, and fully annotated guide to Internet resources on Africa. The information on the Web site is organized by country, region, and topic.

University of Pennsylvania Electronic Guide for African Resources on the Internet

www.africa.upenn.edu/K-12/AFR_GIDE.html

The guide aims to assist not only teachers, librarians, and students, especially those in elementary and high schools, but also university faculty and students in locating online resources on Africa that can be used in the classroom.

H-Africa

www.h-net.org/~africa/ (Michigan State University)

H-Africa is an international scholarly discussion list on African culture and the African past. The focus is on university-level teaching and research, with up-to-date reviews of new books and online discussions about research questions and classroom resources.

B. Maps

Afriterra Foundation

www.afriterra.org/

Contains a searchable database of more than five thousand maps focused on Africa 1480–1900 in the Afriterra collection. More than one thousand of these maps are available as ultra-high-resolution digitized images.

Central Intelligence Agency (CIA) *World Factbook*

https://www.cia.gov/library/publications/the-world-factbook/index.html /

Site maintained by the Central Intelligence Agency. Contains up-to-date maps of every country in the world.

David Rumsey Historical Map Collection

www.davidrumsey.com/directory/where/Africa/

Contains approximately two hundred high-quality digitized historical maps of Africa, especially those from the 1700s and the 1800s.

Oscar I. Norwich Collection of Maps of Africa and Its Islands, 1486 to ca. 1865
(Stanford University)
www-sul.stanford.edu/depts/spc/maps/norwich_african_maps.html
One of the most comprehensive collections of historical maps of Africa, especially those of southern Africa, with 315 high-resolution maps available online.

C. Regional and/or Specialist Web Sites

African National Congress (ANC)
www.anc.org.za/show.php?doc=ancdocs/history/
The historical section of the ANC's official Web site contains documents that either were produced by the ANC, relate to the role of the ANC and its allies in the struggle for liberation, or are directly concerned with the ANC. The collection includes speeches, pamphlets, books, and photographs. New documents are continually being added to this section as they become available.

Aluka
www.aluka.org/
Aluka (derived from a Zulu word meaning "to weave") provides access to three collections. One focuses on cultural heritage sites and landscapes and includes photographs, 3-D models, GIS data sets, site plans, aerial and satellite photography, excavation reports, field notes, nineteenth-century European travelogues, and Arabic manuscripts from Timbuktu. Another collection focuses on African plant species and includes photographs, drawings, botanical art, field notes, and reference works drawn from published and unpublished material, especially from the Royal Botanical Gardens in Kew, London. The third collection includes material relating to the southern African peoples' struggle for freedom from colonial rule, including oral histories, speeches, nationalist publications, newspaper articles, fully digitized books and monographs, regional periodicals and magazines, posters, and pamphlets.

Centre Æquatoria Centre de Recherches Culturelles Africanistes
www.aequatoria.be/English/HomeEnglishFrameSet.html
This site contains full-text material on two major projects dealing with Belgian rule in the Congo. The first focuses on Belgian educational policy and practice from 1926 to 1972 and includes lists of students, inspection reports, exam results, statistics, school board regulations, several local disputes, curricula discussions, and circulars. The second project focuses on colonial schoolbooks and makes available online the full text of more than six hundred schoolbooks and religious textbooks dating from 1897. Originally published in more than thirty-five Congolese languages, an increasing number of these texts are being translated into French and English and made available online to researchers.

Digital Innovation South Africa (DISA)
www.disa.ukzn.ac.za/
DISA is a freely accessible online scholarly resource focusing on the sociopolitical history of South Africa, particularly the struggle for freedom during the period from 1950 to the first democratic elections in 1994. There are two primary collections of material: DISA 1, titled *South Africa's Struggle for Democracy: Anti-apartheid Periodicals, 1960–1994*, focuses on the Sharpeville massacre in March 1960, the rise of the black consciousness movement in the 1960s and 1970s, the independent trade unions, and the revival of the African National Congress after the Soweto uprising of June 1976 through the first democratic elections of 1994. The collection contains forty-five journals representing a wide spectrum of political views on a diversity of subjects such as trade unions, health, culture, and gender (e.g., *FOSATU Worker News, Sash, Isizwe, Clarion Call, Grassroots, African Communist*); DISA 2 is titled *Southern African Freedom Struggles, c. 1950–1994* and includes documents, interviews, articles, posters, commissions,

trials, and legislation under the umbrella theme of freedom struggles, with carefully selected content in areas such as human rights, leadership, political parties, urban struggles, land issues, trade unions, and student unions.

Heritage Foundation
www.heritage.org/
Insight into conservative thinking about Africa and especially position papers that focus on the future energy concerns of the United States.

Human Rights Watch, Africa
www.hrw.org/doc/?t=africa
The first place to look for information about issues of contemporary significance such as child soldiers, Darfur, or conflict in the Congo.

National Intelligence Council (NIC) 2020 Project
www.dni.gov/nic/NIC_2020_project.html
The National Intelligence Council (NIC), a U.S. government body, is the intelligence community's center for midterm and long-term strategic thinking.

D. Trials

International Criminal Trial for Rwanda
http://69.94.11.53/
Up-to-the-minute, full transcripts of the daily proceedings of the trials of individuals charged with genocide and other crimes.

The Trial of Charles Taylor
www.charlestaylortrial.org/
Funded by the Soros Foundation, this website provides daily updates and full transcripts of the trial of the man viewed as being primarily responsible for the carnage in Sierra Leone and Liberia during the 1990s and the beginning of the twenty-first century.

Truth and Reconciliation Commission Maintained by the South African Department of Justice
www.doj.gov.za/trc/trccom.htm
This searchable, full-text site contains transcripts of the testimony of more than twenty-two thousand individuals who identified themselves as victims of the horrors of apartheid, as well as of the more than four thousand people who applied for amnesty for crimes committed during the apartheid era.

INDEX

ABOUT THE AUTHORS

WILLIAM H. WORGER is professor of history at the University of California, Los Angeles. A graduate of the University of Auckland, New Zealand, and Yale University, he previously taught at the University of Michigan and Stanford University. His research focuses on the history of South and southern Africa in the nineteenth and twentieth centuries.

NANCY L. CLARK is dean of the Honors College and professor of history at Louisiana State University. She studied African history at the University of California, Los Angeles, and at Yale University. She is completing a history of South Africa during World War II, which focuses on the war's impact on African and female workers.

EDWARD A. ALPERS is professor and chair of the Department of History at the University of California, Los Angeles. In 1994 he served as president of the African Studies Association. Alpers has published widely on the history of East Africa and the Indian Ocean. His current research focuses on Africans in the Indian Ocean.

CPSIA information can be obtained at www.ICGtesting.com
Printed in the USA
LVOW03s1704020115

421187LV00003B/6/P